W9-BMI-371

The
American
Right
Wing

The American Right Wing

READINGS IN POLITICAL BEHAVIOR

Edited by
ROBERT A. SCHOENBERGER
The University of Michigan

HOLT, RINEHART AND WINSTON, INC.
NEW YORK CHICAGO SAN FRANCISCO ATLANTA DALLAS
MONTREAL TORONTO LONDON SYDNEY

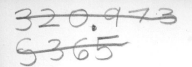

Preface

This collection of essays grew out of a search for empirical and nonpolemical materials on the modern American right wing. Although theory and hypothesis-testing techniques have expanded hugely in recent decades, they have rarely been employed in the study of the attitudes and behavior of ideologues. In the selections that follow, all but two of which were written specifically for this volume, the authors have attempted to combine a serious interest in the substance of rightist political characteristics with both a rigorous scholarly distance from the passions that have distorted so many other attempts to deal with these phenomena, and the application of research and analysis methods that are appropriate to the controversial nature of the topics discussed.

I am grateful to Morris Janowitz for helpful suggestions; to Herbert J. Addison and Jeanette Ninas Johnson of Holt, Rinehart and Winston, Inc., for their editorial help and guidance; to my contributors for making my editorial tasks an unexpected pleasure; and to my wife, Barbara, for the gift of another season of happiness.

ROBERT A. SCHOENBERGER

Ann Arbor, Michigan
April 1969

Contents

The American Right Wing

Introduction

Throughout the liberal democratic community the political far right stands condemned as the enemy of social and racial justice, shared prosperity, and liberty. Although proponents of traditional and libertarian conservatism are generally, if often grudgingly, accepted as part of the broad democratic community, most observers and practitioners of American politics view the extreme right with varying mixtures of fear and contempt. Indeed, a large epithetical vocabulary has been developed to characterize the rightist fringe groups and their supporters: radical, extremist, paranoid, authoritarian, fundamentalist, superpatriotic, pseudoconservative. When doubt arises, the cautious analyst may resort to such labels as ultra- or archconservative.

The antagonism explicit in the use of these terms is justified on the grounds of both political goals and political procedures. The past "Golden Age" toward which the far right faces in all nations is, in the United States, identified with the partly mythic pioneer virtues of thrift, morality, religiosity, independence and, above all, individualism. These do not, of course, harmonize with the universal leftist focus upon equality, collective responsibility, and secular perfectibility.

But the gap is widened and made less bearable by the propensity of the far right to attach, to their current conservative doctrines (for example, laissez-faire economics, limited government, states' rights), chauvinistic nationalism, a conspiratorial theory of history and politics (occasionally blended with a "devil theory") and a Manichean and apocalyptic imagery of social and political conflict.[1] (The latter two traits are not uncommon on the "new left.") Thus the conflict is joined not merely over what constitutes desirable public policy but also over the ground rules of the conflict, the rules of the game.

It is assumed by most theorists of democracy that the stability of such a system is endangered when political rhetoric changes from one of reasonable civility to that of violence, hostility, and distrust. Yet in their indictments of elected and appointed officials as, at best, "dupes" and, at worst, traitors; in their insistence upon direct, unflinching, and final confrontation with the Soviet Russian and Chinese Communist enemy, and in their certainty that time for victory—or survival, or freedom—is about to run out, spokesmen for the far right add only passion, fear, and hatred to the political struggle, each of which is a commodity already in plentiful supply.

The major task of social science, whether motivated by fear or fascination with the right wing, is not argument and prescription—or even proscription—but understanding and prediction. In this context, answers must be supplied to essentially exploratory questions about rightists: who are they? how many are there? where are they located? how cohesive are their belief systems and what are their dominant components? In addition, hypotheses and theories intended to account for rightist beliefs and behaviors must be tested. Are rightist attitudes products of certain psychological predispositions or

---

[1] See Richard Hofstadter, *The Paranoid Style in American Politics and Other Essays* (New York: Alfred A. Knopf, 1965), Part I; Benjamin R. Epstein and Arnold Forster, *The Radical Right* (New York: Random House, Inc., 1967); John H. Redekop, *The American Far Right* (Grand Rapids, Mich.: Wm. B. Eerdmans Publishing Co., 1968); Daniel Bell (ed.), *The Radical Right* (New York: Doubleday & Company, Inc., 1963).

maladjustments? Are they related to special problems of status mobility or status inconsistency? Do such beliefs take root especially in un-structured, disorganized, or politically distinctive environments? Are they associated with extrapolitical but stylistically or motivationally similar attitude structures?[2]

Until very recently, it was impossible to offer persuasive responses to any of these questions. Right-wing organizations, by whatever defi-nition employed, were few and their memberships limited, ephemeral, or secret. Many were fascist or racist-fundamentalist residues from the post–World War I and depression years.[3] While similar groups exist today in the form of the Minute Men, the National States Rights Party, the American Nazi Party, and the various Ku Klux Klans, *inter alia*, the late 1950s and the decade of the 1960s have witnessed a major surge of more "respectable" right-wing formations. Although the rhetoric of this new American right is as fevered as that of the old, the targets have been changed or reordered. Communism is the great implacable enemy and all the other phenomena, actual or imaginary, which stimulated rightist wrath have either been identified somehow with the totalitarian enemy or downplayed or dropped from the rightist lexicon.

So welfare programs, economic and business regulation, the income tax, the Supreme Court, civil rights agitation and legislation, student rebelliousness, and urban violence are each assumed to be part of a master plan to communize America. At the same time, overt anti-Catholic, -Semitic, -foreign, and -Negro propaganda are much less likely to be fundamental elements of the public rhetoric of the new right.[4]

The familiar prejudices and hatreds which the old nativist and fascist right played upon have long and deep roots in Western culture. It is their decline rather than their persistence which may be con-

---

[2] The search for causes and associations of rightism in the field of abnormal psychology and in fluid or frustrating social situations implicitly assumes away an obvious but unasked question: can a normal, stable, informed, and logical individual possibly accept the far right view of political reality? To social scientists, as well as other academics and intellectuals, the combination contains an internal contradiction. To be emotionally and intellectually sound prohibits, by definition, the acceptance of the rightist *Weltanschauung*.

[3] Arnold Forster and Benjamin R. Epstein, *The Troublemakers* (New York: Doubleday & Company, Inc., 1952); John Roy Carlson, *The Plotters* (New York: E. P. Dutton & Co., Inc., 1946), and *Undercover* (New York: E. P. Dutton & Co., Inc., 1943). See also Morris Janowitz, "Black Legions on the March" in Daniel Aaron (ed.), *America in Crisis* (New York: Alfred A. Knopf, 1952).

[4] Compare Epstein and Forster, *The Radical Right*, pp. 64–66.

sidered remarkable. But many of the objects of radical right resentment are real; bureaucracy, collective behavior, big government (and big labor), and Soviet and Chinese Communism are not products of the rightist imagination. It is the conceptual and perceptual distortions of their genesis and purposes and the proposed or implied methods of dealing with them (and their defenders) that disturb the committed democrat.

The essays that follow explore many of the questions raised above, predominantly through the methods of survey research. They possess in common, in addition to their focus upon elements of the American right, the commitment to analysis of rightists defined in terms of behavior—some act of membership, public or private communication, or political support—which permits them both to be classified, sometimes temporarily, on the right and to be distinguished from a preponderantly nonrightist population.

The positive utility of this approach resides in its clarity. The classification of rightists (or conservatives, or Goldwaterites) is based on the voluntary acts of respondents rather than upon the doubtful perfection of abstract operational definitions. The concomitant weakness results from the impossibiliity of defining an inclusive rightist universe through specific group sampling and purposive sampling. Our hope is that these contributions provide, in combination, a broadly accurate political, social, and psychological description of the American right wing in the third quarter of the twentieth century.

The group survey approach to the analysis of rightists characterizes five of these essays. Raymond Wolfinger and his associates offer a wide-ranging description of the "students" at a San Francisco area "school" sponsored by the Christian Anti-Communism Crusade. Sheilah Koeppen, in addition to replicating the earlier study which concentrates upon political opinion and social status variables, explores the nature and prospects of the Crusaders' commitment to democracy.

Fred Grupp's survey of a national sample of members of The John Birch Society—the only time such a project has been permitted by the leaders of this semisecret organization—focuses upon the problem of cohesiveness in opinions, attitudes, and behavior among Birchers. Scott McNall uses both Birchite protest mail and a sample survey of fundamentalist rightists to test hypotheses relating the growth of the rightist movement to problems of social disorganization.

While the politics of rightists comprise much of the content of the first group of essays (McNall's excepted), the psychic and social stimuli to rightist behavior have been a dominant theme of ideological analysis in America since the publication of *The Authoritarian Personality*.[5] Alan Elms, analyzing a Dallas sample, attempts to determine the power of psychological factors, derived from depth interviewing and extensive use of questionnaire material, to explain radical rightists. Mark Chesler and Richard Schmuck examine and explain the responses of midwestern "super-patriots" to a battery of social-psychological scales, and Ira Rohter, employing similar scales, attempts to create both a model of rightist causation and a subideological typology.

The right is not exclusively the home of ideological extremists. The special political traits which characterize the radical rightist do not also subsume those termed conservative. The concluding essays provide two views of modern American conservatives. McEvoy, analyzing a national sample of the electorate, tests many of the hypotheses intended to account for extremism against a subsample of Goldwater supporters in 1964. The editor explores the political commitments of members of the New York State Conservative Party, also testing the quality of fit of some hypotheses about extremism—political, social, and social-psychological.

---

[5] T. W. Adorno, Else Frenkel-Brunswik, Daniel J. Levinson, and R. Nevitt Sanford, *The Authoritarian Personality* (New York: Harper & Row, Publishers, 1950). See also, H. J. Eysenck, *The Psychology of Politics* (London: Humanities Press, Inc., 1954); Milton Rokeach, *The Open and Closed Mind* (New York: Basic Books, Inc., 1960). The modern seminal work relating politics to psychology is Harold D. Lasswell, *Psychopathology and Politics* (New York: Cambridge University Press, 1930). An excellent bibliography of relevant material is Roger Brown, *Social Psychology* (New York: The Free Press, 1965), pp. 655–656. The fount of the sociologically derived hypotheses is D. Bell (ed.), *The New American Right* (New York: Criterion Books, Inc., 1955), revised and updated as *The Radical Right*.

PART 1

THE EXTREME RIGHT: POLITICAL AND ORGANIZATIONAL PERSPECTIVES

America's Radical Right: Politics and Ideology[*]

RAYMOND E. WOLFINGER
BARBARA KAYE WOLFINGER
KENNETH PREWITT
SHEILAH ROSENHACK

Extreme right-wing movements have been a recurring feature of American political life. The antilibertarian pronouncements and tactics of these movements, as well as the frequently deviant character of their demands, lead many observers to consider them a threat to prevailing political values. For

* Reprinted with permission of The Macmillan Company from *Ideology and Discontent*, edited by David E. Apter. Copyright © 1964 by The Free Press of Glencoe, a Division of The Macmillan Company 1964. The authors are more than ordinarily indebted to people whose generosity and skill aided them at every stage of this research. Hugh Schwartz played an important role in planning the data collection, which was done by an unusually talented and dedicated group of students at Stanford University. At succeeding stages, we profited greatly from the advice of Bo Anderson, Adam Haber, and Morris Zelditch, Jr. Ian Dengler and Peter Lyman kindly volunteered their services for coding. Charles E. Lindblom, Dean Manheimer, Nelson W.

the most part, their influence has not been enduring at the national level. They seem to have their greatest success in local communities, chiefly in intimidating educators and librarians. But at every level of government these movements influence the course of events by distracting and limiting political discussion. The profound dissatisfactions they express seem to reflect deep stresses in American society. For this reason, social scientists have tried to understand the sources of right-wing extremism and to discern the characteristics of the people who are attracted to it.

The manifestation of this political tendency in the early 1960s is known as the radical right. It has attracted much scholarly and journalistic attention.[1] While a good deal is known about the radical right's organizations, doctrines, tactics, and leaders, there is little information, albeit much speculation, about the composition and motivations of its following. This article describes a study of the attitudes, political behavior, and demographic characteristics of 308 people who attended and supported an "Anti-Communism School" presented by the Christian Anti-Communism Crusade in Oakland, California, early in 1962.

THE CHRISTIAN ANTI-COMMUNISM CRUSADE

The numerous groups on the radical right express a wide range of policy proposals and a variety of perceptions of the political world. All of them share a central concern with communism. To the radical right, the main communist danger does not come from the Soviet Union and Communist China or from the appeal of communism to the underdeveloped nations. Instead, rightists emphasize the threat of domestic communism. They tend to attribute unacceptable events to communist influence and to characterize their critics as communists or dupes. This preoccupation with

Polsby, Martin Shapiro, Aaron Wildavsky, and Professor Zelditch made many helpful comments on earlier drafts of this article. Drs. Fred C. Schwarz and Joost Sluis graciously gave free tickets to the interviewers. Additional financial support was provided by the Stanford Committee for Research on Public Affairs, the Dean of the Stanford Garduate School, and the Stanford Computation Center. A previous version of this article was read at the 1963 Annual Meeting of the American Political Science Association in New York City.

[1] The radical right has been covered at great length in most newspapers and national magazines. Several popular books have been written about it, including Roger Burlingame, *The Sixth Column* (Philadelphia: J. B. Lippincott Company, 1962); Mark Sherwin, *The Extremists* (New York: St. Martin's Press, Inc., 1963); and Donald Janson and Bernard Eismann, *The Far Right* (New York: McGraw-Hill, Inc., 1963). The only scholarly book on this subject to date is Daniel Bell (ed.), *The Radical Right* (New York: Doubleday & Company, Inc., 1963). One issue of *The Journal of Social Issues* was devoted largely to the radical right: Vol. 19 (April 1963). The semimonthly *Reports* of Group Research, Inc. (Washington, D.C.) contain a great deal of topical information on the radical right.

the danger and pervasiveness of communism has come to be the defining characteristic of the radical right.

Among the dozens of groups and leaders of the radical right, only Robert Welch and his John Birch Society have attracted more attention than the Christian Anti-Communism Crusade and its president, Dr. Fred C. Schwarz.[2] The Crusade's manifest objective is to fight communism by means of radio and television broadcasts, rallies, banquets, pamphlets, and other techniques. At the peak of its popularity, it had a paid staff of thirty in its southern California headquarters and an annual income in excess of $1 million.[3] By early 1963, more than a million copies had been sold of Dr. Schwarz's book, *You Can Trust the Communists*,[4] the primary source of Crusade doctrine. "Schools" are the Crusade's best known activities. Sponsored by local ad hoc committees and staffed by a dozen or more experienced speakers, these affairs have been held in a number of cities, most successfully in the area extending from southern California to the Gulf Coast.

Almost every social scientist or journalist who has described the Crusade considers it a radical-right organization. Schwarz vigorously denies this contention. He insists that the Crusade is a nonpolitical educational organization dedicated to promoting the proposition that communism is a monstrous threat and to encouraging people to fight it through "a continued program of study and applied citizenship to transform acquired knowledge into local, national and international programs." [5] There are good reasons for skepticism about Schwarz's protestations. The speakers at Crusade schools usually have an intemperate style seldom associated with educational activities. Some are well known for advocacy of measures to restrict freedom of expression in the name of anticommunism.[6] Crusade speakers often suggest or allege that secret communist influence lies behind

---

[2] Probably the most complete description of Dr. Schwarz and the Crusade can befound in the Anti-Defamation League's publication, *Facts*, November-December 1962, entitled "The Case of Fred C. Schwarz." The Crusade has been described in some detail in virtually every national magazine. Books on the radical right usually devote a chapter to it.

[3] In 1961, the Crusade's gross receipts exceeded $1.2 million; they fell to just over $1 million in 1962. These figures do not include money paid indirectly to the Crusade, such as contributions for televising Crusade programs.

[4] Dr. Fred Schwarz, *You Can Trust the Communists* (Englewood Cliffs, N.J.: Prentice-Hall, Inc., 1960). The book was issued in a paperbound edition in 1962.

[5] *Christian Anti-Communism Crusade News Letter* (henceforth cited as *News Letter*), April 1962, p. 2.

[6] One Crusade speaker, a Republican member of the California State Assembly, has introduced a bill to forbid teaching in California schools any theory "opposed to recognized religious sectarian doctrines" (*San Francisco Chronicle*, May 22, 1963, p. 1). Schwarz has said that "Americans should be willing to renounce a certain measure of personal freedom in the battle against Communism" (quoted in *Facts*, p. 253).

many sorts of behavior, from foreign-policy decisions to the authorship of *Lolita*.[7] Although Schwarz chooses these "faculty members," he disclaims responsibility for them, explaining that they have academic freedom and that "the viewpoint expressed by every speaker is not necessarily the official policy of the school." [8]

The inevitable corollary of the central Crusade message is an insinuation of major communist penetration of American institutions.[9] Schwarz has predicted that at the communists' present rate of progress, they will win control of the world by 1973.[10] He suggests that this progress is so advanced that Americans are reluctant to express anticommunist sentiments openly. In this alarming situation, Schwarz sees his own role as crucial. Contemplating an impending Crusade school, he said, "many are praying that this event will mark a turning-point in the heretofore disastrous battle with Communism." [11] His assessment of a completed school: "For the first time the forces of the Communist appeasers are on the defensive. People are proud to be classed as anti-Communists." [12] Schwarz commonly suggests that criticism of the Crusade is a function of communist influence.[13]

Crusade officials estimate that the organization has inspired the formation of more than 5000 local "study groups." [14] The only available information about these groups comes from two psychologists who belonged to one of them in Ann Arbor, Michigan.[15] They report that the group's

---

[7] See, for example, *Oakland Tribune*, February 1, 1962, pp. A-1, E-11; *Facts*, p. 254; and *San Francisco Examiner*, February 2, 1962, p. 10.

[8] *News Letter,* April 1962, p. 3.

[9] In a letter to the Crusade mailing list, Schwarz remarked, "Few people would dispute the contention that a deeper understanding of Communism is desperately needed by those who formulate the national policies and programs on which the survival of freedom depends (letter dated July 19, 1963). Speaking in St. Louis, he said, "We can cry out about how awful the Communist influence is in radio, TV, the press, in government. We can just regret it all. Or we can light a candle. . . . We can personally bring our own program of light, education . . ." (quoted in *Facts*, p. 254). Schwarz also attributes a good deal of procommunist influence to American colleges and universities; see, for example, *You Can Trust the Communists*, pp. 17, 28, 33, 35, 60.

[10] See, for example, U.S. House of Representatives, Committee on Un-American Activities, *International Communism* (Staff Consultation with Frederick Charles Schwarz), 85th Congress, 1st session, May 29, 1957, p. 14. Hundreds of thousands of copies of this testimony have been distributed by a manufacturing firm in Wisconsin.

[11] *News Letter,* August 1962, p. 7.

[12] *News Letter*, December 1960, p. 2.

[13] See, for example, *News Letter*, November-December 1961 and May 1962, p. 6; *San Francisco Examiner*, February 2, 1962, p. 10.

[14] Two Crusade publications, "Establishing a Local Study Group," and "Meeting Manual for the Local Study Group," suggest a variety of radical-right material and offer help from headquarters to local groups.

[15] Mark Chesler and Richard Schmuck, "Participant Observation in a Super-Patriot Discussion Group," *Social Issues*, 19 (April 1963), 18–30.

programs were largely indoctrinations in such radical right-wing doctrines as the pervasiveness of communist influence in American life revealed by progressive education, fluoridated water, Supreme Court decisions, and so forth. The other group members shared these views of the world.

There is some conjecture that the main effect of the Crusade is to activate potential recruits or organizations that have more explicit extremist doctrines and more direct action programs than the Crusade itself. Robert Welch has said, "Dr. Schwarz is doing a grand job of waking up people to the Communist menace. Many of our members help to set up Dr. Schwarz's schools . . . and we frankly do our best to take the people who have been stirred up and awakened and alarmed by him to get them together into the John Birch Society as action groups to do something about it all." [16] In Michigan, Crusade study groups are working with an organization called Freedom-in-Action. This organization, based in Houston, has a rather extreme ideology.[17]

We have described the Crusade in some detail because of Schwarz's contention that it is not a right-wing organization. Actually, even some of his followers seem to disagree with him. We asked the 94 pro-Schwarz respondents who were personally interviewed what other organizations were active in the same cause as the Crusade. Unfortunately, 50 of these respondents either claimed that they did not know of any similar organizations or refused to answer the question. But of those who did answer, 82 percent named right-wing groups, chiefly The John Birch Society.

THE RESEARCH

The San Francisco Bay Region School of Anti-Communism was held in the Oakland Auditorium from January 29 through February 2, 1962. Tuition for the week was $20.00. Ministers, teachers, students, policemen, firemen, and servicemen were admitted for half price. A number of free passes (called "scholarships" by Dr. Schwarz) were distributed; almost 30 percent of our respondents did not pay for their tickets. Classes ran from 9 A.M. to 10 P.M., with breaks for lunch and dinner. The faculty included Senator Thomas Dodd (D. Conn.), Representative Walter H. Judd (R. Minn.), and a variety of speakers from the right-wing circuit.

---

[16] Quoted in *Life*, February 9, 1962, p. 117. Schwarz has doggedly refused to evaluate the Birch Society, explaining, "I don't know very much about the John Birch Society" (quoted in Janson and Eismann, p. 63). The *New York Times* has quoted him as saying, "You know sometimes I get the notion Welch follows me around the country, signing up the people after I've worked them up" (reported in *Facts*, p. 249).

[17] See Janson and Eismann, p. 139; and Willie Morris, "Houston's Superpatriots," *Harper's*, October 1961, p. 56.

Dr. Schwarz spoke in the mornings and evenings. Evening classes were televised.

The school was preceded by an extensive publicity campaign, featuring a number of appearances around the Bay Area by Dr. Schwarz. At one of these appearances, he suggested that San Francisco was a particularly appropriate locale for his school because Nikita Khrushchev had selected the city's Mark Hopkins Hotel as the site for his headquarters when the Soviet Union took over the United States in 1973.[18]

Previous Crusade schools evidently had not encountered much local opposition. But in the San Francisco area the school met a barrage of criticism. One newspaper was vociferously and conspicuously hostile, two were cool, and only the Knowland family's *Oakland Tribune* gave the school enthusiastic backing and a great deal of space. The Northern California-Nevada Council of Churches, the Alameda County Central Labor Council, the Attorney General of California, and several groups of prominent citizens publicly denounced the school. The secretary of the local ad hoc school committee resigned with an attack on the organization. At the end of the school, when it was clear that it was not so successful as had been hoped, the chairman of the ad hoc committee attributed this disappointment partly to the Communist Party's alleged strength in the Bay Area.[19]

The controversy surrounding the school probably had the effect of providing cues about the school's place on the political spectrum, and thus reducing the number of nonconservatives who attended. Conversely, it probably enhanced the rightist composition of the student body.

We used two methods of data collection, personal interviews and a mail questionnaire. Most of the questions in these instruments were taken from The University of Michigan Survey Research Center's national election studies, Samuel A. Stouffer's research of a decade ago for *Communism, Conformity and Civil Liberties*,[20] and Martin Trow's study of attitudes toward Senator Joseph McCarthy in Bennington, Vermont.[21] We thus had normative data with which we compared our respondents' replies. The questions in our personal interviews and mail questionnaires were similar, but the latter contained additional items on political activities and attitudes.

The interviewing and the distribution of questionnaires were carried out by the authors and by students in an advanced undergraduate seminar in

---

[18] *San Francisco Chronicle*, January 9, 1962, pp. 1, 16.

[19] *New York Sunday Times*, February 4, 1962, p. 51.

[20] Samuel A. Stouffer, *Communism, Conformity and Civil Liberties* (New York: Doubleday & Company, Inc., 1955).

[21] Martin Trow, "Small Businessmen, Political Tolerance, and Support for McCarthy," *Amer. J. Sociol.*, 64 (November 1958), 270–281. For a complete report on this research, see Trow, "Right Wing Radicalism and Political Intolerance: A Study of Support for McCarthy in a New England Town," (Unpublished doctoral dissertation, Columbia University, 1957).

political science at Stanford University. The students were briefed on interviewing techniques and conducted practice interviews prior to the data collection. The interviews for this study were conducted during the afternoon and evening of the second day of the school. The mail questionnaires, covering letters describing our project as a manifestation of Stanford students' interest in the political opinions of their elders, and stamped envelopes addressed to the Stanford Department of Political Science were distributed on the second and three subsequent days of the school's operation.

A description of our reception at the school will aid understanding of both the character of the audience and the limitations of our data. There were several factors in our favor: Although Dr. Schwarz had given us free tickets, he was unaware that we were interested in his audience rather than in his message until we had collected a good many interviews and had attracted the attention of the press.[22] A number of respondents evidently felt that, since Schwarz had given us "scholarships," he approved of our research. Stanford has a respectable, upper-class reputation in the Bay Area. The interviewers' wholesome, youthful appearance seemed to evoke a desire on the part of many respondents to "save" them from the malign influence of subversive professors.

Observation of the atmosphere at the school made it clear that it would be necessary for our interviewers to abandon the customary researcher's air of impartiality if we were to gather much data. The Stanford students clapped when the audience did and rose for the numerous standing ovations.

Nevertheless, we encountered suspicion, hostility, and abuse. It appeared that the greatest immediate causes of these responses were the interviewers' academic connections and their clipboards, which suggested to the Crusaders that petitions were being circulated.[23] Most of the unfriendly re-

---

[22] At the end of our first evening of data collection, after he and the Northern California director of the Crusade had carefully studied the mail questionnaire, Schwarz agreed not to condemn the study to his audience, although he warned, "With one sentence, I could kill your whole project." He declined, however, to announce publicly that we had no polemic intent and that we were not associated with critical student pickets who had been vehemently denounced by members of the faculty. These negotiations were witnessed by several reporters and were described in the *San Francisco News-Call Bulletin*, January 31, 1962, p. 4. This account appeared after the personal interviews were completed and before most of the mail questionnaires were distributed. Since there were no appreciable differences between responses to the two types of instrument, we concluded that this incident had no important influence on our data.

[23] In addition, there was a good deal of generalized xenophobia. The *Oakland Tribune* remarked on the Crusaders' determined and unusual reluctance to give names to reporters (January 30, 1962, p. G-11). During the evening, a lady stood on the front steps of the auditorium holding a sign bearing a crimson handprint, an American flag, and the words "Remember Hungary." She was constantly harassed by passing Crusaders, who often called her a communist and advised her to "go back" to Russia. Her critics were unmoved by her plaintive reply: "But I'm on your side."

marks were made before the interviewers could say more than a few words or were volunteered by people who had not been approached. The undergraduates bore the brunt of these accusations, but, in some instances, they were regarded merely as dupes of their professor. Some Crusaders evidently assumed that since he was a professor he was also a communist, but one claimed more specific knowledge, telling one interviewer that the latter's Stanford instructor had been the leader of a local communist front for the past seven years.

We were unable to use systematic sampling methods in this situation. Strictly speaking, we do not have a sample, and, therefore, we shall not use tests for significance of difference. Interviewers were instructed to pick potential respondents to "represent" the audience in terms of age, sex, and style of dress. They tried to avoid choosing only people who seemed most willing to be interviewed. They also tried to avoid interviewing or giving questionnaires to minors or more than one person in a family. (Questionnaires inadvertently given to minors have been excluded from the analysis.) About forty people refused to be interviewed, and about 100 refused even to accept mail questionnaires. Since these refusals often were accompanied by invective and accusations of subversive intent, it is likely that the most extreme members of the audience are underrepresented in our sample. Those who refused appeared to be no different from the respondents in age, sex, dress, or manner of speech.

One hundred and eight personal interviews were completed. About 625 mail questionnaires were distributed, of which 244, or 39 percent, were returned. The attitudinal and demographic findings on the mail and personal samples are virtually identical. It is possible, however, that the educational distribution in each group is skewed upward: in the mail-questionnaire group for the obvious reason that such instruments are more congenial to the educated and in the personal-interview group because the undergraduates may have tended, despite instructions, to approach people who appeared closest to themselves in socioeconomic status. There is no way of knowing how representative of the population attending the school our "sample" is. Several independent observers, including a newspaper reporter, have estimated that about 2000 people came to one or more sessions of the school. While the representativeness of our sample is unknown, our respondents therefore constitute a good proportion of the total population.[24]

Eighty-eight percent of the respondents said that they were in favor of Schwarz and the Crusade. The following analysis is based on the attitudes

---

[24] Of the estimated 2000 people at the Crusade, perhaps 200 were minors and, at a conservative estimate, at least 500 came with spouses. Of a total possible population of about 1300, more than a quarter were interviewed or completed a questionnaire.

and characteristics of these 308 supporters of the Crusade, of whom 94 were interviewed and 214 completed and returned mail questionnaires. Previous empirical studies of radical rightists and McCarthyites have been concerned with respondents who, in one form or another, expressed approval of The John Birch Society or of Senator McCarthy. Our respondents meet a stronger test—they are not passive supporters of the Crusade but active participants. They were concerned enough to attend the school, in most cases at some cost in money and time.

Four cautions must be expressed against generalizing from our data to the contemporary radical right as a whole: The Crusade's name and some aspects of its publicity tactics probably minimize its attraction to Catholics and Jews and maximize its appeal to devout Protestants; the Crusade does not take positions on many public issues and therefore has a more generic appeal than many other radical-right groups; compared to many of these organizations, the Crusade is rather moderate; while attendance at the Oakland school demonstrated more than passive endorsement of the Crusade, it was a relatively mild form of activity compared to putting cards on Polish hams, forming discussion groups, or disrupting PTA meetings.

DEMOGRAPHIC CHARACTERISTICS OF THE RESPONDENTS

This sample is strikingly different from the San Francisco Bay Area population with respect to demographic characteristics. Although 12 percent of the area's population is Negro and Oriental, all our respondents are white.[25] In attending the school for five days, we saw no more than a handful of nonwhites.

The Crusaders are predominantly an upper-status group. More than half are businessmen or professionals or have husbands in such occupations; [26] this proportion is twice that found in the white Bay Area population. Forty-one percent of the Crusaders reported annual family incomes in excess of $10,000, compared to 26 percent of the Bay Area population. Almost 80 percent have attended college, and 52 percent have been graduated. This figure is exactly four times the percentage of college graduates in the adult white population of the area. The sample contains a somewhat disproportionate number of people over the age of fifty. These data are summarized in Table I.

---

[25] For this reason, we present normative data for the white population whenever possible. Unless otherwise indicated, "Bay Area" refers to the San Francisco-Oakland Standard Metropolitan Statistical Area as defined by the Census Bureau. All but nine of our respondents come from this region.

[26] All discussion of the Crusaders' occupations is based on the occupation of the head of the respondent's household.

TABLE 1

Demographic Characteristics of the Sample and the White Bay Area Population (in Percent)

	CRUSADERS N = 308	WHITE RESIDENTS OF THE BAY AREA[a]
Occupation of head of household [b]		
Professional and technical	31	14
Businessmen, managers, and officials	27	12
Clerical and sales personnel	14	17
Skilled, semiskilled, unskilled, and service workers	11	50
Other	6	1
No answer	11	6
	100	100
Annual family income before taxes		
$15,000 and over	21	8
$10,000 to $14,999	20	18
$7000 to $9999	22	28
$4000 to $6999	20	30
Below $4000	9	16
No answer	8 [c]	
	100	100
Education [d]		
Completed college	52	13
Some college	26	14
Completed high school	11	29
Some high school	5	19
Grammar school or less	3	25
No answer	3	
	100	100
Age [e]		
Under fifty years old	52	64
Fifty years old and over	45	36
No answer	3	
	100	100

[a] Source: U.S. Bureau of the Census, *U.S. Census of Population: 1960, General Social and Economic Characteristics. California. Final Report PC (1)-6C* (Washington: U.S.G.P.O., 1962).
[b] Bay Area occupation data are for all employed males, including non-whites.
[c] Most of these respondents had high-income occupations.
[d] Normative data are for people twenty-five years old and older.
[e] Normative data are for all white urban residents of California twenty years old and older.

Slightly more than three-quarters of the Crusaders are Protestants. Only 8 percent are Catholics, compared to about 24 percent of the white Bay Area population.[27] The Crusaders' rate of church attendance is quite simi-

---

[27] The best available source of information on the religious characteristics of the Bay Area population is: National Council of the Churches of Christ in

lar to that of northern white Protestants who have attended college.[28] In sum, these data suggest that the Crusade's appeal is to the well educated and well-to-do.[29]

Seymour M. Lipset has analyzed California Poll data on attitudes toward The John Birch Society.[30] He reports that "A supporter of the Society is more likely . . . to be better educated, and to be in a higher economic category."[31] His findings are consistent with ours, with one exception: He found that Catholics were slightly more likely than Protestants to endorse the Birch Society. This difference may be due to the religious aspects of the Crusade's image. This point should be kept in mind as an important qualification of generalizations about the radical right on the basis of our data.

THE CRUSADERS' POLITICAL AND ATTITUDINAL CHARACTERISTICS

The Crusaders are almost unanimously Republican in their voting behavior. Ninety-two percent of those who voted in the 1960 presidential election supported Richard M. Nixon. Sixty-six percent of the Crusaders identified themselves as Republicans, 19 percent as independents, and 8 percent as Democrats.[32] Furthermore, they lean toward the conservative

---

the U.S.A., *Churches and Church Membership in the United States*, Series C, no. 59, 1957. According to this source, there were 595,153 Catholics in the Bay Area; this figure is 24 percent of the white population in 1960. The problem of defining church "membership" makes it an inadequate source of normative data on Protestant church affiliations.

[28] Source: the national sample survey of the 1960 presidential election conducted by the University of Michigan Survey Research Center. All SRC election data used in this article were obtained from the Inter-University Consortium for Political Research. We are grateful to Ralph Bisco, Michael Kahan, Warren E. Miller, and Linda Wilcox of the Consortium staff for their advice and assistance. The SRC data used in the preliminary version of this article that was given at the 1963 meeting of the American Political Science Association were computed by the authors from IBM cards supplied by the Consortium. The originals of these cards subsequently were "cleaned" by the Consortium. The SRC data in this article are from the clean cards, which accounts for a few minor differences in the SRC data presented in the two versions.

[29] The scarcity of lower-status persons in our sample cannot be adequately explained by the well known finding that such people have relatively low rates of political participation. While their rate of participation is lower, such persons still account for a good proportion of the audience at other kinds of public political meetings. For instance, of the white northerners who attended one or more political meetings during the 1960 election campaign, 62 percent had not attended college, and 65 percent had annual family incomes of less than $7,500 (source: the 1960 SRC election study).

[30] Seymour M. Lipset, "Three Decades of the Radical Right: Coughlinites, McCarthyites, and Birchers—1962," in Bell, pp. 353–357.

[31] Lipset, p. 354.

[32] Of the 25 Democrats in the sample, four are Jews, five are Catholics, and five were born in the South. There are eight Jewish respondents in all.

wing of the Republican Party. When asked to choose between Nixon and Senator Barry Goldwater for the 1964 Republican presidential nomination, 58 percent of those who chose one of the two men picked Goldwater. When our data were collected, Nixon was by far the leading candidate, in the nation as a whole, for the 1964 nomination. At about this time, the Gallup organization asked a national sample of Republicans to choose among 10 leading contenders for the 1964 Republican nomination. Forty-six percent chose Nixon, and 13 percent picked Goldwater.[33] It seemed possible that the Crusaders' preference for Goldwater might have been even higher, except for Nixon's long participation in California politics. Many of the old-time Californians in our sample may, in assessing the two candidates, think of Nixon chiefly in his former role as the scourge of domestic communists. Accordingly, we analyzed preferences for the two men by length of residence in the Bay Area. As Table 2 indicates, we found that respondents who had lived in the Bay Area since the beginning of Nixon's career split about evenly in their support of the two men, while newcomers to the area were two to one for Goldwater.[34]

TABLE 2

Preference for Nixon or Goldwater as Republican Presidential Candidate in 1964—by Crusaders' Length of Residence in the Bay Area (in Percent)

	CRUSADERS WHO HAVE LIVED IN THE BAY AREA[a]	
	16 YEARS OR LESS	MORE THAN 16 YEARS
Prefer Goldwater	66	47
Prefer Nixon	34	53
	100	100
N	115	111

[a] "No answers" and "no preference" responses have been removed from the bases.

In addition to their Republican inclinations, the Crusaders are united in their fears of internal subversion. When asked, "How great a danger do you feel that American Communists are to this country at the present time?" nine out of ten Crusaders replied "great" or "very great," as

---

[33] Source: *San Francisco Chronicle*, March 5, 1962, p. 34.

[34] Another possible explanation of this finding is that newcomers to California are more likely to be conservative, for there is some indication that newcomers are more favorably disposed to the Birch Society than are old residents (see Lipset, p. 363). The old-time Nixon supporters, however, are more conservative on issues than the newcomers for Nixon. The old residents for Goldwater are by far the most reactionary of the four groups.

Table 3 indicates. This figure is double the proportion of college-educated respondents who made such replies in Stouffer's study, which was conducted at the height of the McCarthy period.

TABLE 3

Perceptions of the Internal Communist Threat by Crusaders and College-Educated Americans, 1954 (in Percent)

	CRUSADERS	COLLEGE-EDUCATED AMERICANS[a]
Think internal Communist threat is		
A very great danger	66	18
A great danger	21	24
Some danger	9	43
Hardly any danger	2	10
No danger		2
Don't know and no answer	2	3
	100	100
N	308	485

[a] Source: data from the national survey conducted by the National Opinion Research Center in 1954 for Stouffer's study of attitudes toward communism and civil liberties, obtained from the Inter-University Consortium for Political Research.

Seventy-one percent of our respondents said that the danger to this country from domestic communists is greater than the danger from the Soviet Union and Communist China.

We also asked questions about communist influence in several specific sectors of American life. As Table 4 shows, 91 percent of the Crusaders

TABLE 4 *

Crusaders' Perceptions of Substantial Communist Influence or Presence in Various Aspects of American Society (in Percent)

	AGREE	DISAGREE	DON'T KNOW	TOTAL
Communists have a lot of influence in				
"Colleges and universities"	91	9		100
"The Democratic Party"	55	38	7	100
"The Republican Party"	20	72	8	100
"Communists live in my neighborhood"	36	36	28	100

* In this and all subsequent tables marked with asterisks, the bases have not been reported because the tables include different questions, to which the number of "No answers" varied.

thought that communist professors had a great deal of influence in colleges and universities. About half thought that communists had a great deal of influence in the Democratic Party, and a fifth even thought they were influential in the Republican Party. More than a third of the Crusaders said that communists were living in their neighborhoods.

What kinds of people in this country do the Crusaders think are likely to be communists? Twenty-nine percent nominated professors and intellectuals, and 45 percent mentioned youths, students, and "the ignorant." Only 7 percent mentioned foreigners or members of minority groups, and hardly any mentioned government officials. These answers are interesting both for what they include and for what they omit. The prime villains are not defined in ethnic, economic, or governmental terms. Rather, they are those people who communicate ideas and information and those who are most vulnerable to being misled. Stouffer reported somewhat similar findings. Most of his respondents were unable to give more than the vaguest kind of generalized answer ("they do bad things") when asked what communists do. But 42 percent were able to give more specific replies: Eight percent said that communists committed acts of sabotage, and 8 percent more thought they were spies; 28 percent said that they converted people to communism and spread their insidious ideas.[35]

The Crusaders' responses suggest that, to adherents of the radical right, "communists" are people who spread a kind of mental infection that causes people to adopt repellent ideas. One can also infer that the Crusaders reject the idea that communism may feed on deprivation or injustice. The Crusaders' recommendations on what the government should do to fight communism in this country reflect their view that communism is an intellectual malady. Forty-eight percent of the Crusaders recommended education, chiefly on the evils of communism;[36] 15 percent were in favor of supporting present anticommunist policies and institutions; and 46 percent called for harsher measures, ranging from the death penalty to denial of citizenship.[37]

It is sometimes asserted, most often by left-wing commentators, that adherents of the radical right are warmongers, eager for a nuclear exchange with the Soviet Union. At least one writer has explained the radical right's strength in California in these terms: Since the state's economy is dependent on defense spending, Californians will support any movement advocating a more belligerent policy toward communist countries.[38] Our data do not support this proposition. We asked the Crusaders the same question that

---

[35] Stouffer, p. 158.

[36] This figure may reflect Schwarz's emphasis on the need for anticommunist "education."

[37] These percentages total more than 100 percent because some respondents made more than one suggestion. A few Crusaders recommended withdrawal from the United Nations or cessation of all relations with communist countries.

[38] Fred J. Cook, "The Ultras," *The Nation*, June 30, 1962, p. 571.

Stouffer used a decade ago: "Of these three ways of dealing with Russia, which do you think is best for America now?"[39] As Table 5 shows, less than a fifth of the Crusaders were in favor of fighting Russia. Furthermore, a good many of these respondents indicated, by marginal comments, that they interpreted "fight" to mean "vigorously oppose."[40]

TABLE 5

Attitudes toward Dealing with the Soviet Union (in Percent)

	CRUSADERS	NATIONAL SAMPLE, 1954 [a]
Believe the United States should		
Talk over problems with Russia	28	61
Have nothing to do with Russia	37	17
Fight Russia	18	14
Other	2	
Don't know	1	8
No answer	13	
	99 [b]	100
N	308	4933

[a] Source: Stouffer, p. 77.
[b] Does not add up to 100 percent because of rounding.

The current tendency to describe attitudes on policy toward the communist nations on a belligerence-negotiation dimension obscures another aspect of American opinion, one that dominated our perspectives on foreign policy until the Second World War: isolationism. As Table 5 shows, the Crusaders' most striking difference from Stouffer's sample is the extent of their aversion to any involvement with the Soviet Union. We suggest that isolationism, rather than aggressiveness, is the hallmark of many radical rightists' foreign-policy sentiments.

So far we have seen that, although the Crusaders are united in their alarm about the dangers of internal subversion, they display considerable diversity of opinion on proposals for dealing with communism in both its foreign and domestic manifestations. As Table 6 shows, the same pattern occurs on other foreign policy issues; the Crusaders are somewhat conservative but by no means unanimously so on any particular issue. About 40 percent of them support American involvement in the United Nations, and about two-thirds are in favor of foreign aid, although some of the latter group would give aid only to friendly nations. Those respondents with the most extreme perceptions of the power of American communists,

[39] Stouffer, p. 77.
[40] Dr. Schwarz and some of his students complained that the three alternatives given in the question provide an inadequate set of choices. We agree.

TABLE 6 *

Attitudes on Foreign Policy Issues (in Percent)

	AMONG CRUSADERS WHO SEE COMMUNIST INFLUENCE IN BOTH MAJOR PARTIES	AMONG ALL OTHER CRUSADERS
Proportion saying		
"The United Nations is bad for the U.S."	69	58
"The U.S. should give little or no foreign aid" [a]	40	30

[a] Thirty-two percent of the respondents who favor more aid are opposed to present methods of administering the aid program or are against giving aid to communist or neutral nations.

the 56 respondents who think that communists have a great deal of influence in both major political parties, are consistently more conservative than the rest of the sample. But even these alarmists are rather heterogeneous in their attitudes on substantive issues.

The Crusaders share a general feeling that the federal government is too bountiful: Eighty-six percent agreed that "the American people would have more get up and go if the government would stop giving them things." But on a less general level, 40 percent to 60 percent of the Crusaders took liberal positions on several specific issues, as Table 7 shows. For instance, almost two-thirds of them are opposed to the southern position on desegregation, and more than half are in favor of at least some federal aid to education. Once again, the alarmists about domestic communist influence are somewhat more conservative on substantive issues.

TABLE 7 *

Attitudes on Domestic Issues (in Percent) [a]

	AMONG CRUSADERS WHO SEE COMMUNIST INFLUENCE IN BOTH MAJOR PARTIES	AMONG ALL OTHER CRUSADERS
Proportion saying		
"South is right on integration"	44	35
"Opposed to federal aid to education"	56	40
"Opposed to medicare" [b]	69	59
"Unions do more harm than good"	60	56
"Big corporations control too much business"	35	27

[a] With the exception of the last two items in Table 7, the questions in Tables 6 and 7 were asked on the mail questionnaire only.
[b] Answers to this question did not vary appreciably with age.

The Crusaders' level of political tolerance is somewhat uncertain. Our comparative measure is three questions from Trow's Bennington study modified to agree-disagree form: "In peacetime the Socialist party should *not* be allowed to publish newspapers in this country"; "Newspapers should be allowed to criticize our form of government"; "Members of the Communist Party in this country should be allowed to speak on radio and television." [41] Trow's respondents were men, and, since the Crusaders are no exception to the generalization that women are less tolerant than men,[42] we compared only the male Crusaders to Trow's Bennington respondents. We controlled for education, since tolerance usually increases with years of schooling. As Table 8 shows, those Crusaders who have

TABLE 8 *

Political Tolerance of Male Crusaders and the Bennington Sample— by Education

	PERCENTAGE AGREEING	
	AMONG MALE CRUSADERS	AMONG BENNINGTON RESPONDENTS[a]
"Socialists should be allowed to publish newspapers"		
High school graduates or less	69	60
Some college	79	90
College graduates	89	93
"Newspapers should be allowed to criticize our form of government"		
High school graduates or less	79	81
Some college	88	91
College graduates	92	97
"Communists should be allowed to speak on radio and television"		
High school graduates or less	24	20
Some college	24	31
College graduates	33	47

[a] Recomputed by the authors from data in Trow, "Right Wing Radicalism," p. 261.

attended college are slightly less tolerant than the corresponding group of Bennington residents. The Crusaders' slightly higher tolerance at the lowest educational level is probably due to the fact that 60 percent of the Crusaders in that group had been graduated from high school compared to 38 percent of the corresponding Bennington respondents.

---

[41] Trow, "Right Wing Radicalism," p. 261. Trow's respondents were chosen by modified quota-sampling methods.

[42] See, for example, Stouffer, pp. 131–155.

We are not satisfied that the Crusaders are even as tolerant as Table 8 indicates. For one thing, they tend to be particularly intolerant of communists' civil rights, and, as we have seen, they tend to believe that a great many people are communists. Second, the respondents who score as tolerant on the Bennington questions are only slightly less likely to support harsh measures against American communists than are the intolerant Crusaders. It is safest to conclude that our sample's level of tolerance compared to the general population is an unknown quantity. For purposes of intrasample comparison, we will use a four-point intolerance index constructed from the three Bennington items, giving one point for each intolerant response.

Numerous studies have shown that, in the general population, attitudes on political issues ordinarily are strongly related to demographic characteristics like income, education, sex, and age.[43] These relationships are remarkably weak in our sample. For example, well educated Crusaders are not notably more tolerant than those who did not attend college, while the Bennington respondents' responses vary greatly by education (see Table 8). While conservatism on domestic welfare issues normally increases with income, this trend is visible only among the Crusaders with annual incomes above $15,000, as Table 9 indicates.[44] Similarly, conservatism increases with age only among respondents over 60 years old. The demographic variable that produces the largest difference is sex. Women generally are somewhat more conservative than men, particularly on issues concerning

TABLE 9

Domestic Conservatism—by Income (in Percent)[a]

Score on Domestic Conservatism Index	Below $7,000	$7000 to $10,000	$10,000 to $15,000	$15,000 and Over
Low 0	39	34	38	23
1	32	30	27	26
High 2	29	36	35	51
	100	100	100	100
N	44	47	52	47

[a] "No answers" have been removed from the bases.

---

[43] A great deal of research on this point is summarized in V. O. Key, Jr., *Public Opinion and American Democracy* (New York: Alfred A. Knopf, 1961).

[44] Domestic conservatism is measured by a three-point index, with one point each for replies against medicare and aid to education. Conservative responses on the other three items in Table 7 were so weakly associated with one another and with these two questions that we did not include them in the index. The foreign-policy index has four points, with one point each for opposition to foreign aid and to the United Nations and choice of the "fight Russia" or "have nothing to do with Russia" responses in Table 5.

communism; [45] even here, however, the relationships are not strong among the Crusaders.

No matter what cross tabulations we made or what independent variables we controlled, we were unable to find meaningful distinctions related to demographic variables. This failure may be a consequence of the sample's limited range in both demographic factors (most respondents are upper-status) and political predispositions (the Crusaders are conservative). There may not be sufficient range within each set of variables for them to interact significantly.

The relative unimportance of demographic variables in intrasample variation may have a specific meaning in this context, however. It is possible that, once an individual has pledged his political allegiance, once he has become an active member of a political organization, ideological considerations become salient for him. Commitment to other reference groups may yield to the pressures of political commitment. If this proposition is true, we should expect that, among people active in the Democratic Party for example, attitudes would not vary so much by demographic factors as they would among a group of inactive Democrats. This proposition has not been tested with voting behavior data.

Crusaders who engage in more than one form of campaign work are more likely to take conservative positions on issues than are those who are less active. For example, 47 percent of the former group was opposed to both federal aid to education and federally financed medical care for the aged, compared to 24 percent of the latter group. This disparity is in line with findings that the political attitudes of people deeply involved in politics tend to be more consistent and congruent with their party identification. [46]

The voting behavior studies have shown that relationships between party identification and attitudes on political issues are often very weak; Republicans often are as likely to endorse a particular liberal position as Democrats. [47] Trow found that, with education controlled, McCarthy supporters were no more intolerant than the Senator's opponents, while Lipset reports weak relationships between attitudes toward McCarthy and conservative positions on a number of foreign-policy issues. [48] Despite this evidence, there seems to be a tendency to assume that supporters of the radical right

---

[45] Compare Lipset, "The Sources of the Radical Right—1955," in Bell, *The Radical Right*, pp. 303–304.

[46] See Key, pp. 439–440; and Angus Campbell, P. Converse, W. Miller, and D. Stokes, *The American Voter* (New York: John Wiley & Sons, Inc., 1960), p. 208.

[47] See, for example, Campbell, Converse, Miller, and Stokes, chap. 9.

[48] Trow, "Small Businessmen," pp. 272–273; and Lipset, "Three Decades," pp. 338–340. Since support for McCarthy was related negatively both to Democratic allegiance and education, relationships between McCarthyism and conservative issue positions might have been found if party identification had been controlled.

have a consistent set of attitudes far outside the normal political spectrum. Instead, it appears that extremism is not unidimensional; deviant opinions in one area may coexist with quite conventional views on other issues.[49]

Many leaders of the radical right have attracted a good deal of derision for their policy proposals, which range from military adventurism abroad to complete laissez-faire in domestic matters. The Crusaders share the alarmist attitude toward subversion characteristic of the radical right. Their attitudes on various political issues incline to the conservative pole, but they are by no means united on any of these issues. Thus attempting to deduce their attitudes from radical-right ideology would be no more valid than would deducing the opinions of a group of Republicans from the Republican platform.[50]

Failure to distinguish between the pronouncements of political leaders and the opinions of their supporters involves some grave risks in attempting to explain the appeal of the radical right. In the first place, it is not very wise to reach conclusions about the right's sources of support on the basis of an examination of its ideology. Second, the appeal of the radical right is not limited to those individuals who will accept extreme doctrines in their entirety. Any particular bizarre doctrinal point is not sufficient to destroy a right-wing group's attractiveness to all prospective members. Robert Welch's famous remark about President Eisenhower's communist allegiance has not put an end to the growth of The John Birch Society. Although such embarrassments undoubtedly do not make recruiting easier, they do not seem to have destroyed the Birch Society's appeal. The potential supporters of the radical right are therefore more numerous than might be assumed from an examination of its ideology.

THE SOURCES OF THE RADICAL RIGHT

In the past dozen years, a good deal of intellectual effort has been expended in attempts to explain who is attracted to movements like the radical right and for what reasons. Much of this effort has been offhand speculation, but some has been based on sophisticated social-science theory and has produced provocative hypotheses. Some of these propositions are derived from theoretical orientations growing out of attempts to explain Nazism and other extremist movements. Senator McCarthy's impact on

---

[49] We do not mean to suggest that opposition to medicare, for example, is an extreme or bizarre opinion. Our point is that support of medicare is evidence that an individual does not hold extreme rightist views on at least that issue. Regrettably, we did not ask questions about some of the more celebrated radical-right positions, such as abolition of the income tax.

[50] Trow makes this point with respect to McCarthyism; see "Small Businessmen," pp. 280–281.

American political life resulted in another stream of investigations. Most recently, attempts have been made to explain the radical right. There is thus a body of propositions that we can use to examine our data.

Most of these propositions are concerned with ethnicity or socioeconomic status. The San Francisco Bay Area is a suitable testing ground for these propositions, since it is characterized by demographic heterogeneity. It has a variety of ethnic groups in various stages of assimilation, as well as many white Protestants in the process of bettering their positions in life. The area has been settled long enough to have established wealthy families, and its continuing economic growth produces plenty of nouveaux riches. In fact, the Bay Area contains sizable numbers of almost every group considered receptive to the radical right, with the exception of Texas oil millionaires. We shall begin by examining several propositions that are not congruent with our data and then proceed to more fruitful hypotheses.

ALIENATION

One of the most popular—and untested—themes in modern social science is "alienation." Uprooted from his customary setting by industrialization and urbanization, cut loose from the assured life of a stable class structure and traditional mores, deprived of meaningful associations and satisfactions by the formless bustle of modern life, alienated man is regarded as the most malleable and volatile of creatures. In his quiet state, he is apathetic, withdrawing from politics as from all forms of civic activity. But such quietude only increases his desperation, which must be expressed in some form of political extremism: "Mass theory leads to the expectation than the unattached and alienated of all classes are more attracted to extremist symbols and leaders than are their class-rooted counterparts." [51]

There are difficulties in designing research on alienation, which perhaps explain why these ideas have remained unverified. It is uncertain what objective indicators can be used to measure alienation. For example, using group membership as an index of class alienation, as we do, poses a question: Can we conclude that an individual without formal group memberships is any less "class-rooted" than one who belongs to half a dozen organizations? Are such superficial experiences as membership in a Rotary Club proof that an individual is not alienated? Furthermore, the literature on alienation is by no means clear about the nature of the "extremist movements" that supposedly appeal to alienated men.

Our findings relevant to alienation should be examined with these qualifications in mind. First, the Crusaders do not seem to be social isolates. As Table 10 shows, they have a somewhat higher level of membership in

---

[51] William Kornhauser, *The Politics of Mass Society* (New York: The Free Press, 1959), p. 180.

TABLE 10

Group Memberships of Crusaders Compared to Business, Professional, and Clerical Heads of Household in National Sample, 1952 (in Percent)

NUMBER OF GROUP MEMBERSHIPS	CRUSADERS	NATIONAL SAMPLE, 1952 [a]
None	11	26
One	29	28
Two	27	16
Three or more	34	30
	101 [b]	100
N	294	164

[a] Source: SRC 1952 election study.
[b] Does not total 100 percent because of rounding.

all kinds of organizations—church committees, civic groups, veterans organizations, and so forth—than do the business, professional, and white-collar respondents in the 1952 Survey Research Center study.

It is quite conceivable that one can be socially integrated yet feel politically alienated. We used the index of sense of political efficacy developed by the SRC to measure our respondents' feelings of political effectiveness.[52] It does not appear that the Crusaders are possessed by feelings of powerlessness. As Table 11 shows, they have a slightly higher sense of political efficacy than do white northerners who have attended college.

Some writers have taken the view that the radical right offers a means of political expression for people detached from or frustrated by the American two-party system. Our data suggest that the opposite is the case. Fully 98 percent of the eligible Crusaders reported that they voted in the 1960 presidential election, while 54 percent of all respondents said that they had sent letters, postcards, or telegrams to government officials during the previous year. As Table 12 shows, the Crusaders' rate of participation in political campaigns is extraordinarily high. Almost two thirds of them make financial contributions to political parties or candidates. The same proportion attends meetings or rallies, and more than a third does

---

[52] This well known measure of sense of political efficacy is based on these questions: "I don't think public officials care much what people like me think"; "Sometimes politics and government seem so complicated that a person like me can't really understand what's going on"; "Voting is the only way that people like me can have any say about how the government runs things"; "People like me don't have any say about what the government does." Efficacy is measured on a five-point index, with one point for each negative answer. For a detailed discussion of this measure, see Angus Campbell, Gerald Gurin, and Warren E. Miller, *The Voter Decides* (Evanston, Ill.: William Clowes & Sons, 1954), pp. 187–194.

TABLE 11

Crusaders' Sense of Political Efficacy Compared to College-Educated White Northerners (in Percent)

SENSE OF POLITICAL EFFICACY	CRUSADERS [a]	WHITE NORTHERN COLLEGE-EDUCATED [b]
High 4	40	29
3	32	39
2	18	23
1	6	5
Low 0	4	4
	100	100
N	269	262

[a] Respondents who did not answer all four questions in the political efficacy index were excluded from this table.
[b] Source: SRC 1960 election study.

other kinds of campaign work. Seventy-nine percent of the Crusaders engaged in at least one type of campaign activity. It should be noted that these items do not refer indiscriminately to any kind of political activity but to activity in the two-party context—more specifically, to work for the Republican Party. As we have seen, the most politically active Crusaders were more conservative than the inactive ones.

TABLE 12 *

Crusaders' Political Campaign Activity Compared to That of College-Educated White Northerners

	AMONG CRUSADERS [a]	AMONG WHITE NORTHERN COLLEGE-EDUCATED [b]
Percentage saying they		
"Give money or buy tickets to help the campaign for one of the parties or candidates"	62	23
"Go to political meetings, rallies, dinners or things like that"	62	13
"Do any other work for one of the parties or candidates"	37	8
"Belong to any political club or organization"	27	9

[a] These questions were asked on our mail questionnaire only.
[b] Source: SRC 1960 election study. The questions were the same in both studies, except that the first three questions were phrased in the past tense in the SRC study.

STATUS ANXIETY

The best known efforts to identify the sources of Senator McCarthy's support are the essays by noted social scientists collected in *The New American Right*.[53] This book, supplemented by articles on the radical right, has recently been reissued.[54] Several contributors to these books base their explanations of McCarthyism or the radical right on what they call "status politics," that is, a situation in which people project their anxieties about social status onto political objects. Since "status anxiety" is a very broad concept and can be applied to so much of the population, it has little explanatory value.[55] We shall discuss several specific applications of this notion that attribute susceptibility to the radical right to particular groups in the population.

The first and simplest formulation is that upward mobile people are inclined to support the radical right. Presumably such people, newly arrived in the middle class, feel some sort of status insecurity, which they express by superpatriotism and exaggerated hostility to "communists." This proposition is not confirmed by our data. We compared the fathers' occupations of the businessmen and professional Crusaders to those of the white northern businessmen and professionals interviewed in the 1956 SRC election study. As Table 13 indicates, Crusaders have at least as much status stability as the comparison group. Furthermore, within our sample, the status-stable businessmen and professionals were more likely than the upward mobile ones to choose conservative positions on every attitude measure. The status-stable were also much more active politically.

A second proposition asserts that downward mobile individuals are attracted to the radical right because it provides both an explanation for their misfortunes and a scapegoat for their consequent hostility. This proposition does not seem to explain the Crusade's appeal, for few of our respondents had experienced downward mobility.

A third explanation is also based on social mobility—but in the context of ethnic hostility. In this view, upward-mobile second- and third-generation Americans affirm their patriotism and new middle-class status

---

[53] Daniel Bell (ed.), *The New American Right* (New York: Criterion Books, Inc., 1955).

[54] Bell, *The Radical Right*.

[55] The inclusiveness of "status anxiety," the diversity of the various groups that were thought to support McCarthy because of this anxiety, and the scarcity of evidence to support these speculations have led several writers to comment critically on *The New American Right*. See especially Trow, "Small Businessmen," pp. 270–271; and Nelson W. Polsby, "Toward an Explanation of McCarthyism," in Polsby, Robert A. Dentler, and Paul A. Smith, eds., *Politics and Social Life* (Boston: Houghton Mifflin Company, 1963), pp. 809–824. Polsby has an amusing table listing the many categories of people who are considered McCarthyites by one or more of the contributors to *The New American Right* (p. 813).

TABLE 13

Occupational Mobility of Businessmen and Professionals (in Percent)

	BUSINESS AND PROFESSIONALS ONLY	
	AMONG CRUSADERS [a]	AMONG WHITE NORTHERNERS [b]
Father's occupation		
Businessmen and professionals	41	37
Clerical and sales	8	6
Blue-collar	12	38
Farmer	16	16
No answer	23	3
	100	100
N	179	290

[a] In the case of married female respondents, fathers'-in-law and spouses' occupations are used.

[b] Source: SRC 1956 election study.

by supporting the radical right. As Hofstadter puts it, "Many Americans still have problems about their Americanism and are still trying, psychologically speaking, to naturalize themselves." [56] Also, to the extent that right-wing sentiments involve attacks on old-family liberals, revenge may play a part in attracting ethnic-group members to the radical right; what better way to take advantage of one's new position than by turning on the old Yankees who patronized one's ancestors? This proposition was based on survey findings that Catholics were more likely than Protestants to support McCarthy, as well as on McCarthy's attacks on the Harvard-Acheson-striped-pants set.

Another proposition mingling mobility and ethnic hostility suggests that the ethnics' success drives old Americans toward the right:

> These people, although very often quite well-to-do, feel that they have been pushed out of their rightful place in American life, even out of their neighborhoods. Most of them . . . have felt themselves edged aside by the immigrants, the trade unions, and the urban machines in the past thirty years. When the immigrants were weak, these native elements used to indulge themselves in ethnic and religious snobberies at their expense. Now the immigrant groups have developed ample means . . . of self-defense. . . . Some of the old family Americans have turned to find new objects for their resentment among liberals. . . .[57]

[56] Richard Hofstadter, "Pseudo-Conservatism Revisited: A Postscript—1962," in Bell, *The Radical Right*, p. 84.

[57] Hofstadter, "The Pseudo-Conservative Revolt—1955," in Bell, *The Radical Right*, p. 72.

Whatever the utility of these assorted ethnic hostility theses as explanations for the appeal of McCarthyism, they seem to have very little relevance to today's radical right. For one thing, it is clear that the attack of the right is on intellectuals, not on old Americans. More important, it is in New England and the Middle Atlantic states, where old-settler hostility to immigrants was most pronounced, where ethnic hatred was—and is—bitterest, and where the political and geographic displacement of Yankees by ethnics is more thorough, that the radical right has been least successful.[58] In contrast, its promoters find their warmest reception in areas where hostility between immigrants and old settlers has been minimal, in the wide-open societies of the Rocky Mountains, the Southwest, and southern California.[59] Finally, although the underrepresentation of Catholics in our sample may be a function of the title of the Crusade, we find no overrepresentation of recent immigrants. On the contrary, when we compared our non-Catholic respondents to the white, non-Catholic respondents in a representative sample of San Francisco adults,[60] we found that the former group had a much smaller proportion of foreign-born respondents and a somewhat smaller percentage of second-generation Americans, as Table 14 shows.

Another status hypothesis is that right-wing movements draw support from individuals with "status discrepancies," that is, from people whose education, income, and social standing are not congruent—from college-educated truck drivers and illiterate businessmen. As Lipset puts it, "such status incongruities were presumed to have created sharp resentments about general social developments, which predisposed individuals to welcome McCarthy's attack on the elite and on the New Deal." [61] As this statement suggests, one of the difficulties in trying to verify the hypothesis is that it refers as much to a state of mind as to an objectively definable condition.

---

[58] Lipset, "Three Decades," pp. 350–352. A Crusade school held in New York in 1962 was a popular and financial fiasco; the estimated deficit was $75,000 (*Facts*, pp. 261–262). Of a listing of rightist groups published in 1962, 19 percent of the organizations were located in California, chiefly in the Los Angeles area (source: Chesler and Schmuck, "On Super-Patriotism: A Definition and Analysis," *J. Social Issues, 19* (April 1963), 38.

[59] There are a great many second- and third-generation Irish and Italians in the Bay Area and appreciable numbers of them elsewhere in the West. Scandinavians and Germans are also plentiful in the area. But none of these ethnic groups encountered anything like the hostility that was so salient a feature of immigrant life in the Northeast. The ethnic groups that have suffered the most from discrimination in the West, Orientals and Mexicans, display no interest at all in the radical right.

[60] Data on San Francisco are from a sample survey of adults in that city, conducted for the California Department of Public Health under the direction of Drs. Ira Cisin and Genevieve Knupfer. We are grateful to them for these data, and to Edward R. Tufte for help in tabulating the data.

[61] Lipset, "Three Decades," p. 333.

TABLE 14

Comparison of Nativity and Parentage of Non-Catholic Crusaders and White Non-Catholic, Adult San Franciscans (in Percent)

	CRUSADERS	SAN FRANCISCANS [a]
Foreign born	8	23
Native born of foreign parents	20	26
Native born of native parents	67	51
No answer	4	
	99 [b]	100
N	283	576

[a] Source: California Department of Public Health cross-section study of San Francisco adults.

[b] Does not total 100 percent because of rounding.

Perhaps for this reason, attempts to relate objective status discrepancies to support for McCarthy were not successful.[62]

We had the same experience with the Crusaders. We compared the occupations of three educational groups with those of white northerners in the 1960 SRC study, as shown in Table 15. If the status-discrepancy hypothesis had any validity for our respondents, we would expect to find that more of the well educated Crusaders had menial jobs or more of the poorly educated ones were in high-status occupations. There are scarcely any differences between the two samples at the two higher educational levels, except for a slight tendency for more Crusaders, at each level, to be businessmen. With respondents who have attended high school but not college, this difference becomes quite marked; 37 percent of the Crusaders in this group are businessmen, compared to 12 percent of the SRC group. There are, however, only 43 Crusaders in this group; the difference from the SRC group accounts for only 11 respondents. This difference appears to be the result of chance and the generally higher occupational level of the Crusaders.

American society is characterized by a relatively high degree of occupa-

---

[62] Lipset cites California Poll data that show a tendency for individuals with status discrepancies to be disproportionately favorable to the Birch Society ("Three Decades," p. 363). He reports that the number of cases is far too small to warrant much confidence, however. He also cites an unpublished paper by Robert Sokol showing that persons who felt that their pay was not commensurate with their education were more likely to support McCarthy ("Three Decades," pp. 333–334, 374). Another study uncovered relationships between status discrepancies and conservative attitudes; see Gerhard C. Lenski, "Status Crystallization: A Non-vertical Dimension of Social Status," *Amer. Sociol. Rev., 19* (August 1954), 405–412.

TABLE 15

Occupation by Education—Crusaders and White Northerners (in Percent)

	COLLEGE GRADUATES		SOME COLLEGE		ATTENDED HIGH SCHOOL [a]	
Occupation [b]	Cru- saders	North- erners [c]	Cru- saders	North- erners [c]	Cru- saders	North- erners [c]
Professional	54	59	25	34	7	6
Businessmen	31	19	30	17	37	12
Clerical and sales	11	14	22	23	26	20
Blue-collar	3	9	22	25	30	62
	99 [d]	101 [d]	99 [d]	99 [d]	100	100
N	140	108	63	149	43	545

[a] Since only 3 percent of the Crusaders did not attend high school, no lower educational category has been used.
[b] Farmers, students, and "no answers" have been excluded from bases.
[c] Source: SRC 1960 study.
[d] Do not total 100 percent because of rounding.

tional mobility, quite high levels of education, and a rather weak system of status ascription by inheritance. One would expect that such a fluid social system would continue to produce a good deal of "status anxiety" in various forms. For this reason, explanations linking these phenomena to McCarthyism and the radical right may be considered pessimistic. It should therefore be a source of some comfort that, whatever the causes of the radical right, they do not seem to include strains resulting from the characteristic openness of the American social system.

PROVINCIALISM

According to another proposition, the radical right feeds on provincial resentment of the increasing social, economic, and cultural dominance of large cities. The radical right, like Prohibition and the Scopes trial, is interpreted as another rear-guard action against modernity. As Daniel Bell puts it, "what it seeks to defend is its fading dominance, exercised once through the institutions of small-town America, over the control of social change." [63] If this explanation were valid, we would expect to find a greater proportion of people with farm and small-town backgrounds in our sample than in the general population. Comparing Crusaders to white San Franciscans and to the white northerners in the 1960 SRC study, we do not find that a disproportionate number of Crusaders comes from farm fami-

---

[63] Bell, "The Dispossessed—1962," in Bell, *The Radical Right*, p. 12.

lies, as Table 16 shows. Nor do we find that a highly disproportionate number was raised in small towns.[64]

So far we have discussed hypotheses that, whatever their utility in explaining other manifestations of right-wing sentiment, are not helpful when applied to the Crusaders. Now we shall look at some propositions that do seem to have value in explaining our respondents.

TABLE 16

Proportion of Respondents Whose Fathers Were Farmers—by Occupation

	PERCENT WITH FARMER FATHERS [a]		
	Crusaders	White Northerners [b]	White San Franciscans [c]
Occupation of head of household			
Businessmen and professionals	16	11	14
Clerical and sales	12	15	13
Blue-collar	32	31	25

[a] "No answers" have been excluded from the bases.
[b] Source: SRC 1960 study.
[c] Source: Public Health San Francisco study.

---

[64] We asked our respondents, "Were you brought up mostly on a farm, in a small town, or in a large city?" The only roughly comparable normative data available came from the Public Health San Francisco study, which asked, "Where did you live before the age of 15—on a farm, in the country but not on a farm, or in a town or city?" If respondents answered "town" or "city," the population size was asked, and the replies were coded by size. The 25,000-to-100,000 category presents some difficulties for us, since it probably includes both "small towns" and "large cities"; 10 percent of the San Francisco sample are in this category. A second difficulty is that in a sample of a large city one would expect that a higher proportion of the respondents had been raised in large cities than in a metropolitan-area sample where only some of the respondents come from the core city. In the light of these considerations, we can hardly claim to have comparable data, but the following table indicates that the Crusaders probably are not markedly unrepresentative of the Bay Area with respect to rural or small-town backgrounds.

Size of Place Where Raised

	Crusaders	San Franciscans
	(*percent*)	
On a farm (and in the country)		
Businessmen and professionals	20	19
All others	25	23
Small town (up to 100,000 population)		
Businessmen and professionals	37	24
All others	34	25
Large city (over 100,000 population)		
Businessmen and professionals	43	57
All others	41	52

FUNDAMENTALISM

A number of writers have noted that the radical right seems to be attractive to fundamentalist Protestants.[65] Various explanations have been offered for this attraction. The most convincing ones point to affinities between fundamentalist dogma and radical-right interpretations of history. Belief in the literalness and purity of Biblical teachings makes fundamentalists resistant to social and cultural change; they are affronted by moral relativism, increasingly lenient sexual mores, the decline of parental authority, and other aspects of the secular modern world. The fundamentalist sees "the world as strictly divided into the saved and the damned, the forces of good and the forces of evil." [66] The main danger to the faithful is from the corrosion of faith by insidious doctrines—a danger from within. This argument is given added credence by the revivalist style and trappings of many "anticommunist" leaders.[67]

Slightly more than three quarters of the Crusaders are Protestants. Twenty-six percent of the Protestant Crusaders are Baptists or members of minor fundamentalist denominations, compared to 13 percent of the white, college-educated Protestants in the San Francisco sample. These fundamentalists, who comprise 20 percent of the total sample, are not significantly different from the other respondents on either demographic or attitudinal measures. But a more sensitive measure of the intermingling of politics and religion isolates a group that seems to confirm the explanations of affinities between the radical right and fundamentalists.[68] We asked our respondents how they happened to come to the Crusade. Those who came because of church influence (forty-three respondents) are different from the rest of the sample in a number of ways, as Table 17 demonstrates. They are not nearly so well off or well educated. They are slightly more likely to have rural backgrounds and considerably more likely to be devout, religiously active members of fundamentalist denominations.

---

[65] The most extended discussion of this relationship, although without the benefit of data, is by David Danzig, "The Radical Right and the Rise of the Fundamentalist Minority," *Commentary*, April 1962, pp. 291–298. See also Lipset, *Political Man* (New York: Doubleday & Company, Inc., 1961), p. 108; Bell, *The Radical Right*; and Victor C. Ferkiss, "Political and Intellectual Origins of American Radicalism, Right and Left," *The Annals of the American Academy of Political and Social Science*, 344 (November 1962), 6.

[66] Danzig, p. 292.

[67] There are several right-wing movements, chiefly in the Southwest, with a strong revivalist flavor. Schwarz and other officials of the Crusade have backgrounds in various types of religious activity; see *Facts*, pp. 250–252. Schwarz's speaking style often reflects this background.

[68] It should be noted that persons with fundamentalist points of view are found, in varying numbers, in all Protestant denominations. Within some denominations whose theological positions are liberal, there are individual churches that adhere to more fundamentalist positions.

TABLE 17 *

Comparison of the Demographic Characteristics of the "Church Group" (Those Who Came because of Church Influence) and All Other Crusaders

	AMONG "CHURCH GROUP"	AMONG ALL OTHER CRUSADERS
Percentage who		
Are fundamentalists	66	15
Attend church regularly	90	45
Belong to church committees	89	37
Were raised on farms	30	19
Are clerical or manual workers	54	24
Have annual incomes under $10,000	78	51
Belong to unions	21	15
Did not complete college	62	44

The members of the "church group" are considerably more liberal on domestic issues than is the remainder of the sample. Only 8 percent of them favor the southern position on segregation, compared to 42 percent of the other respondents. Almost twice as many of the church group are in favor of medical care for the aged and federal aid to education. This relative liberalism is not merely a reflection of their lower status. Among nonchurch-group Crusaders, low-income respondents are as conservative on domestic issues as high-income respondents.

These data suggest that members of the church group were not attracted to the Crusade by economic self-interest.[69] We suggest that their religious beliefs lead them to look on communism as an earthly manifestation of the devil. As one of these Crusaders put it, "I'm a Bible student and am convinced that the Communist movement is satanic in its origins, principles, and ultimate aims." While only a third of the church group named atheists as likely to be communists, this proportion was three times that in the rest of the sample.

Although members of the church group are more liberal than the other Crusaders, they are even more extreme in their perceptions of the extent of communist infiltration in American life, which suggests that for them "communism" is a handy label for all the works of the devil, from sexual immodesty to permissive child-rearing practices. It appears that people who came to the Crusade through their churches were attracted for essentially

---

[69] Some writers interpret fundamentalist support of the radical right as a consequence of a recent rise from economic deprivation to prosperity; see Bell, *The Dispossessed*, pp. 20–21.

TABLE 18 *

Comparison of Attitudes of the "Church Group" and All Other Crusaders

	AMONG "CHURCH GROUP"	AMONG ALL OTHER CRUSADERS
Percentage who		
"Prefer Nixon to Goldwater"	60	39
"Are low on index of domestic conservatism"	56	30
"Do *not* regard unions as harmful"	62	41
"Are opposed to the South's position on integration"	92	58
"Are opposed to teaching Darwin's theories in schools"	52	30
"Believe atheists are persons likely to be Communists"	31	11
"Are high on index of perception of internal Communist danger" [a]	64	50
"Engage in no more than one form of political activity"	57	41

[a] Perception of the internal communist danger is measured by a five-point index, with one point each for thinking that American communists are a very great danger, that communist professors have a great deal of influence, that communists are very influential in the Democratic Party, and that they are very influential in the Republican Party.

religious reasons, an interpretation supported by their lower level of political activity.

It is possible that the Crusade's religious aura was an essential part of its appeal to such people, who might not find all radical-right organizations equally attractive. They might more likely be drawn to a group like Billy James Hargis's Christian Crusade than to a secular organization like the Birch Society.

OLD-FASHIONED INDIVIDUALISTS

Just as fundamentalists are hostile to the secularism and moral looseness of contemporary society, some other people are supposedly resentful of another modern trend: the development of immense bureaucratic organizations that have crowded individual enterprise to the wall. Such old-fashioned types have "a wistful nostalgia for a golden age of small farmers and businessmen and also . . . strong resentment and hatred toward a world which makes no sense in terms of older ideas and which is conducted in apparent violation of old truths and values of economic and political life." [70] It has been suggested that such people have been drawn to sup-

---

[70] Trow, "Small Businessmen," p. 275.

port of McCarthy and the radical right because they have a "political orientation which has no institutionalized place on the political scene."[71] Small businessmen are thought to be the chief examples of this type.

There are 38 self-employed businessmen in our sample. They do not differ from other respondents in any meaningful pattern, except that half of them report making more than $15,000 a year, which raises some question about all of them being small businessmen.

Testing this antibureaucratic hypothesis with respect to McCarthyism, Martin Trow isolated a group of his Bennington respondents whom he called "nineteenth-century liberals." This group consisted of those respondents who were hostile both to labor unions and big business, the major examples of impersonal mass institutions. Trow found that these "liberals" were much more likely to approve of McCarthy than people who were favorable both to unions and big business or favorable to one and hostile to the other. He interpreted their support of McCarthy as an expression of hope that the Senator would turn back the tide of gigantic bureaucracy.

We used the same questions about unions and big business to isolate a similar group of "nineteenth-century liberals" among the Crusaders. These "liberals" composed 14 percent of Trow's sample and 17 percent of ours. (Only two of our "liberals" are also in the church group.) These respondents are a fairly distinct group. As Table 19 shows, they are characterized by political intolerance, a low sense of political efficacy, conservatism on foreign policy, low political participation, and belief that there is no difference between the Democratic and Republican Parties.

TABLE 19 *

Comparison of the Attitudes of "Nineteenth-Century Liberals" and All Other Crusaders

	AMONG "NINETEENTH-CENTURY LIBERALS"	AMONG ALL OTHER CRUSADERS
Percentage who are		
"High on index of intolerance" [a]	53	24
"Low on index of sense of political efficacy" (score of 0, 1, or 2)	48	24
"High on index of foreign policy conservatism"	74	51
"Engage in no more than one form of political activity"	59	40
"Believe that there is no difference between the major political parties"	43	18

[a] Intolerance is measured by a four-point index, with one point for a "disagree" response to each of the three items in Table 8; "high" is a score of two or three.

[71] Trow, "Small Businessmen," p. 276.

The most remarkable feature of these findings is the "liberals'" lack of involvement in two-party politics; unlike the other Crusaders, they seem to be estranged from conventional means of political expression. Many of them apparently feel that neither political party is a vehicle through which they can protest the eclipse of individualism. If "communism" represents secularism to the fundamentalists, it may well symbolize bureaucratic organization to the "liberals."

The church group and the nineteenth-century liberals together account for about one-third of the sample. It does not appear that the presence at the Crusade of the remainder of the sample can be explained by any of the sociological propositions that we have discussed. In pursuing this problem further, it may be useful to consider who was *not* susceptible to the appeal of the Crusade.

Most obviously, the Crusade was not attractive to Jews, Orientals, Negroes, or Catholics.

Second, it did not seem to have much appeal to lower-status people, except for fundamentalists. On this point, the radical right may differ from McCarthyism, which had considerable appeal for people with less education and more menial jobs.[72] This difference between the two movements may be due to several factors. One possibility is that, at present, the radical right lacks a single commanding leader who dominates the movement and symbolizes it to the public. McCarthy, of course, was more than a symbol; he was the embodiment of his movement. For people with little education, unaccustomed to thinking in abstract terms, a single highly visible leader offers a much easier point of reference. Another possibility is that the ideology of the radical right does not offer much that is attractive to lower-status people.

Studies of public opinion and voting behavior have shown that communist subversion was not a salient issue to many people in the early 1950s, despite the volume of political oratory on the subject.[73] There are some indications that McCarthy's popularity with lower-status people was due to his denunciations of the old American upper class, an attack that would appeal both to Yankee-hating ethnic-group members in the Northeast and to Middle Western anglophobes. Trow's research suggests that many of McCarthy's Bennington supporters saw him as a kind of spiritual Robin Hood, taking the rich and well-born down a peg in behalf of the common man.[74] There is none of this antipatrician tone in the radical right, which

---

[72] Lipset, "Three Decades," pp. 331–333.

[73] Campbell, Gurin, and Miller, p. 52; Campbell, Converse, Miller, and Stokes, p. 51; and Stouffer.

[74] For evidence on this point see Trow, "Small Businessmen." Various articles in Bell, *The Radical Right*, discuss likely sources of lower-class support for McCarthy; see, in particular, Hofstadter's articles and Peter Viereck, "The Revolt Against the Elite—1955."

enshrines in one of its slogans the proposition that the United States is not a democracy.

Third, on the basis both of our data and our contacts with the Crusaders, we do not believe that they are social or psychological cripples. Most of them hold responsible positions in business or the professions, and the vast majority is active in a variety of community organizations. Unfortunately, we do not have data on personality variables. Possibly the Crusaders would score higher than members of the general population on a measure of authoritarianism. Indeed, some research on McCarthy supporters suggests that this would be the case.[75] The Crusaders' beliefs about the extent of internal subversion may be regarded as paranoid, but, despite the deviant quality of some of their political attitudes, they are functioning members of society.

Fourth, and most important, the Crusade was not for Democrats. The most striking single distinguishing characteristic of our sample is the scarcity of Democrats. This scarcity is not a reflection of our respondents' high socioeconomic status, since party identification is quite imperfectly related to SES. Furthermore, the working-class Crusaders are no less Republican than the rest of the sample; 90 percent of them voted for Nixon in 1960. It does not appear that the absence of Democrats is merely a reflection of concern about the dangers of domestic communism, since Stouffer reports that about as many Democrats as Republicans thought that this danger was "relatively great," [76] and it therefore does not appear that Republicans have a monopoly on worries about subversion. Evidently this fear is not a sufficient stimulus to participation in a radical-right movement. By the same token, many Democrats have conservative attitudes on welfare issues, foreign policy, and civil liberties, particularly in California, where there are many southern Democrats. Yet even members of the "church group," who were considerably more liberal than the rest of the sample and came to the Crusade for essentially religious reasons, were as Republican as the other Crusaders.

The strong relationship between party identification and support of the radical right should not be surprising, for party is the most powerful inde-

---

[75] High authoritarianism scores are increasingly related to support of McCarthyism as educational level increases; see Lipset, "Three Decades," pp. 342–344. An extraordinary study of students at Ohio State University indicated that members of a right-wing organization had considerably higher F-scale scores than either uncommitted or left-wing students. The number of cases is quite small, however. See Edwin N. Barker, "Authoritarianism of the Political Right, Center, and Left," *Social Issues*, 19 (April 1963), 63–74.

[76] Thirty-four percent of the Republicans and 30 percent of the Democrats saw the internal Communist threat as "relatively great" (Stouffer, p. 211). Stouffer reports that a number of other surveys have produced the same finding (p. 217).

pendent variable in many other areas of political behavior.[77] For most people, party identification is the most important point of reference in evaluating political phenomena. While the attention paid to domestic communism in political oratory has varied a good deal, it has still been one of the major themes of political discourse—particularly in California— and it is a Republican theme.[78] These cognitive clues were reinforced by the statements of party leaders. By early 1962, a number of prominent Democrats had attacked the radical right, and the Democratic Attorney General of California had denounced Dr. Schwarz and the Crusade specifically. Few leading Republicans had criticized the radical right at that time. The local controversy about the Oakland school occupied a good deal of newspaper space. Politically conscious Democrats in the Bay Area, aware that their party had been belabored on the communist issue for years, could hardly have failed to conclude that a Democratic Crusader would be something of an anomaly.[79]

THE SOCIAL AND POLITICAL CONTEXT OF THE RADICAL RIGHT

If Republicanism and the prevalence of rightist attitudes were the only factors determining the size and importance of radical-right groups, we should expect to find such organizations throughout the country. Yet there are marked variations in the level of radical-right activity. It is most intense in certain regions like southern California and the Southwest and seems to be almost nonexistent elsewhere, especially in the Northeast. The uneven level of radical-right activity seems to be a function of the interaction of two factors: the presence of compatible attitudes and a favorable balance between institutional constraints and rewards for right-wing political agitation. We shall argue that variations in this second factor may account for variations in the strength of the radical right.

The right seems to be most successful in those states that are under-

---

[77] Polsby was the first to draw attention to the importance of party identification as an explanation of support for McCarthy.

[78] Remarks about relationships between Republicanism and support for the radical right are not applicable to those one-party states of the South and Southwest where party identification loses most of its function as a cognitive clue.

[79] In polls taken within a few months after the first widespread public disclosure of the existence of The John Birch Society, Democrats compose 33 percent of the pro-Birch respondents in a national sample (by Gallup) and 28 percent in California (Lipset, pp. 352, 356). It is not reported how many of the 25 pro-Birch Democrats in the Gallup national sample are from the South. As time has passed and the controversy about the radical right has continued, it is quite possible that previously pro-Birch Democrats have learned the "proper" relationship between their party and the Birch Society.

going both major economic growth and marked changes in economic bases, life styles, and cultural geography. It may be that the politically relevant aspects of these conditions involve not so much individual gains and losses in objective social status as what might be called "lateral social change." That is, the cause may be the strains produced by the interpersonal and institutional instability that comes with rapid economic growth. There are arguments attributing the radical right's popularity in California both to rootless newcomers and discomfited old-timers. We have no normative data with which to compare our findings on the length of time the Crusaders have lived in the Bay Area and in California, and we cannot therefore contribute to this discussion.

All the states where the radical right is most active have in common a political characteristic that is conspicuously lacking in the Northeast, where the right is feeblest. Where the radical right flourishes, political party organizations are weak and lack continuity. Control of a major party is an important inducement to right-wing activity in a number of states. But where party organizations are strong, where established leaders have formidable resources for protecting their positions from challengers, and where the rewards for political action run more toward tangible benefits than ideological satisfaction, the difficulty of taking over the party discourages potential right-wing activists. The presence of a strong party organization also impedes other radical-right activity like the intimidation of school teachers and librarians.

In California and in much of the West and Southwest, "organization" is a misnomer for the collection of personalities, factions, and ideological inclinations that comprise the Democratic and Republican Parties. Party leadership is generally fragmented, in large measure because there are few resources available to co-ordinate and discipline party activists.[80] The leaders' vulnerability to concerted attack is a temptation to rebels from the right.

The second major political contextual restraint on the radical right is the presence of a Republican in the White House.[81] At the party-organiza-

---

[80] Two recent case studies of Democratic nominations in California and Connecticut, respectively, illustrate the striking differences in party cohesion in the two states. See John H. Bunzel and Eugene C. Lee, "The California Democratic Delegation of 1960," in Edwin A. Bock and Alan K. Campbell, eds., *Case Studies in American Government* (Englewood Cliffs, N.J.: Prentice-Hall, Inc., 1962), pp. 133–174; and Joseph P. Lyford, *Candidate* (New York: Holt, Rinehart and Winston, Inc., 1959). Bunzel and Lee describe the difficulties experienced by California Democrats in preventing complete fragmentation of their party over the 1960 presidential nomination. The Governor and other leaders were unable to control the delegation. In contrast, Connecticut Democratic leaders succeeded in 1958 in forcing their convention to nominate for Congress an unknown army officer who had not lived in the state for more than 20 years.

[81] Several writers in Bell, *The Radical Right*, have made this point; see Bell, p. 1; and Lipset, pp. 296–297.

tion level, rightist attempts to take control of a state party during the Eisenhower years would have been restrained by awareness of the disadvantages of opposing the President. A president's ability to influence directly the outcome of a power struggle within a state party is limited but by no means negligible. Indirectly, however, his rightist critics face a considerable problem if he is Republican, for they cannot so easily attack his policies. The allegations of communist influence that play so large a part in right-wing propaganda are less convincing to the public when a Republican is president. Hope, party loyalty, and organizational alliances all restrain right-wing leaders at such times. As the case of Senator McCarthy showed, ambitious men who ignore these constraints encounter a basic truth: A concerted attack on a Republican president from the right will inevitably lead to a confrontation in which Republican politicians are forced to choose between their president and his critics. This fact is a Republican president's ultimate weapon against the radical right.

All these conditions are reversed when the White House changes party hands. There is no incumbent president to restrain right-wing dissidents in the state parties. One or more of the politicians contending for the next presidential nomination are likely to encourage radical-right activity as a means of building their own strength. Professional politicians, largely indifferent to ideological considerations, may encourage radical-right accusations as a weapon against the Democrats. During a Democratic administration, alarmism about communism is more plausible to many people.

Recent fluctuations in radical-right activity have conformed to this pattern. The current resurgence occurred after the 1960 presidential election. Although the John Birch Society was founded in 1958, it was not until 1961 that it grew enough to attract public attention. The Christian Anti-Communism Crusade was an obscure organization for the first seven years of its existence, but, in the first year of the Kennedy administration, its income increased 350 percent.[82]

CONCLUSION

We have attempted to answer two interrelated questions in this paper: What kinds of people participate in the Crusade? Why are they attracted to this movement? With the exception of Lipset's and Polsby's work, previous consideration of such questions produced sociological explanations dealing with status anxiety, cultural resentment, ethnic hostility, and the like. By and large, these propositions do not seem consistent with our data. In particular, their utility is vitiated by the most salient fact about the Crusaders: Whatever else they may be, they are not Democrats.

---

[82] The Crusade's reported income was $364,535 in 1960 and $1,273,492 in 1961 (*News Letter*, August 1962, p. 6).

The most economical answer we can give to the first question is that the Crusade draws its support from Republicans, chiefly those of higher socioeconomic status. The Crusaders' support for Goldwater suggests that they are Republicans dissatisfied with their party's stance in national elections. The best inference we can draw from this dissatisfaction is that it is due to acceptance of the welfare state by Republican presidential candidates. As the great reigning evil of our time, communism seems to be, for many people, a shorthand symbol for unacceptable political trends. The Crusaders' fears about the influence of communism were restrained during the Eisenhower administration by the improbability that Eisenhower was soft on communism. With Republicans out of power, "anticommunism" is a way to express resentment with maximum emotional impact and a minimum of divisiveness within the Republican Party.

The political strategy of the radical right is limited by its lack of mass appeal. It is likely, then, to be most effective in those aspects of politics where numbers are not crucial: not in general elections, but in pressure politics, party conventions, and the like. Our respondents' tremendous rates of political participation suggest that they are well placed to pursue their goals in the internal politics of the California Republican Party, pressing for control of the party's various organs, nomination of conservative candidates, and a commanding voice in determining party policy. They appear to have had some success in these endeavors.[83] Their ability to achieve both intraparty success and electoral victories has not yet been demonstrated, however, and it may well be that the interests of the radical right are not compatible with those of the Republican Party.

---

[83] Ultraconservative forces gained control of the national Young Republicans at the organization's 1963 convention in San Francisco. For a discussion of their activities in the Republican Party see T. George Harris, "The Rampant Right Invades the GOP," *Look* (July 16, 1963), pp. 19–25.

The Radical Right and the Politics of Consensus

SHEILAH R. KOEPPEN

Right-wing movements are characteristic phenomena of American politics. Their support comes from persons who express extensive discontent with contemporary political events. These people believe that government policies could well annihilate all that they value, and they charge that these policies are the handiwork of a group of Americans intent on undermining the nation. Since the late 1940s the target of much of this hostility has been American communists.

In the early 1950s Senator Joseph McCarthy's allegations about communists in government served as the rallying cry for the right wing. Following his censure by the Senate, McCarthy's value as a focus declined, although his subsequent death provided a martyr for some right-wing movements, and communists and fellow travelers remained the bête noire of American rightists. In the early 1960s increased activity by associations having as their mission the combating of domestic communist influence earned for themselves the label of the "radical right."

Most analysts of the radical right suggest that its supporters seek to achieve undemocratic ends by undemocratic methods. Their refusal to abide by democratic norms is explained as resulting from the radical right's fear that many political leaders are really communists or communist sympathizers.[1]

This essay examines the alleged association between support for the radical right and lack of support for democratic politics, with reference to data secured from the second of two surveys of supporters of the Christian Anti-Communism Crusade, a radical-right movement. Analysis of the findings of the first survey became the basis of the study by Raymond E. Wolfinger and associates, "America's Radical Right: Politics and Ideology." [2] This study, which refuted many of the propositions about the attributes of radical-right supporters current in the literature, encouraged me to collect more data on the Crusaders. In addition to replicating the Wolfinger survey, the second survey was specifically designed to gather data relevant to the extent of support given by the radical right to the principles of American democracy.[3]

THE RESEARCH

THE SUBJECT AND METHOD OF THE RESEARCH

One tactic of the radical right has been to offer the public an alleged education on communism. Radical-right organizations have offered or

---

[1] The essays collected by Daniel Bell (ed.), *The Radical Right* (New York: Doubleday & Company, Inc., 1963) present aspects of this argument. Richard Hofstadter, one of the contributors, reiterates the argument, generalizing it to refer to what he calls a main theme of American politics, in *The Paranoid Style in American Politics and Other Essays* (New York: Alfred A. Knopf, 1965). The essays in the *J. Social Issues, 19* (April 1963), devoted to the subject of extremist movements, find this disaffection typical of the radical right. A general study of political cynicism suggests that supporters of radical right movements are among the most cynical. Robert E. Agger, Marshall N. Goldstein, and Stanley A. Pearl, "Political Cynicism: Measurement and Meaning," *J. Politics, 23* (August 1961), 494. A similar appraisal of the politics of the radical right is made by journalists. See footnote 6.

[2] Raymond E. Wolfinger, Barbara Kaye Wolfinger, Kenneth Prewitt, and Sheilah Rosenhack, "America's Radical Right: Politics and Ideology," in David Apter (ed.), *Ideology and Discontent* (New York: The Free Press, 1964), pp. 262–293.

[3] For a full report of the research, see Sheilah Rosenhack Koeppen, "Dissensus and Discontent: The Clientele of the Christian Anti-Communism Crusade" (unpublished doctoral dissertation, Stanford University, August 1967).

sponsored seminars, lectures, and courses to teach Americans about communist philosophy and strategy. The classes of the Christian Anti-Communism Crusade were perhaps the best-known example of this movement in the early 1960s, and its president, Dr. Frederick C. Schwarz, the movement's leading pedagogue.

Dr. Schwarz has claimed that the sole purpose of his organization is to provide an education about communism, and that it does not advocate explicit partisan activity or endorse political candidates and does not deserve the label "radical right." The Crusade does lack the more gaudy paraphernalia of some modern radical-right movements, such as secret meetings and drills, and it provides no means for active support in the movement unless Crusade programs are held in the would-be supporter's area. The only contact between the Crusade and its supporters is provided by free subscription to a news letter.[4]

Yet the Crusade has been considered a radical-right movement by academicians,[5] lay writers,[6] and leaders of other right-wing organizations, most notably The John Birch Society.[7] The Crusade espouses the key belief of the American radical right: the chief danger to the United States is communism, and communists hold key positions in American society.[8]

The first Bay Area anticommunism "school" of the Crusade, which

---

[4] At the time of the survey a year's membership in the Crusade costs $10.00; a life membership, $100.00. Fees (typically $20.00) are charged for attendance at a school of anticommunism organized by the Crusade, but the Crusade is liberal in providing "full scholarships" for high school and college teachers, students, and clergymen, and half scholarships for such public employees as firemen and policemen.

[5] The Crusade is categorized as a radical-right organization that is moderate in its tactics by Barbara B. Green, Kathryn Turner, and Dante Germino in "Responsible and Irresponsible Right-Wing Groups: A Problem in Analysis," *J. Social Issues, 19* (April 1963), 3–17.

[6] Descriptions by journalists of Dr. Schwarz and the Crusade as radical-right phenomena include: Fred J. Cook, "The Ultras: Aims, Affiliations and Finances of the Radical Right," *The Nation, 194* (June 30, 1962), pp. 1–68; R. Dudman, *Men of the Far Right* (New York: Pyramid Publications, Inc., 1962); Benjamin R. Epstein and Arnold Forster, *The Radical Right: Report on the John Birch Society and Its Allies* (New York: Random House, Inc., 1967); Philip Horton, "Revivalism on the Far Right," *The Reporter, 25* (July 20, 1961), pp. 25–29; Donald Janson and Bernard Eismann, *The Far Right* (New York: McGraw-Hill, Inc., 1963); Harry and Bonaro Overstreet, *The Strange Tactics of Extremism* (New York: W. W. Norton & Company, 1964); Mark Sherwin, *The Extremists* (New York: St. Martin's Press, 1963).

[7] Robert Welch endorsed the Crusade in a speech to the Commonwealth Club, January 12, 1962, San Francisco, California, reported in the *San Francisco Chronicle*, January 13, 1962, p. 8. Praise for the Crusade was attributed to a Birch Society coordinator in J. Allen Broyles, *The John Birch Society* (Boston: The Beacon Press, 1964), pp. 132–133.

[8] For Dr. Schwarz's interpretation of this theme see his *The Mind, the Heart, the Soul of Communism* (Long Beach: Christian Anti-Communism Crusade, 1957); *Address on the Disease of Communism, Given to the Texas Legislature* (Long Beach: Christian Anti-Communism Crusade, 1959); *You Can Trust the Communists (to be Communists)* (Englewood Cliffs: Prentice-Hall, Inc., 1960). His comments

provided the data for the Wolfinger study, was held January 29 to February 2, 1962, at Oakland, California. When the Crusade planned a second Bay Area school, I prepared a new mail questionnaire to collect more extensive data from Crusade supporters. The revised questionnaire was distributed to adult members of Dr. Schwarz's audiences after each session of the school held in San Mateo, September 17–21, 1962, and after lectures at the Hotel Leamington in Oakland on November 30 and December 1, 1962.[9] The rate of return of the questionnaires was high: 173 out of 300 of the questionnaires distributed at San Mateo (58 percent) and 29 of the 56 distributed at the Hotel Leamington (45 percent). Questionnaires were eliminated if the respondent was opposed to Schwarz or the Crusade, if he was under twenty years of age, or if he had filled out the Oakland questionnaire. The remaining 167 questionnaires provide the data for this essay.

While the Crusade studies employed the survey research technique, neither study was based on a random sample of Crusaders. It is likely that the respondents in both studies are better educated and more articulate than the school audiences taken as a whole.[10] It is also likely that respondents to my questionnaire are more representative of the "hard core" of Crusade supporters. Extensive publicity preceded the first Crusade school, including a well-publicized controversy over the signing, by mayors of Bay Area cities, of a proclamation naming the week of the Crusade "Anti-Communism Week." [11] Little publicity was given the second Crusade school and the subsequent Hotel Leamington meetings.[12] This lack of attention and the cumulative effect of criticism of the first Crusade school [13] may have discouraged moderates from attending the fall Crusade school; certainly there was a sharp decline in attendance.[14]

---

are available also in The Committee on Un-American Activities, *International Communism (the Communist Mind), Staff Consultation with Frederick Charles Schwarz,* House of Representatives, 85th Congress, 1st Session (Washington, D.C., 1957). At the Bay Area Crusade meetings Schwarz constantly repeated this theme.

[9] The methods were similar to those employed by Wolfinger and associates during the Oakland school, and are described in Wolfinger and others, pp. 264–266.

[10] See Wolfinger and others, p. 266.

[11] See *San Francisco Chronicle*, January 6, 1962, p. 2; January 19, 1962, p. 11; and January 23, 1962, p. 1.

[12] Reporters from the *San Mateo Times* and the *Redwood City Tribune* told me at the first session of the fall Crusade that many Bay Area community leaders and the San Francisco newspapers had determined to give Schwarz's second school the "silent treatment."

[13] See *San Francisco Chronicle*, January 9, 1962, p. 38; January 12, 1962, p. 12; January 17, 1962, p. 7; January 30, 1962, p. 17; and February 4, 1962, p. 9.

[14] There were 13,600 "admissions" to the various sessions of the Oakland school, each admission constituting one attendance at one session. See *San Francisco Examiner*, September 18, 1962, p. 11. Only 70 persons registered for the first morning session of the fall Crusade, and the usual daytime attendance was between 50 and 100. About 200 persons attended the Hotel Leamington meetings.

The Crusade studies are based on data from people who not only stated that they endorse a radical-right movement, but who spent considerable time and, in most cases, money, in demonstrating that support by attendance at Crusade meetings. Other empirical studies of radical-right phenomena have been based on general observation,[15] participant observation of meetings,[16] and evaluation of radical-right literature.[17] Studies by Martin Trow and Seymour M. Lipset have employed survey research, but only upon samples of the general population, not on respondents self-selected by their participation in activities of a radical-right movement.[18] Insofar as it is possible to describe the supporters of an amorphous radical-right movement, the Crusade data should provide a better starting point.

CRUSADERS' DEMOGRAPHIC CHARACTERISTICS AND POLITICAL AFFILIATIONS

Data on the fall Crusaders indicates that their demographic characteristics and political affiliations, preferences and activities are strikingly similar to those of the Oakland Crusaders.[19]

---

[15] See the essays in Daniel Bell (ed.); Seymour M. Lipset's 1962 contribution is the exception and is discussed in footnote 18.

[16] Mark Chesler and Richard Schmuck, "Participant Observation in a Super Patriot Discussion Group," *J. Social Issues, 19* (April 1963), 18–30.

[17] Gilbert Abcarian and Sherman M. Stanage, "Alienation and the Radical Right," *J. Politics, 27* (November 1965), 776–796; Barbara B. Green and others (footnote 5); James McEvoy, *Letters from the Right: Content Analysis of a Letter Writing Campaign* (Ann Arbor, Michigan: Institute for Social Research, University of Michigan, 1966).

[18] For his study of sources of support for Senator Joseph McCarthy, Trow surveyed a sample of the male citizens of Bennington, Vermont. "Small Businessmen, Political Tolerance and Support for McCarthy," *Amer. J. Sociol., 64* (November 1957), 270–281. For a complete report of his research, see Trow, "Right Wing Radicalism and Political Intolerance: A Study of Support for McCarthy in a New England Town" (unpublished doctoral dissertation, Columbia University, 1957). Lipset used data from a national survey, a California survey, and the findings of specific research studies, including Trow's, to analyze and compare three right-wing movements. "Three Decades of the Radical Right: Coughlinites, McCarthyites and Birchers," in Bell, 313–377. For his analysis of support for The John Birch Society, Lipset used data from a field survey of 1100 Californians taken in January 1962. On the basis of their responses to two field poll questions, Lipset assigned respondents to one of four categories: favorable to the Society, neutral, unfavorable, and no opinion. Six percent of the respondents were categorized as favoring the Society. Lipset determined the demographic and political attributes of this sampling, and from this generalized the traits of Society supporters. Yet the percentage differences of this sampling from the responses of those neutral to, or in opposition to, the Society are small, and the conclusions are further weakened by the fact that the respondents are not necessarily active supporters of the Society merely because their responses categorize them as favorable to its aims.

[19] The major difference between the two Crusade audiences was the absence, from the fall Crusade data, of a "church group" delineated in the Oakland data by a response indicating the respondent attended because of a recommendation of his church. This church group among the Oakland Crusaders in large part belonged

Table 1 compares certain demographic characteristics of the two Crusade groups with those of white residents of the San Francisco Bay Area, a peer group chosen because Crusaders are invariably white [20] and local residents.[21] Crusaders emerge as well educated, with high status occupations and better than average incomes. More than 90 percent were born in this country.

TABLE 1

Demographic Characteristics of the Sample, the Oakland Sample,[a] and the White Bay Area Population [b] (in Percent)

	FALL CRUSADERS N = 167	OAKLAND CRUSADERS N = 308	WHITE RESIDENTS OF THE BAY AREA
Occupation of head of household [c]			
Professional and technical	35	31	14
Businessmen, managers & officials	33	27	12
Clerical and sales personnel	16	14	17
Skilled, semiskilled, unskilled and service workers	7	11	50
Other		6	1
No answer	8	11	6
Totals	100	100	100
Annual family income before taxes			
$15,000 and over	20	21	8
$10,000 to $14,999	28	20	18
$7,000 to $9,999	25	22	28
$4,000 to $6,999	14	20	30
Below $4,000	5	9	16
No answer	7 [d]	8 [d]	
Totals	100	100	100
Education [e]			
Completed college	48	52	13
Some college	31	26	14
Business or trade school	9	[f]	[f]
Completed high school	7	11	29
Some high school	3	5	19
Grammar school or less	2	3	25
No answer	[g]	3	
Totals	100	100	100

to fundamentalist sects and was less active in politics than the other Oakland Crusaders. See Wolfinger and others, pp. 281–283. Criticism of the Crusade by leading Bay Area clergymen may have discouraged attendance at the fall Crusade by a comparable "church group."

[20] No nonwhites were observed at the fall meetings. Few nonwhites were observed at the Oakland meetings and no interviews conducted with them. Wolfinger and others, p. 267.

[21] Only one of the fall respondents and nine of the Oakland respondents were not from the Bay Area. Wolfinger and others, p. 290, n. 25.

TABLE 1 (cont'd)

*Demographic Characteristics of the Sample, the Oakland Sample,[a]
and the White Bay Area Population [b] (in Percent)*

	FALL CRUSADERS N = 167	OAKLAND CRUSADERS N = 308	WHITE RESIDENTS OF THE BAY AREA
Age [h]			
Under 50 years of age	63	52	64
Fifty years and over	35	45	36
No answer	2	3	
Totals	100	100	100
Country of Birth and Parentage			
Foreign born	4	8	23 [i]
Native born of one or both foreign parents	28	20	26
Native born of native parents	65	67	51
No answer	2	4	
Totals	99 [j]	99 [j]	100

[a] Wolfinger and others, p. 268.
[b] U.S. Bureau of the Census, *U.S. Census of Population: 1960, General Social and Economic Characteristics, California. Final Report DC(1)-6C* (Washington, D.C.: U.S. Government Printing Office, 1962). All of the data are based on the San Francisco-Oakland Standard Metropolitan Statistical Area.
[c] Bay Area occupation data are for all employed males, including non-whites.
[d] Most of these respondents had high income occupations.
[e] Normative data are for persons 25 years and older.
[f] Alternative not available.
[g] Less than 1 percent.
[h] Normative data are for all white urban residents of California 20 years and older.
[i] Source: Department of Health, The State of California, Berkeley, California. There were so few Catholics among Crusaders that data on non-Catholic San Franciscans are used to provide a better basis for comparison.
[j] Does not sum to 100 percent because of rounding.

The vast majority of Crusaders are Protestants.[22] A sizeable percentage of their parents had high status occupations.[23] The Crusaders are either

---

[22] Seventy-eight percent of the fall Crusaders and 77 percent of the Oakland Crusaders are Protestant, and the respective figures for Catholics are 14 percent and 8 percent, for Jews 1 percent and 3 percent. Koeppen, pp. 27–28; Wolfinger and others, p. 278.
[23] See Wolfinger and others, p. 278.

from long-established American families or, if more recent arrivals, descended from North Europeans.[24]

Respondents to both Crusade surveys share the obsession that American communists are a menace to the country. Crusaders answered the same question on the danger from domestic communists as had been asked a national sample of voters in 1954, during the era of Senator McCarthy's well-publicized investigations of communist subversion of the federal government. Table 2 shows that the proportion of Crusaders believing that American communists are "a very great danger," or "a great danger," is about twice that of the respondents in the national sample.

TABLE 2

Perception of the Internal Communist Threat
by Fall Crusaders, Oakland Crusaders,
and the 1954 National Sample (in Percent)

	FALL CRUSADERS $N = 167$	OAKLAND CRUSADERS [a] $N = 308$	NATIONAL SAMPLE, 1954 [b] $N = 4933$
Think internal Communist threat is:			
A very great danger	57	66	19
A great danger	26	21	24
Some danger	15	9	38
Hardly any danger	2	2	9
No danger		[c]	2
Don't know		1	8
No answer	1	1	
Totals	100	100	100

[a] Source: Wolfinger and others, p. 269.
[b] Source: Samuel Stouffer, *Communism, Conformity and Civil Liberties* (New York: Doubleday, 1955), pp. 199–200.
[c] Less than 1 percent.

Both groups of Crusaders are strongly Republican. Table 3 shows that two-thirds of the Crusaders consider themselves Republicans and that an even greater proportion of Crusaders voted for the Republican candidate in the 1960 presidential elections. Crusaders also prefer that the Republican Party nominate conservative, rather than moderate, candidates. For example, twice as many fall Crusaders as Bay Area Republicans in gen-

---

[24] Only 34 percent of the fall Crusaders had one or more grandparents born outside the United States. Ninety-three percent of the foreign-born grandparents were natives of Northern European countries or Canada. See also Wolfinger and others, p. 279.

TABLE 3

*Party Preference and Candidate Preference
of the Fall Crusaders and the Oakland Crusaders (in Percent)*

	FALL CRUSADERS N = 167	OAKLAND CRUSADERS N = 308
Party preference:		
Republican	66	67
Democratic	12	8
Independent	21	19
Vote in the 1960 presidential election: [a]		
Richard Nixon	85	92
John Kennedy	15	8
Preference that a Republican candidate be: [b]		
Moderate	39 [c]	42 [d]
Conservative	61	58

[a] Figures are only for those Crusaders who voted in the 1960 election.
[b] Figures include only those fall Crusaders who voted in the primary and those Oakland Crusaders who stated a preference.
[c] The fall Crusaders were asked whether they voted for Richard Nixon (the "moderate" response) or Joseph Shell (the "conservative" response) in the 1962 Republican gubernatorial primary.
[d] The Oakland Crusaders were asked whether they would prefer Richard Nixon (the "moderate" response) or Barry Goldwater (the "conservative" response) as the Republican Party's presidential candidate in 1964.

eral voted for the ultraconservative candidate in the 1962 guberatorial primary.[25]

As Table 4 indicates, Crusaders are not only staunch Republicans but politically active as well. On the average three times as many Crusaders as college-educated white northerners undertake a political campaign activity.

The similarities between the demographic and political data on the fall and Oakland Crusaders, despite the six-month lapse of time between the two schools and the quite different atmosphere in which the schools were held, is marked. This congruence suggests that the additional data from the fall Crusade on the association between support for the radical right and lack of support for democratic politics may be of considerable validity for all radical-right movements.[26]

---

[25] Thirty-one percent of Bay Area Republican ballots were cast for Shell. Frank M. Jordan, *State of California, Statement of the Vote, Consolidated Direct Primary Election and Special Statewide Election, June 5, 1962.*

[26] Both Wolfinger and associates and I used the foregoing and additional demographic and attitudinal data to test propositions current in the literature on the sources of the radical right. As with the data recited in the text, both groups of Crusaders presented the same patterns. Neither group is (1) alienated from American

TABLE 4

*Crusaders' Political Campaign Activity Compared
to That of College-Educated White Northerners*

	AMONG FALL CRUSADERS $N = 167$	AMONG OAKLAND CRUSADERS [a] $N = 308$	AMONG COLLEGE-EDUCATED WHITE NORTHERNERS [b]
Percentage saying that they:			
"Give money or buy tickets to help the campaign for one of the parties or candidates"	68	62	23
"Go to political meetings, rallies, dinners or things like that"	61	62	13
"Do any other work for one of the parties or candidates"	44	37	7
"Belong to any political clubs or organization"	33	27	10

[a] Source: Wolfinger, p. 277.

[b] Source: Michigan SRC 1960 election study. The same questions were
used in all three studies but in the SRC study the first three questions
were phrased in the past tense.

CRUSADERS AND DEMOCRATIC POLITICS

CONSENSUS AND AMERICAN POLITICS

Many analysts of American politics have dwelt on the "consensus" prevailing in the United States. In very general terms consensus may be
defined as that degree of agreement among Americans necessary for the
orderly functioning of the democratic process—the oil without which the
political machine would cease to operate.[27] Consensus is a necessity be-

social and political life, (2) in a social position inconsistent with its background or
level of education, (3) composed of descendants of newer immigrant groups, or
(4) predominantly from rural backgrounds. There was some evidence in both sets
of data of the attraction of the radical right for Trow's "nineteenth-century liberals,"
those opposed to the development of large organizations. See Wolfinger and others,
pp. 275–281, 283–286.

[27] See generally, Carl Friedrich, *The New Image of the Common Man*
(Boston: Little, Brown & Company, 1960), ch. 5; Ernest E. Griffith, John Plamenatz,
and J. Roland Pennock, "Cultural Prerequisites to a Successfully Functioning Democracy: Symposium," *Amer. Pol. Sci. Rev.*, 50 (March 1956), pp. 101–137; V. O.
Key, Jr., *Public Opinion and American Democracy* (New York: Alfred A. Knopf,
1961), pp. 27–53; A. Lawrence Lowell, *Public Opinion and Popular Government*
(New York: Longmans, Green & Company, 1926).

cause the American political system runs on competition, and competition breeds bitter political differences.

The theorists have differed as to whether the consensus is as to the procedures or the substance, or both procedures and substance, of American politics. As V. O. Key has noted:

> Analyses in such terms usually assume that there exists within society a general acceptance of fundamental values, a widespread agreement on basic goals, or some common concurrence on the rules of the game, which makes it possible to settle the questions that arise from day to day in a manner not intolerable to the losers.[28]

I suggest that trust in governmental officials is an additional and equally important aspect of consensus.

Citizens of a democracy would be expected to agree on such values as liberty, justice, and equality.[29] Survey research conducted by Herbert McClosky, Samuel Stouffer, and James Prothro and Charles Grigg, does indicate an extremely high rate of agreement among Americans on these abstract values of democracy.[30]

None of these researchers, however, believes that the content of consensus is nothing more than agreement on abstract values. The agreement must extend to the manner in which these values are applied in actual political situations. Nearly all Americans may profess a belief in freedom of speech and in justice; but while 89 percent "believe in free speech for all no matter what their views might be," [31] only 27 percent agree with one application of this value, that communists should be permitted to speak in their community.[32]

I will call formal and informal methods of making political decisions "procedures." If these procedures incorporate the democratic values, public support of the procedures establishes and maintains a democracy.[33] Public preference for procedures which reject democratic values undermines the consensus.

The importance to a democratic polity of controlling competing forces has encouraged some theorists to conclude that conformity to democratic procedures alone is sufficient to maintain democracry. According to Carl

---

[28] Key, pp. 39–40.

[29] For such a definition of democratic values, see Pennock's contribution to the "Symposium," p. 131.

[30] Herbert McClosky, "Consensus and Ideology in American Politics," *Amer. Pol. Sci. Rev., 58* (June 1964), 363; Samuel Stouffer, *Communism, Conformity and Civil Liberties* (New York: Doubleday & Company, 1955); James Prothro and Charles Grigg, "Fundamental Principles of Democracy: Bases of Agreement and Disagreement," *J. Politics, 22* (May 1960), 276–293.

[31] McClosky, p. 366.

[32] Stouffer, p. 41.

[33] For an example of a "procedure," see Prothro and Grigg. They claim that consensus rests on an agreement among the adult members of a society on the basic question of how political power is won (p. 276).

Friedrich, constitutional democracy does not require agreement on fundamental issues but only on fundamental procedures. Yet procedural consensus provides too little oil for the political machine.

At the simplest level a theory that democracy rests upon substantive consensus subsumes public agreement about specific goals toward which the government should strive—and specific policies which should be adopted to achieve these goals.[34] The myriad problems which the government must face, the variety of solutions to these problems which might be chosen, and the public's lack of information, all suggest that this theory of substantive consensus is of doubtful validity. Substantive consensus may be more realistically viewed as an agreement on an orientation toward political issues, rather than an agreement on specific policies. An almost infinite variety of policy alternatives may be suggested as the solution to a political problem. If the American public excludes from consideration extreme policy alternatives on the right and left, a form of substantive consensus results.[35]

When the range of policy alternatives is restricted, the difference between the remaining alternatives is likewise restricted. The likelihood that a competing group will find a proposed alternative so repugnant that it will seek to impose its own policy by undemocratic procedures similarily decreases.[36] Substantive consensus is therefore an element in the preservation of procedural consensus.[37]

Restricting the range of policy alternatives may also contribute to the adoption of policies which comport with democratic values. Since most Americans profess a belief in democratic values, policy alternatives selected from the middle range may better approximate the common understanding of the manner in which these values should be translated into particular programs. If the public lends little support to those who would place no restrictions on the publication of "obscene" matter, and is equally cool to those who would forbid publication of any matter more salacious than the *New York Times*, consensus may be said to have narrowed the range of policies which could be adopted to deal with the problem. This substantive consensus may also effectively represent the manner in which

---

[34] See Lowell.

[35] The agreement by Americans to limit the range of policy alternatives has been noted by Robert A. Dahl in *A Preface to Democratic Theory* (Chicago: University of Chicago Press, 1956), p. 132.

[36] Pennock noted that agreement on democratic rules and procedures necessitates that there not be "persistent and widespread cleavage on policy" (p. 132).

[37] Disagreements over policy extensive enough to impede the conduct of democratic politics may still result, despite the restriction of policy alternatives, as where the public is evenly divided for and against a policy and those who support and oppose the policy hold their preferences with the same degree of intensity. The limitation of policy alternatives is a support, not a guarantee, of democratic procedure. For a discussion of such divisions of public opinion, see Robert E. Lane and David O. Sears, *Public Opinion* (Englewood Cliffs, N.J.: Prentice-Hall, Inc., 1964), pp. 107–113.

most Americans believe the value of free speech should be reflected in a legislative program.

Trust in the government would seem an equally important factor in support for democratic procedures, "government" for this purpose being defined as the occupants of those roles through which the formulation and administration of decisions for society are undertaken.[38] The competitive component of American politics requires any interest group to act or see its privileges and prospects limited by the political efforts of a competing group. Action will be by means of democratic procedures only if the interest group believes such procedures can produce results. Trust in democratic procedures requires a trust in the government officials in which all procedures culminate. Peaceful lobbying is futile unless the legislators are open to persuasion. Voting is futile unless election officials accurately count and report the ballots.

The general sense of trust in government as an essential of democracy has been noted by Almond and Verba, who key the concept to a belief in community of interest.

> Constitution makers have designed formal structures of politics that attempt to enforce trustworthy behavior, but without these attitudes of trust, such institutions may mean little. Social trust facilitates political cooperation among the citizens in these nations, and without it democratic politics is impossible. It probably also enters into a citizen's relation with political elites. *We argued earlier that the maintenance of elite power is essential in a democracy. We would now add that the sense of trust in the political elite—the belief that they are not alien and extractive forces, but part of the same political community—makes citizens willing to turn power over to them.*[39]

A more particularized source of trust in government has been suggested by Fred I. Greenstein, who has theorized about the residual effect upon adult attitudes toward elected officials of the benevolent picture of such officials developed by very young children in America.[40] While the sources of popular trust in the government are varied, an indicator of such trust is the pragmatic judgment that results can be achieved because officials can be trusted; and trust in the government is an important aspect of consensus.[41]

Defining the elements of consensus does not reveal its ambit. One

---

[38] As defined by David Easton and Robert D. Hess, "The Child's Political World," *Midwest J. Pol. Sci., 6* (August 1962), 231.

[39] Gabriel A. Almond and Sydney Verba, *The Civic Culture* (Princeton, N.J.: Princeton University Press, 1963), p. 490, emphasis added.

[40] *Children and Politics* (New Haven, Conn.: Yale University Press, 1965), pp. 53–54.

[41] McClosky's survey on the extent of consensus measures trust in political officials, pp. 368–371. See also Pennock, p. 124.

method of evaluating the American consensus is a simple head-count of those in agreement. The authors of two recent studies had assumed that consensus would require the assent to democratic values and procedures of a very large proportion of adult Americans. The proportion suggested by Prothro and Grigg was 90 percent.[42] McCloskey thought that 75 percent agreement would be sufficient.[43]

Both studies found that agreement on vague democratic values such as freedom of expression was indicated by an overwhelming proportion of Americans questioned. But when the respondents were questioned on their agreement with specific democratic procedures, the extent of agreement often fell far short of the minimum level stated by the authors as requisite for consensus. For example, 85 percent of Americans agree that "unless there is freedom for many points of view to be presented, there is little chance that the truth can ever be known," but 50.3 percent believe that "a book that contains wrong political views cannot be a good book and does not deserve to be published." [44]

To explain why the American consensus works with only a minority of Americans in agreement on specific procedures, the authors of these studies suggest that the characteristics of the people who support democratic institutions are more important than absolute numbers.[45] To Prothro and Grigg the minority consensus is effective because people with undemocratic attitudes are not likely to act on behalf of their attitudes.[46] McClosky views the other side of the coin: those people who are active in politics support democratic values and procedures to a greater extent than the less active.[47]

From surveys of the national population and of the population of one community, respectively, Stouffer and Dahl suggest that Americans who have the following attributes are more likely to be trained in and aware of democratic norms than Americans lacking these attributes: education; status as determined by occupation; wealth; a sense of political efficacy; and participation in private and political associations.[48] The proportion of Americans who by possession of these attributes have acquired sufficient education in democracy to make them likely supporters of democratic processes has not been determined by these studies.[49] It would

---

[42] Prothro and Grigg, p. 278.

[43] McClosky, p. 363.

[44] McClosky, pp. 366–367.

[45] In his contribution to the "Symposium" John Plamenatz proposes that democracy needs the active support of only a minority of the people (p. 123).

[46] Prothro and Grigg, pp. 293–294.

[47] McClosky, pp. 261–263.

[48] Stouffer; Robert A. Dahl, *Who Governs* (New Haven, Conn.: Yale University Press, 1961), chap. 26.

[49] Prothro and Grigg conclude that the attribute most likely to yield support of democracy is education (p. 291). Robert E. Agger and associates, in a

appear that the proportion is less than a majority of Americans, and surveys indicating a minority consensus on particular democratic procedures confirm this offhand impression. Democracy can be preserved by these outnumbered "carriers of the creed," as they are termed by Prothro and Grigg,[50] only if the minority is more politically active and influential than the undemocratic majority. An intense minority can impose its preferences when the majority is unorganized.[51]

The proportion of Americans who engage in political activity other than casting votes is small.[52] Surveys have indicated that these political activists, whom Dahl calls the "political stratum,"[53] rank higher than the general population in income, occupation as determined by status, education, sense of political efficacy, and extent of group membership.[54] Since these attributes are the same attributes likely to produce a respect for democratic procedures, the politically active minority should also be the democratically inclined minority.[55]

Studies of particular groups of political activists confirm that activists agree upon democratic values and procedures.[56] Stouffer found greater support for civil liberties from community leaders than from the general population.[57] A decade later McClosky compared the attitudes of dele-

---

report on a survey of the population in Eugene and Springfield, Oregon, state that trust in democratic politics is positively associated with education. Robert E. Agger, Marshall N. Goldstein, and Stanley A. Pearl, "Political Cynicism: Measurement and Meaning," *J. Politics, 23* (August 1961), p. 484. On the other hand, Edgar Litt, sampling registered voters in a middle-class Boston ward, found no association between formal education and political cynicism. Litt points out that lack of trust in democratic politics may be shared by people regardless of their socioeconomic and educational attributes if they live in a community whose political leaders are reputed to be corrupt. "Political Cynicism and Political Futility," *J. Politics, 25* (May 1963), 315–316. His findings lend weight to McClosky's suggestion that education as an isolated factor may be given too much credit for producing support for democracy (pp. 277–278).

[50] Prothro and Grigg, pp. 292–293.

[51] See Robert A. Dahl, *Who Governs*, pp. 314–315.

[52] Lester W. Milbrath, *Political Participation* (Skokie, Ill.: Rand McNally & Company, 1965).

[53] Dahl, *Who Governs*, pp. 90–94.

[54] Milbrath, chaps. 3, 5. See also Dahl, *Who Governs,* chaps. 24, 25.

[55] However, Plamenatz suggests that while democracy is maintained by the politically active, it is not because they comprehend what democracy means, but because they behave in ways that keep it going (p. 123).

[56] Agger and associates report a finding that is contrary to the norm, that some party activists are not more trusting than the rank and file. Among a sample of precinct committeemen and committeewomen and members of political clubs in the Eugene-Springfield area, Democratic party activists are less cynical than rank-and-file Democrats and Republican activists are more cynical than rank-and-file Republicans (and more cynical than Democratic activists) (p. 486).

[57] Stouffer's data show that community leaders are more aware of democratic procedures and have greater respect for the procedures that incorporate the value of tolerance than does the general population.

gates to national political conventions with those of a national sample of the voters. He found the delegates more likely than the voters to believe in procedures by which political competition is conducted, and less cynical and suspicious about politics.

The Crusaders are well-to-do, well educated, in high status occupations, and very active in politics—attributes thought to be conducive to social training in democratic norms, and hence productive of support for democratic institutions. But the Crusaders participate in a radical-right organization whose principle tenet is that communists and communist sympathizers exert a significant and baleful influence upon the government and people of the United States. Those who think that enemies of the nation make use of its political procedures could be expected to doubt the value of these procedures and the norms on which they are based.

Which characteristic of the Crusaders, their demographic traits or their political beliefs, is the better indicator of how much support they give to democratic politics? In short, do the Crusaders share in the American consensus? What association exists between the extent of the Crusaders' political activity and their support of democratic institutions?

PROPOSITIONS

Consensus in a democratic polity exists when citizens: (1) trust in the government, (2) support the values and abide by the procedures whereby political conflict is resolved, and (3) limit the range of alternative solutions they will consider in any dispute over public policy. Because of the Crusaders' intense fear of domestic communist influence, the amount of trust which they are willing to give the government would seem crucial to an evaluation of their role in the American consensus.

To determine the extent of Crusader trust in the government—since this trust is but one of the three variables of consensus, the other aspects will be examined by testing the following propositions:

Proposition 1: Trust in the government is associated with support for democratic procedures.

Proposition 2: Trust in the government is associated with support for a limited range of solutions to public problems.

To determine whether allegiance to the radical-right thesis on the domestic communist menace bears on the Crusaders' support of democratic institutions, these related hypotheses will next be tested:

Proposition 3: A sense of danger from American communists is associated with a lack of support for each aspect of consensus.

As in all organizations, Crusaders differ among themselves in the degree of fervor with which they espouse policies and attitudes. The more active Crusaders would be likely to exhibit greater distrust of government, in accord with Proposition 4.

Proposition 4: A lack of trust in the government is associated with greater activity in a radical-right organization.

Those active in one organization are more likely to be active in other organizations, including political organizations. Proposition 5 tests whether this holds true for Crusaders.

Proposition 5: Greater Crusade activity is associated with greater participation in partisan politics.

The politically active are generally supposed to be more committed to democratic values and procedures than those less active in politics. Proposition 6 assumes the contrary in comparing political activity with an element of consensus.

Proposition 6: Among Crusaders greater participation in politics is associated with a lack of trust in the government.

In an effort to evaluate the motives for Crusader political activity, Proposition 7 was added to Proposition 6:

Proposition 7: Among Crusaders greater participation in politics is associated with a greater sense of danger from American communists.

CRUSADERS' SENSE OF TRUST IN THE GOVERNMENT

Dr. Schwarz and most of his fellow lecturers at the Crusade schools preach the danger to the United States of communist subversion. To these lecturers the communist menace arises not from the number of American communists and communist sympathizers, which they concede to be small in proportion to the population, but from the influential positions in American life which the communist-oriented have achieved.[58]

To determine whether Crusaders believe these positions of influence to include government officials, Crusaders were asked to respond "yes," "maybe," or "no" to a series of questions as to whether "significant com-

---

[58] For Schwarz' comments on this theme see footnote 8. Lecturers at a Crusade school typically will include not only those who have dealt with communists on a national level (such as Herbert Philbrick, former F.B.I. agent and author of *I Led Three Lives*, and Robert Morris, former Chief Counsel of the Senate Internal Security Sub-Committee) but also speakers who claim to have encountered communists in their work or local community. Typical of the latter would be a missionary from Japan, a housewife from Nebraska, and a medical doctor from Michigan.

munist infiltration" existed in specified governmental agencies. The data are summarized in Table 5.

TABLE 5

Crusaders' Perceptions of Significant Communist Infiltration in Various Government Agencies [a]

IN YOUR OPINION IS THERE SIGNIFICANT COMMUNIST INFILTRATION IN:	IN PERCENT			
	No	MAYBE	YES	TOTAL
The State Department	9	27	65	101 [b]
California State Legislature	15	42	43	100
Central Intelligence Agency	33	44	23	100
Congress	36	34	30	100
The Justice Department	37	42	21	100
The White House	41	32	27	100
The Supreme Court	48	27	25	100
Your City Council or local government	52	31	18	101 [b]
Federal Bureau of Investigation	79	17	4	100

[a] No answers and don't knows have been removed from the bases.
[b] Does not sum to 100 percent because of rounding.

The Crusaders' perception of communist infiltration of American government will be used as an indicator of the trust dimension of consensus. This indicator was selected for two reasons: (1) a direct question asking if there is communist influence in a particular agency of government is considerably more definite than any question asking how the respondent "feels about" or how much he "trusts" that agency; (2) to a group of people preselected as concerned about communism by their attendance at a "Crusade" against communism, a belief that communist influence was not present in a governmental agency would seem a sine qua non for trust in that agency. The "maybe" responses have been separately tabulated, but so long as a respondent believes that there "may" be significant communist influence in the agency, his lack of trust in the agency seems likely, particularly since those who volunteered a "don't know" response were omitted.

Table 5 ranks governmental agencies in ascending order according to the degree of trust placed in each by the Crusaders. The picture presented is of pervasive distrust of American government, whether the governmental unit is elective or appointive, national or local.[59]

Only one governmental agency, the Federal Bureau of Investigation, is considered free of communist influence by a large majority of Crusaders.

---

[59] Compare the findings of Robert E. Lane that in the early 1960s Americans in general had greater confidence in their government than at any time since World War II. "The Politics of Consensus in an Age of Affluence," *Amer. Pol. Sci. Rev., 59* (December 1965), 874–895.

This finding is to be expected in light of J. Edgar Hoover's well-publicized campaign against communist subversion. Equally predictable is the over-whelming distrust shown the State Department, which undoubtedly reflects the effect of McCarthy's charges of communist subversion of the State Department, in the 1950s, and perhaps the general distrust of American foreign policy common to most right wing movements. Neither finding is a particularly good measure of Crusader trust or distrust of American government in general.

It is between these extremes that the Crusaders' distrust of government is manifest. Of the federal branches of government, the Supreme Court is slightly more trusted than the White House and considerably more so than Congress. The greater but still quite limited trust given the Supreme Court may reflect a conflict between the traditional American belief that courts are above political influence and the persistent complaint by some radical-right organizations (although not the Crusaders per se) that the Supreme Court is "soft on communists" and guilty of undermining basic American values by certain of its decisions, such as the banning of prayers in public schools.

The relatively low degree of trust in the White House may in part reflect the predominantly Republican loyalties of the Crusaders. Yet the Cru-saders reveal little difference on the basis of party affiliation in their responses to a question as to whether internal subversion had increased or remained the same after President Kennedy took office: 57 percent of Republicans and 53 percent of Democrats said internal subversion had increased.

The overwhelming distrust of the state legislature is also most revealing of the Crusaders' distrust of all government. Because of state preemption in California of many governmental areas formerly of local concern, and because California is but one of 50 states represented in Congress, the focus of political activity for many groups in California is likely to be the state legislature—the government agency of importance most distrusted by the Crusaders.

The Crusaders' responses relate, of course, to the incumbent officials. Responses to another question suggest, however, that Crusader distrust of American government will endure. Sixty-six percent of the Crusaders agree that "the way things are going now, it is likely that the United States will be Communist within the next twenty years."

CRUSADERS' TRUST IN GOVERNMENT COMPARED WITH SUPPORT FOR DEMOCRATIC PROCEDURES AND ACCEPTANCE OF A LIMITATION ON POLICY ALTERNATIVES

Proposition 1 assumes an association between trust in the government and the second aspect of consensus, support for democratic procedures.

A comparison of Crusader attitudes on democratic procedures with those of two college-educated samples indicates that the Crusaders do not withhold support for democratic procedures to the same extent as they refuse to trust in the government, but that those Crusaders who are most distrustful of government are most likely to fail to support democratic procedures.

An example of democratic procedure is the principle of majority rule effected by elections under universal suffrage. The Crusaders were asked two questions designed to reveal whether they would prefer restriction of suffrage by educational or property-ownership qualifications. The same questions have been asked samples of the population of Ann Arbor and Tallahassee by Prothro and Grigg. Table 6 compares Crusader responses with those of college-educated members of the Prothro and Grigg sample,[60] disagreement with the question in each case representing the response in favor of a democratic procedure. Crusaders emerge as slightly more opposed to restricting the suffrage to "well informed" voters than college-educated members of the Prothro and Grigg sample, and much more opposed than the sample to imposition of a property ownership qualification.

Crusader support for this aspect of democratic procedure becomes even more remarkable when a comparison is made between these responses and the extent of Crusader trust in the federal government.[61] As Table 6 indicates, those Crusaders who believe there is no significant communist infiltration of the federal government are considerably more likely to disagree with a statement that the suffrage should be restricted by educational or property qualifications. Those Crusaders who believe there may be significant communist infiltration do not give significantly more support to the principle of universal suffrage than Crusaders certain of communist infiltration.[62] But even Crusaders who are certain that communists have penetrated Congress and the White House are more favorably disposed toward universal suffrage than the college-educated sample of Prothro and Grigg.

With respect to another aspect of democratic procedure, the Crusaders appear less supportive than a comparable group. Freedom of speech is a

---

[60] Because 79 percent of the fall Crusaders attended or were graduated from college, college-educated respondents in the Prothro and Grigg study were used for comparison.

[61] In Table 6 and later tables, Crusader trust in government is evidenced by responses as to communist infiltration of Congress, the White House and the Supreme Court only. These three items give an adequate distribution of Crusader opinion, and facilitate comparisons with the federal domestic and foreign policies to be discussed.

[62] Lending some support to the suggestion made earlier that a belief that communists may have infiltrated a government agency is as good a measure of distrust as a conviction that such infiltration has occurred.

TABLE 6

Support for Democratic Procedures by Crusaders according to Trust in the Federal Government, and by College-Educated Respondents in the Ann Arbor-Tallahassee Sample (in Percent)[a]

SUPPORT FOR DEMOCRATIC PRINCIPLES	TRUST IN THE FEDERAL GOVERNMENT										
	In your opinion is there significant communist infiltration in:									Total	Ann Arbor and Tallahassee [b]
	Congress			White House			Supreme Court				
	Yes $N=44$	Maybe $N=51$	No $N=54$	Yes $N=40$	Maybe $N=47$	No $N=60$	Yes $N=38$	Maybe $N=40$	No $N=72$	$N=167$	$N=137$
People should be allowed to vote in a city referendum only if:											
"They are well informed on the problem voted on"	68	67	78	65	72	82	66	58	81	70	62
"They are taxpayers deciding on a tax-supported undertaking"	43	43	59	35	51	57	34	35	63	48	23

[a] Source: Prothro and Grigg, p. 285.
[b] The figures have been rounded off.

Reprinted by permission of the authors and the Journal of Politics.

basic democratic value which is implemented by tolerance of the use of mass media by those with whom one disagrees. In a survey by Trow, male Crusaders are about as tolerant of newspaper criticism of the American form of government as are male residents of Bennington, Vermont.[63] But college-educated male Crusaders are much less in favor than similar Bennington respondents of permitting socialists to publish newspapers (68 percent to 93 percent) or permitting communists to speak on radio or television (30 percent to 47 percent).[64]

The Crusaders' lack of support for freedom of speech, in contrast to their support of majority rule, may be due to their fear of a communist take-over. Crusaders are taught that communism advances in America because of the persuasive powers of a small group of influential men. It is natural that Crusaders would wish to deny these men general access to the media of persuasion. This explanation accords with the Crusaders' general tolerance of newspaper criticism of the government, a question without a red tinge.

Table 7 compares Crusader support for freedom of speech with their degree of trust in the federal government.[65] As with support for majority rule, those Crusaders who believe there is no significant communist infiltration in the federal government are more likely to support freedom of speech than are Crusaders who believe there is or may be significant communist influence. And just as with majority rule, there is little difference in the support given freedom of speech between those who merely suspect, and those who are sure of, communist infiltration.

Proposition 2 states an association between trust in the government and support for a limited range of solutions to public problems. Comparison of Crusader responses with those of national samples in Table 8 indicates that Crusaders espouse more extreme solutions to problems of domestic economic and foreign policy. Table 8 also compares Crusader support for various domestic and foreign policies with the extent of Crusader trust in the federal government. The Crusaders who believe that significant communist infiltration of the federal government has or may have taken place are slightly more likely to oppose medicare and federal aid for school construction than are those who see no communist infiltration; they are far more likely than the Crusaders who trust in the government to advocate abolition of the income tax, cessation of foreign aid, and relinquishment of United States membership in the United Nations. Differences on

---

[63] Martin Trow, "Right Wing Radicalism and Political Intolerance: A Study of Support for McCarthy in a New England Town," p. 261.

[64] Identical questions had been asked the fall Crusaders, and their responses were similar to those of the Oakland Crusaders summarized above.

[65] The table contains a question not used in the Trow study, on whether books against religion should be removed from the public library.

TABLE 7

Crusaders' Trust in the Federal Government and Their Preference for Freedom of Speech (in Percent)

	TRUST IN THE FEDERAL GOVERNMENT									Total
	In your opinion is there significant communist infiltration in:									
	Congress			White House			Supreme Court			
FREEDOM OF SPEECH	Yes $N=44$	Maybe $N=51$	No $N=54$	Yes $N=40$	Maybe $N=47$	No $N=60$	Yes $N=38$	Maybe $N=40$	No $N=72$	$N=167$
"Newspapers should be allowed to criticize our form of government"	89	86	91	90	81	93	87	75	94	83
"Books against religion should not be removed from the public library"	73	71	96	72	77	85	71	68	83	76
"Socialists should be allowed to publish newspapers"	52	56	76	48	40	60	50	48	79	62
"Communists should be allowed to speak on radio and television"	11	24	33	13	15	38	5	13	39	22

TABLE 8

Opposition to Federal Policies by Crusaders according to Trust in the Federal Government, and by Various National Samples (in Percent)

	TRUST IN THE FEDERAL GOVERNMENT											
	In your opinion is there significant communist infiltration in:											
	Congress			White House			Supreme Court			Total	National Sample
	Yes $N=44$	Maybe $N=51$	No $N=54$	Yes $N=40$	Maybe $N=47$	No $N=60$	Yes $N=38$	Maybe $N=40$	No $N=72$	$N=167$	
Domestic economic programs											
The federal income tax should be abolished	48	45	11	62	36	13	55	45	15	35	a
Oppose social security tax to pay for old age medical insurance:	87	82	71	93	81	68	84	83	74	79	26 [b]
Oppose federal economic aid for local public school construction:	89	75	76	80	92	63	82	88	69	79	25 [c]
Foreign affairs											
Against foreign aid	50 [d]	59 [d]	15 [d]	53 [d]	53 [d]	20 [d]	58 [d]	60 [d]	15 [d]	38	30 [e]
U.S. should give up membership in the U.N.	55	55	19	65	49	20	77	43	26	41	8 [f]

[a] Comparative data not available.
[b] Source: American Institute of Public Opinion, June 9, 1961 (Institute Surveys hereinafter stated as "AIPO").
[c] Source: AIPO, February 19, 1960.
[d] Responses indicating qualified approval of foreign aid are not included.
[e] Source: AIPO, February 3, 1963, 35 percent of the Republicans were against foreign aid.
[f] Source: AIPO, November 29, 1963.

public policies between those who suspect, and those who are sure of, communist subversion, are again slight.

CONSENSUS AND THE FEAR OF COMMUNISTS

To this point Crusader distrust in American government has been established by the extent of communist infiltration of governmental agencies which Crusaders perceive, and the associations between Crusader distrust of government and other aspects of consensus explored. It is likely that similar associations will exist between the degree of fear of domestic communists and the degree of support given democratic institutions, as stated in Proposition 3. Table 9 confirms this assumption.[66] The more danger a Crusader sees in American communists, the more likely is that Crusader to believe in communist infiltration of government agencies, to reject freedom of speech (the aspect of procedural consensus in which the Crusaders made the poorest showing), and to opt for extreme solution to public problems.[67]

Crusaders were also asked whether they believed "communists have a lot of influence" in the Democratic and Republican parties. Because a political party is the major vehicle for political participation available to an individual in America, the Crusaders' attitude toward the parties is perhaps as important a measure of their support for democratic institutions as their attitude toward Congress or the White House. Sixty percent of all Crusaders believe that communists have great influence in the Democratic Party, but only 12 percent of Crusaders believe communists are as influential in the Republican Party. Trust in both parties increases markedly with the decrease of perception of danger from domestic communists. The Democratic Party is viewed with suspicion by 89 percent of the Crusaders

---

[66] As indicated in Table 2, Crusaders could respond that domestic communists presented "no danger" and "hardly any danger," in addition to the responses listed in Table 9. No Crusader responded that the communists constituted no danger, and less than 2 percent indicated hardly any danger; these latter responses accordingly were collapsed in Table 9 into the category of "some danger." The variation in the center of the list of governmental agencies in Table 9 from the order in Table 5 results from the inclusion in Table 9 of "no answer" responses.

[67] It is interesting that Crusaders are in greater agreement, whatever their degree of fear of communists, on *proposed* federal programs than on existing federal programs. At the time of the survey medicare had not been adopted, and federal school aid was less extensive than at present. At that date, however, the federal income tax had been in effect nearly 50 years and the various federal foreign commitments for 15 to 20 years. This may indicate a Crusader belief that domestic communists are more likely to benefit from new programs. It is more likely that opposition to medicare and school aid represents merely a conservative, not an extremist, position, and accordingly no strong association exists between such opposition and fear of communists. Compare the associations on abolition of the federal income tax.

TABLE 9

Danger Seen from American Communists and Consensus (in Percent)

CONSENSUS	THINK AMERICAN COMMUNISTS ARE:			Total $N = 167$
	Very Great Danger $N = 94$	Great Danger $N = 43$	Some Danger $N = 24$	
Trust in the government				
"There is *no* significant communist infiltration in":				
The State Department	2	7	21	9
California State Legislature	4	12	42	14
The Justice Department	17	35	79	32
Congress	18	28	88	32
Central Intelligence Agency	20	33	50	29
The White House	26	40	79	36
The Supreme Court	30	44	88	43
Your City Council or local government	31	56	71	44
Federal Bureau of Investigation	63	79	75	69
Preference for freedom of speech				
"Newspapers should be allowed to criticize our form of government"	88	93	100	83
"Books against religion should not be removed from the public library"	69	81	100	76
"Socialists should be allowed to publish newspapers"	59	69	91	62
"Communists should be allowed to speak on radio and television"	10	36	39	22
Opposition to federal policies				
Domestic economic programs				
The income tax should be abolished	49	23	5	35
Social security should not cover old age medical insurance	90	87	71	79
Federal government should not give aid to public school construction	84	81	78	79
Foreign affairs				
Against foreign aid	49	39	12	38
The U.S. should give up its membership in the U.N.	56	38	9	41

most fearful of American communists, as compared with 22 percent of the Crusaders who consider communist subversion only "some danger." No Crusaders who see "some danger" from communists, and only 8 percent of the Crusaders who perceive communists as a "great danger," believe that the Republican Party is influenced by communists. Even among Crusaders who think communists a "very great danger," no more than one-fifth suspect the Republican Party. The G.O.P. is considered about as trustworthy as the F.B.I.[68]

ACTIVITY IN THE CRUSADE AND SUPPORT FOR DEMOCRACY

The informal structure of the Christian Anti-Communism Crusade [69] requires that the only meaningful measure of the "greater activity in a radical-right organization" contemplated by Proposition 4 be attendance at both Crusade schools held in the San Francisco Bay Area. Respondents at the fall school were asked whether they had attended the earlier Oakland school; those Crusaders who had attended the Oakland school are hereinafter referred to as "oldtimers," and distinguished from "newcomers" attending their first school.

Table 10 indicates that oldtimers are somewhat less trusting of govern-

TABLE 10

Exposure to the Crusade and Trust in the Government (in Percent)

	EXPOSURE		
TRUST IN THE GOVERNMENT	Newcomers $N = 88$	Oldtimers $N = 77$	Total $N = 167$
There is no significant *communist infiltration in:*			
The State Department	14	4	9
California State Legislature	19	7	14
Congress	33	31	32
Central Intelligence Agency	34	25	29
The Justice Department	38	29	32
The White House	40	31	36
Your City Council or local government	42	47	44
The Supreme Court	48	39	43
The Federal Bureau of Investigation	62	72	69

ment than are newcomers. The percentage differences are not great except with regard to the State Department and the California State Legislature, which are trusted by roughly three times as many newcomers as oldtimers. Oldtimers evince greater trust in local government and the F.B.I. The attitude of repeater Crusaders toward the F.B.I. may result from

---

[68] As to Crusaders' attitudes toward institutions farther removed from the government, 82 percent of all Crusaders believe that "communist professors have a lot of influence in American colleges and universities." Crusaders who think domestic communists a very great danger are two-and-a-half times more likely to distrust American higher education than are Crusaders who regard American communists as merely some danger.

[69] See text accompanying footnotes 3–9.

nothing more than two exposures to Crusade speaker Herbert Philbrick, but when coupled with the extreme distrust shown the State Department by oldtimers, suggests that hard-core Crusaders are more aware of, or more responsive to, publicity about alleged communist infiltration.[70]

Oldtimers also give less support than do newcomers to the other aspects of consensus. Only 13 percent of the oldtimers would permit communists to speak on radio and television, as compared with 30 percent of the newcomers. Oldtimers are more likely to favor abolition of the income tax (39 percent to 26 percent), and withdrawal from the United Nations (50 percent to 36 percent).[71]

This picture of the oldtimers as more distrustful of government, more fearful of domestic communists, and less willing to accept certain values and programs of modern America, presents an interesting problem in cause-and-effect. Are the oldtimers more radical than the newcomers because of their double exposure to the teaching of Crusade schools, as well as their possible exposure to Crusade materials sent them during the interval between the schools? Or are the oldtimers more radical than the newcomers because only the already dedicated would think it worthwhile to attend two more-or-less repetitious schools? Is the militancy of the oldtimer learned from the Crusade or preexisting and merely expressed through the Crusade?

No clear answer can be given. Certainly the self-selection of the dedicated by willingness to endure part or all of two week-long programs of strikingly similar content during a seven month period is an important factor. This may in part be balanced by the less favorable community climate at the time of the fall school,[72] which suggests that anyone attending the fall school would be likely to be radical, since he would choose to attend despite little publicity, and that unfavorable. The newcomers at the fall school might thus themselves be preselected as extremists.

The data provides some support for the thesis that oldtimers are made, not born. A recurring theme of the Crusade, and one which most Americans would not accept, is that domestic communists are as great a danger

---

[70] Oldtimers also display a greater fear of the domestic communist menace. Ninety-four percent think American communists are a "very great danger" or "great danger," as compared with 75 percent of newcomers. Seventy-four percent of oldtimers felt that communist subversion had increased during the Kennedy administration; only 57 percent of newcomers agreed. These percentage differences respecting the increase of subversion hold true when only Republican oldtimers and newcomers are compared.

[71] A nearly equal percentage of each group favors foreign aid, but oldtimers are four times as likely to volunteer that their support of foreign aid is conditioned on that aid going only to noncommunist countries. With respect to Medicare and federal aid for school construction, oldtimers are only slightly more in opposition than newcomers.

[72] See text accompanying footnote 14.

to the United States as the communist nations of Russia and China. To equate the danger from communists within and without America, Schwarz uses this illustration: "When a ship is sinking, which is the greatest threat: the water inside the ship or the water around the ship?" [73] Since oldtimers are more fearful of domestic communists than are newcomers, they would likely be more fearful of foreign communists as well unless Schwarz's teachings have borne fruit. But 58 percent of the oldtimers state that they are "not at all worried" about the chance of an atomic war, as compared to 40 percent of the newcomers,[74] and oldtimers are almost twice as likely as newcomers to believe that "Russian claims about achievements in space are false."

CRUSADER POLITICAL ACTIVITY

It might be assumed that participation in a radical-right organization would decrease participation in political organizations, on reasoning that having found an organization which embraces his beliefs, the rightist will be unwilling to work in a political organization more or less unreceptive to him. Proposition 5 states the contrary, that those Crusaders most active in the movement are also most active in partisan politics. Table 11 confirms this proposition.

TABLE 11

Exposure to the Crusade and Political Activity (in Percent)

	EXPOSURE		
POLITICAL ACTIVITY	Newcomers $N = 88$	Oldtimers $N = 77$	Total $N = 167$
Generally speaking, do you think of yourself as:			
A Republican	62	71	66
A Democrat	12	12	12
An Independent	26	16	21
Number of party campaign activities [a]			
0 and 1	30	14	22
2 and 3	40	34	37
4 and 5	30	52	39
Wrote letter(s) to a government official	55	74	63
Attended meetings of a Republican Assembly	25	43	30

[a] Party campaign activities in Tables 11 and 12 are those listed in Table 4.

[73] *Speech at the Philadelphia School of Anti-Communism*, November 1960 (tape). Schwarz used this same illustration at both the Oakland and fall schools.

[74] Thirty-seven percent of college graduates in a national sample indicated that they were not at all worried about atomic war. AIPO, July 14, 1961.

On its face, this association between activity in the Crusade and political activity is not surprising. The Crusade is a quasi-political organization, although its leaders carefully avoid any endorsement of candidates or issues, and it is likely that persons interested enough in the Crusade to attend two schools will also be interested in more direct political participation. But in light of the correlation between extent of Crusade activity and dissensus established by Proposition 4, the association between Crusade activity and political activity would predict, in accordance with Proposition 6, that among Crusaders greater participation in politics is associated with a lack of trust in the government. Table 12 indicates that this association exists. In rough compass, the more likely a Crusader is to evidence distrust in the government by envisioning communists in a particular governmental agency, the more likely is that Crusader to participate in political campaign activities and to write letters to a government official.

Why should the Crusaders reverse the usual correlation between greater political participation and increased support for democracy? One explanation is that Crusaders participate in politics from a negative standpoint: they wish to prevent that which they most fear, communist subversion, and are driven into the political arena by their fear. Proposition 7 reflects this interpretation by assuming an association between greater political participation and fear of domestic communists. The data provide some support for this proposition. Forty-six percent of Crusaders who think American communists a "very great danger" commonly take part in four or five party campaign activities; only 17 percent of Crusaders who think communist subversion is only "some danger" engage in so many campaign activities.[75] In the 1962 California gubernatorial campaign, Joseph Shell was considerably more outspoken in his opposition to communism than was Richard Nixon. Shell was the choice of a majority of Republican Crusaders; but as Table 12 indicates, he got a far higher percentage of votes from Crusaders who distrust the federal government than he received from the others. Comparisons between oldtimers and newcomers also support this interpretation. Oldtimers are more politically active. They are also more prone to vote for those politicians who wave the banner of anticommunism. Of Crusaders voting in the 1962 gubernatorial primary, 64 percent of the oldtimers preferred Shell as against 58 percent of the newcomers. In the 1960 presidential election, 90 percent of the oldtimers voted for Nixon, but only 78 percent of the newcomers.[76]

---

[75] The attitudinal and activity syndrome typical of Crusaders is similar to that of Negro law students in the South. The most cynical students were more active in politics. Agger and others, p. 501.

[76] The greater Republicanism of the Crusaders does not account for the difference. Among Republican Crusaders only, 92 percent of the oldtimers and 83 percent of the newcomers voted for Nixon.

TABLE 12

Crusaders' Trust in the Federal Government, Their Party Preference, Candidate Preference, and Political Activity (in Percent)

TRUST IN THE FEDERAL GOVERNMENT

In your opinion is there significant communist infiltration in:

	Congress			White House			Supreme Court			Total
	Yes $N=44$	Maybe $N=51$	No $N=54$	Yes $N=40$	Maybe $N=47$	No $N=60$	Yes $N=38$	Maybe $N=40$	No $N=72$	$N=167$
Party preference										
Republican	62	75	61	65	66	62	66	70	63	66
Democratic	18	8	11	13	9	15	13	8	14	12
Independent	18	14	28	18	23	22	18	18	22	21
Candidate preference in 1962 Republican Gubernatorial Primary [a]										
Richard Nixon	36	18	32	20	34	28	32	33	28	29
Joseph Shell	50	61	35	58	51	38	50	58	38	45
Number of political campaign activities engaged in										
0 and 1	7	24	24	5	22	28	10	13	27	22
2 and 3	32	38	48	30	36	45	42	33	39	37
4 and 5	62	36	27	66	43	45	52	53	30	39
Wrote letter(s) to a government official	71	59	54	67	64	55	61	65	58	63

[a] Percentage of all respondents to trust in government questions. Percentages total far less than 100 because some respondents to trust questions were ineligible to, or did not vote in, the primary.

An additional explanation of the Crusaders' singular degree of political participation may lie in their high educational level and socioeconomic status. Their high rank in the community may provide the self-confidence necessary to permit them to take part in a political system for which they manifest considerable distrust, and their education has acquainted them with the techniques of political power.[77]

At least Crusader party campaign activity may also be explicable by its Republican nature. A large majority of Crusaders consider themselves Republicans. An even larger majority believe there has been no significant communist subversion of the Republican Party. By participating in Republican politics Crusaders take part in the affairs of a political organization as trustworthy as the F.B.I.

PARTY POLITICS AND THE RADICAL RIGHT

Four themes run through the Crusader data. First is the Crusader's consuming fear of domestic communists. Because communists are a grave danger to America, most governmental agencies must have been infiltrated by communists and should be viewed with distrust. Because communists may make use of mass media, they must be denied the right to use these media. To the extent a Crusader fears communist subversion, then to that extent he will declare for extreme solutions to public problems, solutions no longer acceptable to the bulk of Americans.

Second, this dissent from consensus is selective. Communist subversion may be prevalent, but a Crusader is more likely to perceive it in the White House, Congress, and the California State Legislature than in the Supreme Court or local government. Communists should be denied freedom of speech, but all other Americans should have the right to criticize our form of government and elects its officials. To a hard-core Crusader (although not to a milder one) the clock should be turned back to repeal governmental policies in effect for decades; but with respect to certain proposed governmental policies, Crusaders of all shades unite to oppose policy alternatives to about the same extent as would be expected of the conservative Americans who do not see communists behind every bureaucratic desk.

Third, Crusaders are clearly within the "political stratum" and, on the average, all of them are more politically active than most other Americans, and the most dedicated are even more active. Yet this activity occurs in an aura of massive distrust of the government and its procedures. The

---

[77] Almond and Verba present data indicating that education is closely associated with a sense of political efficacy (chap. 7). Agger and others report a strong association between political potency and a high level of education, and a positive but less significant association between political potency and a high income (pp. 484 and 487). But the latter authors find that political cynicism among the well-educated inhibits political activity (p. 498).

more distrustful a Crusader is of government and democratic values, the more active politically he is likely to be—the more active politically, the more active in the Crusade.

Finally, Crusaders are predominantly Republican, and Republicans who trust in that party more than any formal governmental entity.

The conclusions to be drawn from these Crusader themes as to the radical right in general must be less definitely stated. The most obvious is that party identification would appear to be the most significant ascertainable factor in predicting the sources of support for the current radical right. Earlier studies by Nelson W. Polsby [78] and Seymour M. Lipset [79] had emphasized the importance of the Republicanism of supporters of Senator Joseph McCarthy, in contrast to the demographic and psychological factors which others had speculated characterized the radical right.[80] Although Richard Hofstadter has termed interesting the association between a preference for the Republican Party and support for a radical-right movement revealed by Polsby and the Wolfinger Crusade study, to Hofstadter this association is not as important to an analysis of a radical-right movement as the socioeconomic and psychic stresses which underlie party preference.[81] However, there is as yet no empirical data available to determine what those common stresses may be, but the ardent Republicanism of the Crusaders is patent.

Their party identification has failed to socialize the Crusaders in democratic values. It has been suggested that acquisition of a party preference may induce adherence to the existing political system, by impeding participation in new political movements.[82] Partisan political activity itself has been proposed as a source of confidence in the political system.[83] It is

---

[78] The first study asserting the importance of party identification in assessing support for the radical right was Nelson Polsby's "Toward an Explanation of McCarthyism," *Political Studies, 8* (October 1960), 250–271. Polsby analyzed Gallup survey data and election returns to determine voter support for candidates who took a stand with respect to McCarthy's activities. He concluded that affiliation with the Republican Party was more closely associated with support for McCarthy than any other voter characteristic.

[79] Seymour M. Lipset, using SRC election data for 1954, agreed that Polsby was correct in stressing Republicanism as an important factor in predicting support for the radical right (p. 329).

[80] See generally the essays in Daniel Bell (ed.).

[81] Bell, pp. 85–86.

[82] Greenstein, p. 84.

[83] See Herbert McClosky's data on the greater extent of support for democratic politics among delegates to national conventions (pp. 364–371). Samuel Eldersveld, from a survey of voters in Detroit, reports that people in contact with political parties have greater knowledge about government, slightly more confidence in the political campaign process, and are more optimistic about being able to play a role in the political system. He concludes that "parties may be efficacious in strengthening the system." *Political Parties: A Behavioral Analysis* (Skokie, Ill.: Rand McNally & Company, 1964), p. 501.

doubtful that any number of declarations by Republican leaders about the values of free speech would convince the Crusaders that a communist should have that privilege. The Crusaders' ideology, their manic belief in the danger from domestic communism, limits the effect of their party identification.

So long as the radical right retains the requisite degree of trust in the Republican Party, they will continue their high level of political activity within the Party. Because they are more active than the generality of party members, it is likely that they will have a voice in party affairs out of all proportion to their numbers. An American party is a loose coalition of groups united as much by animus toward the opposing party as by mutuality of interests, and liberal and moderate Republicans may often choose to swallow the vagaries of their radical-right compatriots in return for their valuable volunteer work and financial resources. Commencing in 1964, the "eleventh commandment," which all California Republicans were advised to follow, is to refrain from criticizing any Republican candidate for office, whatever his views.

However, if their party should ever appear to endorse the hate-object of the radical right, the rightists would face a serious conflict between ideology and party identification. The ability of the radical right to discriminate among policies as witness their selective nonsupport for democratic values, would suggest that a limited amount of distrust of their party would not be fatal to their loyalty. Party preference may be retained despite conflicting preferences, as evidenced by the strong ties to the Democratic Party maintained by some white Southerners who are vehemently opposed to that Party's civil rights policies.[84] The radical right might even be motivated to "capture" control of the party organization to rescue it from the enemy. In recent years the right wing has captured much of the local Republican Party machinery in California. Many of those active in this movement have been mere conservatives, but the radical right has played a role. By the election of Senator George Murphy and Governor Ronald Reagan, this movement has shown that they could recapture the party without destroying it.

At some point the alliance between the chosen party and the hate-object of the radical right may appear so patent to the radical right as to destroy its trust in the party. The radical right would then face a choice of political inactivity or the building of a protest organization outside the party system. Neither the strength of the Crusaders' ideology, nor the intensity of their political activity, suggests that political quiescence will be the choice.

---

[84] Donald R. Matthews and James W. Prothro, "Southern Images of Political Parties: An Analysis of White and Negro Attitudes," *J. Politics, 26* (February 1964), 110.

The prospect of the Republican Party's endorsing communism seems a bit remote, although one might speculate as to the effect on a radical-right group of a Republican-directed recognition of Communist China or a precipitate withdrawal from Vietnam. However, the object of radical-right fears need not remain domestic communism.

The Political Perspectives of Birch Society Members

FRED W. GRUPP, JR.

Relative to their country's overall population, few Americans evidence a high degree of political sophistication. There appears to be little genuine interdependence or constraint among the political beliefs of most citizens, and what little evidence there is indicates that only a small percentage of the population can be considered ideological in its approach to politics.[1] For example, in one study less than four percent of the American electorate was classified as ideological, even with the generous inclusion of doubtful cases in the category of ideologues.[2] A similarly small proportion

---

[1] The most thorough study based on panel survey data is Phillip Converse, "The Nature of Belief Systems in Mass Publics," in David Apter (ed.), *Ideology and Discontent* (New York: The Free Press, 1964), pp. 206–261.

[2] Angus Campbell and others, *The American Voter* (New York: John Wiley & Sons, Inc., 1960), pp. 216–265.

of the adult population holds membership in political clubs or organizations.[3]

IDEOLOGY AND MEMBERSHIP

When confronted with ideological phenomena such as the radical right, it is tempting to assume that rightists demonstrate the high degree of interdependence between their political beliefs that is associated with ideological thinking. The temptation to ascribe the organizational ideology to the membership must be even stronger when the organization is controversial and semisecret. It is not surprising that many studies of extremist organizations such as The John Birch Society have focused on the policy statements of the organizational elite. This may be the only information available. Too often, however, what the organization stands for is assumed to be representative of the views of the membership; the individual member is assigned an "ideology by proxy." [4] That there are risks in analyzing the sources of support for the organization this way is apparent and probably results more often from a lack of knowledge about the distribution of beliefs among the members than from a scholarly conviction that membership is a shorthand statement of an ideological position.

I contend that what the membership of The John Birch Society shares is a strongly developed sense of dissatisfaction with the political policies currently pursued in the United States. But there is little agreement among the members about the particular policies on which they disagree, or in the remedies they propose. Furthermore, it will be demonstrated that membership in the Society serves more than an ideological or belief-orienting function for most Birchers.

The purpose of this paper therefore is to examine data about the political perceptions of individual Birch Society members. What issues are for them the most salient? How close is the "fit" between the political orientations of the members and that of the organizational elite? How likely is it that the mass membership of The John Birch Society can be mobilized into a pursuit of a particular ideological goal? It is to questions like these that data about the issue orientation of Birch members will be brought to bear.

---

[3] In the University of Michigan Survey Research Center 1964 Election Study less than 3 percent of the national sample acknowledged that they were or ever had been members of organizations such as the NAACP, CORE, KKK, Black Muslims, Christian Anti-Communism Crusade, ADA, American Communist Party, or The John Birch Society.

[4] Campbell, p. 220.

THE RESEARCH

Undertaking a mail survey of a sample of the national membership of The John Birch Society became possible early in 1965 as the result of contact with a Wisconsin member of the Council of the Society, the organization's 24-man governing board. My contact hand-carried copies of the proposed questionnaire to the monthly meetings of the Council and acted as liaison with the Birch hierarchy. Approval for the project was granted in the late spring of that year, and the Society selected a sample of their national membership. Preaddressed envelopes—and a cover letter signed by Robert Welch, mildly endorsing the project—were mailed to my contact in Wisconsin. He stuffed each envelope with a copy of the cover letter, the questionnaire, and a return envelope addressed to himself. The mailing took place in July of 1965. When they were returned, the completed questionnaires were removed from the envelopes by my contact and forwarded to me. Thus, not even the postmark on the return envelope was available as a clue to the respondent's identity.

These procedures, which were necessary in order to get the Society to agree to the survey, placed some formidable methodological strictures on the data. Not only was there no control over the drawing of the sample, but without access to the mailing list it was impossible to utilize normal follow-up procedures. As a result the response rate of 35 percent, while respectable for a first-wave mailing,[5] is sufficiently low to cast some doubt on the validity of the data.[6]

While a spokesman for the society adjudged the 650 responses representative of the geographic distribution of the membership, the results may overrepresent the better-educated and higher-status Birch member. The questionnaire was lengthy and contained several open-ended questions which should have been most congenial to the more literate segment of the Society. In addition, 138 of the respondents (21 percent) indicated that they were chapter leaders or other officials in the Society. Since there should be only one chapter leader for every 10 to 20 members, these more involved Birchers appear to be overrepresented as well.

Even though it is unlikely that the questionnaire was mailed only to

---

[5] Raymond Wolfinger and his associates had a response rate of 39 percent when dealing with a group of Christian Anti-Communism Crusaders. See "America's Radical Right: Politics and Ideology," in Apter, pp. 262–293 at p. 266.

[6] Some recent research found that mailed questionnaires provided representative responses with an even lower rate of return. See E. C. McDonagh and A. L. Rosenblum, "A Comparison of Mailed Questionnaires and Subsequent Structured Interviews," *Public Opinion Quart., 29* (1965), pp. 131–136.

handpicked members of the Society, or that unflattering responses were weeded out,[7] the representativeness of the data is sufficiently questionable so that no use will be made of statistical tests of significance.

CORRELATES OF MEMBERSHIP

It is to be expected that enlargement of the membership of a militant organization to include more disparate elements would inevitably dilute the ideological fervor which characterized a younger and smaller movement. This is the classic dilemma; the weight of numbers is needed to make an impact, but expansion leads to bureaucratization, and to the degeneration of the ideological commitment of the members.

A brief look at the demographic correlates of membership will illustrate the diversity that exists among Birchers. In addition, a look at the political and social setting in which the Bircher operates will provide a background against which to interpret his perceptions of the political system.

AGE

Contrary to the commonly held notion that political conservatism increases with age, the data indicate that the Birch Society is drawing its members from among the youngest strata of American society—the average Bircher is 41 years old. And the modal point for the John Birch Society is the age grouping 30–39, while among the United States population it is in the over-60 category. These distinctions are detailed in Table 1.

That most Birchers are young contradicts the conventional tenet which holds that conservatism is a concomitant of increased age. Instead of a growing political conservatism, what the more mature may share is a stiffening of political attitudes—liberal or conservative. Donald Matthews, for example, in his study of senatorial behavior found that the ideological stance of individual senators remains markedly consistent through several Congressional sessions, even though there were sizable shifts in the ideological makeup of the Senate during the period that he investigated.[8] To this point, Lipset has stated:

---

[7] Additional evidence for this point of view is presented in more detail in my "Political Activists: The John Birch Society and the ADA," a paper presented at the 1966 Annual Meeting of the American Political Science Association, and in "Social Correlates of Political Activists: The John Birch Society and the ADA," unpublished Ph.D. dissertation, University of Pennsylvania, 1968, Appendix I.

[8] Donald R. Matthews, *U.S. Senators and Their World* (Chapel Hill: University of North Carolina Press, 1960), pp. 234–235.

If, in fact, generations tend to vote left or right depending on which group was in the ascendancy during their coming of age, then it may be necessary to reconsider the popularly held idea that conservatism is associated with increasing age. . . . If a society should move from prolonged instability to stability, it may well be that older people would retain the leftist ideas of their youth, and the younger generations would adopt conservative philosophies.[9]

For the purposes of this study it is sufficient to note that The John Birch Society has been able to appeal to those portions of the American population who came of age after the major depression of the 1930s. For many, even World War II may not have been very salient. By not having directly experienced the rigors of the depression, a large portion of the membership of The John Birch Society presumably is not overly responsive to economic need. They should be less impressed with governmental attempts to stabilize the business cycle and with associated welfare programs than are older Americans. Furthermore, over half of the Birchers came of age after World War II ended. For most Birchers it has been communist, rather than fascist, intransigence which has been the most prominent feature of world politics. Therefore, the two major historical factors conditioning the political perspectives of the younger Birchers would seem to be economic prosperity and international instability with a Cold War accent.

TABLE 1 [a]

Comparative Distribution of Birch Members and U.S. Sample by Age (in Percent)

AGE	POPULATION		DIFFERENCE
	JBS	U.S.	JBS - U.S.
Under 30	22	19	3
30–39	28	20	8
40–49	23	21	2
50–59	14	18	— 4
Over 60	12	22	—10
Total	99 [b]	100	
(N)	(644)	(1571)	

[a] The U.S. sample data in this and subsequent tables is from the University of Michigan Survey Research Center 1964 Election Study and was made available by the Inter-University Consortium for Political Research.

[b] Column does not total 100 percent due to rounding error.

[9] Seymour M. Lipset, *Political Man* (New York: Doubleday & Company, Inc., 1963), pp. 282–283.

COMMUNITY CHARACTERISTICS

The Birch Society has been able to recruit disproportionately from less populated states, from small-town America, and in those states with the greatest population flux.

Other studies have found a direct relationship between population density and political activism; political activity increases with population density.[10] Table 2, however, reveals a negative incidence of population density and Birch Society membership. An explanation for this unexpected finding is that several of the least densely populated states, notably Utah and Arizona, are among those with the greatest percentage of their population residing in urban areas. In fact, five of the ten states classified as least densely populated are more urban than is Delaware, which is one of the ten states with the greatest population density. Furthermore, it is the more sparsely populated states which are characterized by the greatest population flux. It is these states (California is a notable exception)[11] which show the greatest percentage increases.

TABLE 2 [a]

Percentage of the Birch Membership and United States Population (1960) Residing in the 10 Most/Least Densely Populated States

AREA	POPULATION	
	JBS	U.S.
Most dense	22	37
Least dense	9	4

[a] Based on 1960 Census data. Most densely populated states: Rhode Island, New Jersey, Massachusetts, Connecticut, New York, Maryland, Pennsylvania, Ohio, Delaware, and Illinois. Least densely populated states: Alaska, Nevada, Wyoming, Montana, New Mexico, Idaho, South Dakota, North Dakota, Utah, and Arizona. JBS (*N*) for most dense states 134; least dense 66.

Other observers also have seen population flux as contributing to the growth of the radical right. Murray Havens in his study of right-wing extremism in the Southwest noted:

---

[10] See, for example, Robert E. Lane. *Political Life* (New York: The Free Press, 1959), p. 267.

[11] California ranks third in percent population increase in the period 1960–1965 with an increase of 18 percent. Nevada had the greatest percentage increase, a staggering 54 percent, but California with its lower rate attracted over a million new residents compared to Nevada's 200,000 or so newcomers. See U.S. Bureau of the Census, *Pocket Data Book U.S.A. 1967* (Washington, D.C.: Government Printing Office, 1967), p. 38.

Much more significant than the sheer size of the community are the direction and magnitude of changes in its population. Virtually without exception, the cities in the Southwest in which the radical right has produced the most serious political consequences have been those in which the most rapid increases in population have taken place. Where the size and composition of the local population are relatively stable, it is far more difficult for the rightists to gain a political foothold.[12]

The 18 states whose population increased between 1960 and 1965 at a greater rate than the national average of 8.5 percent contain 55 percent of the Birch members, compared to only 35 percent of the United States population.[13]

In Table 3 the distribution of the Birch membership and the United States adult population by size of community of residence is compared. One of every six Birchers lives in the small, 10,000–25,000 population community and well over half (60 percent) live in communities of less than 50,000 people.

TABLE 3 [a]

Comparative Distribution of Birch Membership and 1960 U.S. Population by Size of Community (in Percent)

SIZE OF COMMUNITY	POPULATION	
	JBS	U.S.
Under 2,500	15	38
2,500–9,999	11	10
10,000–24,999	17	8
25,000–99,999	23	12
100,000–249,999	14	7
250,000–999,999	11	12
Over 1,000,000	10	12
Totals	101 [b]	99 [b]

[a] Source: *Pocket Data Book U.S.A.*, p. 37.
[b] Columns do not total 100 percent due to rounding error.

While it remains somewhat of an open question why the Birch Society program is so well received in the smaller communities of the United States, two possible explanations have appeal. The first of these is the association of rural and small-town life with the Protestant Ethic. The

---

[12] Murray C. Havens, "The Radical Right in the Southwest," Paper delivered at the 1964 Annual Meeting of the American Political Science Association, p. 3.

[13] The states are: California, Texas, New Jersey, Florida, Virginia, Georgia, Louisiana, Maryland, Connecticut, Colorado, Arkansas, Arizona, Utah, Hawaii, New Hampshire, Delaware, Nevada, and Alaska.

illusion of local independence and individual responsibility are particularly strong in these areas, especially among the "old aristocrats and traditional farmers" which lead them to organize their lives around the values of the "good old days." [14] These individuals are attracted to the Society because of its espousal of similar values. They are belief-oriented members, ones who respond to the Society's emphases on morality and personal accountability.

Similarly, among the "old middle class" in these communities, such as the small business man, the family doctor, or the local judge, may be found the second explanation—a decreased sense of social deference, a gap between the status accorded to them and that to which they feel entitled. Perceived status deprivation is more apt to occur in newly settled areas, in communities characterized by rapid population flux. Such areas are least likely to have a well-developed consensus about community status rankings and many old-time residents, as well as the newcomers, are apt to suffer status uncertainty. For some Birchers, both commitment to traditional values and concern with status may combine to impel membership in organizations like the Society.

RELIGIOUS FUNDAMENTALISM

There are several reasons for suspecting an affinity between religious fundamentalism and membership in the Society. First, both Robert Welch, the founder, and John Birch, the first martyr of the Society which bears his name, were raised as fundamentalist Baptists. While Welch "broke through the intellectually restrictive bonds," [15] John Birch's commitment was sufficiently strong for him to bring heresy charges against five of his professors at Mercer University. Second, there is the parallel geographic distribution of the fundamentalists and the Birch respondents. Both tend to be located in the South and West and in smaller towns and cities, as opposed to metropolitan areas. And Robert Welch is clearly aware of the nexus between fundamentalism and the Birch Society as the following excerpt from the *Blue Book* illustrates:

> Now I know that there are still millions of devout Catholics, fundamentalist Protestants, and faithful Jews in this country who still believe unquestioningly in the divine Truths and Powers which their Bibles reveal to them, and whose conduct and relations with their fellowmen are guided strictly by the precepts of their religious faith. . . .
>
> Let us all thank whatever God we severally worship that there is so

---

[14] Arthur J. Vidich and Joseph Bensman, *Small Town in Mass Society* (New York: Doubleday & Company, Inc., 1958), pp. 304–306.

[15] Robert Welch, *The Blue Book of the John Birch Society*, 13th printing, Copyright © 1961 by Robert Welch, p. 152.

large a remnant of the really true believers still left. We honor them. We need their steadying adherence to the rock of reverence, and their aspiration of unwavering obedience to ancient and divine commandments. We desperately need their unshakable confidence in absolutes, eternal principles and truths, in a world of increasing relativism and transitoriness in all things. We admire them. In fact, as will become clear tomorrow, the young man I admire most of all those America has produced was a fundamentalist Baptist missionary named John Birch. . . .[16]

Finally, specific secular targets of the fundamentalists have included Catholics, non–Anglo-Saxon immigrants and minorities, radical labor, big government, liberal institutions such as the National Council of Churches, international institutions such as the United Nations, and foreign (non-American) influences such as perfidious allies, neutrals, and above all, communism and socialism, between which they find it difficult to distinguish.[17]

The emphasis here is on the similarity of beliefs between religious fundamentalists and rightists. Both stress individual responsibility. Man's fate is determined by his own actions, rather than through intermediaries such as church or state. And the Birchers share with the fundamentalists a disenchantment with social and political forms of collectivism, which David Danzig labels "the modern fundamentalist's secular counterpart of atheism." [18]

In Table 4 the religious affiliation of the Birch respondents is compared to that of a sample of the adult population. Birchers overrepresent fundamentalist Protestants. When occupation is controlled, this relationship becomes even more evident; among business and professional Birchers 12 percent are fundamentalists while only 6 percent of the business and professionals in the United States adult population are religious fundamentalists. Furthermore, religious fundamentalism is not associated solely with sects but may be found in every Protestant denomination and among Roman Catholics. Many of the Birchers nominally categorized as liberal Protestants in Table 4 may in fact hold fundamentalist beliefs.

Thus far, it has been the cognitive or belief aspect of fundamentalism that has been of interest. There are status considerations as well. High-

---

[16] *Blue Book*, pp. 58–60.
[17] William G. McLoughlin, Jr., *Modern Revivalism* (New York: The Ronald Press Company, 1959), pp. 361–365, 401, 435, 443–454, and 464; David Danzig, "The Radical Right and the Rise of the Fundamentalist Minority," *Commentary* (April 1962), pp. 292–293; Richard Hofstadter, *Anti-Intellectualism in American Life* (New York: Alfred A. Knopf, 1963), pp. 117–141; John Higham, *Strangers in the Land* (New Brunswick, New Jersey: Rutgers University Press, 1955), pp. 181, 293, and elsewhere; and Stewart Cole, *History of Fundamentalism* (Hamden, Connecticut: The Shoe String Press, Inc., 1931).
[18] Danzig, p. 292.

TABLE 4

Religious Affiliation of the Birch Membership and U.S. Sample (in Percent)

AFFILIATION	POPULATION	
	JBS	U.S.
Fundamentalist Protestant	20	10
Roman Catholic	23	22
Liberal Protestant	49	60
Jewish	[a]	3
No religion	4	4
Other	3	1
Totals	99 [b]	100

[a] Less than 1 percent.
[b] Does not total 100 percent due to rounding.

status churches are identified with the political liberalism decried by Birchers, while the fundamentalist churches and sects which should be congenial to them politically have low social status. Birchers with fundamentalist beliefs may claim affiliation with a liberal Protestant church because nominal affiliation will permit the accrual of status benefits without seriously challenging their values. To the extent that this is true, liberal Protestant Birchers should have lower rates of church attendance than fundamentalist Birchers. The logic of this approach is identical to that used by Benton Johnson in his discussion of the apparent paradox of liberal Protestant Republicanism and fundamentalist Protestant tendencies to vote Democratic.[19] This explanation has been summarized this way:

> Religion, therefore, would seem to affect political choice in two independent ways, as a source of beliefs and as a determinant of status. And the two variables operate at cross-purposes among Protestants. Active membership in a liberal high-status church pulls one toward political liberalism; nominal adherence primarily serves as a source of status and hence strengthens the political conservatism associated with high position. And the opposite pattern operates among the inactive and active adherents of the more fundamentalist low-status groupings.[20]

The expectation, then, is that the fundamentalist Birchers will attend church relatively regularly indicating integration in the religious life of

---

[19] Benton Johnson, "Ascetic Protestantism and Political Preference," *Public Opinion Quart., 26* (1962), 35–46.

[20] Seymour M. Lipset, "Religion and Politics in the American Past and Present," in Robert Lee and Martin E. Marty (eds.), *Religion and Social Conflict* (New York: Oxford University Press, 1964), p. 102.

their church or sect, while the liberal Protestant Bircher—who is suspected of fundamentalist beliefs—will be less faithful in attending church services.[21]

The findings, presented in Table 5, indicate that the fundamentalists do attend church more regularly than the liberal Protestant members. This suggests that some Birchers with liberal Protestant affiliations maintain a fundamentalist religious orientation.[22]

TABLE 5

Comparison of the Liberal and Fundamentalist Protestant
Members of the John Birch Society by Frequency
of Church Attendance (in Percent)

AFFILIATION	FREQUENCY OF ATTENDANCE		
	Regularly-Often	Seldom-Never	*N*
Liberal Protestant	62	38	(322)
Fundamentalist Protestant	79	21	(131)

EDUCATION

Birchers are more highly educated than the national average; 64 percent of the Birch Society membership has had exposure to at least some college, while among the United States sample only 24 percent have attended college.

The high level of education attained by Birchers was not unexpected because the political activist is more able than most Americans to translate content into political terms that are meaningful to him. This translation process is, in turn, related to the ability to deal with abstractions, which is abetted by increased education. Political activists have relatively well-developed concepts about politics; the ideologue "understands" why things

---

[21] To the extent that liberal high-status churches have adopted fundamentalist beliefs in some areas, it will work against the test of the hypothesis. See Danzig, p. 293. Furthermore, students of religious practices in the United States have found a positive relationship between class and church attendance—lower classes attend church less frequently, even among Catholics. Since fundamentalism has had its greatest appeal among the lower classes, this, too, will work against the test of the hypothesis. Finally, church attendance is not a particularly satisfactory measure of religious involvement. Consider, for example, the following response from a Bircher:

I am a branch of the Lord Jesus Christ. He is the Vine. I am not a member of a steeple house, if this is what you mean. (*J.B.S. Q.* #304)

These factors will combine to reduce the differences essential to validate the hypothesis.

[22] Both sets of Birchers attend church more frequently than does the general population. Of the 1964 SRC sample, 42 percent attend church "regularly" and another 16 percent attend "often."

TABLE 6

Comparison of U.S. Sample and Birch Membership by Level of Attained Education (in Percent)

Education Level	Population		Difference
	JBS	U.S.	JBS - U.S.
Less than 8th grade	2	12	−10
Completed 8th grade	3	13	−10
Some high school	7	20	−13
High school graduate	24	31	− 7
Some college	33	13	20
College graduate or more	31	11	20
Totals	100	100	

occur as they do because his ideology reveals the "true" relationships between phenomena. It is precisely this point that Lane and Sears stress:

> If a person has some information and some more or less clear concepts into which it fits, he is ready to do a little political thinking. His success along these lines depends a good deal on his ideas of causation, especially social causation.[23]

It has been observed that the fundamentalist's views of causation are keyed to the Bible. Illustrative of the fundamentalist position is this comment by a Bircher:

> Six thousand years of history tells us that no heathen nation ever did as well as our American nation with its strong Christian background. No Professor can really understand what is going on unless he has thoroughly read both old and new testaments in the *King James Bible* —then he can begin to comprehend the forces that are at work.[24]

Because Birch respondents cleave to the individualism associated with the Protestant Ethic and other traditional American values—the individual alone is responsible for his behavior and achievements—they discount or are unaware of the impact of impersonal social forces. Instead, conspiratorial explanations of social events are both personalized and attractively simple. The educational backgrounds of most Birchers have served either to reinforce the conspiratorial view or to insulate them from exposure to other explanations. Among college-educated Birchers there has been little

---

[23] Robert E. Lane and David O. Sears, *Public Opinion* (Englewood Cliffs, N.J.: Prentice-Hall, Inc., 1964), p. 68.

[24] *J.B.S. Q.* #463, emphasis in original. Similarly, Wolfinger, p. 283, quotes a Christian Anti-Communism crusader as saying, "I'm a Bible student, and am convinced that the Communist movement is satanic in its origins, principles, and ultimate aims."

meaningful exposure to the social sciences. An understanding of the political process requires a realistic view of social causation, and the political predispositions with which students enter college are not likely to be challenged in the natural sciences or other technical fields.

Tables 7 and 8 reveal that the Birch membership has had a noticeable lack of exposure to liberal arts and the social sciences and that they have attended the lower quality colleges and universities of the United States. Less than a fifth of the college-educated Birchers majored in liberal arts or a social science.[25] In terms of the total membership only one of every 10 Birchers has had extensive exposure to social-science explanations of political phenomena.

TABLE 7 [a]

Major Field of Study of College-Educated Birch Members

Major Field	N	Percent
Social science	(65)	18
Humanities	(47)	13
Natural science	(32)	9
Engineering	(66)	18
Other	(153)	42
Totals	(363)	100

[a] Fields of study based on University of Wisconsin usage, liberal arts included in the social science category. Other includes agriculture, education (including physical), medical, commerce, and dental as the major fields.

TABLE 8 [a]

Quality of Education of College-Educated Birch Members

Quality	N	Percent
Highest level	(38)	10
Second level	(50)	14
Third level	(51)	14
Lowest level	(227)	62
Totals	(366)	100

[a] Universities rated according to Bernard Berelson, *Graduate Education in the United States* (New York: McGraw-Hill, 1960); and colleges rated according to James Cass and Max Birnbaum, *Comparative Guide to American Colleges* (rev. ed.; New York: Harper and Row, 1965). In this and the following tables the not ascertained responses are omitted, which results in *N*'s of varying sizes.

[25] Outside of engineering, the largest single area of specialization among Birchers is commerce with 58 majors. Only 10 Birchers majored in political science; only nine in sociology.

SOCIAL CLASS

Birchers exhibit class characteristics that generally reflect their high level of attained education. Over 50 percent are drawn from the high-status business and professional ranks and a similar portion indicated 1964 family incomes in excess of $10,000. In 1964, less than 25 percent of the white families in the United States had incomes that high. Comparisons between the Birch respondents and the general population by occupation and income are presented in Tables 9 and 10.

TABLE 9

Comparison of U.S. Sample and Birch Members by Occupation of Head of Family (in Percent)

OCCUPATION	POPULATION	
	JBS	U.S.
White-collar		
Professional	25	10
Businessman	30	16
Clerical and Sales	18	10
Total white-collar	73	36
Blue-collar		
Skilled and semiskilled	14	28
Unskilled, service	3	10
Total blue-collar	17	38
Other		
Farm operative	3	5
Student, retired, unemployed, etc.	8	22
Total other	11	27
Totals	101	101

While Birchers overrepresent upper- and upper–middle-class characteristics, they do not all present consistent class images. It has been hypothesized that persons whose status rankings are inconsistent, that is, the individual with a high-status occupation and little formal education (for example, the banker who did not finish eighth grade), will develop anxiety or tension because of the status discrepancy. Memberships in organizations, it is suggested, may serve to buttress the individual's sense of self-esteem. One scholar argues that status frustration produces a predisposition to become a radical rightist,[26] and another scholar found a tendency among discrepants to express approval of The John Birch Society.[27]

---

[26] Ira S. Rohter, "Why People Become Radical Rightists: An Empirical Study," January 1966, p. 4 (mimeographed).

[27] Seymour M. Lipset, "Three Decades of the Radical Right," in Daniel Bell (ed.), *The Radical Right* (New York: Doubleday & Company, Inc., 1964), p. 437.

TABLE 10 [a]

*Comparison of U.S. Population and the Birch Members
by 1964 Family Income*

| INCOME | POPULATION | | |
| | JBS | | U.S. |
	N	Percent	Percent
Under $3000	(17)	3	15
$ 3000–6999	(121)	20	36
$ 7000–9999	(163)	26	24
$10,000 plus	(319)	51	24
Totals	(620)	100	99

[a] All income data is before taxes and includes all sources. Data about U.S. population from Bureau of the Census, *Pocket Data Book, USA 1967*, Table 233, p. 191. Unrelated individuals and nonwhite families excluded from the United States percentages in order to make the data more comparable.

Birchers do have more status discrepancy between their educational and occupational rankings than does a sample of the general population (see Table 11). Among discrepant Birchers, however, there are distinctly different behavioral consequences associated with the discrepancy patterns; those with high occupation-low education profiles are the least satisfied with current federal policy, while the high education-low occupation Birchers are politically more interested and more active. The behavior of the more highly educated is very similar to that of the congruent member whose education and occupational rankings are consistent.

For the members whose occupational attainments outstrip their education it is clear that any future achievement will only make the discrepancy

TABLE 11 [a]

*Comparison of Discrepancies between Education and
Occupation Rankings among The Birch Members
and the U. S. Sample (in Percent)*

| STATUS DISCREPANCY | POPULATION UNIVERSE | |
	JBS	U.S.
None	45	63
Education higher	36	18
Occupation higher	19	19
Totals	100	100

[a] United States figures from Elton F. Jackson, "Status Consistency and Symptoms of Stress," *Amer. Sociol. Rev.*, 27 (1962), 469–480. See Table 1, p. 473. JBS (*N*) 578; United States (*N*) 1673.

greater. On the other hand, one cannot lose his education in the way that one can lose his job. Thus, these highly educated respondents have a more firmly established class position, which suggests that it is primarily the high-occupation discrepants who derive status support from membership in the Birch Society. The reduced political activity of this group also supports this interpretation. Furthermore, the high-occupation discrepants are more likely than other Birchers to be conscious of their class standing, as the data in Table 12 indicates.

TABLE 12

Middle-aged [a] *Birch Status Discrepants Who Think about Class, by Discrepancy Pattern*

STATUS DISCREPANCY	PERCENT	N
None	56	(181) [b]
Education higher	53	(137)
Occupation higher	61	(79)

[a] Analysis was restricted to middle-aged in order to increase the likelihood that the status discrepancy would be perceived by the Birch member.

[b] Numbers in parentheses indicate the base on which the percentage is calculated.

There is some additional evidence bearing on the status frustration thesis. Birchers tend to be engaged in occupations with declining prestige. Of the 349 Birchers whose occupations could be identified in terms of the 1947 and 1963 surveys of occupational prestige in the United States, two-thirds had reduced prestige rankings.[28] It might also be argued that the low-status Birchers—those with incomes of less than $3000 annually, unskilled laborers, and those with little or no education—receive status benefits from membership in the Birch Society. By and large, however, the upper–middle-class complexion of the Birch membership makes support for the economic conservatism espoused by the Society consistent with the assumption of class, rather than status, politics.

PARTISAN IDENTIFICATION

A smaller percentage of the Birch membership (62 percent) identified with a major political party than did the 1964 SRC sample (75 percent) in response to the question, "Generally speaking, do you think of yourself as a

---

[28] Robert W. Hodge and others, "Occupational Prestige in the United States: 1925–1963," in Reinhard Bendix and Seymour M. Lipset (eds.), *Class, Status, and Power* (New York: The Free Press, 1966), pp. 322–334.

Republican, a Democrat, an Independent, or what?" (See Table 13.) When probed further, however, the Birchers almost unanimously think of themselves as closer to the Republican Party. Only 22 of the 650 Birch respondents maintain an Independent posture or lean to the Democratic Party. The comparative distribution of the Birch membership and the 1964 sample across the SRC scale is shown in Table 14.

TABLE 13 [a]

Partisan Identification of the Birch Membership

IDENTIFICATION	PERCENT	N
Republican	60	(389)
Democrat	2	(15)
Independent	22	(143)
Conservative	7	(46)
Conservative Republican	4	(24)
Independent Republican	1	(6)
Hyphenated Democrats	3	(21)
Not ascertained	1	(6)
Totals	100	650

[a] Responses to the question, "Generally speaking, do you usually think of yourself as a Republican, a Democrat, an Independent, or what?"

TABLE 14 [a]

Comparison of the Distribution of Party Identification among the Birch Members and the U.S. Sample (in Percent)

ORG.	PARTY IDENTIFICATION								
	SD	WD	ID	I	IR	WR	SR	Other	Total
JBS			1	4	32	16	46	2	101
U.S.	26	25	9	8	6	13	11	2	100

[a] The categories of party identification across the top of the table are: Strong Democrat, Weak Democrat, Independent Democrat, Independent, Independent Republican, Weak Republican, and Strong Republican. Other includes not ascertained. Totals exceed 100 percent due to rounding error.

For the uninvolved, party label is a great convenience for it sorts into understandable categories political data which would otherwise be confusing. Among Birchers, however, a partisan identification indicates a competing reference group: Those Birchers who strongly identify with the Republican Party are more satisfied with the political outputs of the federal government and are less involved politically than the Independent (but Republican-leaning) Birchers. Furthermore, the strong Republican Bircher is less likely to consider his Birch membership his most important associational membership, and is more likely to have named the party's presidential nominee (Barry Goldwater) as his choice for President of the United States in mid-1965. Also, he is more apt to channel his campaign activity through the regular party organization than is the Independent Bircher.

REGIONAL DIFFERENCES

The Society has been able to recruit most successfully in the West and South, with two-thirds of the membership residing in those two regions. Furthermore, these regions provided even greater percentages of the early joiners; almost three out of every four long-time Birchers are from the West or South.

TABLE 15

Region of Residence of Birch Members by Length of Membership (in Percent)

REGION	LENGTH OF MEMBERSHIP		
	Less than 1 Year	1 to 2 Years	Over 2 Years
East	24	16	12
Midwest	23	20	16
South	21	23	30
West	32	41	42
Totals	100	100	100
N	(223)	(140)	(282)

The differences among the members are greater than those of latitude and longitude. For example, southern Birchers are most likely to have been reared on a farm, be a fourth-generation or more native-born American, and have ancestral ties to northern and western Europe. They are also the most highly educated of the Birchers, have the highest prestige jobs, the highest incomes, and are the most Protestant and the most Fundamentalist religiously. Thus the southern Bircher presents a social profile—old family, well-to-do, Anglo-Saxon, Protestant, and professional—that contrasts sharply with that of the eastern Bircher, who is more apt to have recently joined this Society, to be Catholic, blue-collar, lower income, and so forth. These and other relationships are displayed in Table 16.

In addition to variations in social characteristics among the regional subsets, there are political differences as well. It is in the South and West that ideological dissatisfactions are of the longest standing. Southern Demo-

TABLE 16[a]

*Regional Differences Among Birch Members by Selected
Characteristics (in Percent)*

CHARACTERISTICS	REGION			
	East	Midwest	South	West
Where raised age 5–15				
Farm	8	15	24	20
Generation native-born				
Fourth or more	34	43	70	44
Ethnic background (paternal)				
North and West Europe	49	53	60	49
Length of residence in community				
Over 8 years	62	58	59	55
Education				
High school graduate or less	52	39	23	38
Occupation				
Business or professional	49	70	72	58
Blue-collar	30	13	11	22
Religion				
Roman Catholic	48	30	9	20
Fundamentalist Protestant	13	15	34	30
Liberal Protestant	32	50	53	43
Income				
Less than $10,000	54	48	42	45
Over $10,000	46	52	58	55
Length of membership				
Less than 1 year	49	42	28	29
Over 2 years	31	36	53	48

[a] Cells represent percentage of regional respondents sharing a characteristic—that is, 8 percent of eastern Birchers were raised on a farm.

crats who have been ideologically excluded from the national Democratic party are attracted to the Republican party,[29] while western and midwestern conservative Republicans have long complained about domination of their party by its liberal eastern wing. Also, southern and western Birchers live in those states with the least stable or permanently organized political parties. In other words, those conservatives who feel most aggrieved live in the states where they have the best opportunity for doing something about it. In California and in much of the Southwest there are no strong party organizations which can impose their direction on dissidents. Instead, the "parties" of these areas, as well as those of the one-party South, consist of factions formed around personalities or other unstable divisions of the population.

---

[29] It is illustrative that Strom Thurmond, recent addition to the Republican Party, was their second choice, behind Goldwater, for President as of mid-1965.

SUMMARY

The Society has been most successful in areas characterized by population flux and rapid changes in cultural geography; in areas with weak or unstable political parties; from among Republican and Republican-leaning conservatives; from among the young and the upper-middle class; from among those with a personalized and individualistic sense of social causation, particularly religious Fundamentalists and the technically educated; and from among the status discrepant.

MEMBERSHIP COHESION

The members of The John Birch Society differ sufficiently over a variety of measures to indicate that it is doubtful they will be committed evenly to the organizational ideology. Yet it would be a mistake to count on social differences to necessarily produce discontinuities. Individuals may hold inconsistent positions on different dimensions of their belief systems. Furthermore, a particular policy position may be consistent with more than one ideology. Thus one might oppose the graduated income tax out of simple self-interest, a commitment to laissez-faire economics, or because the taxes seem to be a major tool of the Conspiracy.

ISSUE ORIENTATIONS

The major source of information regarding the ways in which Birchers view the political system comes from an open-ended question about their perceptions of problems which exist in the United States. In addition to identifying problem areas, alternative policies were solicited. The Birchers advanced 2,707 discrete responses to the question, "What changes in federal policy would you like to see?"

It was possible to subsume the responses in eight general categories dealing with domestic and foreign policy issues as perceived by the Birchers. This reduction in items greatly increases the capacity to deal with them meaningfully. However, this simplification is achieved only at some cost in verisimilitude.

Of the eight categories revealed in Table 17, six deal with domestic politics in the United States and the remaining two are foreign policy-oriented. The respondents were asked which of their proposed changes they considered the most important, and the most important responses were distributed more evenly than might have been expected. Although two thirds of the Birch membership is disenchanted with the United States domestic policies, foreign affairs are prominent: the largest single category of Birch responses are the 22 percent who would change United States policies with regard to foreign trade, aid, and the like. In all, the pattern of responses indicates a rather thorough dissatisfaction with all phases of federal policy.

TABLE 17

*Percentage of Birch Members Desiring Changes
in Federal Policy by Category
and Importance of Change*

CATEGORY	MOST [a] IMPORTANT	TOTAL [b] MENTIONS
Separation of powers	5	8
Federalism	13	12
Social policy	16	13
Dissatisfaction with administration	9	10
Economic and fiscal policy	14	17
Civil rights	2	4
Foreign policy	14	14
Aid, trade, disarmament, U.N.	22	20
Other	2	2
Not ascertained	3	
Totals	100	100

[a] Based on 650 respondents.
[b] Based on 2707 total responses.

With regard to the *separation of powers* there are two principle areas of controversy among the Birchers, each of which would lead to reduced federal activity if their proposals were adopted. The first has to do with Congressional-executive relations and takes the form of either advocating a weakening of the Presidency or a strengthening of Congress. The second has to do with the activities of the Supreme Court, and here even greater percentages of Birchers urge a reduction in activity. Some Birchers recommended changes in the criteria by which federal judges are selected, such as making the positions elective rather than appointive, while others suggested a sharply limited term of office. Others would impose certain criteria of eligibility, such as previous judicial experience prior to being seated on the Supreme Court, and a handful (7 percent) urge the impeachment of Justice Warren. Thus about a third of the Birchers see Congress being overshadowed by the Executive and the Court. Of these respondents, the majority (147 to 60) perceive the Court as the most guilty of "usurpation" of power and the most in need of restraining.

It should be remembered that the questionnaires were distributed in the summer of 1965 shortly after one of the most productive periods of federal law-making in American history. In view of this, the Birch reaction about strengthening Congress is to be expected.

Birch concerns about *federalism* were of two kinds: expressions of support for states' rights and protestations that the federal government was too big and should be reduced in size. Of the latter group, a sizable minority suggested limiting or abolishing federal grants-in-aid—which they consider the prime cause of the expansion of federal power at state expense. And another 9 percent favor the Liberty Amendment.

On the whole, the advocates of states' rights did not explain how they would achieve the redress in balance of power they seek, nor were they very explicit about the ills that occur because states' rights are not being promoted. While there was a small, but vociferous, group of 20 respondents who indicated that the state should regain control over education and that "God should be put back into the schools," most of the states' rights advocates did not elaborate on their position.

The *social policies* pursued by the federal government attracted two types of responses from Birchers. The first and by far the largest of these were general statements about the policies of the federal government being too liberal or "socialistic," thus deviating too far from the principles of the "founding fathers." Other general statements about welfare-statism, galloping socialism, "Great Society" give-aways, or Fabian socialism were of the same type. Characteristic of these is the fact that no evidence or examples are given to illustrate the complaint. There were 278 responses such as these.

The second type of response is similar to the first in terms of hostility to the social welfare programs of the federal government, but differs by being much more explicit about the perceived evil. This type of response either gave evidence to the particular type of programs which the Bircher found distasteful, such as Medicare, social security, or the T.V.A., or illustrated the complaint against "socialism" by indicating the harm being done by these programs to the individual in the form of weakened initiative and self-reliance, reduced individual freedom, and "the breeding of generations of leeches and parasites." There were 108 of these more specific responses.

The tendency on the part of Birchers to make general statements without empirical referents is sufficiently clear to suggest the need for further analysis. These differences are of the type discussed by Berelson and associates under the headings of "style" and "position" issues. Style issues are those which are symbolic in nature and which tend to be associated with non-material or status rewards, while position issues are less "fuzzy" and tend to be associated with material rewards and class politics.[30] The statements made by most of the Birch respondents are of this symbolic kind.

---

[30] Berelson, Lazarsfeld, and McPhee, *Voting* (Chicago: The University of Chicago Press, 1954), Chapter 9, and Lewis A. Froman, Jr., *People and Politics* (Englewood Cliffs, N.J.: Prentice-Hall, Inc., 1962), pp. 24–26.

There are two interrelated explanations for this tendency toward style issues on the part of Birch respondents. The first is the familiar claim of the status-frustration thesis that the old-time and still-cherished values of hard work and individual responsibility associated with the Protestant Ethic are being flouted and undermined by the social welfare programs of the federal government. This explanation has a great deal of appeal. However, it seems most reasonable as an explanation of the behavior of the minority of Birchers who identified the corrosive effects of those federal policies on the old-time virtues. It appears less well-suited to explain the more frequent generalized antiwelfare statist comment. As a supplement to the proposal that it is the derogation of cherished values which has led to the antiwelfare attitudes among Birch respondents, it may be that they also hold strong position-issue orientations regarding governmental economic and fiscal policies. In other words, opposition to welfare statism as a style issue is a corollary of a low tax position issue. To be sure, these two explanations are not in conflict and for many Birchers may reinforce one another.

Indeed, Birch proposals for federal policy changes in the area of *economic and fiscal policy* fall into three main categories. The first of these has to do with fiscal responsibility and takes the form of urging a reduction in federal spending, a return to hard currency, a balanced budget, or a return to the gold standard. The second major area in Birch discontent has to do with government regulation of business and labor. Here the Birchers advocate an end to farm subsidies, the elimination of government competition with business, a return to the "free operation of the law of supply and demand," and increased anti-union legislation. Finally, Birchers advocate policies with regard to taxation ranging from the complete elimination of all taxation through elimination of the graduated aspect of the income tax (which stifles initiative) to a mild advocacy of a reduction in overall tax rates.

With regard to *satisfaction with the Administration*, about 8 percent of the total Birch responses indicate the need to filter out subversive personnel from among the ranks of government employees. At the most extreme, 30 Birch respondents urge an awakening of the public to the Communist conspiracy which is taking place at the federal level of government. Another 147 would remove Communists or Communist sympathizers from the ranks of government officials, would expand the activities of the House Un-American Activities Committee, outlaw the Communist Party of the United States, or strengthen antisubversive laws. Another 51 have similar views but restrict their suspicions to the State Department.

In view of such open hostility and suspicion of disloyalty within the Administration, it is well to remember that less than 10 percent of the Birch Society see this as the most important problem facing the United States and, over all, it is less often cited than five of the other seven areas.

This is a particularly interesting finding because some of the analysts of the Radical Right distinguish rightists from the rest of society on the basis of a preoccupation with communism. Ira Rohter, for example, claims:

> But there is a unique radical rightist theme which allows an *empirical* distinction to be made between the variety of divergent groups and ideas lumped together as rightist. This theme is believing there exists a conspiracy of Communists who have secretly worked their way into positions of great power and influence throughout the world, and particularly in the *internal* affairs of the United States.[31]

It is noteworthy that the overall Birch membership does not consider communism in government to be of particular importance, even though a very small percentage consider it to be of the utmost importance. With the exception of those few who see traitors in all high places, the targets of affection and disaffection are the policy outputs of government, not the occupants of governmental roles.

If the Birch indifference to internal communism was unexpected, even more surprising is the absence of comment in the area of *civil rights*. In 1965, in the four months—April to July—preceding the distribution of the questionnaires, the *Bulletin* of The John Birch Society (which contains the monthly agenda items for the membership) stressed the need to "fully expose the 'civil rights' fraud and you will break the back of the Communist conspiracy." In those four issues, a total of about six times more space was given to this program than was expended on any one of the Society's other programs, such as "The Movement to Impeach Earl Warren," or "The United Nations—Get Us Out." In addition, the April issue of the *Bulletin* was accompanied by a 16-page pamphlet, *Two Revolutions at Once*, which dealt exclusively with the civil rights movement. In spite of the organizational emphasis on this issue, only 14 of the 650 Birch respondents perceive the civil rights movement as the problem area most in need of correction in the United States. Furthermore, in terms of overall responses, this category received the least number of total mentions.

Only one third of the Birch responses were *foreign policy*-oriented. There are no "doves" in the Birch Society and dislike of a "no win" foreign policy is a frequent complaint of its membership. By far the largest block of responses (212) urge a "tougher," "more realistic" foreign policy dedicated to "winning." United States interests, they hold, should come first and should aim for the "total defeat of Communism." Thirty-nine Birchers want "complete victory in Viet Nam," nineteen others want the same thing in Cuba, and six use the phrase "turn Chiang loose." Another nineteen would enforce the Monroe Doctrine (the United States had troops in the Dominican Republic at the time the questionnaires were distributed). Twenty-five

---

[31] Rohter, p. 2, emphasis in original.

urged an end to diplomatic relations with communist countries and another six advocated retreat to fortress America and an end to relationships with the rest of the world, as they find allies as untrustworthy as enemies.

There was also a block of Birch foreign policy responses which were critical of the United States strategic or military policy. These respondents are primarily of two types—those who disapprove of the limited nature of the war in Viet Nam and would use "all force necessary to win" and a second type of response expressing disapproval of the Defense Department procedures or decisions, such as the shift in emphasis from manned bombers to missiles as the country's major nuclear weapons delivery system.

The Birch commitment to military force as a useful foreign policy tool is nowhere better exemplified than by their views on *foreign aid*, trade with foreign, particularly communist, countries, and the relative merits of the United Nations. The United Nations evoked the greatest number of responses. Birchers support the Society's program, "the United Nations—Get Us Out," with 166 responses to that effect. An additional 29 responses indicate willingness to see the United States remain a member of the United Nations while at the same time expressing disapproval of current U. N. policies. There were no Birch supporters of the United Nations.

A clear statement of the nature of the Society's grievances with the United Nations is revealed in the following quotation from the *Bulletin*:

> There are more communists in the United Nations building in New York than there are in the Kremlin. Every action taken by the United Nations serves communist purposes. A primary purpose of these conspirators is to undermine the traditions, the morals, the economic system, and the independence of the United States. Yet without the direct and indirect financial support of the United Nations by our government, the whole gigantic but hollow shell would collapse in six months.[32]

There is little diffuse support for other nonmilitary foreign policy techniques. For example, 81 Birch respondents would stop all foreign aid, 42 would decrease the amount of foreign aid authorized, and 182 others urged an end to foreign aid and/or trade with communist, socialist, or neutral countries. With regard to disarmament, the Birchers who ventured an opinion are unanimously opposed to it; they would repeal the Test-Ban Treaty and abolish arms control agencies.

In summary, Birchers are opposed to existent federal domestic policy in a variety of issue spheres and advocate increased state responsibility in those areas. The Supreme Court serves as a convenient target for Birch complaints about the direction of federal activity. With regard to foreign affairs, the Birchers seek a hardline "hawkish" foreign policy and evidence little faith in nonmilitary and diplomatic techniques. Their rejection of

---

[32] *Bulletin*, May 1965, p. 10.

"dovish" approaches to foreign affairs includes opposition to United States membership in the United Nations, which conveniently symbolizes for them those approaches.

One way of assessing the cohesiveness of the organizational membership is to compare their issue orientations with the programs and goals of the organizational elite as revealed in their house organ, the *Bulletin*. It might be argued that the comparison of responses to open-ended issue question is a poor measure of member support for avowed organizational goals. Different results might have been attained if the members had been asked point blank whether they approved of those goals. However, there are alternative grounds for preferring the unstructured approach. The open-ended responses are probably a better measure of issue saliency among the members; free answers tell more about the problems and difficulties perceived as important by the respondent than would structured questions.

The six Birch programs emphasized in the *Bulletin* were:[33]

1. Impeach Earl Warren
2. Promote The Liberty Amendment
3. Save the Panama Canal
4. Get the U.S. out of the U.N.
5. Expose the Civil Rights Fraud
6. Support Your Local Police

Comparing the issue orientations and important problem perceptions of the Birch members with the programs advocated by the organizational elite does not reveal very strong support for those programs. In Table 18 the proportion of the Birch membership is categorized by the number of times that their issue orientations coincided with an organization-sponsored program.

Society emphases have changed since the distribution of the questionnaires. First, the official Birch position is now in opposition to U.S. involvement in the Vietnam War,[34] even though analysis of the issue orientations of the members indicates that many of them sought out the Society because of a disenchantment with U.S. foreign policy. Opposition to the war has undoubtedly hampered recruiting for the Birch Society. The second major change occurred in late 1966 when the Society officially altered its view of the communist conspiracy to the extent of relabeling the real

---

[33] These were the agenda items in the four monthly *Bulletins* (April–July 1965) just prior to the distribution of the questionnaire. The problem of overlap is more complex than this, however, for organizations do not advocate all goals equally. The Society dedicated 33 pages to Expose the Civil Rights Fraud, 10 pages to the Impeach Earl Warren campaign, and only one and one-half pages to the anti-U.N. program, and yet this is the only program the members supported in their open-ended responses.

[34] The John Birch Society first took this position in the August 1965 *Bulletin*, pp. 18–20.

TABLE 18

Comparison of Member Issue Orientations and Elite Sponsored Organizational Programs by Degree of Overlap (in Percent)

OVERLAP	TOTAL RESPONSES	MOST IMPORTANT RESPONSE
0	65	93
1	27	7
2	7	
3	1	
4	[a]	
Totals	100	100

[a] Less than one percent.

conspirators as the INSIDERS. Typical of their activities in the United States, according to the Society, is the adoption of the graduated income tax, the establishment of the Federal Reserve System, and the direct election of senators. In effect, the new approach stresses even more than before the conspiratorial nature of world events, while at the same time playing down the communist role in the conspiracy. According to the text, the communist movement is a tool of the larger conspiracy, not its guiding force as once had been claimed.[35]

These changes in official ideology have not been accomplished without cost.[36] Several high-level Birch members have left the Society. The extent to which ordinary members have also resigned over these issues is not known, but it is clear that Birch members did not see the world that way when the questionnaires were distributed.

. SATISFACTIONS OF MEMBERSHIP

A second measure of membership cohesion comes from the responses to questions about the reason for joining the organization and the personal satisfaction stemming from being a member. While most Birchers join the Society for ideological purposes, a greater percentage have come to prize it for other than ideological reasons. In particular, the major shrinkage which occurs between motivation and satisfaction of membership takes place among those Birchers who joined for ideological reasons.

---

[35] See *The Truth in Time*, reprinted from *American Opinion*, November 1966. This reprint is a copy of the text narrated by Robert Welch in a film as part of the recruiting effort of the Society.

[36] See John H. Fenton, "Birch Society Is Shaken by 'Acrimonious Disputes,'" The *New York Times*, Sunday, August 28, 1966, p. 68.

TABLE 19

Most Important Reason for Joining and Satisfaction Derived from Membership among Birchers by Category (in Percent)

CATEGORY	REASON FOR JOINING	SATISFACTION
Become informed	11	16
Ideological	62	21
Associate with like-minded people	18	19
Need for political commitment	8	36
Other (including not ascertained)	2	8
Totals	101 [a]	100

[a] Column does not total 100 percent due to rounding.

The category most in need of definition is that of the need for political commitment. Coded in this category are those Birchers for whom satisfaction of membership stems from the activity itself or from an awareness or knowledge that something is being done of which the member is a part. It is true that if probed further about the activities of which they approved, these Birchers would probably name programs or goals with distinctly ideological casts to them. What is being suggested, therefore, is not that these Birchers are without ideological orientation, but that there is a difference between the activist who derives his pleasure from the action or sharing in the excitement, rather than from the advancement of particular goals. Illustrative of this type of Bircher is the one who finds his satisfaction in "knowing that liberals are bothered by me" and the one who derives his pleasure "from the knowledge that I am aware and *doing* something." [37]

Rudolf Heberle drew essentially the same distinction in his study of social movements. He proposed two types of active participants:

> The enthusiast (*Schwaermer*) is primarily inspired by the ideals of the movement, while the fanatic (*Eiferer*) is primarily concerned with action. . . . The fanatic, as a type, is essentially identical with the political activist who seeks and finds fulfillment in political action as such. To him the goals of the movement do not mean as much as the life of combat and the experience of group action. [38]

The research of Sven Rydenfelt concerning the sources of Swedish communism also provides some supportive evidence for this kind of interpretation. He found in two counties in Sweden (each with a high percentage

---

[37] *J.B.S. Q.* #267 and 383. Emphasis in original.
[38] Rudolf Heberle, *Social Movements* (New York: Appleton-Century-Crofts, 1951), pp. 114–115.

of extremist voting) that "The Communists and the religious radicals . . . seem to be competing for the allegiance of the same groups." [39] It is in this sense that some Birchers might be as satisfied passing out antifluoridation pamphlets or copies of *The Watchtower* as getting signatures on "Impeach Earl Warren" petitions.

Less than 3 percent of the Birchers express dissatisfaction with their membership and 81 percent consider The John Birch Society to be their most important organizational attachment, therefore it is an important finding that over a third of the members are either information- rather than action-oriented, or derive social satisfaction from mingling with like-minded people rather than promoting organizational goals. Furthermore, there are social and political differences associated with the satisfaction of membership types.

TABLE 20

Variations over Selected Social Characteristics among Birch Members by Satisfactions of Membership (in Percent)

CHARACTERISTICS	SATISFACTIONS OF MEMBERSHIP [a]			
	Informed	Ideological	Like-Minded	Political Commitment
Sex				
Male	70	61	69	65
Age				
35 or less	41	31	31	40
35 to 65	51	63	59	54
Over 65	8	6	9	7
Education				
College graduate or more	35	28	28	30
Occupation				
Professional	40	22	27	26
Businessman	28	32	35	31
Religion				
Roman Catholic	28	22	26	26
Fundamentalist Protestant	27	31	20	30
Liberal Protestant	45	47	54	44
Income				
Over $10,000	48	51	57	53
Ethnic background				
North and Western Europe	49	55	51	54
Generation native-born				
Fourth or More	43	44	48	57
Where raised age 5–15				
Farm/Town	53	43	42	39

[a] The upper left-hand cell should be interpreted to mean that 70 percent of those Birchers deriving satisfaction from being informed are males.

---

[39] Cited in Lipset, *Political Man*, p. 100.

TABLE 21

Variations over Selected Political Categories among Birch Members by Satisfactions of Membership (in Percent)

CHARACTERISTICS	SATISFACTIONS OF MEMBERSHIP [a]			
	Informed	Ideological	Like-Minded	Political Commitment
Rates federal government				
Totally unsatisfactory	33	51	47	52
Interested in national politics?				
Extremely	72	70	69	73
Party identification				
Strong Republican	48	44	52	46
Rate of political activity				
High	71	75	70	79
Work or money given to:				
Regular party	39	29	30	31
Citizen's group	29	33	33	25
Both	32	38	37	44
Who would like as President?				
Goldwater	74	56	59	58
Ever been officer in Society?				
Yes	20	28	16	24
How learned of Society				
News	34	32	35	39
Friends	55	54	53	47
Relatives also members?				
Yes	45	52	54	48

[a] The upper left-hand cell should be interpreted to mean that 33 percent of those Birchers deriving their satisfaction from being informed by the Society consider the job being done by the federal government to be totally unsatisfactory.

To briefly summarize the data presented in Tables 20 and 21, it is apparent that the information-seeking Birchers differ in important ways from the other respondents. They are younger, better educated, and most often involved in a professional occupation. Examination of their political attitudes and behavior (detailed in Table 21) reveals that they are by far the least dissatisfied of the Birchers, that they are the most likely to have worked through the regular party organization during the 1964 campaign, and that they chose Goldwater for President in the summer of 1965 in much larger percentages than the other Bircher respondents. In other words, they most resemble the conservative, but not extremist, strong Republican identifier of the voting studies literature.

Those Birchers whose satisfaction with membership comes from associating with like-minded people evidence political behavior patterns much like those just discussed. They tend to have the least active political profiles, they are the least likely to occupy leadership positions in the Society, they are more apt to have relatives who are also members, and yet they are more apt to consider membership in the Birch Society their most important in a national organization. This category of Bircher also identifies strongly with the regular political party, is least likely to consider himself an Independent, and has both moderate (for Birchers) rates of dissatisfaction with the job being done by the federal government and levels of interest in national politics.

While these two satisfaction types may be characterized as the most moderate third of the Society's membership, having the lowest rates of political activity and dissatisfaction, they differ markedly in other ways. The social Birchers tend to be the least educated and to overrepresent businessmen and liberal Protestants. Furthermore, they enjoy the highest percentage of incomes in excess of $10,000. These are the Birchers who have the most disparate social profiles and who are most likely to suffer status discrepancies; it is this 19 percent of the membership which lend support to the status frustration thesis. Business, as an avocation, has fallen in prestige while education has come to be more prized. Therefore membership in the Society may serve to enhance the self-esteem of members suffering a sense of status deprivation.

The remaining two-thirds of the Society are the hyperactives who tend to operate more often outside of the formal party structure, yet do more party work in the process than even the strong party identifiers. The difference between the ideological Birchers and those with the need for political commitment is the degree to which they associate membership with the achievement of particular goals. This distinction between goal-oriented and activity-oriented members is of great importance, for the Society is not making visible progress toward any of its stated objectives. To the extent that this becomes apparent to the membership, the effect upon the ideologue will be much more profound than for the nongoal-oriented activist. Those whose satisfaction stems from the promotion of ideological goals either leave the Society in greater numbers than the others or come to prize their membership for other reasons.

These two groups tend to overrepresent religious fundamentalists and Anglo-Saxon backgrounds, and both include larger percentages of blue-collar workers than any of the other categories. The possibility of high ascribed, low achievement status discrepancy among some Birch respondents in these two categories is thus indicated.

While these two types of Birchers are characterized by the intensity of their political attitudes and their high rates of political activity, there are differences as well. There appears to be a more conscious rejection of party by the ideological Birchers, with a higher percentage of them claiming to be Independents. This group was less likely to name Goldwater as their choice for President in 1965. Furthermore, the ideologically oriented Birchers were more apt to restrict their contributions to a citizen's group than were the politically committed, and this suggests the intent on the part of the ideologues to promote a particular candidate or policy. The political-commitment Birchers were the most inclined to support both the regular party and the citizen's groups; a staggering 44 percent of these respondents gave money *and* work to both types of organizations in 1964.

Important implications flow from these findings. First, those members whose satisfaction derives from the achievement of particular goals stand a good chance of becoming disenchanted with the Society if there is no progress toward those goals. In contrast, the larger group from whom the activity has been hypothesized to be the source of satisfaction are the closest approximation of the zealous army of workers often attributed to The John Birch Society. However, since they are action-oriented rather than goal-oriented there will tend to be problems in containing these members. They will be difficult to control, to keep working in Society programs and away from unsponsored projects. Indeed, unauthorized activity occurs frequently among the membership,[40] and in addition to posing a discipline problem, these political-commitment Birchers are fair game to be recruited into other action-oriented organizations. It should be clear, however, that many of them will remain content in their particular activity (such as circulating "Impeach Earl Warren" petitions), even though no real objective is achieved. But for the ideologue, this lack of achievement may be sufficiently disturbing to cause defection from the organization. Moreover, it will be these Birchers who will be most uncomfortable with changes in organizational ideology, such as the Society's recent abandonment of communism as the symbol of the "International Conspiracy."

RECRUITMENT TRENDS

The final look at membership cohesion will focus on recruitment trends within the Society. The categories of length of time served as a member in The John Birch Society used in this analysis are less than one year, one to two years, and more than two years. This categorization coincides with politically relevant time periods. Those Birchers who had been members for less than one year before the distribution of the questionnaires joined the Society after Barry Goldwater had been nominated by the Republicans for the 1964 Presidential election. These Birchers (one third of the total membership) entered the Society during the period of political enthusiasm

---

[40] Almost without exception the *Bulletin* each month contains a plea from Robert Welch to the membership not to engage in activity which has not been cleared by the national leadership. For example, of four 1965 *Bulletins*, see April, pp. 4–6, 12–13; May, pp. 1–3, 14–17, 20; June, none; and July, pp. 29–31.

surrounding the 1964 election, which was magnified for them by the ideological implications of Senator Goldwater's candidacy.

On the other hand, the 22 percent who joined the Society during the previous year did so at a time when a strong ultraconservative effort was being expended to assist Goldwater in achieving the nomination—and when politics had not yet obtruded so far into the public consciousness. The significantly greater number of males in this middle membership group, coupled with their slightly higher rate of having relatives who were also members of the Society, suggests the purposeful recruiting of some of the respondents during this critical period.

Long-time Birchers have a more patrician social profile—three-fourths have had at least some exposure to college, and a third earn over $15,000 annually—and they are more active politically than the newer members. The gradual dilution of ideological intensity among the membership has in fact been speeded up by the more recent additions.

The data in Table 22 reveals that the more recently recruited Bircher is more satisfied with the job being done by the federal government, is less interested in national politics, and is more apt to identify as a strong Republican than as an Independent. He is less active politically, but is more

TABLE 22

Variations over Selected Political Characteristics among Birch Members by Length of Membership (in Percent)

CHARACTERISTIC	LENGTH OF MEMBERSHIP		
	Less than 1 Year	1 to 2 Years	Over 2 Years
Society most important member?			
Yes	85	81	79
Interested in national politics?			
Extremely	67	71	71
Rates federal government			
Totally unsatisfactory	43	50	50
Party identification			
Strong Republican	51	47	44
Independent	34	38	41
Rate of political activity			
High	64	72	85
Work or money given to:			
Regular party	38	30	30
Citizen's group only	28	33	30
Both	34	37	40
Who would like as president?			
Goldwater	71	60	52
Most important issue orientation			
Foreign policy	51	35	35
Social and economic	41	45	49

likely to have rendered his services or given his money to the regular party organization than to a citizen's group. Thus in a variety of important ways, the new Birchers are more moderate politically than are the early joiners.

CONCLUSION

The enlargement of the Society's membership has been achieved at some cost in cohesiveness; the more moderate views of the newcomers will have to be accommodated if they are to maintain a meaningful relationship with the organization. Members who are unwilling to accept evolution toward less extreme goals will seek other memberships or be purged, as will the leaders who do not moderate their views to embrace those of the membership.

This does not preclude a gap between official statements of organizational goals and the actual activity of the organization. Indeed, the official statements of the ideology of an organization must be expected to evolve a great deal slower than changes in the behavior of its members in order to supply some continuity to the movement.

With The John Birch Society in particular there has always been a gap between the organization's statement of the problems to be faced and the policies proposed for their solution. In 1965, for example, Robert Welch described for the membership the nature of the battle facing them:

> . . . for this may be the most important letter I have ever written. On its results may well depend the freedom and the lives of those to whom it is addressed, as well as the future of our country and even the survival of your civilization. And the time has truly come for some realistic bluntness.
> THIS IS NEITHER EXAGGERATION NOR FANTASY—. These terribly—and reluctantly—melodramatic phrases are based on the following considerations, which I honestly believe to be the stark and simple truth: (1) The Communist conspiratorial apparatus is now closing in, with every conceivable pressure and deception, on all remaining resistance to the establishment of its police state over our own country.[41]

Welch continues by declaring that only the Society has a chance to prevent this disaster from occurring, that there is still time to "slow down, stop and eventually rout" the Communists, but that the only measures which have a chance of "stopping and reversing the long patient progress of this conspiracy" are those which are "*fantastic* enough to be *realistic* in proportion to the danger."[42]

---

[41] Robert Welch, "A Stick of Dynamite" in the *Bulletin*, July 1965, p. 4.
[42] "A Stick of Dynamite," p. 4, emphasis in original.

If the programs advocated by the Society—the distribution of literature and the organization of study groups—in no way reflect the same sense of urgency, the gap between the leadership's perceptions of the problems and their responses to them results from their acceptance of a conspiratorial view of history. It was suggested earlier in this paper that the sharing of this conspiratorial view of social causation is probably the most common denominator among the Birch respondents. And it explains the emphasis the Society places on pamphleteering—"For the one and only thing which neither the Communist conspiracy nor any conspiracy can withstand," says Robert Welch, "is a sufficient amount of daylight turned onto its dark activities."[43]

A more compelling illustration of the effect that this way of looking at things has on individuals was provided for the author personally when a prominent Birch member brought forth a Society-sponsored film of the civil rights movement to be shown to a group of college students. The film, *Anarchy U.S.A.*, attempted to document the Birch claim that the civil rights movement in the United States is being directed by the communist conspiracy for communist purposes. There was little or no attention paid in the film to the effects of unemployment, poor and overcrowded housing, broken homes, crime, illiteracy, and so on in contributing to the unrest of the nation's cities. In discussing the film with students after the showing, the Birch member remarked that "all of the civil rights problems in this country would disappear if only everyone had a chance to see the film."

Furthermore, discrepancies between the official policy statements of the political perspectives of the members will not be perceived as equally distressing by all Birchers. Such differences will be most painful for the belief-oriented Bircher, whose membership may prove dysfunctional. On the other hand, the Society may provide needed status support for the social Birchers, as well as harnessing the energies of the political-commitment members in projects which, if not particularly useful, do not threaten the stability of the political system. Thus, the relationship between these members and the Society may be functional both for themselves as individuals and for the political system generally.

It seems unlikely that the national membership of the Birch Society can be mobilized in pursuit of particular goals, except in most general terms. None of the Society's current projects appears to have gotten off the ground. On the other hand, within a region, state, or community where the members are sufficiently in agreement about the goals which are to be sought—for example, repeal of Proposition 14 in California [44]—there is considerably

---

[43] "A Stick of Dynamite," p. 5.

[44] In August, 1967, a Birch Society Chapter Leader in Michigan told me that two of every three Society dollars spent on recruiting was being spent in California.

more likelihood of concerted action. This would seem to be particularly true in states which lack strong political parties or in local, nonpartisan, elections. In neither of these situations does there exist a functioning political organization of sufficient strength to be able to discourage idiosyncratic behavior on the part of the Birchers. Where the conditions of rapid social change and fragmented political parties coincide, the impact of Birch strength will be most evident.

Social Disorganization and Availability: Accounting for Radical Rightism*

SCOTT G. McNALL

A major problem in attempting to answer questions and formulate hypotheses about radical-rightist [1] groups is obtaining samples of their *memberships*. Many studies of rightist groups turned out to be only studies of their leadership, and conclusions about the followers are based on the leaders' characteristics. Other studies have used "samples" taken from letters-to-the-editor, but these are also inadequate for drawing conclusions

* I would like to thank my colleagues Don McTavish, Murray Straus, and Irving Tallman for their critical comments on an earlier version of this paper.

[1] The term radical rightist will be used here to refer to someone who believes in a communist conspiracy and sees communists as having infiltrated civil rights movements, peace movements, the State Department, and other government agencies.

about rightists in general. This paper will deal with two samples which may give us the answer to some of the questions about the membership of rightist groups. First, let us consider the general societal variables which are responsible for a person's membership in a radical-right group.

We will begin our analysis with a review of social disorganization and its relationship to rightists. It was Louis Wirth's contention that one should study ideologies to find indications of social disorganization;[2] if we find an ideology which is at variance with the rest of society, then disorganization exists. Now it may or may not be true that disparate ideologies are the result of disorganizing circumstances, and that deviant behavior is a response to, or a result of, the situation. This is our problem.

THE JOHN BIRCH SOCIETY

There is a wealth of literature dealing with the problem involved in delimiting the social areas of a city,[3] and attributing certain behavior patterns found in those areas to their particular social conditions. Anyone who has attempted to characterize an entire city in terms of "areas" has made one basic assumption: that people who live close together tend to be more alike than people who live far apart. The book by Shaw and McKay, *Juvenile Delinquency in Urban Areas*, postulated that delinquents will be found in certain areas of any city.[4] Homogeneity is the key to this study, as it is to any study that makes use of social areas. One problem, however, is that often aggregate data is used to make predications about individual behavior.[5] Consequently, if one is going to try to deal with rightist behavior by constructing indices to account for it, these indices must be based on individual and not aggregate correlations.

The first problem that I will deal with is: given the names and addresses of 1600 members of The John Birch Society throughout the United States, can we account for where they live in terms of indices of disorganization? (This group of 1600 will hereafter be referred to as the McNall sample.)

---

[2] Louis Wirth, "Ideological Aspects of Social Disorganization," *Amer. Sociol. Rev.,* 5 (August 1940), 472–482.

[3] See for instance: Theodore R. Anderson and Janice A. Egeland, "Spatial Aspects of Social Area Analysis," *Amer. Sociol. Rev.,* 26 (June 1961), 392–398; Wendell Bell, "The Social Areas of the San Francisco Bay Region," *Amer. Sociol. Rev., 18* (February 1953), 39–47; Eshref Shevky and Marilyn Williams, *The Social Areas of Los Angeles, Analysis and Typology* (Berkeley, California: University of California Press, 1949).

[4] Clifford R. Shaw and Henry D. McKay, *Juvenile Delinquency in Urban Areas* (Chicago: University of Chicago Press, 1942).

[5] The problems of dealing with ecological correlations has been discussed by William S. Robinson, "Ecological Correlations and the Behavior of Individuals," *Amer. Sociol. Rev.,* 15 (June 1950), 351–357.

Do the general social areas in which these people live share a common characteristic?

In the 1964 *Bulletin for November* Robert Welch told the followers of the John Birch Society:

> On Sunday, December 6, the magnificent new Music Center will be opened in Los Angeles. Built on municipally owned land, in the Civic Center at Grand Avenue and First Street, this new pride of a great city was built with private funds, raised largely under the leadership of Mrs. Norman Chandler, who had been chairman of the building fund since the project was started in 1959. Mrs. Chandler and all of her associates are to be congratulated, and deserve great credit and much applause.
>
> But a horrible red fly has now crawled into the ointment. At a luncheon meeting of dignitaries in the Los Angeles County Hall of Administration . . . Mr. Robert A. Riddell, coordinating chairman for the United Nations Week Activities, presented a United Nations flag for the Music Center. . . . And it was officially announced that this UN flag would be flown over the building.[6]

It is now beside the point that this story was not true. Members were urged to send an "immediate flood of letters" to nine of the sponsors, patrons, and officials of the Music Center. Among the nine were Mrs. Norman Chandler and Walt Disney, who was chairman of the Bucks Bay Committee. It is important for the representativeness of our sample that Welch's story was not carried in any other rightist publication at the time. This means that of the letters received by the nine people to whom the Birchers were supposed to write there were likely to be few from any other group.

The nine people listed in the *Bulletin* were contacted and asked if they would be willing to release the letters that they received so that a content analysis could be made. Several of them agreed and over 1600 letters were received for analysis. The letter-writers tended to concentrate on names that were familiar to them; thus Walt Disney received an overwhelming majority (80 percent). A content analysis of the letters was made and one finding is of special importance here.

In the *Bulletin for November* members were told:

> As always, keep your letters friendly, polite, factual, and carefully reasoned. Your most effective argument, it seems to me, might be along this line. The Music Center is a tremendous accomplishment, a tribute to the free-enterprise American system which produced the private wealth that made it possible, a tribute to the public-spiritednesss of the very people to whom you are writing, and a tribute to the cultural

---

[6] *Bulletin for November* (Belmont, Massachusetts: The John Birch Society, November 5, 1964).

standards of the people of Los Angeles County. It is something of which all the millions of good citizens of southern California should, and normally would, be very proud indeed. Then why on earth mar that accomplishment, dampen that enthusiasm, and needlessly convert it into a symbol of what so many millions of even these same good people in southern California, regard as a dangerous enemy of our country and threat to the future freedom of our children? . . . .[7]

The *Bulletin* then went on to list the sources from which the writers could quote. In the content analysis of the 1600 usable letters one of the things looked for was whether or not the content of the letters was the same as that suggested by the Birch Society publication. The assumption was that if it was the same, then the sample of letter-writers represented Birch Society members and not other groups. Of the total, 27 percent of the letters took exact quotations from the *Bulletin*, 56 percent paraphrased them, and the remaining 17 percent did not follow the format suggested by the Society. Following is an example of a paraphrased letter from a husband and wife which begins:

> You are to be congratulated on your new Music Center. It is a tremendous accomplishment and a tribute to your public spiritedness and to the cultural standards of the people of Los Angeles.

> It is something of which all the good citizens of Southern California should and normally would be very proud indeed. But the flying of the U.N. flag over the Music Center would only serve to mar that accomplishment, dampen that enthusiasm, and needlessly convert it into a symbol of what so many millions of even these same good people of southern California regard as a dangerous enemy of our country and a threat to the future of our children. . . .

Further confirmation that this sample is representative of the residential distribution of Bircher letter-writers comes from a comparison of two other studies of letters written by superpatriots. The first was a study conducted by Wartenburg and Thielens of a letter-writing campaign by Birchers against the United Nations.[8] The second was a study conducted by McEvoy of letters written to a national magazine protesting a story which to some rightists seemed "subversive." [9] (Here again, the monthly *Bulletin* interpreted the story as being subversive, and urged a letter-writing campaign.) As Table 1 indicates, a comparison of the three studies reveals marked similarities in regional distribution.

---

[7] See footnote 6.

[8] Hannah Wartenburg and Wagner Thielens, Jr., *Against the United Nations: A Letter Writing Campaign by the Birch Movement*, New York, Columbia University Bureau of Applied Social Research, 1964 (mimeographed).

[9] James McEvoy, *Letters from the Right: Content-Analysis of a Letter Writing Campaign*, Ann Arbor, Michigan, University of Michigan Center for Research on Utilization of Scientific Knowledge, 1966 (mimeographed).

TABLE 1

Distribution of Rightists by Census Region (in Percent) [a]

REGION	NATIONAL POPULATION	WARTENBURG AND THIELENS STUDY	McEVOY STUDY	McNALL STUDY
California	8.8	33	30	34
Other Far West	6.8	9	11	9
South	30.7	29	29	22
North Central	28.8	18	19	19
Northeast	24.9	11	10	16
Unknown			2	
Totals	100.0	100.0	100.0	100.0

[a] Source: Data shown above for both the Wartenburg and Thielens study and the McEvoy study comes from James McEvoy, p. 17.

There is a small percentage of difference between samples in terms of the representation from the South and Northeast. McNall's sample has a smaller percentage from the southern states and a greater number from the northeastern states than the earlier studies. California is separated for analysis as it accounts for one third of all letter-writers in the three samples. It might have been expected that the McNall sample would have had a preponderance of writers from California, as the issue of the U.N. flag over the Music Center was a local one. However, the very fact that there were no more responses from California for this cause than there had been in the other two cases indicates that McNall's sample is representative of the letter-writers and that one third of the Birch Society's members are in California. Given the fact that we have what can reasonably be called a representative sample of writers, let us see how we can account for the existence of this group of people.

As we noted previously, ideologies and area of residence are often linked. We do know that crime rates are higher in areas of the city marked by low socioeconomic status, high in- and out-migration, and other variables characteristic of an unstable environment. We know also that in periods of general societal disorder (for example, wars or depressions), there tends to be an increase in membership in religious organizations and social movements. The general thesis that both Kornhauser and Nisbet have put forth when speaking about the mass society is that the movements or organizations which people join are a means of handling the disorganization in their environment. In the mass society those old settings in which the individual has received support for his ego, that is, his ideologies and self concepts, are fragmented. The intermediate groups which spring up in the mass society are a direct response to the social needs of the isolated person.

We know that the Birch Society has a distinctive ideology and that it represents a distinctive subculture within the larger society. Is there anything in the larger environment which can account for a person's movement into society? Note that we are not talking about what causes an individual to join the Birch Society instead of some other group. We are asking: "Are there predisposing conditions for group membership in general in the larger environment?" Can one derive empirical measures of a mass society?

Four indicators were taken as possible measures of disorganization.[10] They were: (1) percentage of migration in and out of a state, (2) the number of suicides in a state, (3) the median age of the population in a state and, (4) the amount of theft and larceny in a state. We started on the state level to see whether it would be possible to account for the variation from state to state in the number of Birchers. The census data for individuals was taken for each state and interitem correlations computed. Table 2 shows the relationship between these variables and the residential location of our group of 1600 Birchers.

It was decided to use migration as a measure of disorganization because a high degree of migration in either direction can cause a breakdown of stable referents. Community facilities can be strained by an influx of newcomers; strangers with new social and physical needs can cause disruption. As for out-migration, this could be caused by unemployment and other factors which also signal potential disorganization. As the figures on migration indicate, there is a strong relationship (.51) between amount of migration and membership in the Birch Society. This finding gives support to the notion that rapid changes in familiar environments can act as an impetus to radical political behavior. In the case of California, which is second only to Nevada in amount of migration, we find a particularly strong relationship between in-migration and membership in the Birch Society. It should also be noted that it is in-migration and not out-migration that seems to be related to membership in the Birch Society.

In the case of in-migration we have a situation in which newcomers to an area may not be readily absorbed by the existing institutions and may, in fact, challenge those institutions. The newcomer to an area may feel isolated and rejected because of different values. He may, for instance, be a recent migrant from a stable rural area. Or, he may be an old member of the community who does not accept strangers and reacts by seeking

---

[10] It should be noted that the index of disorganization is being taken as an operational indicator of mass society. For our purposes, disruption of stable events which allow a person to locate reference points to validate his self and meet his social needs, is seen as that which creates a mass society. There are a variety of other phenomena which have been seen as the *result* of mass society, for example, alienation, anomie, and so forth. It is, however, difficult to measure these phenomena on a societal level, and claim that a mass society does, or does not exist.

TABLE 2

Relationship of Selected Items and Membership in John Birch Society on a State Basis

VARIABLES	1	2	3	4	5	6	7	8	9
1 Percent of total population who are Protestants [a]		.77	.31	—.24	—.23	—.49	—.40	—.35	—.26
2 Percent Protestant according to religious faith [b]			.51	—.21	—.11	—.46	—.50	—.37	—.13
3 Percent of Protestants who are Fundamentalists [c]				—.26	—.29	—.38	—.21	—.26	—.07
4 Migration [d]					.52	—.04	.67	.67	.51
5 Suicide [e]						.11	.34	.50	.27
6 Age [f]							.04	.11	—.07
7 Theft [g]								.82	.38
8 Larceny [h]									.48
9 Membership in Birch Society [i]									

[a] Percent of total population who are Protestants is the population of each state in 1950 divided into the total number of Protestants. Source: *Churches and Church Membership in the United States.* Series A, No. 3, Table 4. (New York: National Council of the Churches of Christ in the U.S.A., 1956).

[b] Percent Protestant according to religious faith refers to the number of Protestants in a given state divided by all reported church members for that state. Source: *Churches and Church Membership*, Series A, No. 4, Table 7.

[c] Percent of Protestants who are Fundamentalists was calculated by adding the number of reported church members for the Fundamentalist churches in a given state and dividing by the total reported Protestant church members. Groups classified as Fundamentalist were such groups as: Seventh-Day Adventists, Assemblies of God, Church of God, Church of the Nazarene, United Brethren, Pentecostal Holiness, and International Church of the Foursquare Gospel. Source: *Churches and Church Membership*, Series B, Nos. 5, 6, 7, and 8, Table 12.

[d] Migration refers to the percent of total population change between 1950 and 1960. Source: U.S. Bureau of the Census. *Statistical Abstract of the United States: 1960* (81st ed.), Washington, D.C., 1960.

[e] Suicide refers to the number of suicides in a given state per million population. Source: U.S. Bureau of the Census. *Vital Statistics of the United States: 1960*, Washington, D.C., 1960.

[f] Age refers to the median age of the population for a given state. Source: U.S. Bureau of the Census. *U.S. Census of Population: 1960, Characteristics of the Population*, Washington, D.C., 1963.

[g] Theft refers to the number of known offenses exceeding $50 for a given state per 100,000 population. Source: *Uniform Crime Reports, 1960.*

[h] Larceny refers to number of known offenses exceeding $50 for a given state per 100,000 population. Source: *Statistical Abstracts of the United States: 1962.*

[i] Membership in The John Birch Society refers to the Minnesota analysis of 1600 letters.

out others who share his political philosophy, which advocates exclusion and isolation, and which sees the newcomer as subversive. We do not know, however, whether these Birch Society members are recent migrants to the areas in which they now reside. In the case of Southern California, where almost a third of them are located, we do know that it is in-migration which has accounted for its rapid population growth, because this growth is not due to an abnormally high birthrate. It is likely that those who are members of the Birch Society are also recent migrants to the area, and the in-migrating population is likely to contribute a greater share to the Society than does the general population.

The number of suicides is a classic measure of the amount of disorganization in a given area. As Emile Durkheim pointed out, anomic suicide was a direct response to a situation in which the individual could no longer orient himself to a familiar world.[11] Old norms, rules, and definitions of situations being no longer adequate, the individual was disoriented and usually isolated from the protective influence of a primary group. His alternatives were to reintegrate with a social body or commit suicide. But in a state of maximum disorganization, the individual's opportunities to integrate into an ongoing social group and to protect his ego are limited.

In Table 2 we can see that the relationship between migration and suicide is substantial (.52). However, there is a lower-order relationship between suicide and rightist behavior (.27). This raises the question of alternatives. We can speculate that in an area characterized by disorganization (as measured by migration), there is a tendency for deviant behavior to occur. This is why there is a strong relationship between migration and suicide and migration and rightist behavior, but not between suicide and rightist behavior. Both are a response to the disorganization. But to the extent that suicide is another alternative to rightist membership, we would expect a high negative correlation between suicide and rightism, both as an individual and a state basis. This is partly true, but we have other variables operating. Suicides do occur in places in which there are high rates of disorganization. So does rightist behavior. Consequently, we have this relationship between suicide and rightist behavior. This means that suicide and rightism are two ways of handling the same problem. If one alternative is taken (and the most frequently chosen is group membership) then the other alternative will not be. But to underline the fact, disorganization (and suicide is a direct reflection of disorganization) is related to rightism.

That suicide is a variable of a different level is evidenced by an examination of two other measures of disorganization in Table 2. As can be seen, theft relates to rightism (.38) as does larceny (.48). A much higher

---

[11] Emile Durkheim, *Suicide*, translated by John A. Spaulding and George Simpson (New York: The Free Press, 1951).

relationship exists, however, between these variables and migration (both at the .67 level). The relationship between suicide and theft is .35 and between suicide and larceny, .50. One may interpret all of these relations as follows.

In these cases, migration is the independent variable, and larceny, theft, suicide, and rightism are responses to it—but on different levels. The mobility of people into and out of a region generates anomie for several reasons. As noted above, when the movement is outward, it may signal the dissolution of old ties and the breakup of friendship patterns which contribute to individual stability. Where the movement is inward, it can strain established relationships and organizations that are not equipped to assimilate the newcomers. There are two levels of response to changing definitions of the situation. One may opt out of the system by committing suicide, or one can respond to the changes.

As Kai Erickson has pointed out, deviance, which contributes to and is the result of disorganization, is one way that a society defines its boundaries.[12] Deviance, quite simply, is what a society chooses *to label* as deviant. The function of the society's labeling is to make disorganization a means for defining the boundaries of the system. In this sense, moderate disorganization can be thought of as system-maintaining. This applies to our case, because rightism can be considered a response to the changing boundaries. It is an attempt on the part of the people involved to find themselves in the system. This search is a complicated process, and involves an attempt to find validation for a way of life and an image of it. Theft and larceny are also responses to the changes in the boundaries brought on by migration. The opportunities for deviant acts may increase as the boundaries change. However, there is a lower order of relationship between theft and larceny and rightism because of different responses to boundaries. High migration can contribute to high crime rates, and rightist political behavior often springs up in these areas. But the rightists's response is to support drives to hire more police and define the boundaries so that "criminal" behavior is brought under control. This would lower the rates of crime and consequently lower the relationship between crime and rightism, but would maintain a stronger relationship between rightism and migration because migration is the independent variable.

The one measure of disorganization which seemed to have no relationship to rightism was age. Age was included in these measures because in an urban setting the old are often cut off from those ties which are necessary to maintain a sense of integrity and general well-being. In addition, the composition of some radical-right groups has often been envisioned as made up of the elderly, and the elderly tend to live in urban areas and

---

[12] Kai T. Erickson, "Notes on the Sociology of Deviance," *Social Problems, 9* (1962), 307–314.

not in the suburbs. However, this is a sample of members of the Birch Society, and Birchers tend to be fairly well-educated, financially secure, and thus likely to be living in the suburbs.

Much has been made of the relationship between rightism and fundamentalistic religion. When people think of radical rightists they often think of men like Billy James Hargis, Carl McIntyre, and others who combine a fundamentalist rhetoric with their politics. In addition, attention has been given to the fact that religions in this country generally support the status quo and also call for support for values and ways of life that are characteristic of the nineteenth century. It is reasonable to conjecture that because of these relationships, religion would be related to membership in rightist groups such as the Birch Society.

Three variables were selected in order to deal with this question. The first—the percent of total population who are Protestants—is a rough indicator of how many people in a given state profess membership in a given church. It also provides a rough estimate of how many people are likely to go to church. The next category, the percent of church-goers according to religious faith, is the number of Protestants divided by the number of members in all other religious faiths. This category was included along with the first so that we would have some idea of the number of Catholics in a given state. This way we could test assumptions relating Catholicism and increasing conservatism in some segments of the Catholic Church to conservative politics. Finally, I wished to isolate the Fundamentalists for separate analysis because they possess an eschatological ideology which is similar in content to much of the ideology of radical rightists. Also, it was necessary to isolate the Fundamentalists from the main body of Protestants because some states are dominated by liberal Protestant denominations such as the Methodists.

The first fact that is evidenced from Table 2 is the lack of any relationship between rightism and religion. Two things are operating here—the nature of the sample and the relationship of religion with our other variables. Our measures of disorganization, for example, migration, suicide, theft, and larceny, are all negatively related to religion. This can be explained by the fact that membership in religious bodies is not related to high rates of disorganization. (One of the major problems facing the urban church is how to retain its membership.) As for the sample, it can be noted that although the bulletins of the Birch Society stress support for religious values they do not incorporate religion as part of their appeal. The only appeals are of the vague "mother, God, and country" type. In addition, membership in rightist groups may partially substitute for membership in religious bodies. Primarily, Table 2 shows that membership in rightist groups and membership in religious bodies are independent phenomena.

The information up to this point does not furnish us with data on individual behavior, nor does it allow us to adequately answer the question: "How do you account for rightist behavior?" We have, however, gone part way. There is a strong relationship between disorganization at the state level and rightist membership in a particular state, but we do not know whether this disorganization operates on a local level. In short, do rightists live in *areas* of a state or in *areas* of cities characterized by disorganization and, if so, is it this disorganization that accounts for their joining a rightist group?

THE CASE OF CALIFORNIA

Southern California is the undisputed center of Birch activity in the United States. One third of our sample and one third of the Michigan and Columbia samples are concentrated there. Does Southern California differ significantly from the rest of California? Let us examine the counties. Sixty-eight percent of all Birchers in our sample live in five counties. These counties comprise 53 percent of the total population of California. We selected six variables for comparing these counties with the remainder of California's counties. The percent of increase in population from the 1950 to 1960 census was taken as a measure of disorganization. We did not use the items of theft, larceny, and so forth, as we did in our comparisons of states, because as we have seen these variables are highly related to amount of migration. As some rightist propaganda has often had a distinct ethnocentric bias and because Southern California has a large proportion of foreign born, we included a measure of the percent of foreign born. The populations were also compared in terms of median years of school, rates of unemployment, number of professionals in the civilian labor force, and median family income. This is due to the fact that Birchers, as Lipset indicates in his review of the data from California, tend to be fairly high educated and middle-class.[13] Table 3 gives us our relevant comparisons.

It is immediately evident from Table 3 that the major difference between these five counties and the rest of California is in the increase in population between 1950 and 1960. While the total state experienced an overall increase in population of 48.5 percent, all except one of our five counties far surpassed that figure. The county of Santa Clara, for instance, had an increase in population of 121.1 percent. There is distinction between the other five variables for the specific counties. This distinction is not, how-

---

[13] Seymour Martin Lipset, "Three Decades of the Radical Right: Coughlinites, McCarthyites, and Birchers," in Daniel Bell (ed.), *The Radical Right* (New York: Doubleday & Company, Inc., 1963).

TABLE 3

Comparison of Five Counties in Which Birchers Are Concentrated within the Larger State of California (in Percent) [a]

COUNTY	INCREASE IN POPULATION 1950–1960	FOREIGN BORN	MEDIAN YEARS OF SCHOOL	RATE OF UNEMPLOY- MENT	NUMBER OF PROFES- SIONALS	MEDIUM FAMILY INCOME
Los Angeles	45.5	9.5	12.1	5.7	14.8	$7046
San Bernardino	78.8	5.7	11.7	6.2	10.7	5998
San Diego	85.5	6.3	12.1	6.2	15.2	6545
Santa Barbara	72.0	9.9	12.2	3.6	14.9	6823
Santa Clara	121.1	7.9	12.2	4.6	19.2	7417
CALIFORNIA	48.5	8.5	12.1	6.1	13.5	6726

[a] Source: U.S. Bureau of the Census. *U.S. Census of Population: 1960, vol. 1, Characteristics of the Population.* Part 6, California. U.S. Government Printing Office, Washington, D.C., 1963.

ever, consistent. What *can* be said is that the only significant variation comes in migration, which is taken as a measure of disorganization.[14] There is increasing evidence that disorganization can account for membership in rightist organizations like the Birch Society, but this proposition needs to be tested at still another level. Can rates of disorganization within a city and/or city's census tracts account for differential rates in membership in rightist groups? To test this proposition we will make use of another sample.

THE FREEDOM CENTER

The reason for changing samples is that in some cases the home address of our Birch sample was not obtainable. For example, the person may have signed his name, but neglected to include a street address. The postmark was usually used to locate him in a town, but we could not locate the town's census tracts. Also, it would be almost impossible to construct indices for social disorganization for every census tract for every city in the United States. There would be further problems in comparing different cities, regions, and so forth. Consequently, we concentrated on one city for which we had an identifiable sample of active members. As we are postulating that the same factors will contribute to participation in all radical-rightist movements it does not matter whether we shift from Birchers to Freedom Center members. This point will be raised again as it bears on the problem of "availability" of movements.

The sample of Freedom Center members was collected as a result of our involvement as a participant observer in a radical-rightist organization.[15] In the course of this study we were able to obtain the names and addresses of 266 members in Portland, Oregon. This was a complete listing of all those who had contributed money and time to the organization. It was a list of *involved* participants. Without going into detail, it should be noted that this group's membership was composed primarily of lower– to lower–middle-class men and women, most of them over the age of 50, who lived in an urban area. The organization was also made up of people who had fundamentalist religious backgrounds, and the rhetorics from this background found continual expression in the meetings of the Freedom Center.

---

[14] That 32 percent of the Birchers in California live outside of the areas characterized by extremely high rates of population growth still does not mean that disorganization does not play its part in explaining where the remainder are located. It must be remembered that California itself experienced a more rapid rate of growth between 1950 and 1960 than did the other states in the country.

[15] Reported in my dissertation, *The Freedom Center: A Case Study of a Politico-Religious Sect* (Eugene, Oregon: University of Oregon Press, 1965).

Our problem in dealing with the location of the residences of 266 Center members was to try and account for this location in a systematic fashion. We constructed two indices, one of social status, and one of social disorganization. The index of social status was composed of the variables: average value of dwelling, average contract rent, median years of school completed, median family income, and percentage of labor force unemployed.[16] These variables are highly correlated, but are they "logically" related? The median income of a family, by itself, will not be a good representation of social status, but combined with such factors as the median years of school completed for the population in the census tract, it takes on more meaning. A high income, a high education, and an expensive home is a still better indicator. Yet all of this could occur in a disintegrating area, as measured by low rents and the number of unemployed. We then listed the pertinent information for each of our five variables for 95 census tracts. In the case of four census tracts, which comprise a major part of Portland's skid row, "arbitrary" rankings had to be given. After listing all of the necessary information for the census tracts and then ranking *each* census tract in terms of the particular values for that tract, we arbitrarily assigned the lowest ranks to skid row. Next, after having ranked each census tract for five variables with possible ranks of one to 96, we calculated the average rank for each census tract. Theoretically, it was possible for a census tract to have an average rank running from one to 96; the actual range was from three to 95. Finally, we ranked the average ranks so that the values ranged from zero to 95. The reason for doing this was to facilitate the statistical comparison between this measure and the measure of social disorganization to follow. (The Spearman rank order correlation between the measure of social status and the measure of social disorganization for the selected census tracts is —.70.) We then divided this scale into eight parts, for the purpose of constructing a graphic scale to depict the various social status "areas" of the city. The names and addresses of the 266 Center members were then plotted and compared with the eight areas. The results are indicated in Table 4. An inspection of the two percentage columns indicates that the percentage of members found in a given social area differs from the percentage of the total population for that area in an "inverse" manner. There is a slightly smaller percentage of members found in high

---

[16] The percentage of the labor force unemployed was computed by dividing all of those males listed as unemployed by the total civilian labor force for any given census tract. These same variables have been used by a variety of researchers in constructing indices of social status based on census tract data. See for example: Calvin F. Schmid, "Generalizations Concerning the Ecology of the American City," *Amer. Sociol. Rev., 15* (April 1950), 264–281; and Eshref Shevky and Wendell Bell, *Social Area Analysis, Theory, Illustrative Application and Computational Procedures* (Stanford, Calif.: Stanford University Press, 1955).

TABLE 4

Social Status Areas in Which Center Members Reside [a]

| | (High Status) | | | Scale Values | | | | (Low Status) | |
	0	1	2	3	4	5	6	7	T
Number of members	23	29	25	34	37	37	46	35	266
Percentage of members	8.65	10.90	9.40	12.78	13.91	13.91	17.29	13.16	100
Percentage of total population	11.21	15.53	11.27	11.18	14.62	12.03	13.33	10.83	100
Percentage difference	− 2.56	− 4.63	− 1.87	+ 1.60	− .71	+ 1.88	+ 3.96	+ 2.33	

[a] $\chi^2 = 12.00$ P $>$ .05. Difference between expected and observed number of members.

social status areas compared to the percent of the population for the given area. Conversely, in the lower status social areas there is a greater percentage of members than would be expected on the basis of simply the percentage of total population for that area. It would appear, on the basis of this information, that there has been a tendency for Freedom Center members to be concentrated in the low-status areas of the city.

However, if we use the percentage of total population for a given social area to compute the expected frequency of occurrence for residence of Freedom Center members, we find that our *chi*-square is not significant at the .05 level. Still, a clear trend appears even though it is not statistically significant. Perhaps the explanation is to be found by looking at areas of social disorganization.

In our measure of social disorganization we included the variables in percent of dwelling units deteriorating and dilapidated; percent of black population; rate of family disruption; and median age of males.[17] Of course a high percentage of black people in a census tract does not mean high rates of social disorganization. The contrary may be the case where there is a closely knit ethnic group that punishes deviations. Yet when one combines the various factors which compose our index of disorganization, the situation changes radically. The procedure here was the same as that for the last index in terms of assignment of values and ranking of the census tracts. Again the residences of the 266 Center members were compared to the resulting areas. Table 5 gives the results of this analysis. As can be seen, six of the eight percentages occur in an expected direction. The total percentage difference in the expected direction for social status, however, was approximately 20 percent. Here it is only 11.72 percent. The corresponding *chi*-square is also lower for this table than for the previous one. In this case disorganization per se does not account for rightist behavior in this city.

In order to determine whether or not an index combining low social status with high rates of disorganization would afford a better predictive device we combined all of the indices. Following the same procedures as we did for the separate indices, it was found that all of the percentage differences were in the expected direction, and the results were significant at the .10 level. But the relevant point is that, again, we could not ade-

---

[17] The percent of dwelling units deteriorating and dilapidated was computed by dividing the total number of dwelling units in these conditions by the total number of dwelling units for the census tract. The rate of family disruption was computed by adding together the sums of those divorced, widowed, and separated and dividing it by the total population age fourteen and over. It was decided to compute this latter figure only for the white population, even when the colored population in the census tract was larger than the white. This was because the rates for family disruption were similar for both whites and colored in the same census tract.

TABLE 5

Areas of Social Disorganization and Residence of Center Members [a]

	(Low Disorganization)			Scale Values			(High Disorganization)		
	0	1	2	3	4	5	6	7	T
Number of members	22	32	35	34	38	41	35	29	266
Percentage of members	8.27	12.03	13.16	12.78	14.28	15.41	13.16	10.61	100
Percentage of total population	11.97	14.29	13.58	11.81	14.41	12.06	12.05	9.83	100
Percentage difference	− 3.50	− 2.26	− .42	+ .97	− .13	+ 3.35	+ 1.11	+ 1.08	

[a] $\chi^2 = 7.45$ P > .05. Difference between observed and expected number of members.

quately account for rightist political behavior by the use of demographic data alone. Another variable operates.

In his discussion of the peyote religion among the Navaho, David F. Aberle uses a model that has relevance here. In order to account for the level of peyote use in specific areas, Aberle took into account more than a dozen variables that have been used to study Navaho culture. Towaoc was the community that had the earliest history of extensive peyote use, and it was found that the use of peyote in other Navaho communities could be best accounted for by their distance from Towaoc.

> The best predictor for early peyotism is the availability measure—mileage from Towaoc, in a logarithmic transformation. The shorter the distance the higher the level of peyotism . . .[18]

The concept of availability can also account for membership in other organizations. Availability means more than how close a person is to the source of a phenomenon. It also has to do with the number of intervening opportunities which present themselves.[19] In the case of the peyote users they were few, for example, other religious organizations, fraternal organizations, and so forth. Availability therefore involves at least two major variables—distance from the phenomenon and/or the number of alternatives available to an individual for involving himself in some other group.

This applies to the Freedom Center in two ways. First, 25 percent of the members lived within the census tract of the Center, or in ones immediately adjacent. Second, and more important, the members' opportunities to become involved in this organization were rigidly channeled.

In studying the recruitment mechanisms of this organization it was found that friendship matrices accounted for much of the membership. For instance, when we asked members how they had heard about the Center, we were given standard replies such as: "Oh, Mrs. Jones told me about it," "I heard it from somebody in my church," "I had been interested in this sort of thing all along and a friend took me to a meeting," and so on. Further friendship ties were evidenced during other phases of interviewing. One of the techniques for finding out who was in the Center, as well as obtaining names of potential respondents, was to ask the person interviewed to name some "friends" in the Center who might be willing to talk to me. In every case two or three people were mentioned. We found a vast interlocking of friendship groups.

---

[18] David F. Aberle, *The Peyote Religion among the Navaho*, Publication #42 (Wenner-Gren Foundation for Anthropological Research, Inc. (New York: 1966), p. 31.

[19] For a discussion of the theory of intervening opportunities, see: Samuel A. Stouffer, "Intervening Opportunities: A Theory Relating Mobility and Distance," *Amer. Sociol. Rev., 5* (December 1940), 845–867.

A question that can be asked at this point has to do with whether or not these friendship patterns formed before or after movement into the group. It was possible to interview a random sample of 54 people out of the original list of 266. In asking these people about other affiliations it was found that 72 percent of them were concentrated, previous to joining the Center, in four fundamentalistic churches. Even among the remaining 28 percent there was evidence that they had had old friends in the Center before they were, or that they had recruited friends. (Obviously there are cases where, because of a person's interest in radical groups, he will be independently attracted to the group and does not fit into a friendship matrix.) Two factors are operating in the case of this organization: distance, and the number of other organizations around. Both of these dimensions constitute availability.

AN APPLICATION

Could this analysis apply to our Birch sample? Let us extend it and consider what follows in terms of possible explanations. At this stage, we are not seeking definitive statements, but suggestive ones. The available data limits the conclusions that we can draw, but it need not limit our perspectives.

We cannot trace out the friendship matrices, but we can deal with one of the other dimensions of availability, that is, what other alternatives present themselves to a person who is predisposed to join a deviant political organization. If we assume that the mass society thesis is sound, that intermediate associations, for example, arise as a means of dealing with problems of alienation (the greater the disorganization the greater the number of intermediate associations), then we can postulate that in those areas where disorganization is high, there will be more Birch activity. We have seen that there is a strong relationship between disorganization and residential location of Birchers and Centerites. By this logic one could explain the high concentration of Birch membership in Southern Caliornia, and in California in general. It was *the* available organization for people who were predisposed by disorganization to join a movement. California experienced a rapid rate of population growth, and as was noted previously, the old associations were not capable of assimilating the newcomers. When an organization such as the Birch Society came along it served a double purpose. On the one hand, it channeled the impulse of people who were predisposed to this type of group into a singular activity and, on the other, it served as a means of assimilating a new population. In short, the Birch Society is successful in California because there was not a series of older established groups to which people with deviant impulses could be attracted. Had there been a choice of similar organizations there first, the Birch Society would not have the strength it does.

This idea can be represented schematically by Figure 1. In a system, *A*, "spinoff," or drift from the dominant society will be widely distributed, and no single group will be prominent. But in a system, *B*, where there

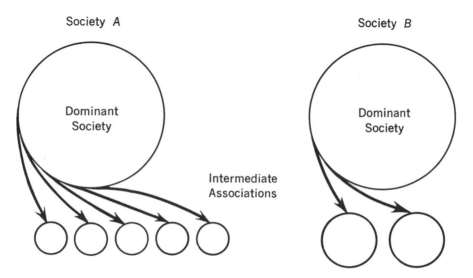

FIGURE 1

are few associations, the power and prominence of the single group will be maintained because there are limited alternatives for the deviants. In order to further support this line of reasoning, let us turn to the South. On the basis of our indicators, we would expect that, because many areas of the South are characterized by disorganization, they would also be prime areas in which the Birch Society might grow. But the Birch Society is not dominant in the South (see Table 1). We contend that this is because people who would be likely to join the Society have been channeled into organizations such as the White Citizens Councils and the Ku Klux Klan. In addition, Billy James Hargis, and others like him, have organizations which are more available. To test this proposition it would be necessary to have the membership lists of groups such as the Klan so that we could more accurately deal with the relationship between disorganization and membership in deviant political systems.

The position taken here is similar to Kai Erickson's. There is a certain amount of ideological deviance in any system at any given time. Therefore, when we attempt to account for rightist political behavior, it is necessary to keep in mind the fact that when it seems to dominate in a given area we need not assume anything other than that it was the only alternative available.

CONCLUSION

In order to explain rightist political behavior two approaches were examined. First, we attempted to account for membership in The John Birch Society by making use of measures of disorganization. It was found that the level of disorganization was strongly and consistently related to membership on a state level. The same analysis was applied on a county basis in California, and it was found that those counties in which Birchers were concentrated differered from the rest of the state in the amount of possible disorganization. Then, to apply this analysis to the census tracts within a city, we made use of a new sample composed of members of a fundamentalist radical-right organization—the Freedom Center. Again it was found that disorganization could account for part of the relationship. However, in explaining why a particular person joined a particular group it was necessary to shift the level of analysis. A new concept—availability —was employed to show that after one isolates predisposing conditions for membership in deviant organizations, it is necessary to examine the processes by which involvement and recruitment take place, to explain individual involvement.

The means of dealing with the pressures that a mass society imposes on the individual are varied and can take the form of joining a religious group or a deviant political organization, therapy, and so forth. The alternatives that one has at his disposal will of course vary with such standard variables as age, sex, socioeconomic status, and race. What determines the particular group that a person will join (for example, a lower-class fundamentalist group, a political group, and so forth), has to do with the availability of a particular group when the individual has the impulse to join.

PART 2

THE EXTREME RIGHT: SOCIAL AND PSYCHOLOGICAL PERSPECTIVES

Psychological Factors in Right-Wing Extremism

ALAN C. ELMS

Psychological interpretations of right-wing extremism have usually involved assumptions of extreme predispositional factors. One of Lasswell's [1] cases, a major opponent of the League of Nations, was able to deal successfully with paranoid delusions by "reinforcing his identification with the interests of the nation and God, and displacing his suspicions upon more generalized foes." Adorno and others [2] proposed that "the antidemocratic individual, because he has had to accept numerous externally im-

[1] Harold Lasswell, *Psychopathology and Politics* (Chicago: University of Chicago Press, 1930; Compass Books edition, 1960), p. 120.

[2] T. W. Adorno, Else Frenkel-Brunswik, Daniel J. Levinson, and R. Nevitt Sanford, *The Authoritarian Personality* (New York: Harper and Row, Publishers, 1950), p. 239.

posed restrictions upon the satisfaction of his needs, harbors strong underlying aggressive impulses . . . one outlet for this aggression is through displacement onto outgroups leading to moral indignation and authoritarian aggression." Bell [3] argued that "Social groups that are dispossessed invariably seek targets on whom they can vent their resentments, targets whose power can serve to explain their dispossession," and that radical rightists have indeed been dispossessed of their social or psychological status, at least in their own eyes. Hofstadter [4] suggested additionally that radical rightism often involves "the projection of interests and concerns, not only largely private but essentially pathological, into the public scene." Toch [5] concluded tentatively that the rightist belief in conspiracy "may be the final effort to maintain an unrealistic self-concept, on behalf of which one's own weaknesses, failures, and inadequacies have to be explained away."

Such hypotheses about psychological processes underlying extreme rightist positions generally presuppose the projection of internal problems onto external objects. Smith, Bruner, and White suggested, rather than "projection," the broader term "externalization" to describe a process which

> occurs when an individual, often responding unconsciously, senses an analogy between a perceived environmental event and some unresolved inner problem. He adopts an attitude toward the event in question which is a transformed version of his way of dealing with his inner difficulty. By doing so, he may succeed in reducing some of the anxiety which his own difficulty has been producing.[6]

It has not always been assumed that extreme rightists are clinically paranoid, as Lasswell's example seems to have been. But even when they are described as "more or less normal people" who are simply using "paranoid modes of expression," [7] the implication usually seems to be that their extremism has developed largely through the process of externalization, and that they therefore must have started out with relatively extreme psychological problems.

Such assumptions, particularly with regard to the radical rightists of the past decade, have seldom been based on direct psychological assessment. Depth interviews, which were the basis of Lasswell's original research and

---

[3] Daniel Bell, "The Dispossessed," in Daniel Bell (ed.), *The Radical Right* (New York: Doubleday & Company, Inc., 1963; Anchor Books edition, 1964), p. 3.

[4] Richard Hofstadter, "Pseudo-Conservatism Revisited: A Postscript," in Daniel Bell (ed.), *The Radical Right*, p. 100.

[5] Hans Toch, *The Social Psychology of Social Movements* (Indianapolis: The Bobbs-Merrill Company, Inc., 1965), p. 57.

[6] M. Brewster Smith, Jerome Bruner, and Robert W. White, *Opinions and Personality* (New York: John Wiley & Sons, Inc., 1956), p. 43.

[7] Hofstadter, *The Paranoid Style in American Politics* (New York: Alfred A. Knopf, 1965), p. 4.

which contributed significantly to the conclusions drawn by Adorno and his associates, have been little used by others. Recent research has centered largely on analysis of right-wing literature [8] or on short-answer questionnaire data.[9] Such research is useful, but it does not provide a substantial basis for the evaluation of complex, perhaps unconscious psychological processes.

Most research and writing on extreme rightists has also suffered from one or more other problems: the lumping together of active extremists with those who merely agree with a certain percentage of "extreme" items on opinion questionnaires; the assumption that rightist leaders, who may be more accessible to questioning or more easily located, are similar in motivation to the mass of their followers; the assumption that motivations of right-wing activists are similar in politically heterogeneous communities and in communities where political conservatism is common.

The present study was undertaken to gather psychologically meaningful information on a relatively small number of extreme rightists and comparison groups of nonrightists, in order to evaluate the possible continuing usefulness of previous psychological explanations of radical conservatism. The study did not involve the depth of psychological probing found in the case studies of Lasswell or Adorno and others; but it did include the collection of information which was of more personal psychological relevance than that included in most recent studies of rightists. Further, the present sample was drawn from a geographical area whose extreme rightists have received almost no careful psychological study, and from individuals of insufficient importance or prominence in the rightist movement to gain any of the financial rewards, and little of the power or prestige, which may go to rightist leaders. The study did not include a systematic sample of any significant part of the national population, so whatever its results, the possible usefulness of previous psychological hypotheses about right-wing extremism would remain. But their inclusiveness might be called into serious question.

METHOD

SUBJECTS

Forty adult volunteers from the Dallas, Texas, metropolitan area were given psychological tests and interviews from February through July 1966. Names were initially selected from letters-to-the-editor columns of area

---

[8] For example, Hofstadter, chap. 1.
[9] For example, Herbert McClosky, "Conservatism and Personality," *Amer. Pol. Sci. Rev., 52* (March 1958), 27–45.

publications, primarily the two major daily newspapers, on the basis of apparent extremity of expressed political views in either rightist or leftist direction. A soliciting letter was mailed to each individual chosen.[10] The letter was designed to appeal both to rightists and to leftists, though it was assumed that rightists in particular might be reluctant to participate in a psychological research project at the sponsoring institution, which several years earlier had come under considerable local attack for harboring leftists. (The writer of the soliciting letter, however, was not known in the community for the advocacy of any political views.)

The letter referred to recent criticisms of public opinion polls and stated, "As a social psychologist interested in opinions, I personally feel that some of these criticisms of opinion polls are correct. But little scientific research has been done to find which criticisms are accurate, and whether the polls should be changed in some way or restricted to private use. I have started a research project designed to answer some of these questions." It went on to say that the writer was also interested in "the range of opinions held by normal individuals. . . . Because you are active in community life, or have recently expressed your opinions to a local newspaper, I am asking for your assistance," and emphasized that he wanted to talk "with a variety of persons with many different opinions." Payment of $15.00 was offered for six hours of completely confidential participation, during which the volunteer would be asked "to answer opinion questionnaires, discuss your opinions in more depth, etc."

The interested volunteer was asked to fill out a card—giving his name, age, occupation, years of education, and telephone number—and return it in the stamped, addressed envelope. Specific appointments were then made by telephone. Since the study focused on psychological rather than sociological or demographic variables, matching of rightist and leftist subjects as to age, educational level, and broad occupational category was attempted. A shortage of female rightist volunteers, and the eventual necessity of categorizing some volunteers as moderates (rather than as rightists or leftists), defeated this attempt in specific detail. But at least no age, educational, or occupational group was heavily disproportionate among the rightists as compared to the leftists.

There were disproportionate rates of response to the soliciting letter, however, between those initially categorized as rightists and as leftists. Excluding those who had moved out of the area or were physically incapacitated, 52.5 percent of right-wing men to whom letters were mailed

[10] This study was conducted at Southern Methodist University, and was partially supported by grants from that university's Council of the Humanities and Office of Research Services, whose assistance is deeply appreciated. The soliciting letter was mailed under an SMU letterhead, but sources of funds were not mentioned unless a volunteer or potential volunteer requested such information.

volunteered to participate; 60 percent of left-wing men; 17.9 percent of right-wing women; and 68.2 percent of left-wing women. These percentages should be reduced by a small number who initially volunteered and then refused to participate further, either prior to or during the first interview session: 8.5 percent of right-wing men; 8 percent of left-wing men; 3.6 percent of right-wing women; and 4.5 percent of left-wing women. Further, some of the would-be volunteers were not accepted, either because they could not be matched closely enough on demographic variables with subjects in the opposite ideological category (this was particularly true of several male rightists of advanced age and little education), were too young (below 21), or were connected directly with the sponsoring institution. Thus, though the percentages of volunteers (other than right-wing women) were relatively high for a mail solicitation of this kind, the percentages actually participating were considerably lower: 25.4 percent of right-wing men; 32 percent of left-wing men; 12.5 percent of right-wing women; and 45.5 percent of left-wing women. Considering the varying degrees of author- and self-selection represented by these percentages, as well as the self-selection involved in writing a strongly worded political letter to a newspaper, no claims of representativeness are made for the groups of volunteers studied here. However, this unrepresentativeness does not lessen the possible significance of psychological phenomena to be observed in these individuals.

PROCEDURE

Once accepted, each volunteer came individually to the author's campus office on three separate occasions, usually one week apart, for approximately two hours at a time. (Occasionally a particular session was completed more quickly.) At the first session, a graduate assistant [11] administered the following questionnaires in this order: an Omnibus Opinion Survey; the Tomkins Polarity Scale; [12] and an Information Survey. The Omnibus Opinion Survey consisted of these items, in more or less random sequence but with an item and its reversal always separated by unrelated items: 29 items from the California F Scale, Forms 40–45; [13] 29 reversals of these items; the 40 items of Rokeach's Dogmatism Scale; [14] reversals of 20 of these; 18 items from the Ethnocentrism Scale, Suggested Final Form; [15] reversals of 9 of these; and a 30-item Conservatism-Liberalism

---

[11] The help of Carl D. Jacobs is gratefully acknowledged.
[12] Silvan S. Tomkins, "Left and Right: A Basic Dimension of Ideology and Personality," in Robert W. White (ed.), *The Study of Lives* (New York: Atherton Press, 1963).
[13] Adorno and others, pp. 255–257.
[14] Milton Rokeach, *The Open and Closed Mind* (New York: Basic Books, Inc., 1960).
[15] Adorno and others, p. 142.

Scale, composed half of statements commonly thought of as liberal, and half of conservative statements.[16]

Subjects responded to the Omnibus Opinion Survey by checking agreement or disagreement with each item on a six-point scale ranging from +3 (strongly agree) to —3 (strongly disagree), with no zero point. The Polarity Scale was answered on the standard published questionnaire form (Fourth Edition), where subjects could agree with one, neither, or both choices in 59 pairs of humanistic and normative statements. (On both the Omnibus Opinion Survey and the Polarity Scale, subjects were asked to answer all items but to circle those they wished to qualify or discuss later.) The Information Survey included 15 questions dealing with current events or political issues, ranging from the population of the United States to the contents of the First Amendment to the U.S. Constitution.

At the conclusion of the first session, each volunteer was given a two-page suggested outline [17] and asked to spend not more than two hours during the following week writing his autobiography, to be turned in at the second session. The subject was told he could omit any items in the suggested outline if he wished, though it was emphasized that a complete and accurate autobiography would help the researcher to understand better the development of opinions. Volunteers were assured throughout the study that they would remain completely anonymous and that their names would never be associated publicly with any of the data collected. (For that reason, unimportant biographical details are omitted or altered in descriptions of subjects later in this paper; significant details are altered when necessary in ways which will protect the respondents' identities without distorting the psychological processes involved.)

Each volunteer was interviewed by the author at the second and third sessions. These interviews were tape-recorded in full, with the knowledge and acquiescence of the volunteer. During approximately the first half of the second session, a 12-card series from the Thematic Apperception Test was administered.[18]

Following the TAT, the volunteer was asked to discuss in greater

---

[16] Reversals of scale items were taken largely from Richard Christie, J. Havel, and B. Seidenberg, "Is the F Scale Irreversible?" *Journal of Abnormal and Social Psychology,* 56 (January 1958), 143–159; and from Dean Peabody, "Attitude Content and Agreement Set in Scales of Authoritarianism, Dogmatism, Anti-Semitism, and Economic Conservatism," *J. Abnorm. Social Psychol.,* 63 (June 1961), 1–11. The Conservatism-Liberalism Scale was drawn from Peabody's Conservatism Scale, Rokeach's Opinionation Scale, and items constructed by the author. A copy of the Omnibus Opinion Survey, including specific sources of all items, is available from the author.

[17] Based on Henry Murray, *Explorations in Personality* (New York: Oxford University Press, 1938), pp. 413–415.

[18] Henry Murray, *Thematic Apperception Test Manual* (Cambridge: Harvard University Press, 1943).

detail his feelings about, or qualifications of, the items he had circled on the Omnibus Opinion Survey. He was then asked to discuss further approximately 50–60 other items from this questionnaire, including 32 items about which all subjects were questioned, and several others which the subject had answered in a manner apparently different from his general pattern of response (though he was not told the basis for selection of these items). This interview procedure was continued during the third session, and was extended to the Polarity Scale if time permitted. Such questioning was designed to explore the actual political positions of respondents in considerably greater detail and complexity than a simple survey with six-point response scales permits; to gain information particularly on respondents' sophistication and level of knowledge about ideologically relevant issues; and to study (without seeming to over-emphasize the political orientation of the research) such things as the respondents' sources of information on political issues, their relatives' and associates' political positions, and the principal influences involved in their own adoption of a general political orientation.[19]

In addition, questions were asked at the beginning of the third session to clarify or supplement the respondents' written autobiographies; and if there was enough time at the session's conclusion, each subject was also questioned concerning his feelings about the Dallas area as a place of residence, the degree and kinds of extremist political activity (right or left) which he perceived in the area, his reaction to the Kennedy assassination, and similar material. He was then paid by check and was asked not to discuss the research project with other individuals until its conclusion, at which time he would be sent a summary of the results.

Six subjects in an earlier pilot study were sent generally the same soliciting letter, but were asked to come to four 2-hour sessions, of which one session was used mainly to administer the Rorschach Test, and they were not paid for their participation. Because of these differences, and because they were tested approximately one year earlier, their data are not included in quantitative tabulations or comparisons. They will be mentioned briefly, however, with reference to the general psychological dynamics of extremist attitudes.

CATEGORIZATION

Initial categorization of volunteers, by style and content of newspaper letters, was only tentative and did not prove consistently reliable in discrimination of right-wing extremists from more moderate conservatives, or liberals from mixed liberal-conservative moderates. (Fortunately, no

---

[19] Much of this interview material, relevant to the psychological interpretation of survey responses, will be discussed in a subsequent paper.

extreme rightists were initially categorized as liberals, or vice versa. No one who could reasonably be categorized as a "left-wing extremist" or "radical leftist," according to most social-scientific uses of these terms, was discovered in the sample.) It became apparent during interviews that certain individuals were only single-issue rightists (or liberals), or utilized a tone in published letters which was not apparent in general expression of political beliefs. Therefore, in order to facilitate the examination of factors central to rightist extremism but not to moderatism or liberalism, subjects were regrouped into three categories: right-wing extremist; conservative-to-moderate; and liberal. This recategorization was made before questionnaire data were tabulated.

Categorization as "right-wing extremist" was based on proclaimed membership in The John Birch Society; strong endorsement of its views and frequent enthusiastic reading of its publications; or strong advocacy of belief in communist infiltration of the nation's major institutions, combined with strong belief in other positions now usually regarded as "extreme rightist," such as rejection of virtually all public welfare measures as destructive of national or personal moral fiber. (Since all participants in the study had written letters to newspapers on these or related topics, public advocacy of such positions was also involved.)

Liberals were categorized by self-identification as liberal; by general endorsement of New Deal-type programs without serious reservations; and by advocacy of other positions usually classified as liberal, including support of extensive civil rights activities. Conservative-to-moderate subjects were those falling between these two positions: either individuals generally conservative but rejecting the positions of the Birch Society and similar groups as too extreme, or individuals holding a strong mixture of liberal and conservative positions. (Data presentation and discussion will be devoted mainly to the more clearly differentiated groups, the liberals and the extreme rightists.)

Recategorized in this way, subjects in the main part of the study included 15 extreme rightists, 11 conservative-to-moderates, and 14 liberals. (Seven conservative-to-moderates were initially categorized as rightists, four as leftists.) Of the 15 extreme rightists, five explicitly identified themselves as John Birch Society members; five more may have been Birch Society members, judging from their reading patterns, opinions, political activities, and so on, but did not identify themselves as members when given the opportunity to do so. Of those definitely not JBS members, one agreed substantially with the Society's views and wished particularly to get rid of the "atheistic, Communistic United Nations"; one was not a member because he "already knew most of the stuff" he had seen in JBS publications. One had read "a tremendous amount" of JBS literature and felt generally in sympathy with it; one was an enthusiastic Ayn Rand

Objectivist, felt collectivists had taken over the country, and in referring to Communists stated that "a rose by any other name is still a man who is a collectivist"; one had campaigned for far-right candidates and felt the Communists had infiltrated government, education, and the disarmament movement, but was particularly concerned with trying to root Communists or sympathizers out of her church denomination. Of the six pilot-study subjects, three appeared likely to be JBS members, based on the above criteria, but did not acknowledge membership; the fourth gave frequent antisocialist speeches and read or listened to tapes of much far-right material, but preferred to work within the Republican Party rather than in the Birch Society; the fifth indicated general agreement with the Society but specifically denied being a member; and the sixth was an active participant in American Nazi Party activities. None except the Nazi admitted membership in any other far-right organizations, although the others also read such far-right but non-Birch publications as the *Liberty Lobby Newsletter, Human Events*, and the *Dan Smoot Report*.

Among liberals in the sample, most were simply liberal Democrats, or unaffiliated individuals who supported liberal programs or voted for liberal candidates. The most extreme were one man who had campaigned for Henry Wallace for President and had belonged to several "front" groups in the 1940s (but who had since withdrawn from such groups and felt himself to have become more moderate), and a second person who had worked for many years in labor union organizing, and whose rather mild socialistic position was expressed in Texas through support of the state's liberal Democratic faction rather than the conservative state Democratic organization.

RESULTS

Questionnaire scores, presented in Table 1, support the above divisions into left and right, though it is not really possible to make a determination of "extremism" on the basis of short-answer questionnaires.[20] On the Conservatism-Liberalism Scale contained in the Omnibus Opinion Survey, all rightists' total scores were to the right of center, all liberals' total scores were to the left of center, and there was no overlap between rightists' and liberals' scores. (A small degree of overlap was found between rightists and moderates, and between liberals and moderates.)

The Conservatism-Liberalism Scale is composed of items involving

---

[20] Since neither systematic sampling nor experimental manipulation was used in this research, means are presented only as descriptive indicators, and further statistical analysis was avoided.

TABLE 1

Mean Self-Report Questionnaire Scores per Item [a]

SCALE	RIGHTISTS ($N = 15$)	MODERATES ($N = 11$)	LIBERALS ($N = 14$)
Conservatism-Liberalism	+ 1.71	+ 0.08	− 1.43
California F	− 0.14	− 0.62	− 1.08
Reversed California F	+ 0.11	+ 0.70	+ 1.45
Dogmatism	− 0.20	− 0.62	− 0.57
Ethnocentrism	− 0.69	− 1.67	− 2.13
Polarity	− 1.73	−22.55	−26.43

[a] The range of possible scores for all scales, with two exceptions, was −3 to +3, plusses indicating the assumed rightist end of the continuum. On the Reversed F Scale, minuses indicate the assumed rightist end of the continuum. For the Polarity Scale, means are given for total number of right-wing agreements minus total number of left-wing agreements; the range of possible scores was −59 to +59.

direct assessment of political ideology. Other scales containing more indirect measures of rightist proclivities did not yield such strong indications of right- and left-wing polarization, but generally substantiated the distinctiveness of the rightist and liberal subject groups. On the Tomkins Polarity Scale, one rightist (a Birch Society member) had a higher left-wing score than the liberal with the lowest left-wing score. On the California F Scale, there was greater overlap: six rightists scored as "less authoritarian" than the two "most authoritarian" liberals.

Reversals of the California F Scale and parts of the Dogmatism and Ethnocentrism Scales were included mainly for use in a separate study of response set phenomena; scores on the latter two sets of reversals probably have little meaning in themselves. An indication that agreement response set did not artifactually elevate California F Scale scores for right-wing subjects is that both rightists and liberals averaged roughly the same number of double agreements on the scale (agreement both with an authoritarian statement and with its reversal), the rightist mean being 5.60, the liberal mean 5.86. However, rightists showed double disagreement with substantially more F Scale items than the liberals, the means being respectively 5.33 and 3.14. On both the Dogmatism and the Ethnocentrism Scales, liberals showed somewhat less double agreement and somewhat less double disagreement than rightists. (For Dogmatism, rightists' double agreement mean was 4.73, double disagreement mean, 2.73; liberals' means were 4.14 and 2.07. For Ethnocentrism, rightists' double agreement mean was 1.27, double disagreement mean, 1.07; liberals' means were 0.79 and 0.57.)

Neither rightists nor liberals showed clear superiority on the Information Survey. Out of 15 questions, liberals answered eight more accurately on the whole; rightists answered six more accurately; liberals' and rightists' accuracy was fairly similar on one item. On certain items involving quantitative estimates, ideological bias appears to have influenced answers regardless of which group was the more accurate: a majority of rightists underestimated the average hourly wage of Russian factory workers, while a majority of liberals overestimated; both overestimated the percentage of Negroes in the U.S. population, but rightists did so to a greater degree; both overestimated the percentage of nonmilitary expenditures in the U.S. budget, the rightists again to a greater degree; liberals considerably more often underestimated the number of felonies in the U.S. per year. On one nonquantitative item, liberals were considerably superior at listing the contents of the First Amendment to the Constitution; several rightists erroneously described the contents of the Tenth Amendment (dealing with states' rights) instead.

In addition to the data above, collected in easily quantifiable form, tabulations were made of 21 different categories of autobiographical or personal data drawn from volunteers' written autobiographies and interview statements. The categories were developed after data collection had been completed, and were largely selected as representing the most likely areas of difference (other than ideological) between rightists and liberals in the sample. In most of these categories, quantification was difficult and clear quantitative differences were not apparent. Findings from these tabulations were as follows:

Similar numbers of rightists and liberals mention prestigious ancestry (grandparents or beyond). But only one rightist mentions minority status or possibly negative reputation among ancestry (a reference to a well-to-do German ancestor, forced to emigrate to the U.S. because of political repression), while six liberals, nearly half the sample, mention such characteristics (ancestors who were Jewish, carpetbaggers, polygamous Mormons, and so on). Geographical origin of subjects and their parents, and subjects' length of stay in the Dallas area, were similar for rightists and liberals.

The liberal sample was somewhat older (averaging 44.6; rightists averaged 39.8), and included more women (7 females, 7 males; among rightists, 3 females, 12 males). Eight rightists had earned a bachelor's degree, compared with three liberals; but the three liberals had also earned graduate degrees, a level achieved by no rightist. A greater number of liberals appeared to have been very poor through most of childhood (5 to 1). Rightists were more likely than liberals to be (or to be married to) businessmen or high-income salesmen (8 to 3). Occupational background otherwise showed little difference; so did occupational mobility and father's occupation.

Rightists and liberals recalled roughly similar discipline as children, though rightists were more likely to recall a pattern of usually mild discipline combined with occasional strong physical punishment (5 to 1). Degree of marital success or failure seemed generally similar. Both rightists and liberals seldom appeared happy with the actual content of their jobs. Self-esteem levels appeared roughly similar, as did general degree of mental stability (that is, absence of noticeable psychological symptoms). Rightists showed greater religious activity and concern than liberals: five liberals rejected or were disinterested in religious beliefs, compared with one rightist, while on the other hand eight rightists were very active or very concerned with religious matters, compared with one liberal. Rightists were more active in political party work (in addition to work for the Birch Society or other extremist groups, which they considered nonpolitical): ten rightists had done substantial work for party organizations or had held local party offices, as compared with four liberals.

The point should be made once more that these data are only suggestive, and cannot be treated as confirming or contradicting any hypotheses, since the subject populations were small and nonrandom. However, in several instances to be discussed further (for example, lack of differences in mental stability), they do offer interesting contrasts to most published data and speculations. In a few instances (such as degree of religious activity), they appear to support earlier research.

DISCUSSION

Before broader issues are considered, the question should be raised of whether the extreme rightists in this study were really "extreme." They were, of course, members of organizations usually considered extremist, such as The John Birch Society, or subscribed to positions very similar to those of the Birch Society, particularly with regard to anticommunism. Further, they were willing to endorse such positions publicly, in letters to newspapers. In these respects they were more carefully selected as extreme than the "extremists" of several earlier studies. Further, they differed sharply from either liberal or moderate volunteers on the Conservatism-Liberalism Scale used in the study. However, the scale has not been standardized on populations of known ideological stance; and there are other indications that the rightists of the present study were not the most extreme of extremists.

For one thing, these rightists were willing to be tested and interviewed by the author. Nearly half of the right-wing men to whom soliciting letters were sent did not volunteer, nor did over four-fifths of right-wing women. Presumably some had valid reasons for not participating, such as lack of time, as a few indicated. Others, however, may have been so fearful of talking with a psychologist, or of associating themselves with so "liberal" an institution as the author's university, that they avoided volunteering. Several volunteers (right and left) questioned the author or his assistant carefully about the study's sponsorship and purpose before consenting to participate. One rightist seemed convinced that the study was being sponsored secretly by the Ford Foundation or the Center for the Study of Democratic Institutions, and was never fully persuaded otherwise; he participated reluctantly and remained reticent. (On the other hand, a liberal volunteer became angry at the high number of "Birch-type" statements on the Omnibus Opinion Survey and walked out midway through the first session, never to return.)

Further, rightists' scores on most of the short-answer questionnaires were not as extreme as might have been expected from earlier studies. The rightist mean on the California F Scale was —0.14, indicating a slight amount of *disagreement*, on the average, with each authoritarian statement. Since Adorno and his associates used a seven-point scale with a zero point, direct comparisons with scores on the present six-point scale are difficult. But the rightists' mean was certainly not high, and in fact appears fairly close to the mean for the least authoritarian group of men in the Adorno study. The Dogmatism Scale mean of —0.20, though indicating a slight degree of disagreement with dogmatic positions, was close to the mean of a small group of "highly dogmatic" college students studied by Rokeach.[21] Those students happen also to have been clearly conservative, though they were not selected on that basis. But the present study's rightists were nowhere near as dogmatic on Rokeach's scale as were the highest-scoring nonstudent samples he tested.[22]

Rightists' scores on the Ethnocentrism Scale averaged somewhat on the nonethnocentric side (—0.69). Since the form used was a final version recommended but never actually employed by Adorno and his associates, no comparison means were available; but at least it is clear that the rightists more often disagreed than agreed with ethnocentric statements. For the Polarity Scale as well, adequate comparison means were unavailable, since Tomkins so far has published little actual data on the scale; but the rightists did agree with slightly more leftist than rightist statements.

Shall we conclude from such data that the extreme rightists of this study were nonauthoritarian, nonethnocentric, not particularly dogmatic, not very extreme, and indeed not even rightists? Unfortunately for the results of these questionnaires, the volunteers were undeniably rightist in marking agreement with explicitly ideological statements; and by the standards which most social scientists have used in studying such phenomena, they were clearly extreme rightists in behavior and in stated attitudes. Is it likely that they were simply lying on the questionnaires, or at

---

[21] P. 104.
[22] P. 90.

least were selecting those responses which seemed to them most socially desirable? Presumably most of the volunteers in the study, right, left, or middle, shaded some of their answers in a more socially acceptable direction. But during the extensive interviews exploring questionnaire responses in greater detail, rightists showed no unusual proclivity for doing so. They seemed generally to have described their opinions accurately in the questionnaires, and were quite willing to provide additional supporting information and explanation for most answers.

One factor evident in the interviews may have accounted in considerable part for the rightists' unexpectedly low scores on certain of the scales. Several rightists seemed unusually concerned about verbal subtleties in the scale statements, to such a degree that they disagreed with otherwise acceptable statements because of quibbles over the meaning of specific words or phrases. Liberals occasionally did the same, but apparently not to the same extent. (There is quantitative as well as impressionistic support for this inference, in the rightists' greater number of double-disagreement responses on the F Scale; that is, the rightists more often disagreed both with a statement and with its reverse than did the liberals.)

Further distortion of scale scores may have come from rightists' tendency to interpret key words in certain questionnaire statements idiosyncratically or ideologically, so that the statements came to have implications different from those apparently intended by the questionnaires' authors. The most obvious instance is an item from the Dogmatism Scale, "The highest form of government is a democracy and the highest form of democracy is a government run by those who are most intelligent." Agreement with the statement is presumed to be an indication of dogmatism, disagreement an indication of open-mindedness. The rightists in the study uniformly and dogmatically disagreed with the statement (as did some liberals, so much has Dallas political colloquy been influenced by The John Birch Society) because, of course, "This is a republic, not a democracy—let's keep it that way!" Likewise with such items from the California F Scale as "Most people don't realize how much our lives are controlled by plots hatched in secret places," or "Every person should have complete faith in some supernatural power whose decisions he obeys without question." Either most people *do* realize, but are too apathetic to do anything about the plots; or else the plots aren't hatched in secret places at all but in Washington, plain for him who has eyes to see; and certainly one should have faith in God, or Jesus Christ, but not in "some supernatural power."

These subtleties of interpretation may not account completely for rightists' depressed scale scores, but they seem partially responsible. It also appears likely, from interview data, that the rightists of this study really are *not* unusually authoritarian. They are more strict with their children, on the whole, than are the liberals; but their strictness does not appear harsh, and they give little indication of authoritarian relationships with other people. They are dogmatic, as their scale scores indicate; but most do not convey an impression of real fanaticism or "True Believer-ism." They do not appear as strongly normative as Tomkins seems to have had in mind in contrasting the normative rightist with the human-istic leftist, though there is some indication of normative emphasis in rightist volunteers' frequent references to "firmness" in dealing with chil-dren; to the "respectability" of parents or ancestors; to the "high char-acter" or specific praiseworthy traits possessed by the spouse, rather than to romantic love. (In this regard, the data are similar to those of Rohter,[23] who observed that rightist interviewees frequently mentioned morals or values. However, certain of Rohter's other findings, with regard to such things as feelings of anomia among rightists, received little support from the present study.)

It appears so far that most of the rightist volunteers show sufficient evidence, in other areas than specific ideological beliefs, of tendencies toward conservatism; but insufficient evidence of any bases for extremism. Here a simple hypothesis is proposed for further discussion: individuals without unusual personality needs or strong predispositions toward authori-tarianism, dogmatism, or normativism, may adopt an extreme rightist posture, because a set of political opinions of any kind would be func-tional for them (in helping to explain complex public events efficiently, for example); because through personal experience or parental training, a conservative political position is most acceptable to them; and because community standards make an extreme rightist position as acceptable as most other positions.

The present study does not provide sufficient evidence to support this hypothesis definitively; but examination of further data may at least show that the hypothesis is not clearly contradicted. Is there evidence of ex-treme psychological abnormality or unusual experience which would pre-dispose the rightists in this sample specifically to adopt an extreme ideological position?

The rightists themselves would probably argue that theirs is a case of extreme knowledgeability—that they have adopted their stance because they are much better informed on political and social issues than most people. If scores on the Information Survey (dealing with facts which would presumably supply an important basis for ideological discussion) are any indication, the rightists were no more well-informed, and perhaps less so, than individuals with distinctly different political orientations.

---

[23] Ira S. Rohter, "Some Personal Needs Met by Becoming a Radical Rightist," paper presented at American Psychological Association Convention, Chicago, 1965.

Interview responses dealing with issues of great interest to the rightists, such as the distinctions between a democracy and a republic, or between liberalism and conservatism, confirmed this impression.

Certain sociologists would argue instead that the rightists are likely to have suffered from social mobility, either excessively upward or excessively downward, with attendant status anxieties. Unfortunately, the rightists in the current sample showed no unusual mobility compared with the liberals, and seldom showed unusual anxieties about status or job. Nor did they seem to feel unusually "dispossessed" of any kinds of property, status, or moral stance.

There remains the possibility of severe psychological affliction, past or present, externalized through political opinions. However, most subjects, both rightist and liberal, displayed little in the way of neurotic or psychotic tendencies, and for those who did, the proportions were similar in the two groups.

Two rightists and two liberals had had periods of extreme depression, resolved by religious or semireligious conversions. For the two rightists, this involved conversion in association with organized religious groups, fundamentalist in orientation. For one liberal, the conversion did not involve a religious group but a personal mystical experience of hearing a comforting voice, as from God, saying "Lo, I will be with thee always." For the other liberal the conversion was to a Jungian psychological-philosophical position, which the subject saw as "a religious attitude toward life," prepared for by a three-year self-analysis but specifically precipitated by two archetypal dreams. This liberal and the two rightists felt that their emotional problems had been largely resolved, and indeed they seemed no longer disturbed by them. The other liberal still had occasional periods of depression, which were considerably milder than before the mystical experience and which did not significantly interfere with various constructive activities.

In three other instances, symptomatology was more severe. One liberal had had a "very serious emotional disturbance" in late adolescence, was hospitalized for a brief time, and was treated at three different psychiatric facilities over two years. When the third course of treatment "went bad," he fell into a prolonged depression. Toward the end of this period, he developed an active interest in politics and began joining groups with a "strong leftist trend," including several now on the Attorney General's subversive list. In 1948, he worked actively for Henry Wallace's presidential candidacy. He felt his activities in these groups "represented a socialization of myself," that is, they helped him to recover from his depression and to become more social. He then began to feel he had become too deeply involved in these organizations, and when he had an opportunity to move to Dallas he divorced himself from such activities.

He later had another depressive episode, but not as serious, and had noticed, on the whole, "an improvement in my psychological health" since coming to Dallas. At the time of this study, he was moderately active in liberal politics on the precinct level.

One rightist had severe marital difficulties followed by a "seminervous breakdown" involving suicide threats. When he was dismissed from his job, he began searching for answers "to why I had lost everything when according to contemporary standards of morality everything should have worked out with a happy-ever-after ending instead of the tragedy that it was." He began to read voraciously in Freud, Jung, Fromm, Philip Wylie, and others, but "found no rational answers" until he discovered a book by Ayn Rand. In the three years prior to his interviews, he had memorized large portions of her books, had taken several courses in Objectivism, and had come to feel he was a more serious student of Objectivism than anyone he had met. He felt he "didn't start living until I discovered Rand," that he "was just a piece of meat just being." But he had by no means resolved his problems: he felt he was still "desperately in need of a psychotherapist"; felt that he had been an ideal husband but that certain of his and his wife's relatives had destroyed his marriage and had him fired; and he was almost obsessively concerned about the poor impression of Ayn Rand's philosophy which he conveyed to others.

Another rightist was the only one of the six pilot-study subjects to indicate severe psychological difficulties. He had apparently never been referred to a psychotherapist, but mentioned a number of very hostile encounters with close relatives, sometimes including physical violence and usually involving the feeling that he had triumphed over their attempts to do him grave injustice. The culminating event, with which he dealt at great length both in response to a blank TAT card and in a later interview, involved his striking a neighbor on the head with a crowbar (in self-defense, according to the subject), and then being railroaded into a conviction for "assault with intent to murder" by the neighbor's sons and a hostile court. He was given a long-term suspended sentence and a large fine. Apparently he was not at that time specifically concerned with political ideology; but several years later he had an accident which left him inactive and out of work for a time. During this period, he began reading political literature and became concerned with the fate of the nation. When interviewed, he was active in several small extremist organizations, particularly the American Nazi Party (he had not joined The John Birch Society because he couldn't afford the dues, and had subsequently come to suspect it of being a Communist-front organization). In his autobiography he wrote that "For all practical purposes, we are now under Communism," but that people "are so brainwashed with the JEW

CONTROLLED NEWS MEDIA that they refuse to believe the ridiculously heinous things planned by the WORLDWIDE JEWISH CONSPIRACY for our beloved Nation. . . . By the reverse of righteousness by the ANTI-CHRIST Patriotism has become a liability rather than an asset! Patriots now have to work underground because the FEDS have joined the enemy in the BLACK REVOLUTION against the WHITE PATRIOTS."

Several other subjects had psychological problems apparently more minor than the seven already cited. One rightist complained of periodic feelings of intense depression, lasting for a day or two at a time; he felt they were probably hereditary (his father having had similar symptoms), and rather than seeking to resolve the difficulty he had simply learned to avoid most social contacts and to do detail work rather than any work involving decision making during the depressive periods. He also had recurrent nightmares about his divorced wife, to whose mental illness he felt he had contributed; but his feelings of depression antedated these indications of guilt feelings by many years. His psychological symptoms appeared to have no specific connection with his religious or political convictions.

The rightist who feared that the study was supported by the Ford Foundation has already been mentioned. Other than his general suspiciousness and reticence, there was little to indicate psychological disturbance. Several rightists had marital histories indicative of neurotic problems (for example, an unconsummated marriage ended by divorce; two successive marriages to divorced women with children); but these were no more prevalent than among the liberals. Among liberals, one woman had recently been given estrogen treatment for menopausal depression, apparently not of a serious nature; one man had lost several jobs through arrests for drunkenness, drunken driving, and so forth, but was apparently controlling his drinking at the time of the study; one man had had severe marital problems as a result of his wife's recurrent schizophrenia, and had himself recently "failed" in a high-level job, but was continuing to try to cope with his wife and felt he was coping with his new job successfully.

Other than these instances, which do not constitute a majority of either liberals or rightists, there was little evidence of anything except reasonably adjustive responses to normal life stresses.[24] One might speculate

---

[24] Two other recent studies similarly report extreme rightist subjects generally to have few psychological impairments: Raymond E. Wolfinger, B. K. Wolfinger, K. Prewitt, and S. Rosenhack, "America's Radical Right: Politics and Ideology," in David E. Apter (ed.), *Ideology and Discontent* (New York: The Free Press, 1964); and Mark Chesler, Richard Schmuck, and James Whiteside, "Social Backgrounds and Personality Predispositions of Super-Patriots," paper presented at American Psychological Association Convention, Chicago, 1965.

that the rightists had succeeded so well at projecting their personal problems onto politics, that their problems had disappeared or at least been restricted to the area of projection. Neither the interview material, the autobiographies, nor TAT responses would support such speculation for most subjects who have not already been specifically discussed. Subjects were questioned about childhood experiences, about successes and failures in life, about attitudes toward close relatives, and so on; it is unlikely that indications of extreme psychological problems, past or present, would have escaped notice in more than a very few instances. For pilot-study subjects, not only the TAT but the complete Rorschach Test was administered, again without indication of severe problems except in the case of the Nazi activist.

It may be of interest that the two rightists with apparently the most extreme psychological symptoms took ideological paths distinctly different from the usual Birchite anticommunist circuit: one became a fanatical Objectivist, the other affiliated with the American Nazi Party. Likewise, the liberal with the most extreme history of mental illness differed distinctly from others in the sample in having once belonged to several far-left groups, including reputed Communist-front groups. In each of these cases, as well as in the four instances of subjects with depressive episodes followed by religious or semireligious conversion, adoption of a rightist or leftist political position seemed rather directly associated with resolution of the psychological problem, or appeared to be a direct outgrowth of it. (Even in the Jungian's case, the archetypal dreams and his acceptance of his unconscious were followed shortly by a change from conservatism to liberalism, and he himself associated this change with his psychological conversion.)

Other subjects attributed their ideological choice to a wide variety of influences, and the choice could not usually be tied to attempts to deal with repressed psychological conflicts, severe status anxieties, or similar phenomena. Most rightists felt they had been "raised as conservatives," but had attained specific ideological direction only upon encounter with Birchite literature, the Goldwater campaign, or such things as (in one case) a businessmen's briefing by the "head of Naval Intelligence," who officially revealed Eleanor Roosevelt's key role in the Communist Conspiracy. A few mentioned negative reactions to Democratic legislation directly affecting them, such as higher taxes or restrictions on the oil business, as being precipitating factors. (With one exception, all rightists affiliated with a political party were Republican.) Liberals also frequently mentioned the influence of parents or high-school teachers; in addition, several referred to their own childhood poverty or later economic difficulties (for example, being fired from jobs unjustly) as leading to sympathy with the poor and downtrodden, and thus to liberalism.

It is difficult to advance a single set of factors which predisposed the rightists in this study to select relatively extreme ideological positions. Neither unusual political sophistication (the rightists' own explanation) nor unusually strong status concerns (a standard sociological explanation) seems to account for the extremism of any volunteer. For a few rightists —three out of fifteen in the main study, one out of six in the pilot study— extremist political activity seems to have been initiated by attempts to deal with severe psychological problems. For two or three others, neurotic conflict may have contributed to ideological extremism without being the controlling factor. For the remainder, about two thirds of the sample, no nonideological factors, singly or in combination, seem sufficiently extreme to account for ideological extremity.

Certainly, the political attitudes of all these rightists served psychological functions, as did the political attitudes of the less extreme liberals and moderates in the study. Smith, Bruner, and White, Katz,[25] and others have discussed such functions at length—social adjustment, value expression, object appraisal, and so on. These functions need not be served by extreme attitudes or activities; they may involve standard political party activity, or political apathy, or coin collecting, or an interest in Elizabethan literature, as well as John Birch Society membership.

Why then did these rightists choose The John Birch Society rather than numismatics or the Shakespeare-Bacon controversy? For most, it appears to have been first because they had been early indoctrinated with conservatism by parents and other influential figures; and second, because the literature and organizations of the extreme right were already easily available to them in the Dallas area. Most rightists in the sample had not been interested or active in extreme right-wing movements before 1960, the majority not before 1964. The social and historical circumstances which had led Dallas political discussion by that time to be influenced heavily by extreme conservatism, and particularly by the editorial policies of the *Dallas Morning News*, are too complex and too unclear to be discussed here. But it seems apparent that once such a situation existed, most of these rightists found that adoption of an extremist position and involvement in extreme political activities was a rather easy process, meeting ready acceptance from most friends and acquaintances and opposition from few (other than the easily discounted national news media); resulted in no disruptions of careers or marriages; and provided an interesting pastime associated with various kinds of ego gratification and ready-made explanations of troubling, but not overwhelming, questions. For most, radical rightism involved all the advantages and few of the disadvantages of coin collecting: there appear to be many more rightists than numis-

---

[25] Daniel Katz, "The Functional Approach to the Study of Attitudes," *Public Opinion Quart., 24* (Summer 1960), 163–204.

matists in Dallas; rightist social events are more frequent; the hobby is not very expensive; the relevant literature is easy to come by, and eliminates the necessity to spend time on biased national newscasts or mass publications; and certainly radical rightism deals with more important issues than numismatics. Few people have a pleasant hobby which can also help save the world from disaster.

All this is not to deny the importance of factors advanced by other researchers as accounting for radical rightism, but to argue that these other factors, usually extreme in nature, are not always required. Among other things, the local community context may make radical rightism so available and so acceptable that the only extreme precipitating factor necessary is living there. (And even that, of course, may not be an "extreme" behavior if, as in Dallas, the community provides a substantial number of other reasons for coming to or remaining in the area.) Wolfinger and associates [26] have suggested a somewhat similar concept, though the necessary supporting data were not available to them. The present study does not provide such data on a large or readily quantifiable scale, and comparable data are needed from other communities throughout the country before definite conclusions can be drawn. The present results do suggest strongly that although extreme psychological disturbance may be a sufficient precipitating factor for political extremism, it is not a necessary one.

---

[26] P. 286.

Social Psychological Characteristics of Super-Patriots

MARK CHESLER
RICHARD SCHMUCK

Super-patriotism is a manifestation of the ideologies and energies of persons who resist and reject many aspects of contemporary American social and political life. This particular manifestation is an outgrowth of a unique form of adaptation between a person's individual needs, values, and role conceptions, and broad changes in the social order. To place super-patriotism in proper perspective, we initially define it and highlight it against a background of contemporary social changes. Then we review data from content analyses and interviews suggesting factors in cultural backgrounds, social roles, and personality characteristics that may account for the emergence of super-patriots as active agents of political and social change.

DEFINING CHARACTERISTICS

Previously, we sketched a definition of super-patriot belief systems based on a content-analysis of protest literature and a review of prior, scholarly studies.[1] We have suggested that super-patriotism is characterized by political conservatism and fervent nationalism, by active participation in conservative social and political organizations, and by the perception of a major and dangerous internal communist conspiracy operating to influence many areas of American life. For purposes of the empirical study to be described here, the variable of super-patriotism was operationalized by questions aimed at these three areas of belief and activity. One was *patriotic and nationalistic conservatism:* super-patriots were partly defined as persons who strongly agreed with the statement, "Whereas some people feel they are citizens of the world, that they belong to mankind and not to any one nation, I, for my part, feel that I am first, last, and always an American." They were also defined by an espousal of a conservative political belief system, identifying most strongly with Republicans who favored more conservatives and fewer liberals or moderates in control of their party. A second defining characteristic was their vigorous *anticommunism*, not only with regard to international affairs, but especially focused upon the internal danger of subversion. Persons defined as super-patriots viewed communists as having considerable and dangerous influence in government and within both the Republican and Democratic parties. Finally, a third defining characteristic of super-patriotism was their clear *commitment to action*. The action may have involved becoming educated about communism, educating others, protesting, or politicizing. We viewed this commitment to some action as a necessary component of super-patriotism, although we recognized that there could be some people with a super-patriot ideology who do not act upon it. Such "potential super-patriots" are not focused on here, but they may be a source of latent and perhaps future super-patriot strength. It may well be that educational and political activity are the primary routes through which anti-Communist and patriotic conservatives are socialized into fervent and active super-patriotism.

To study empirically some social-psychological characteristics of super-patriots we interviewed 134 Midwesterners, many of whom we had reason to believe were super-patriots on the basis of organizational membership lists, literature and announcements, public petitions, and letters to the editors of newspapers. On the basis of the defining dimensions discussed above, approximately 50 percent of this sample was actually categorized as super-patriots. The so-called conservatives, making up about 25 percent

---

[1] See R. Schmuck and M. Chesler, "On Super-Patriots: A Definition and Analysis," *JSI, 19* (1963), 1931–50.

of this sample, were defined as politically conservative and fairly nationalistic, but not particularly active—definitely not active in extremist
organizations. Moreover, the conservatives did not believe that communists
have a strong influence in American government or in the political parties.
The moderates—the remaining 25 percent of the sample—ranged from
traditionally moderate Republicans to moderate Democrats. They were the
political normals or "controls" in the study.

Super-patriots, conservatives, and moderates were defined quantitatively
by their respective scores on an index composed of the items described
below. These ideological and behavioral items empirically define the persons
whose views and styles are represented in the rest of the chapter.

QUANTITATIVE BASIS FOR DEFINING SUPER-PATRIOTS,
CONSERVATIVES, AND MODERATES

1. *Patriotic political conservatism* (5 points possible)
   A. Preference for the Republican party (1)
   B. Preference for Goldwater as the Republican standard bearer [2] (1)
   C. Preference for some Democrat significantly more conservative
      than Johnson as the Democratic standard bearer (1)
   D. A response of Agree (1) or Strongly Agree (2) to "Whereas
      some people feel they are citizens of the world, that they belong
      to mankind and not to any one nation, I, for my part, feel that
      I am first, last, and always an American"

2. *The perception of a dangerous conspiracy* (5 points possible)
   A. Perception of many communists having *great* (2) or *some* (1)
      influence in American government
   B. Perception of *much* (3) or *some* (1) Communist influence in
      both major political parties, or *much* (2) or *some* (1) influence
      in one of the major parties

3. *Commitment to action as reflected in involvement in, and active
   approval of, patriotic and conservative organizations* (4 points possible)
   A. An implied (1) or vigorous (2) approval of The John Birch
      Society
   B. Statement of membership (1) or leadership (2) in a politically
      conservative group

The total index score possible is 14. For the purpose of this study, super-
patriots were identified as those scoring 9 or more points; conservatives

---

[2] The original data in this study was collected in the spring of 1964,
when Goldwater, Rockefeller, Nixon, and Scranton were contenders for nomination
as the Republican presidential candidate.

included those who scored between 5 and 8 points; moderates scored 4 or below.

Before turning to an analysis of the data pertaining to these defining characteristics, it would be useful to establish a context for considering and understanding the character and growth of this phenomenon. It is our contention that pervasive institutional changes in the American society have set the stage for substantial modifications of occupational and organizational roles and values, and that super-patriotism can best be seen as a series of potential responses to these changes.

INSTITUTIONAL CHANGE AND SUPER-PATRIOTISM

The pace of contemporary social and cultural change is so rapid that in many ways American society has changed more in the past 30 years than in the 200 years preceding. Moreover, all current predictions estimate an even more rapid series of changes for the next 30 years. The importance of change in American society and in the world is highlighted by the growing number of individuals, private agencies, and governmental organizations concerned with predicting and controlling the future.[3]

Outstanding areas of social change during the past several decades have been the ecological, age distribution, and migration patterns of the population; the nature of the economic system; the structure and operations of government, politics, and partisan political activity; educational systems and techniques; religious and moral institutions; and still others including leisure, work, and family organization. No segment of daily existence or of the population has been left untouched by these far-reaching changes. Not all of these changes are merely quantitative extensions of previous trends; some are qualitative shifts, and are creating a different America, with different life opportunities, values, and styles.

The nature of these changing patterns and structures of society demands new forms of relations between the individual, his small groups, and the larger collectivities to which he belongs. Some years ago American society was more individuated; the individual and his small group, at work, in the family, or in leisure activities, were generally politically and economically autonomous from the larger society. More recently, the individual and others are called upon more often to accomplish tasks together, and small groups and larger collectivities are more interdependent. Visible accomplishments for individuals are no longer easily available, and the single person may often feel more anonymous, more secure, and less responsible.

---

[3] For instance, see the discussions in: Michael, D., *The Next Generation* (New York: Random House, Inc., 1965); "Toward the Year 2000: Work in Progress," *Daedalus*, 1967 (Summer).

One result of this secure and unresponsible anonymity may well be an increased sense of bewilderment over the meaning and boundaries of self and other, and of the individual and his referent groups. The resultant search for personal identity and human community have become catch phrases of our times. The blurring of these boundaries and the emphasis on work in larger and larger groups makes it difficult to answer personal questions about meaning and direction but, at the same time, reassures the individual that he no longer stands alone. He can depend, and must depend, on others for productivity, creativity, and social support.

Another major characteristic of contemporary life is a revolution in the world of knowledge. An increased scientific understanding of many aspects of our own world, and indeed other worlds as well, has led to dramatic growth in an emphasis upon the utilization of science in industry and government. Industrial researchers and developers plan not only new products and markets, but new forms of production and internal management. The public sector, too, invests heavily in basic and applied research in the physical and social sciences. It has become more and more important for Americans in all institutions to be informed of recent discoveries in their own fields. This tremendous knowledge explosion threatens to make standards of the past irrelevant and outmoded; and calls into question many previously held assumptions about man's social and physical existence. The result is that modern man is called upon to take less for granted and to maintain fewer unquestioned or unquestionable assumptions and behavior patterns. No matter what the area of belief, value, behavior, or tradition, the knowledge gatherers and researchers of the present may challenge accustomed ways of thinking and behaving with new information and implications at any time.

Major changes in the social structure and institutional patterns reach individuals through their connection with the larger society in their work, leisure time activities, and community roles. In addition, parents and educators pass on their personal views and experiences of the world and its demands through the ways in which they socialize their children. Changes in institutional structures and norms, manifesting themselves in demands for change in role prescriptions and proscriptions, have placed great strain on various portions of the population. At the same time, some people adjust more easily to social changes and new value patterns than others. It is difficult for everyone to adapt continually and effectively to changing demands, and some people are left to flounder in political, economic, or moral confusion. It is both the nature of social change and the character of persons, and not merely change itself, that must be understood to interpret how many super-patriots, or protesters of any sort, are responding to these times.

Most Americans, at least on the surface, continuously adjust to these social changes without serious political, economic, or moral consequences. They have altered their life styles and their personal values and aspirations, and have managed to be relatively comfortable, if not sometimes enthusiastic, in the contemporary world. Others, especially adolescents and young adults, have had a more difficult time, either because of an inability to meet new demands or because of serious dissonance between the ways they have been trained and the way the world is, or because of a deeply felt commitment to resist adjusting to the demands of this changing social order. One group of adults who appear to resist many of these changes actively, and to resist in moral and ideological ways, are super-patriots. Super-patriots seem to be socialized by their social backgrounds, psychological styles, and belief patterns, in ways that do not support or facilitate many of the emerging themes and role demands of our changing society.

It is *not* our contention that changes in social structures, institutional procedures, and roles and norms cause super-patriotism. They do, however, seem to constitute a necessary, although not sufficient, condition. The phenomena of super-patriotism are the effects of a complex interaction of social structural and normative conditions on the one hand, and individual personality styles and beliefs on the other. These societal changes set the stage upon which super-patriots act out their frustrations and beliefs, and provide a background for understanding and highlighting the varied bases of super-patriotism. In addition, since a preeminent characteristic of most American super-patriots is their direct focus upon certain changing societal and personal life styles and goals, it seems doubly appropriate to take a brief look at their stated reactions to some of the major structural and normative changes in the American society over the past several decades.

ECOLOGICAL PATTERNS AND THE SUPER-PATRIOTS

Major changes have occurred in the American society in the geographic distribution of the population and its accompanying mobility. New centers of population have developed rapidly, especially in cities close to new areas of economic growth. In addition to mobility occasioned by shifts in work and living sites, people move about more in pursuit of their leisure activities. The number of passenger miles traveled has more than doubled over the past 25 years, and the increase in air travel clearly testifies to the migratory character of contemporary America.

Several studies of super-patriots tend to locate their major centers of activity in or near those areas of the nation undergoing the greatest population mobility. McEvoy, Chesler, and Schmuck, as well as Wartenburg and Thielens, report an overrepresentation of Californians among super-patriot letter writers.[4] Moreover, it appears that Southern California accounts for the major proportion of this representation. Other states which contributed letters out of proportion to their population included the growing states of Florida and Washington, and the out-migration states of Alabama and Tennessee. In addition to these findings, a compendium of "rightists groups, publications, and some individuals" [5] reports fully 19 percent of its listing originating in California, with other concentrations in Texas and Florida, all areas experiencing rapid mobility and change.

It is clear that the pattern of letter-writing by super-patriots closely parallels some of the migration and mobility channels suggested earlier. A disproportionate number of the letters studied by McEvoy, Chesler, and Schmuck came from people living in small and medium-sized towns and urban areas with populations ranging from 10,000 to 500,000. These areas include the semi-urban and suburban areas experiencing the greatest percentage of recent influx from more rural areas and from central cities.

It may be argued that the rootlessness of those who are extremely mobile supports their participation in super-patriot groups. Despite their mobility, these transient persons may be quite uncomfortable with a complex and varied series of social settings and constant strangeness. Participation in nationalist activities may then occur because there is little identification with small groups and local organizations, and the rootless person may more easily identify directly with the whole society. In a sense, his home becomes the nation or the state rather than a local group or community. Moreover, the neophyte to a community may quickly feel accepted through his participation in an active, friendly, super-patriot group, and may thereby relieve any tensions created by the strangeness and loneliness of the new environment.

A fascinating feature of some of the more vigorous supporters of Barry Goldwater during the 1964 presidential campaign was their suggestion that we might just "cut off the northeastern seaboard." While not an official part of super-patriot ideology, this position does reflect a growing mistrust of the East among these super-patriots who have moved and are living in the western and southwestern areas of the nation. It also captures part of the essence of super-patriot concern with the relationship among eastern intellectuals, liberal Republicans, and civil rights groups as being dominated

---

[4] J. McEvoy, M. Chesler, and R. Schmuck, "Content Analysis of a Super-Patriot Protest," *Social Problems, 14* (1967), 455–463. Wartenburg, H. and W. Thielens, *Against the United Nations: A Letter Writing Campaign by the Birch Movement* (New York: Columbia University Bureau of Applied Social Research, 1964).

[5] See *First National Directory of "Rightists" Groups, Publications, and Some Individuals in the United States* (Fourth Edition) (Sausalito, California: The Noontide Press, 1962).

by eastern elites. Such an image gains prominence especially among those super-patriots in the southwest crescent and in the southern states.

ECONOMIC CHANGES AND THE SUPER-PATRIOTS

Economic changes in America generally have followed a rural to urban pattern of area development and an entrepreneurial to bureaucratic pattern of social organization. Increasing demand exists for technical, clerical, and service personnel to work in urbanized, complex, large-scale organizations. These bureaucratic structures and occupations necessitate communication and interdependence with colleagues and general interpersonal competencies in dealing with the public. Super-patriots have often been quite critical of the increasing size and complexity of American industrial organizations. They have not taken very clear positions on issues involving monopolies, interlocking directorates, and the like, but they do exhibit a distinct, although general, antipathy to bigness in various forms. In addition to bigness per se, super-patriots exhibit a general opposition to various forms of bureaucracy and service occupations. Often this opposition is highlighted in their direct castigation of the federal governmental bureaucracy, but it can be taken as an attack on that organizational form in general. Bureaucracies are seen often as masses of red tape that do not recognize or reward individual initiative or merit, and thus retard individual achievement and social efficiency.

Even more obnoxious to super-patriots than bigness or bureaucracy in business, however, is such complexity or power in governmental systems or labor union organizations. Attitudes toward labor unions were measured in our interviews by the following statement: "The way they are run now, labor unions do this country more harm than good." The results indicated that 28 percent of the super-patriots strongly agreed with this item, compared with 17 percent of the conservatives and 9 percent of the moderates; 26 percent of the super-patriots disagreed, compared with 39 percent of the conservatives and 64 percent of the moderates who disagreed.

Super-patriots typically are opposed to almost all recently expanding public aid or welfare programs, and they see these developments as "leading the country down the road to Communism." They feel that low-income groups and individuals ought to be able to make out on their own and, if they cannot, private charity is the appropriate American response. Public welfare is seen as an inappropriate burden upon those who do work hard, as a negative incentive for achievement and success, and as an encouragement for those on the public dole to remain there.

In this same context, super-patriot organizations have actively fostered and supported programs to repeal the income tax laws. The graduated, progressive income tax is often seen as a communist invention, and most often seen as a negative incentive for financial success. Programs have also been instituted to preserve the integrity and success of the domestic economy by forbidding any imports from communist dominated or controlled nations. This economic protest has taken various forms, from resolutions by city councils to local laws and informally arranged "card parties," where local merchants are either boycotted or harassed until they bend to such partisan pressure.

GOVERNMENTAL ACTIVITY AND THE SUPER-PATRIOTS

Over the past few decades, we have witnessed a rapid increase in the size and breadth of governmental activities at all levels. The federal government has been especially active in coordinating and centralizing local functions, as well as in providing funds for state and local programs. The net result has been an increase in funding and sometimes control of local programs by public agencies increasingly removed from the local scene.

Some super-patriots are critical of what they perceive to be dangerous trends in the federal contribution to local systems, and particularly in the growing acceptance of public contributions and guidelines to the structure and operation of the American economy. They are especially concerned with governmental encroachments on private production and free enterprise in the form of services and power facilities. This opposition is also vigorously concentrated on almost all governmental ventures to expand the public sector of the economy. Several organizations are lobbying to force the government to relinquish all holdings that compete—or could compete —with private enterprises. To test the degree to which super-patriots strongly supported an economic ideology emphasizing private and free enterprises, we asked our interviewees to indicate their agreement or disagreement with the following statement, "The U.S. government should get rid of all its activities that compete with private industry." Sixty-seven percent of the persons defined as super-patriots strongly agreed with the statement, while only 27 percent of the conservatives and 19 percent of the moderates agreed with it. Only 3 percent of the super-patriots disagreed, while 14 percent of the conservatives and 50 percent of the moderates opposed the statement. Several super-patriots added that they felt the government should stop "immediately" or should "sell TVA now," and "get out of the post office business."

The opposition of super-patriots to federal governmental influence in local and regional affairs is manifest particularly in their perception of encroachments on "states' rights" and local initiatives. The increasing centralization of governmental activity is seen as the first step toward totalitarian rule and the demise of intervening governments and checks on federal power. Relationships are seen among the incidence of decreased local or state control and trends toward democratic centralism, socialism, and communism.

Super-patriots are also concerned with the potential loss of American sovereignty resulting from international trade agreements such as the Common Market. Loss of the United States' economic independence, and the possibility of supporting communist economies, is seen as occurring in our trade relations with the communist nations. International political organizations are viewed as even more dangerous. In this regard, the activities of the United Nations, UNESCO, and citizen groups advocating world government often are accused of being subversive. Our interviews demonstrated that those persons defined as super-patriots much more often were opposed to the United States' membership in the U.N. than were the conservatives and the moderates. We asked our interviewees: "Do you or do you not think it was a good idea for the United States to join the United Nations?" Only 21 percent of the super-patriots answered "yes," against 61 percent of the conservatives and 88 percent of the moderates. We also asked the following question about our relations with China: "What do you think the U.S. should do if Communist China gets into the United Nations?" The answer of "get out" was given by 75 percent of the super-patriots, 33 percent of the conservatives, and 11 percent of the moderates.

Many super-patriots believe that absolutely no compromise or negotiation is possible between communist countries and the nations of the free world. Recent forms of economic and political cooperation are seen as aiding satanic forces in their drive to "enslave" America and destroy Christianity. Therefore, negotiations about international organization and nuclear disarmament between the United States and the Soviet Union are perceived as leading to a loss of national sovereignty and autonomy and a surrender to world communism.

DOMESTIC POLITICS AND SUPER-PATRIOTS

In addition to foreign policy changes, many new practices and trends are discernible in the shape of our political system in recent years. For instance, since 1932 the federal government has largely been run by a Democratic Party hegemony. Young people growing up under a Democratic or moderate Republican political administration have tended to adopt "liberal" public positions, especially concerning domestic problems. Moreover, dissent has become more and more difficult on foreign policy because of the middle-of-the-road approach of most administrations and the growing complexity of international politics.

Many super-patriots express a deep concern for the future of our current political alignments. It is argued by some that Republican candidates have lost consistently because of their attempts to imitate the Democratic party's programs and platforms. The result has been to offer the voters an "echo" of the Democratic party, not a "choice" between the two. The most effective program for Republican victory is seen to be the return to a real two-party politics sparked by Republican espousal of truly conservative positions. The same super-patriots argue that the party would be better off without their complement of such left-wing and moderate Republicans as Rockefeller, Scranton, and Romney.

In the interviews, we asked the respondents who identified themselves as Republicans whether or not they were happy with their party. The three groups—super-patriots, moderates, and conservatives—differed widely with respect to the degree of their satisfaction with the Republican party. Approximately 87 percent of the Republican super-patriots said they were disturbed by the "me-tooism" in the Republican party. This result is in sharp contrast to the 33 percent of the Republican conservatives who felt the same concern.

In addition to these ferments within the ranks of the Republican party, often felt and sometimes created by super-patriots, there are also third or fourth party splinter movements that some super-patriots have considered as antidotes to Democratic and Liberal hegemony. On several occasions, a new party of conservatives has been encouraged or even formed at the national and state levels. While none of these attempts have yet gained national power, they do reflect some super-patriots' dissatisfactions with these trends in the character of America's domestic political machinery.

Some super-patriots see local autonomy being threatened, and the social sciences being used as a tool, by the current advocates of desegregation and social equality. Super-patriots often explicitly charge that various civil rights organizations are communist dominated and thereby have conspiratorial intentions to destroy the American way of life. In the interviews, we specifically asked about the National Association for the Advancement of Colored People, an organization which is generally viewed as taking a moderate stance on civil rights issues. Over 90 percent of the interviewees had heard of the N.A.A.C.P. and of these we asked, "Do you approve of what they're doing?" Only 5 percent of the super-patriots approved, against 44 percent of the conservatives and 42 percent of the moderates. Twenty-five percent of the super-patriots were ambivalent and 70 percent disapproved; 33 percent of the conservatives and 35 percent of the moderates were ambivalent; and 23 percent of the conservatives and moderates disapproved. We probed further: "Some people feel that some of the organizations working for integration, such as the N.A.A.C.P., are communist infiltrated; others feel that this is not true. What are your feelings on this issue?" Fifty-seven percent of the super-patriots answered "yes, they are definitely infiltrated," while 20 percent of the conservatives and 11 percent of the moderates answered similarly.

Some super-patriots argue that there is no clear evidence to support assumptions of either the biologic or the social equality of the races. Others suggest that the theme "civil rights" is being used in the same symbolic manner as was "agrarian reform" in China or Cuba. Racial crises in the South and in northern urban areas are seen as being artificially created by Communist agitators who desire to add racial hatred and conflict to their theories of class war. Martin Luther King was sometimes viewed as a "race agitator," unfit to be called a clergyman, and working hand-in-hand with the communists, dupes, or participants in what one respondent called, "the general left-wing overdrift of our times." One super-patriot noted, "They have been trying since the days of Roosevelt to remake America in the image of their one world, one race ideology."

The complicity of the federal government's executive offices in prosecuting desegregation in education and voting procedures is seen as a dictatorial move. It is also seen as a threat to further erode state autonomy, to place large numbers of illiterates on voting rolls, and to establish federal control over education. The judicial branches of the federal system are particularly attacked. The Supreme Court, and especially Chief Justice Earl Warren, is a target for a great many super-patriot concerns. The "Warren Court" is considered not only a prime agent of desegregation, but as being "soft on Communism." By voiding convictions based upon violations of free speech and assembly rights, the Court is liable for freeing Communists to organize and subvert. We asked the interviewers about the Chief Justice's role: "Some people think of Earl Warren and the Supreme Court as being 'soft on Communism.' How do you feel about this"? Eighty-one percent of the super-patriots answered "yes, definitely," while 10 percent answered "maybe," and 9 percent answered "no." This data is even more striking when we take into consideration the added evidence that a substantial number of super-patriots volunteered the information that "Earl Warren *is* a Communist."

EDUCATIONAL CHANGE AND SUPER-PATRIOTS

New skills are in constant demand in this complex technological society. In order to prepare themselves for more complex jobs, more students are entering college and in general are staying longer in some kind of school. There are relatively fewer school dropouts today than there were a generation ago. For many, education no longer ends when one leaves formal institutions; many industries have their own extensive training programs, and adult education programs are conducted by many universities, state education departments, and private agencies.

The manner in which young people are being educated is a source of concern for some super-patriots who often charge that children are not being educated in the basic academic fundamentals. Contemporary schools are seen as emphasizing irrelevant social adjustment goals and, in the process, "brainwashing" children in amoral and often anti-American values. Also, many of the older standards of respect and obedience toward the teacher are breaking down. Teachers are often charged with being lax in their own administration of discipline, and this, coupled with societal trends toward lawlessness and parental permissiveness, is believed to encourage students to flount and disregard authority.

As a further specific extension on their general ideology with regard to domestic political and economic institutions, super-patriots are critical of the role the federal government plays in educational matters. Federal aid, they believe, will lead to federal and, eventually, international control of educational curricula and practices. Some super-patriots are convinced that communists and communist sympathizers have already infiltrated and now direct various educational systems from the elementary grades through post-graduate and adult education programs. This is felt to be particularly true of schools and educators who practice a "progressive" theory of instruction or learning. The progressive school, according to the super-patriots, is not only lax and adjustment-oriented, but is also committed to the socialist (communist) principles of their founders.

MORAL AND RELIGIOUS SYSTEMS AND THE SUPER-PATRIOTS

The super-patriots are greatly concerned with a variety of moral issues as well as with the moral components of policy issues. They see the increasing crime rate as evidence of a general breakdown in the moral fiber and character of our nation. According to them, this breakdown can be traced to the attempts of "do-gooders" to hamstring the police forces, to permissive patterns of child rearing and schooling which do not teach respect for law and order, to the inappropriate demands and strategies of minorities which legitimate breaking the law, and to conscious infiltration and subversion by communists. Several major programs are underway to gain support for local police forces and to prohibit the formation of civilian police review boards.

Many super-patriots are similarly concerned with the increasing attention paid to mental health and mental illness.[6] Following the statement: "Problems of adjustment and emotional problems have become an increasing

---

[6] See R. Schmuck and M. Chesler, "Super-Patriot Opposition to Community Mental Health Programs," *Community Mental Health Journal, 3* (1967), 382–388.

concern of public schools in recent years. Many schools have hired professional psychologists and social workers to deal with these problems. Some people feel that such persons are beneficial in schools, others feel that they do more harm than good to the children," the interviewees were asked if they thought there should be such services in elementary and high schools. The super-patriots (48 percent) were much more opposed to the psychological services than were persons in the other two categories—29 percent of the conservatives and 13 percent of the moderates. In a similar vein, psychological tests used by the government, industry, and schools are often thought to contain items which are morally repugnant or which expose private matters to public scrutiny.

What is objected to in the mental health ideology is the apparent amorality and lack of focus upon sin. Mental health programs and policies generally are seen to dilute older notions of right and wrong, sin and retribution. In addition, the super-patriots' general concern for giant bureaucracies and governmental activity in the public sector is once again evident in their opposition to expanding mental health facilities and institutions. As a final concern with regard to mental health, some super-patriots feel that there are too many psychiatrists and psychologists who are foreign born, or atheists, or possibly communists. The communists, too, we are reminded, shun belief in God, sin, and morality.

In addition to mental health activities, some super-patriots see evidence of our nation's moral breakdown in the public conduct of our high officials. Many rumors are spread about drinking, illegitimate sexual activity, and even sexual perversion in high government places.

Because many super-patriots are engaged in protests against the moral trends of the contemporary culture, their charges are often directed toward the failures of organized religious institutions as the traditional custodian of societal morality. If the mental health movement has vitiated the concept of sin, it is because the churches, too, have collaborated in its demise. Super-patriots are especially critical of those institutions that do not join them in a "Holy Christian War" against the communists. They are concerned with the growth in size and complexity of some churches and what they see as the resultant impersonalization of religion. Further, super-patriots charge that churches which encourage ecumenicalism and define part of the religious mission as working to improve social conditions and social problems are aiding the communist program. Advocates of this "Social Gospel" are seen as provoking internal strife in American society and as placing the origin of sin in societal conditions rather than in man's nature. Both trends are perceived by super-patriots as advancing communist purposes. One particular target is the National Council of Churches (and certain denominations) which has been charged with infiltration by communists and communist sympathizers.

CHANGES IN NORMATIVE THEMES
AND STRUCTURES

Throughout many of the societal and institutional changes occurring in modern America run several corollary changes in social values, norms, and styles of life. Some of these new normative tendencies create institutional change, some are created by such change, and some occur associationally without clear causal relationships. The central mechanism by which evaluative and normative changes are incorporated into the individual's daily life pattern is through a variety of socialization processes and institutions. Among significant socialization units are the family, school, peer group, and economic-occupational systems. Bronfenbrenner suggests that those persons or families with the greatest access to societal channels and sources of information will incorporate the normative changes more rapidly than their more isolated neighbors.[7] Thus families in urban areas, of middle- and upper-class literate backgrounds are most likely to lead the way in adopting new evaluative modes. There are many examples of major shifts in American values throughout this century; we will explore just a few outstanding ones that may shed light on the dynamics of super-patriotism.

One of the major changes seems to be the movement away from individual glorification and reward for individual effort to a priority upon cooperative and collaborative work in teams. In many areas of life, at work and at leisure, there is more group activity than there was in the past. The space industry is an obvious and constant reminder of teamwork, a far cry from Lindbergh's lone-wolf fame. This trend has also been reflected in some of the institutional changes we have already discussed; in the decrease of small and individually owned farms, in the growth of bureaucracies, and in the increasing demand for people to perform service occupations and interpersonal helping roles. As a result of these normative and structural shifts, the new members of the society are being prepared for adult roles in different ways. Children are being taught collaborative lessons from an early age; and the family and school spend more and more time and energy teaching youngsters to be interdependent and work together. It is clear that this tradition of cooperation, adjustment to group demands, and loyalty to organizations of peers, is in marked contrast to the traditional American standards of individualism and individual effort. We have moved from personal definitions of self-interest to a concern for the interests of others and of the groups to which we belong and owe fealty. In Riesman's terms,

---

[7] U. Bronfenbrenner, "Socialization and social class through time and space." In E. Maccoby, T. Newcomb, and E. Hartley (eds.), *Readings in Social Psychology* (New York: Holt, Rinehart and Winston, Inc., 1958).

aspects of the American character have shifted from a focus upon internal cues and directions to a greater concern for the feelings, reactions, and desires of others.[8]

These trends are reflected in child-rearing patterns which emphasize the interdependence of the child and other children and the parents. More emphasis is placed upon teaching the child to get along with others than upon independent achievement. Parents now express their own feelings of love and affection more freely, and children often learn to search for and depend upon the friendly and rewarding character of social life. In a variety of ways, parents pay more attention to the child's wishes and social needs than they did in the past, thus providing a model for the child's attention to others. A generation or more ago, of course, child-rearing practices were highly scheduled and tended to fit the parent's comfort or established notions of "what's right for baby." As Bronfenbrenner reports current trends, "Over the past quarter of a century, American mothers at all social class levels have become more flexible with respect to infant feeding and weaning." [9] By flexible, he means more willing to adjust to what seems to be the child's comfort and capabilities. In much the same vein, Miller and Swanson document how greater flexibility and permissiveness in child rearing can be connected to demands for interpersonal performance and functioning in our great modern welfare bureaucracies.[10] Bureaucratic and service roles demand and expect more attention to the nuances of feelings between people. Only by having had early training in identifying and verifying one's own feelings can one be sensitive to, and accurate about, the feelings of others. And it takes both skills to manage successful interpersonal relations in complex bureaucracies.

Since one of the hallmarks of modern life is that each man is closer to, and in greater contact with, other men, there is plenty of opportunity for external controls to be shared and applied to behavior. These controls or sanctions can either be applied by impersonal organizations or by peers and family. The prevalence of external controls has made it less necessary for modern man to have, in addition, a strong system of internal controls. The child who is fed and trained on a fixed schedule must learn to control his own impulses and needs in a way that the child reared by demand feeding and training does not. Thus the greater modern permissiveness and flexibility in child rearing corroborates the lessening organizational demands for internal sources of self-control. Additionally, since for many affluent families it is indeed possible to gratify most of their children's demands, there is even less necessity to teach children to learn self-control or to delay gratifi-

---

[8] D. Riesman, N. Glazer, and R. Denney, *The Lonely Crowd* (New Haven, Conn.: Yale University Press, 1961).

[9] Bronfenbrenner, p. 424.

[10] D. Miller and G. E. Swanson, *The Changing American Parent* (New York: John Wiley & Sons, Inc., 1958).

cation. Reared in this tradition, youngsters are less able to delay gratification of all sorts, and often expect and demand immediate gratification and satisfaction.

The increasing prominence of the Freudian and psychiatric traditions of thought during this century reflect another normative shift. The potential existence of an unconscious, the psychological naturalness of Oedipal rebelliousness in youth, the psychological as well as the moral concept of guilt, and the stresses and strains of mental illness are all now important parts of our national culture and thinking. People are concerned about such issues, and apply these explanatory constructs to their own and to others' behaviors. Thirty years ago, relatively few people knew of the existence of psychiatry and its treatments, and its basic assumptions and concerns were clearly not part of the public parlance. Now emotional health or fulfillment is a public and important value for many Americans, and a pseudosophistication about psychological variables is a part of personal dialog and mass media presentations.

This value change also raises serious questions and debates about contemporary man's sense of moral responsibility. To various extents man is seen as consciously responsible for his own actions, or so pushed and pulled by unseen forces that he is only a pawn of inner conflicts? This dilemma is illustrated dramatically in the debate over whether criminality or criminal deviance is a moral or psychological problem. To be able to define the problem clearly in one of these categories, of course, can lead one to decide unequivocally upon the most appropriate personal and societal treatments. The unsettled character of this problem and the lack of public clarity about solutions creates a great deal of value-conflict, and the conflict itself now is a reflection of the increasing prominence of the psychiatric ideology. The prevalence of large bureaucratic structures further compounds the problems of personal responsibility. When groups of men, or impersonal institutional structures, are the major acting units in the economic, political, and social system, what is the unique moral responsibility of each man who is a member of these groups or institutions? Whatever each person's unique response, it seems clear that each member can feel less responsibility for his own actions and especially those actions of the group and institutions to which he belongs, than in the past.

Another changing normative theme is the concern for life goals that may at times be opposed to earlier American concerns with material achievement and success. Since Americans in general have achieved greater material rewards than any other people in history, and are more affluent themselves than ever before, the mere maintenance of that comfortable and sometimes privileged position is for many an important value in itself. Furthermore, the more that bureaucratic enterprises and governmental programs seek to insure and guarantee a steady job and at least a subsistence income for everyone, the more a concern for security is encouraged and supported.

This trend is also reflected in a diminution of adventurous and risk-taking behavior; if most middle-class persons are assured a life of material comfort unless they slip up somewhere, why take a chance of slipping up? The values of playing it safe or cool, or conforming to the expected, are instrumental for many Americans who want to remain secure about their assured futures.

American society is also experiencing a new and troubling prominence of the classically conflicting nature of public values regarding the priorities of order and justice. The "Hobbesian dilemma" of how status, security, and power motivations are controlled and gratified has been brought into new focus by increasing public attention to national and regional problems of injustice and inequality. For the past several decades, and particularly in the mid-1930s and the 1960s, activities in areas of such racial, legal, and economic injustice and inequality have threatened the existence of public order. Protest movements, strikes, riots, and large-scale apathy, illness, and despair threaten the orderly consummation of public life. Many people argue that priorities should be placed upon immediate redress of these injustices and inequalities, with the assumption that such redress would best preserve social order and individual conscience. At the same time, many others argue that we must act instead with priority on the maintenance of order rather than on redress of injustice. Unambiguous priorities of the past that demanded order have given way at least to the legitimacy of this debate, and the possibility of dealing openly with attempts to secure justice and equality.

In addition to these specific modifications in our traditions, the weight of traditions themselves as guidelines for behavior is being lessened by the society's increasing dependence upon scientific information for all kinds of pursuits. The knowledge explosion, and the growth of scientific and intellectual elites, lessens the weight of tradition and institution as epistemological styles of decision making. From establishing foreign policy to repairing a new automobile, from deciding whether to develop and market a new product to hiring new personnel, special kinds of knowledge and specialists in the collection and organization of knowledge are needed and called upon. The expectation that we can derive viable and utilitarian knowledge from scientific and intellectual pursuits, and in fact that these pursuits are essential for personal success and societal advance, leads to new American values regarding science and knowledge.

VALUE CHANGES AND THE SUPER-PATRIOTS

The specific manifestations of super-patriot opposition to many contemporary changes in values are found in earlier portions of this selection, but it seems appropriate to review some of them as they are suggested by the changes cited above. Super-patriot ideology is clear in its concern for the maximization of individual effort, initiative, and reward. Man able to "make it on his own," to grow and work unfettered by the demands of friends and colleagues or the ties of bureaucracies and governments, represents an ideal to the super-patriot. In this context, super-patriots often are opposed to modern conceptions of the need to "get along" with others. Getting along in school, in foreign affairs, or in morality is seen as a potential diminution of man's unique and American heritage. Current child-rearing practices seem, for the super-patriot, to lack a concern for the adequate training of discipline and respect. In this context, discipline is not seen to exclude love and affection, but rather it is seen as a means to achieve them without sacrificing other aspects of human development.

The revolution in knowledge has, according to some super-patriots, caused us to turn away from reliance upon eternal truths and cherished traditions. A greater respect for tradition than for scientific truth typifies the super-patriot ideology. And as tradition lends order to the world, super-patriots also select the maintenance of social order as a keystone to their personal and societal values. Physical as well as moral order is seen as absolutely essential, and moreover, should be primary concerns if America is to survive and preserve as a people.

It must be clear that the value shifts we have been discussing are by no means monolithically accepted and followed by all Americans. And certainly super-patriots are not the only groups or individuals who oppose these movements. Although these trends represent the major movements in American life, there are clearly other, and often countervailing, trends as well. Differential exposure to trends, and different socialization experiences, will help create different personality and ideological styles, and therefore different potential responses to social change.

These changes in the social structure and normative themes of society pose a variety of strains on many Americans. One major strain is felt at the level of psychological identity; another concerns social roles and social behavior; a third involves personal economic survival and security; a fourth primarily concerns social status and the protection of prestige and position; and a fifth involves a firmly held ideology. We have, up to now, documented some of the changing themes and structures and some typical super-patriot responses to them. We now explore the nature and extent of some of these personal and social strains as they are found in the sample of super-patriots who were interviewed.

CHARACTERISTICS OF SOME SUPER-PATRIOTS

The survey into the cultural backgrounds, social roles, and personal styles of midwestern super-patriots was achieved through an intensive two-hour interview. In general, the individuals who were interviewed and categorized as super-patriots were no more alike than leftists or active political moderates. They came from a variety of cultural backgrounds and social strata, and often exhibited quite divergent personal styles. They appeared to join groups for various reasons and thereby gained different personal satisfactions from participation. Some of the wide variety of group memberships represented by persons in this sample included The John Birch Society, The Conservative Federation, The Independent American Party, and The Christian Anti-Communism Crusade.

There are some things that the super-patriots we interviewed clearly were not, and some of these negative results may serve to clarify or dispel common stereotypes. For instance, the super-patriots were not generally psychotic, irrational, or severely disturbed. Most of them seemed to be pleasant, considerate, and law-abiding. They were comfortable and happy with their familial relations and very much in touch with the relationships and events in their interpersonal spheres. The interviews also indicated that they were not suffering from excessive anomie and did not feel especially powerless; indeed, just as many conservatives and moderates felt as powerless as did the super-patriots. Generally, the super-patriots were of no particular age or social status. Our sample included college students, young marrieds, middle-aged, and older persons. They ranged from lower class or lower-middle class to upper-middle or upper class. Further, within this Midwestern sample, they appeared to originate in no particular geographical or ecological region. These negative findings may be helpful in placing this phenomenon in proper perspective, a perspective that does not permit seeing super-patriots as a disturbed or mentally ill minority of "kooks."

But if the above are examples of what they are not, what then are some of the things that they are? The following characteristics did distinguish the super-patriots we interviewed from the conservatives and the moderates in the same sample.

1. Super-Patriots were more often religiously fundamentalistic and pietistically moralistic.

We asked a few questions to measure the degree of religious fundamentalism of the respondents. These questions had to do with belief in God, belief in an afterlife, belief that in the afterlife some people will be punished and others rewarded by God, and belief that the Bible is God's word and therefore completely and literally true. Fundamentalists were defined as those who agreed strongly with all of these items. Modernists disagreed that the Bible is literally true and that punishment occurs in the afterlife, but still agreed that God and an afterlife do exist, while nonbelievers disagreed with all questions. We found 72 percent of the super-patriots to be fundamentalists, compared with 49 percent of the conservatives and 32 percent of the moderates. On the other hand, only

28 percent of super-patriots were classifiable as modernists, against 46 percent of the conservatives and 62 percent of the moderates. A very few of the respondents, 5 percent of the conservatives, 6 percent of the moderates, and none of the super-patriots were nonbelievers.

Along with this religious fundamentalism, there were other indications that the super-patriots were very pietistic and moralistic. Answers to one question in particular indicated a strong aversion to emphasizing pleasures of the senses; for instance, we asked the interviewees to agree or disagree with, "Since life is so short, we might as well eat, drink, and be merry, and not worry too much about what happens to the world." Most respondents tended to disagree with this statement, but 72 percent of the super-patriots, 31 percent of the conservatives, and 26 percent of the moderates disagreed strongly.

Super-patriots' concern for traditional morality and for the moral basis of many aspects of their lives was illustrated in several other ways. We asked the respondents: "Who are the three greatest living Americans? What is it about him or her that is great?" The person most frequently named by the super-patriots was General Douglas MacArthur.[11] But regardless of the choice of person, the reasons for the choice differed greatly between the super-patriots, and the others. Super-patriots differed from the conservatives and the moderates in that they more often contributed greatness to MacArthur on the basis of "his strong moral character," or "his fighting for his principles." Conservatives and moderates who suggested MacArthur, most often did so on the basis of his "service to his country," "great intellect," or "brilliant generalship." When the responses to this question were categorized according to four different images of greatness—power, achievement, humanitarian service, and moral principles and character—the super-patriots overwhelmingly identified with the dimensions of either power or moral character imagery. Conservatives and moderates, on the other hand, much more often chose images of greatness connected with achievement and humanitarian service.

In another, somewhat related, question respondents were asked, "How would you wish your son to be different from you?" The most frequent responses for the entire sample were "more educated" and "in no ways." One outstanding difference between the super-patriots and the others was the super-patriot emphasis on "character improvement." Twenty-five percent of the super-patriots mentioned this moral growth dimension, against only 5 percent of the conservatives and the moderates combined.

2. Super-Patriots were more dogmatic and stereotypic in their cognitive styles.

Those persons categorized as super-patriots scored higher than con-

---

[11] The interviews were all conducted in the early spring of 1964, prior to MacArthur's death.

servatives and moderates on a series of items taken from Rokeach's dogmatism scale.[12] Over 70 percent of the super-patriots scored above the median on the dogmatism scale, while only about 40 percent of the conservatives and the moderates scored in a similar manner. The three groups were also tested on the F scale for authoritarianism, but the same strong differences did not hold. About 55 percent of the super-patriots and 42 percent of the conservatives scored above the median. These differences, while interesting, were not significant, and not nearly as potent as the differences in dogmatism scores.

Additional data analyses were executed to observe more closely the relationships between dogmatism and super-patriotism. We found, for instance, that dogmatism and super-patriotism were most closely related to younger persons between the ages of 20 and 39 and to older persons over 60. There was no indication that the super-patriots between the ages of 40 and 59 were especially dogmatic. Furthermore, dogmatism and super-patriotism were more highly related to persons with farm backgrounds than they were to those who had never lived on a farm. The relationships between dogmatism and super-patriotism were stronger for those persons who were dissatisfied with their jobs. This coincides with the older population as well, highlighting the relatively less satisfactory occupational roles and more constrained cognitive limits of older super-patriots.

The tendency for super-patriots to think stereotypically and to reduce differences and information available in the environment were also indicated. The interview asked, "Some people feel Russia and Communist China are together in an international conspiracy, others feel they are fighting with each other. Do you feel that the differences between Communist Russia and Communist China are 'great,' 'somewhat,' or 'small'?" Sixty-seven percent of the super-patriots, contrasted with 39 percent of the conservatives and 16 percent of the moderates, saw the differences as small. On the other hand, 65 percent of the moderates, 42 percent of the conservatives, and 18 percent of the super-patriots saw the difference as great. Several of the super-patriots added to their perception of minimal differences in commenting, "They're both the same, the Kremlin is the head of both."

Answers to other questions indicated that the super-patriots thought of Jews in a stereotypic manner. They more often strongly agreed that: "In general, Jews are pretty much alike," "Jewish districts in cities are the results of clannishness," and "It is wrong for Jews and non-Jews to intermarry." This data does not mean necessarily that super-patriots were anti-Semitic; although they were prone to making such generalizations, another key element of the anti-Semitic syndrome—that of emotional

---

[12] M. Rokeach, *The Open and Closed Mind* (New York: Basic Books, Inc., 1960).

fervor or hatred—did not appear to be characteristic. In both these areas of foreign affairs and ethnic identifications, stereotypy and information simplification seemed to be general characteristics of super-patriots.

3. Super-Patriots were more concerned with income and security as occupational rewards.

The interviews indicated that super-patriots were typically more concerned with economic and financial rewards and job security, and less concerned with status advancement or interpersonal or affiliative rewards in their occupations. When we asked the respondents to choose the most important factors they looked for in a job, five major categories emerged: "income and security," "achievement and advancement," "friendly co-workers," "making a contribution," and "publicity." Super-patriots most often chose "income and security" as their most important motivator. Conservatives and moderates, in contrast, tended to focus on "friendly co-workers" or "making a contribution" as occupational rewards. Super-patriots and others equally answered "achievement and advancement." Other conversations about job roles and rewards indicated that, in general, super-patriots were much less concerned about the interpersonal aspects of their occupations than were conservatives and moderates.

4. Super-Patriots were more concerned with international and national affairs.

The data indicated consistently that the super-patriots were much more concerned and knowledgeable about national and international events and policies than were the others. The first series of questions in the interview had to do with feelings of happiness or worry about various events. Specifically, we asked: "What are some of the things you worry about these days?" Gurin, Veroff, and Feld found that about 13 percent of their random interviewees were concerned about world conditions and national issues and affairs.[13] Most respondents in their national study were chiefly concerned with family finances, children's education, health, and so on. In our study, we naturally would have expected more respondents to choose international and national affairs because of the set presented to them during the interview. Despite this contextual factor, however, we found the super-patriots to be much more concerned about these more "distal" events than were other respondents. Seventy-three percent of the super-patriots, as compared with 62 percent of the conservatives and 43 percent of the moderates, responded with concerns about world conditions and domestic affairs. This tendency may reflect a super-patriot disposition to externalize conflicts and project distress onto distant and macrocosmic phenomena in the environment.

---

[13] G. Gurin, J. Veroff, and S. Feld, *Americans View Their Mental Health* (New York: Basic Books, Inc., 1960).

DIFFERENT SOCIAL-PSYCHOLOGICAL PATTERNS
AMONG SUPER-PATRIOTS

Despite the interest and value of these general differences between super-patriots and other portions of our sample, some of the differences among the super-patriots themselves were even more provocative. For a more refined analysis, the entire sample was divided into three income levels as indications of social status and into three different age levels. The three status levels were: families with incomes below $5,000; families with incomes between $5,000 and $10,000; and finally those with annual incomes above $10,000. Twenty-three percent of the sample was in the lowest category, 48 percent in the middle category, and 29 percent in the highest category. The median income of the super-patriot group was slightly higher than the national average. Certain occupation categories, of course, coincide with these income levels: persons in the lowest-income groups were most often housewives, retirees, or part-time manual and clerical workers; those in the middle-income group were usually engaged in clerical, service, and skilled trades occupations; and persons in the highest-income group included salesmen, engineers, lawyers, and other professionals.

Almost all of the super-patriots in the lowest-income category were over 60 years of age; most of them were retirees, or the widows of retirees. By and large they had grown up on farms and spent their formative years in relatively poor and low-status families. Farm families undoubtedly were among the last to receive the norms about new child development patterns generated by the mainstream of the middle-class American society.[14] Thus, both because of age and geography, many of these super-patriots underwent early socialization experiences that were divergent from those of their more urbanized peers and that are quite different from more contemporary emphases. Inasmuch as these patterns are reflected in values and cultural styles, we can see how these older persons would be alienated from modern youth and societal trends.

As is typical of persons of this age, their education levels were the lowest in the sample. All but one of these super-patriots demonstrated high levels of dogmatic and stereotypic thinking. Although dogmatism was significantly related in general to super-patriotism, it was associated most strongly in this lowest income group. A rather typical response from one of these aged, lowly educated, dogmatic super-patriots was that he "felt very strongly about many, many issues." Another said he was "100 percent against socialism, 100 percent against the U.N., and 100 percent against the League of Women Voters because women should stay in the home." It may be that dogmatic conceptual patterns coupled with a low education produce a kind of boredom and few alternatives for the satisfactory use

---

[14] Bronfenbrenner, pp. 411–412.

of one's time at or near the end of an unsatisfactory occupational career. Involvement in super-patriot groups may be a means of asserting oneself, or of being involved in something again. For these lesser educated and dogmatic people, super-patriotism may be a means of escaping the ennui and disengagement of retirement.

Indeed, some of these older people manifested signs of pessimism, hopelessness, and despair which were not at all typical of most super-patriots who were interviewed. The anticipation, or expectation, of personal or societal failure was quite prevalent, with one person likening "Noah's flood" to what might befall us today. Others showed overt dissatisfaction and frustration with the products of their occupational careers. One widow said that she and her husband had struggled and saved all their lives, and she still had nothing. She had very little money, did not wish to ask anyone for help, and was sure that, "something's wrong somewhere." One retiree, an ex-farmer, claimed that he was forced out of his semiskilled job by the bureaucrats and intellectuals who were speeding everything up. This man viewed psychology and psychologists as alien, and before his retirement had been a devotee of both Gerald L. K. Smith and Senator Joseph McCarthy. Since he had retired, he had had the time and opportunity to join six conservative organizations and to write numerous letters to his congressman. He told the interviewer that he didn't fully realize what his country meant to him until he retired. His association with openly anti-Semitic organizations was atypical for most of the super-patriots interviewed, but his energy and participation levels were common.

The lowest-income super-patriots, in summary, often were dogmatic and somewhat frustrated about their careers. Generally, they were older, most of them approaching the end of unsatisfactory occupational careers. They were pessimistic about the future and reflected a hopelessness and powerlessness in their views of the nation. Without education, yet valuing it, they sought additional knowledge by reading, listening to tapes of extremist speakers, and forming into discussion groups. Their continual existence in low-status roles and environments supported their desire for greater security, both in their personal lives and in their view of the nation and the world.

The super-patriots in the middle-income group generally were either over 60 years of age or between 20 and 39 years, and the younger age group was more common. These super-patriots tended to show a marked inconsistency between their income level and educational status, with income being disproportionately higher than educational levels. In the non–super-patriot portion of the sample, persons of this age were much more likely to have higher education than income levels. These super-patriots' form of status inconsistency, highlighted by the finding that they were more often high-school dropouts, was accompanied by inferior feelings about educational skills and strong anti-intellectual attitudes. Knowledge of and experience in extremist groups may have added to their feelings of competence and expertise about community and national affairs. Such perceived expertise may have facilitated this group's expressed defiance of the liberal intellectual elites and disparagement of institutions of higher learning. Many of them saw colleges as being infested with left-wing intellectuals and as destroying parts of our traditional ways of life. Young people were described as becoming worse after college attendance—"they are manipulated by liberal and socialist professors," and "they are taught more and understand less."

Status and mobility tensions were more evident among these super-patriots, because they more often came from lower- or upper-status family backgrounds than from their own middle-income group. Coming from such social backgrounds, they manifested a variety of intergenerational economic mobility patterns, with both upward and downward mobility being strongly associated with super-patriotism. Income, rather than sheer security, seemed to be more relevant for them when talking about their job choices and satisfactions. The role strains and psychological adjustments necessitated by substantial status mobility must have set up inconsistencies between material and status satisfactions. Even though he enjoyed relatively satisfactory material comfort, one super-patriot stated: "I am an overconfident son-of-a-bitch and don't worry about being fired; I would like more money and recognition for my work."

These middle-income super-patriots also were likely to be religious fundamentalists who went to church often and who tended to be very moralistic. They were very concerned about what they viewed as immoral policies and events as well as the questionable moral conduct of all Americans. It appeared that, for these people, involvement in super-patriot groups may present an outlet for their status anxieties within a framework compatible with their moralistic and dogmatic view of the world.

The highest-income super-patriots generally tended to be between the ages of 35 and 50 years. They were markedly upwardly mobile, strongly fundamentalist, highly dogmatic, and often from farm or rural backgrounds. This cluster of rural background and observant religious fundamentalism was accompanied by a dominant concern for moral issues, for the role of morality in public affairs, and for the preservation of principles and moral values in public and private conduct.

In contrast to some of the moral confusion, pessimism, lostness, and frustration of the lowest-income super-patriots, these upper-income persons were motivated by their clarity and their engagement in moral protestation and confrontation of contemporary trends. An example of this approach to the world was found in one super-patriot's response to the question of what makes a good American. "A good American," he replied, "is a Christian who attends church regularly and who is informed about important political issues of the country. He should always vote, obey laws, and pay taxes."

Another upper-income super-patriot was disturbed by certain aspects of the news and thus strongly expressed his views: "Amorality is creeping more and more into the media of press or TV and radio. There are pressures by certain groups who only want their personal gain." The concern for morality was also expressed in connection with views of mental health programs and psychological services in the schools: "Rather than psychology in the schools, what is needed is a return to capital or corporal punishment and stronger courts."

While these highest-income super-patriots predominantly were reared in middle-income families, they obviously had "made good" financially. Most had moved upward in status from their generational families and were successful in bureaucratic-managerial and entreprenurial-professional roles. Perhaps the social strains and adjustments incumbent upon movement into the urban technocratic system is partly responsible for the highlighting of value conflicts felt by these super-patriots. For many of this group, entrance into super-patriot roles was a partisan form of community participation and political expression—it did not seem to be designed to fill needs for new meaning, new roles, or new friends. These super-patriots had been socially and financially successful, and unlike their counterparts of lower status, they did not express major needs for security and more income.

Age was also an important factor in differentiating the super-patriots in this sample. The middle-aged ones, between 25 and 50, in general were experiencing rapid status and geographic mobility. As already noted, some of the middle-income super-patriots had moved both up and down the status ladder, while the high-income super-patriots mostly had moved upward. Many of these middle-aged persons' incomes were higher than their formal educations would warrant, and this income-education inconsistency was often associated with a fervent anti-intellectualism. Other personal characteristics included strong commitments to fundamentalist religious beliefs, moralistic and dogmatic styles of thought, as well as concerns about power, income, and moral character. Such personality styles were not generally facilitative of adjustment in a rapidly changing and complex social order. Involvement in right-wing organizations may have satisfied such persons' needs by giving them a sense of intellectual stature, by reducing some of the complexities of our times, and by firmly placing them on the side of moralistic and principled politics.

The older persons, those over 55, were somewhat different. Many of them were retired and had very low incomes. They had not led very successful or satisfactory careers, and harbored a deep wish for more education and greater security. Joining right-wing groups generally enhanced their sense of personal worth and provided additional dimensions of meaning in a confusing world. Furthermore, right-wing groups seemed to reduce the boredom brought about by little education and an inability to use leisure time effectively.

VALUE-TENSIONS AND SUPER-PATRIOTISM

A major source of tension experienced by super-patriots seemed to be the degree of "mismatch" or discrepancy between their values and the major value trends of the American society. The interviews indicated that super-patriots differed from other Americans on many deeply cherished values and especially in the different ways that even common values were implemented in policy and behavior. Moreover, the super-patriots were aware of such differences. These differences are made more crucial by the super-patriots' serious concern about morality and moral values. A value discrepancy, the realization of the discrepancy, and the feeling that such a discrepancy is important, all combine to generate an active protest movement of people who are concerned with resistance to the ideological contradictions to, and encroachments upon, their firmly held values.

It is not merely ideological discrepancies that are involved, but a psychological realization that one is out of step with contemporary morality, or vice versa. The super-patriot understands the situation and reduces tensions by perceiving the society's current trends as being out of step with not only his personal moral code, but with the society's own ultimate verities. Thus, super-patriot positions and fervor are not promulgated in the name of some individualistically generated ideology or sectarian system of values, nor are they proffered as the pathway to a new utopia. Rather, they are presented as being this society's own initial commitments, commitments now being eroded and altered. The super-patriot perceives his end of this evaluative dissonance from a stance of righteous moral stability and indignation in the face of societal change and corruption. In the name of the original moral order, he wishes to retain adherence to a given code of norms and practices. This represents one of the basic reasons that nationalism and patriotism play such an important role in this movement—super-patriots see themselves as the truest Americans, seeking to return a deviant system to its more fundamental and original posture.

This analysis in no way contradicts, or substitutes for, the foregoing discussions of the personality predispositions and social role factors involved in super-patriotism. Rather it complements those perspectives by suggesting that for some kinds of people, in certain role situations, in this changing society, it is precisely the phenomena of evaluative mismatching or value discrepancy that produces the tension which leads to this particular form of symbolic expression and protest.

A focus upon the dynamic contribution of psychological aberration, intellectual obsolescence, cognitive styles, status decrystallization, or political impotence does indeed highlight some of the characteristics of contemporary super-patriotism. But these variables are clearly not typical of a significantly large number of super-patriots in our sample. Moreover, in the hands of some observers, these constructs often serve to explain away rather than confront the phenomena of super-patriotism as an ideological protest framed in political terms. For although ideology and values may serve many psychic masters, it may also *be* master. The super-patriot's realization of, and attempts to redress, his value mismatching presents the rest of the society with a clear strain on their own sense of the limits of political pluralism. And at this level, super-patriotism must be seen *as* a political phenomenon *in* political terms.

CONCLUSION

Super-patriotism in this country will not soon end. The political and social conditions necessary for its continuing growth are clearly present in the shape of the future. The further development and maturity of an affluent society will create greater status strains for middle-income groups, especially those with educations insufficient for a highly automated economy. Also, in the years to come, more successful young professionals who have migrated from small towns to the larger (and ever-larger) urban complexes will find that their status concerns can be met, and their moral value concerns accepted, in right-wing extremist organizations.

The future will bring more early retirees, some of whom will barely be able to make ends meet. Many of these people may work out their frustrations and disappointments, and use their new leisure time, by venturing into politics as an avocation. They will be responsive to the attractions of super-patriotism in much the same way as the dogmatic, frustrated, moralistic, and low-income persons studied in this selection.

In addition to the expanding pools of people subject to these social strains, we can expect that the pace of domestic change will increase, not decrease. Rapid domestic changes will continue; and the interdependent and threatening character of domestic crises and inter-national dilemmas is likely to further create and heighten material, status, and value cleavages in the population. The great concern for moral values demonstrates that value conflicts, as well as various status strains, economic discomforts, and psychological styles, are at work in the genesis of contemporary super-patriotism. The fact that current super-patriot organizations attract men and women from such diverse social backgrounds and strata, and with such widely divergent personal styles, suggests that they will have longer staying power and influence than the single issues and single-class movements of the past.

Social and Psychological Determinants of Radical Rightism*

IRA S. ROHTER

INTRODUCTION

WHO ARE THE RADICAL RIGHTISTS?

Considerable confusion surrounds terms such as "radical rightists," "extremists," "right-wingers," "ultra-rightists," "super-patriots," and the like.[1] They have been used so indiscriminantly that a potpourri of orga-

* While my debts are many, I would especially like to thank Professor Frank Pinner for his constant encouragement, his willingness to read and comment in detail on several drafts of this long study, and most importantly, his constant emphasis on conceptual clarity and correct use of the English language.

[1] Throughout this study "radical right*ism*" will be used to identify the particular set of beliefs which characterize this movement; "right*ists*" refers to individuals who subscribe to these beliefs. The exact nature of these beliefs is spelled out in the following paragraphs.

nizations and individuals advocating views ranging from classic laissez-faire economics (the American Economic Foundation) to openly promulgated racial hatred and violence (the American Nazi Party, the Ku Klux Klan) have all fallen under the rightist label. The more analytical literature, while generally less polemical, is no less ambiguous about who is a rightist, and what exactly constitutes "radical rightism" or its synonyms.[2] Some analysts, for example, equate rightism with a rejection of democracy, civil liberties, and the basic norms of the American political system. Others see rightism as a fundamental and intense opposition to the social and economic changes this country has undergone during the past 30 years. Still other commentators (and sometimes the same ones) characterize radical rightism as a "protest movement," appealing to "alienated" and "dispossessed" individuals and classes, with certain distinctive ideological orientations (nationalism, isolationism, xenophobia, anticommunism).[3]

Such definitions, which try to combine ideologies, appeals, and sociological characterizations, are patently inadequate for the empirical study of radical rightism. They hopelessly intertwine different levels of analysis, confusing the *dependent* variable (indicators which allow rightists and

---

[2] Among the most valuable scholarly works on the radical right are: Daniel Bell (ed.), *The Radical Right* (New York: Doubleday & Company, Inc., 1963), which contains analytically oriented articles by Bell, Seymour Lipset, Richard Hofstadter, David Riesman and Nathan Glazer, Alan Westin, and Talcott Parsons; the entire issue of *The Journal of Social Issues* devoted to "American Political Extremism in the 1960's," *19* (April 1963); J. Allen Broyles, *The John Birch Society* (Boston: The Beacon Press, 1964); R. E. Ellsworth and S. M. Harris, *The American Right Wing* (Washington, D.C.: Public Affairs Press, 1962), an excellent summary of rightist views; and Richard Hofstadter, *The Paranoid Style in American Politics* (New York: Alfred A. Knopf, 1965).

Valuable substantive information on the right is provided by: Arnold Forster and Benjamin Epstein, *Danger on the Right* (New York: Random House, Inc., 1964), *Report on The John Birch Society—1966* (New York: Random House, Inc., 1966), and *The Radical Right* (New York: Random House, Inc., 1967), based on data collected by the Anti-Defamation League; Harry Overstreet and Bonaro Overstreet, *The Strange Tactics of Extremism* (New York: W. W. Norton & Company, Inc., 1964); Fred J. Cook, "The Ultras: Aims, Affiliations and Finances of the Radical Right," *The Nation, 30* (June 30, 1962), p. 68 ff.

[3] For specific discussions of the problems of defining rightism see: R. Schmuck and M. Chesler, "On Super-Patriotism: A Definition and Analysis," *J. Social Issues, 19* (1963), 31–50; G. B. Rush, "Toward a Definition of the Extreme Right," *Pacific Sociol. Rev., 6* (1963), 64–73; R. Hofstadter, "The Pseudo-Conservative Revolt—1955," in Bell (ed.), pp. 63–79; B. Green, and others, "Responsible and Irresponsible Right-wing Groups: A Problem in Analysis," *J. Social Issues, 19* (1963), 3–17. Illustrative of the articles which use mixed definitions are: D. Bell, "Interpretations of American Politics—1955," in Bell (ed.); S. M. Lipset, "Social Stratification and 'Right-Wing Extremism'," *British J. Sociol., 10* (1959), 28; and G. Abcarian and S. M. Stanage, "Alienation and the Radical Right," *J. Politics, 27* (1965), 776–796.

The interested reader can find many additional biographical references in the articles listed here and in footnote 2.

nonrightists to be uniquely classified) with ideological *correlates* (the other beliefs which rightists hold) and *independent* variables such as social and personality attributes which *produce* (that is, causally determine) rightism. If these distinctions are not made and maintained, the ensuing analysis is likely to be theoretically muddled and empirically tautological.[4]

To keep our classes and types of variables separate, I suggest that radical rightism be uniquely defined by its core belief that the United States is deeply in the grip of a massive communist conspiracy which has significant influence on our government, schools, churches, mass media, and so on. Robert Welch, founder and leader of The John Birch Society, puts it this way:

> *Washington has been taken over!* By which we mean that Communist influences are now in full working control of our Federal Government . . . And we believe that the Communists and their dupes, allies, and agents, throughout this vast apparatus of government, now actually determine almost all policies, actions, and decisions.
> *And then look all around you!* For the Communist influence at the top reaches far outside of government. This influence, at times or in some areas amounting practically to control, is visibly well established and entrenched in the mass communications media, in books and magazine publishing, in education, in the labor movement, in the entertainment field, in many other divisions of our national life, and in a great many specific national organizations.[5]

This internal communist conspiracy theme allows us to cut through the divergent groups and ideas which all too often are indiscriminately lumped together and called "rightist." For example, the right covers many of its political arguments in conservative wrappings, and some observers in turn mistakenly *equate* conservatism with rightism, and vice versa.[6]

---

[4] For example, the discovery of a strong empirical association between being a radical rightist and being politically conservative may reflect an original definition of "rightism" which included among its defining characteristics "opposition to modern society." If as seems likely, this trait is a facet of conservatism, then the association noted above may represent simply subscale correlations within a multifacet measure of conservatism.

[5] This excerpt is taken from a pamphlet titled "The Time Has Come," printed and distributed by The John Birch Society, Belmont, Mass. (copyright 1964). Similar statements can be found in the published literature of all rightist organizations.

[6] This line of reasoning has two major faults; it is logically and empirically false. Even if we accept the proposition that all rightists are ideologically conservative, this does not allow the reverse inference that therefore all conservatives are rightists. Furthermore, the assertion that conservatism equals radical rightism is empirically unsupportable. Even if one's personal experiences with persons who are extremely conservative but not rightists does not provide adequate counter-evidence to reject this notion, one can go to more systematically collected data. Two recent studies of members of New York's Conservative Party clearly demonstrate that registrants and party leaders are ideologically conservative but display none of the

The *defining* characteristic of a radical rightist, in my judgment, is his belief that there exists a vast conspiracy of communists who have worked their way (often secretly) into positions of great power and influence throughout the world, and notably, in the internal affairs of the United States. Thus follow claims that the United States is from 60–80 percent controlled by communists,[7] and accusations that former Presidents, Secretaries of State, heads of the CIA and other government agencies, among many others, were (and still are) communist agents.[8]

AN OVERVIEW OF MAJOR HYPOTHESES

Why do so many Americans believe that a large number of our political leaders are outright traitors, and that the United States is tightly locked in the grip of a diabolical clique which is directly linked to crime and civil strife, decline of home life and religion, foreign policy mistakes, poor education, and a vast catalogue of so-called "Communistic" governmental programs such as the progressive income tax, social security, foreign aid, participation in the United Nations, Medicare, and the like?

These views *are* shared by many. Welch speaks officially for about 80,000 dues-paying members of the Birch Society, a well-run organization with

---

other traits loosely associated with radical rightists. Schoenberger's findings (presented in this collection) about registered Conservative voters are buttressed by Marcia Jaquith's study of Conservative county chairmen, club leaders, and executive committee members, "The Conservative Party of New York State: A Study of Third Party Leverage," unpublished honor's paper, Denison University, 1965. (I am indebted also to Professor Frederick Wirth, Miss Jaquith's adviser, for bringing these findings to my attention.) These leaders, who on several occasions showed themselves to be skillful politicians, were, at a specific *policy* level, conservative (the items were taken from H. McClosky, and others, "Issue Conflict and Consensus Among Party Leaders and Followers," *Amer. Pol. Sci. Rev.,* 54 (1960), 408–414). The majority of leaders, however, rejected nine out of twelve propositions which tap more *general* conservative values and orientations (taken from H. McClosky, "Conservatism and Personality," *Amer. Pol. Sci. Rev.,* 52 (1958), 29–30); they were generally well educated and employed in commensurate occupations, and a heightened concern with internal communism was not evident.

[7] *American Opinion, 8* (July–August 1965). This magazine is published by Robert Welch, Inc., and, although technically separate, is certainly a semiofficial voice of The John Birch Society.

[8] Welch originally wrote: "My firm belief that Dwight Eisenhower is a dedicated, conscious agent of the Communist conspiracy is based on an accumulation of detailed evidence so extensive and palpable that it seems to me to put this conviction beyond any doubt." This statement appeared in the original version of Welch's long, circulated letter called "The Politician." (*Christian Science Monitor,* April 1, 1961.) After a great deal of public furor (and intraorganization debate) Welch subsequently release a *revised* edition of "The Politician" in which this particular accusation is muted. See also footnote on p. 278 of *The Politician* (Belmont, Mass.: Belmont Publishing Co., 1963).

Welch also charges former Secretary of State John Dulles and his brother, Allen Dulles, former head of the CIA, among others, with being Communists. *The Blue Book of The John Birch Society* (Belmont, Mass.: Author, 1963), pp. *223–227.*

over 200 employees and more than 75 professional full-time field coordinators, with some 4000 local chapters spread throughout the United States. The Society operates five regional offices, supervises 350 American Opinion Bookstores which distribute books, periodicals, records, tapes, and films, and at the end of 1966 was spending more than five million dollars a year.[9] The Birch Society is only one of literally thousands of organized groups which subscribe to the "Welchian" kind of Communist conspiracy interpretation of history and current events. Membership in these right-wing groups exceeds 300,000 individuals, and these organizations, in total, spend more than $20 million a year advancing their particular views.[10]

Formal membership is only a partial indicator of the magnitude of rightist influence; national opinion surveys consistently show Birch Society sympathizers number between four and six million.[11] And this influence seems to be spreading. The right has stepped up its recruiting efforts, and propagates its views over 5000 radio broadcasts each week and through periodicals whose total circulation exceeds 500,000 copies each month.[12]

Most observers agree that this relatively well organized right-wing movement will continue to exert influence for some time to come. Two strategies for wielding direct political power are now being actively pursued: third party movements have already formed in Michigan, Illinois, Florida, Missouri, Georgia, Pennsylvania, Texas, California, Washington, Oklahoma, Arizona, and Connecticut. (Some evidence suggests Wallace's American Independence Party was the vehicle in 1968.) A second plan, advocated by The John Birch Society and the Liberty Lobby, is to capture the Republican Party by gaining control of precinct and state level organization.[13]

As this collection of articles shows, many answers to this question have been offered. I will try to explain why certain individuals are drawn to right-wing politics by employing a social psychological emphasis.[14] This approach draws particular attention to the manifold goals which men pursue through politics. While the desire for economic gain and material well-

---

[9] These figures are taken from Epstein and Forster, *The Radical Right*. They are consistent with other published data on the Society, including its own reports.

[10] A. Westin, "The Deadly Parallels: Radical Right and Radical Left," *Harper's Magazine*, April 1962, pp. 25–32; Epstein and Forster, *Report on the JBS*.

[11] Gallup Polls, reported in *Chicago Sun Times*, March 6, 1962; *Milwaukee Journal*, Dec. 19, 1965, and an Opinion Research Corporation Poll reported in the *New York Times*, July 31, 1964.

[12] Epstein and Forster, *Report on the JBS*.

[13] Epstein and Forster, especially chap. 4.

[14] I want to state clearly that I explicitly reject a *single* determinant theory which focuses exclusively on psychological or sociological or historical factors in accounting for radical rightism. The phrase "social psychological emphasis" simply means that I am attacking the problem by choosing to focus on the *individual*, as he is affected by a complex combination of his own intrapsychic needs and his social environment.

being is certainly high on any list of political motives,[15] often other, less physically tangible goals are sought in the political arena. In fact, some of the deepest struggles in American political life have emerged over issues not exclusively motivated by economic interests—such as race relations, civil liberties, and moral standards (Prohibition, Blue laws).[16]

The major thesis of this study is that radical rightism represents a form of political behavior resulting from the strongly socialized central values, beliefs, and personality needs of some individuals coming in conflict with certain modern trends in the larger society. More specifically, although still in general terms, rightism attracts adherents because it allows them, through its beliefs and activities, to express their considerable discontent with values and styles of life which differ from their own, to alleviate their sense of powerlessness and confusion, and to achieve a heightened sense of personal worthiness.

The major social and psychological benefits which accrue to rightists through their behavior may be usefully organized into four functional categories.[17] Rightism appeals to some persons because its beliefs provide a simple explanation for a world which seems bewildering and threatening. The right's distinctive conspiracy view thus serves a "knowledge" function by offering its adherents a relatively simple framework to account for those things which distress them and to suggest simple techniques to remedy them.

"Ego-defensive" needs, centering around the protection of self-esteem,

---

[15] As the authors of *The American Voter*, perhaps the major study of voting behavior, state: "economic interests have long been a primary motive impelling political action." A. Campbell and others (New York: John Wiley & Sons, Inc., 1960). The works of Seymour Lipset, V. O. Key, Robert Alford, and other empirically oriented political analysts, stress the strong relationships between socioeconomic position, political behavior, such as party preference, voting, stand on issues, and activity. Lipset's and Alford's comparative studies find the same relationships existing in many nations. Seymour Lipset, *Political Man* (New York: Doubleday & Company, Inc., 1960), V. O. Key, *Public Opinion and American Democracy* (New York: Alfred A. Knopf, 1961), Robert Alford, *Party and Society* (Skokie, Ill.: Rand McNally & Company, 1963).

[16] Discussions of the goals which men seek through politics are contained in Robert Lane, *Political Life* (New York: The Free Press, 1959), M. Brewster Smith, Jerome Bruner, and Robert White, *Opinions and Personality* (New York: John Wiley & Sons, Inc., 1965), and Lipset, *Political Man*, p. 232.

[17] These particular categories are taken from D. Katz's "The Functional Approach to the Study of Attitudes," *Public Opinion Quart., 29* (1960), 163–204. See also Smith, Bruner, and White, *Opinions and Personality*, esp. pp. 278–279. The classic extended discussion of this type of analysis is contained in Robert Merton's *Social Theory and Social Structure*, revised edition (New York: The Free Press, 1957), chaps. 1 and 2. For a logical analysis of functionalism and its many problems see Carl Hempel's "The Logic of Functional Analysis," in L. Gross (ed.), *Symposium on Sociological Theory* (New York: Harper & Row, Publishers, 1959), and Richard Rudner's *Philosophy of Social Science* (New York: Prentice-Hall, Inc., 1966), chapter 5. The use of functional categories in this paper is more heuristic than rigorous.

are met by the often employed rightist tactic of labeling people "communists." Rightists often find their personal status and values challenged by persons with higher social standing, or those who maintain different value-standards. In these trying circumstances the rightist is able to buttress his own positive self-identity by depicting his opponents as "communists," that is, disreputable people whose views are of no account.

The strident anticommunism and fervent patriotism which envelopes the movement allows rightists to express their central values in a status-enhancing manner and gain social acceptance from others who share similar views. This "value-expressive" function of rightism permits the typical rightist to display publicly the type of person he ideally conceives himself to be; virulent attacks against "communist-inspired" atheism and immorality demonstrate symbolically his personal religiosity and high moral standards; his intense nationalism fosters an elevating identification with "Americanism" and its virtues.

Participation in rightist meetings and activities also meets certain "utilitarian" or "adjustive" functions. Being associated with persons sharing similar feelings and common political views provides a network of supportive social relationships, an appeal particularly salient to socially marginal individuals. Older, retired people, for example, find something to busy themselves with—an ennobling cause. By working together on a common Ideal—the restoration of freedom to America—participants reinforce each other's sense of self-worth.

Before I try to analyze these major hypotheses, however, two points should be made quite clear. First, there is a danger that some readers will misinterpret the assertion that personal needs play an important part in the etiology of rightism as implying that our study reduces to one of political psychopathology. This is emphatically not true, and this imputation would be highly misleading. Most rightists seem to be reasonably well-functioning individuals who raise families, hold steady jobs, and in many ways are not terribly different from their neighbors. To say that they have anxieties and frustrations which they resolve in certain political forms, that they are attracted to radical rightism because it satisfies important social and personal needs, or that they selectively perceive information and express their feelings in radical political behavior, is simply to spell out the means which these particular individuals employ to cope with pressing needs. Everyone employs in his daily life such maneuvers, in one form or another, to maintain an emotional equilibrium; in fact, these outlets provide means for avoiding severe and disabling emotional difficulties.

Secondly, it must be emphasized that many diverse needs are satisfied through rightist behavior, and we must guard against trying to explain rightism (or any behavior for that matter) as caused exclusively by any *single* factor. Any social movement attracts persons with diverse needs, and each person's involvement in the movement gratifies a number of them.[18] The statistical nature of the analysis which follows only allows us to make generalization type statements that rightists are *disproportionately* more *x* or *y* or *z*, compared to nonrightists, which clouds some of the finer distinctions between necessary, sufficient, and contributory causes. Nevertheless the set of factors here introduced and explained below are hypothesized to be common to the genesis of rightist behavior.

RESEARCH DESIGN

THE SAMPLE

The empirical data for this study comes from structured interviews administered in 1965 to 169 rightists and 167 nonrightists (who served as a control-comparison group) living in the Pacific Northwest.[19] The 31-page questionnaire, administered by professional interviewers, sought information about social background, political and social activity, attitudes and values, and personality traits.[20]

Practical and theoretical considerations required us to construct a purposive sample of rightists to be interviewed.[21] The major criterion for inclusion in the sample was some form of public activity which seemed to indicate a radical right orientation. Some names were obtained from newspaper articles listing prominent members of The John Birch Society and Liberty Amendment Committee in a large northwestern city; others

---

[18] Hans Toch, *The Social Psychology of Social Movements* (Indianapolis: The Bobbs-Merrill Company, Inc., 1965); Hadley Cantril, *The Psychology of Mass Movements* (New York: John Wiley & Sons, Inc., 1941); Rudolf Herberle, *Social Movements* (New York: Appleton-Century-Crofts, 1951); William Kornhauser, *The Politics of Mass Society* (New York: The Free Press, 1959); Harold Lasswell, *Psychopathology and Politics* (Chicago: University of Chicago Press, 1930) and *World Politics and Personal Insecurity* (New York: Whittlesey House, 1935); Gabriel Almond, *The Appeals of Communism* (Princeton, N.J.: Princeton University Press, 1954).

[19] I would like to express my appreciation to the Center for the Advanced Study of Educational Administration at the University of Oregon for a research grant which greatly facilitated the collection and analysis of these data. I would also like to thank Dr. Philip Runkel and Dr. Harmon Zeigler for their help and encouragement during this period.

[20] Detailed descriptions of the procedures employed in the study are contained in *The Radical Rightists: An Empirical Study*, unpublished doctoral dissertation, Michigan State University, 1967. The interview schedule is also reproduced.

[21] Ideally a probability sample drawn from the total population of rightists would provide the best sample for generalizing the findings from this study. Several practical reasons prevented this however. Limited financial resources did not allow the drawing of a simple random sample of sufficient size to statistically analyze a rightist subsample. Membership lists of rightist organizations normally are guarded secrets, and besides, many ideological rightists are not organizational members. I thus had no choice but to follow the sampling design described.

were found through a content analysis of letters written over a four-year period to "letters to the editor" newspaper columns in two other northwestern cities, one of medium size located in the middle of the state, the other smaller and located in the southern part of the state. A sample of comparably active nonrightist citizens was developed in a similar manner; their names were also taken from referenda petitions, newspaper articles, and letters to newspapers. In addition to the constructed samples, a random sample drawn from a list of active members of a rightist organization gave us another 56 known rightists.[22]

THE DEPENDENT VARIABLE—THE RADICAL RIGHTISM INDEX

Radical rightists were defined earlier as persons who *believe*, to a large degree, in the existence of an internal communist conspiracy which has significantly infiltrated all levels of government and most social institutions in the United States, and who are *involved in action* to counter this communist threat. Applying this attitudinal and behavioral definition to the total sample, individuals were ranked on two empirical dimensions: their extent of belief in, and degree of activities directed against, internal communist subversion. This approach recognizes that some followers are more committed than others to the ideology and practices of rightism, and allows us to work with distinctions of degree (interval and ordinal scales) rather than a simple dichotomy of rightist-nonrightists (a nominal scale).

A multi-item, weighted index, based on 25 separate interview questions, was utilized to classify our respondents' degree of rightism; the 10 most heavily weighted item-indicators are: [23]

---

[22] The method used to collect the sample of rightists leaves much to be desired if, from the findings of this particular study, we wish to make valid generalizations about all rightists. Three basic problems characterize these data: the fact that only rightists living in one of several regions in the U.S. were interviewed, the likely bias inherent in interviewing people who publicly express their views, and the small size of the sample restricts severely statistical analysis using multiple controls to elaborate and specify relationships.

This last statement, about small sample sizes, refers to the classic problem of instituting multiple controls in a cross-tabulation type of analysis, which soon results in individual cells containing so few cases that meaningful interpretation is precluded. I am currently exploring strategies, using multiple correlation and regression techniques, which circumvent this problem. These results will be published in *The Radical Rightists* (Basic Books, Inc., in press).

While conclusive solutions to these problems must await the collection of additional data, it is my considered judgment that the social and psychological variables examined in this study are universal traits of all rightists, and thus are not importantly affected by geographical factors. As to the second major difficulty, are publicly active rightists importantly different from their non-active colleagues, a partial answer is given in the concluding section of the paper.

[23] This large number of items was used to increase the Index's reliability. Since some items seemed at face value better indicators of radical rightism than others, a weighting procedure was used to emphasize more significant items. The technique used to determine relative item weights is based on a logic which allows

1. Approve of the John Birch Society.
2. Talked often to other people, trying to warn them about communist influence.
3. Think there is communist influence in American government today.
4. Agree that "many of the textbooks used in our schools promote socialism."
5. Agree that "America is standing close to the brink of total disaster from communist subversion."
6. Think there is communist influence in American schools and colleges.
7. Voluntarily named other places (churches, labor unions, and so forth) where communists might be found.
8. Attended rallies, study groups, etc., where "anticommunist" or "extremely conservative" matters were discussed.
9. Attended rallies, study groups, etc., of radical-right or rightist-front organization.
10. Problem in America today particularly worried or concerned about is communism, socialism, or extreme conservative concerns.[24]

High scores on the Radical Rightism Index represent persons who both subscribe to subversion beliefs and implement them through action. Persons who share similar beliefs but who do not act on them have scores lower than activitists, but higher than those persons who hold few or no communist-conspiracy beliefs and are completely inactive.[25]

The validity of the Index as a measure of radical rightism is confirmed by three independent tests: the comparison of scores of persons originally

---

the data itself to determine the loadings. This was done by computing the total degree of association between a radical right-type response on each item run against radical right responses on all other type items, and using this degree of association as the weighting. An item's weight represents the extent which a rightist response on the item would predict a rightist response on other items. The wordings are abridgements of the original questions (see footnote 20).

[24] "Extreme conservative concerns" are responses mentioning the concentration of power in the government, its tyranny and usurpation of the Constitution, suppression of basic freedoms, and the like. Such rhetoric is often voiced by rightists, who then, of course, attribute them to internal communism subversion.

[25] This assumption of unidimensionality is supported by two different tests. The product-moment correlation between the belief-components of the Index and the full belief and activity Index score $= .97$. The degree of covariance can be interpreted as a measure of the goodness of fit of the regression lines for the two potentially distinct dimensions; the small amount of variance between the two lines (6 percent) shows that the amount of error in the assertion is quite low. In a separate analysis, Wes Skogan, employing a multivariate technique called discriminant function analysis (See Cooley and Lohnes, *Multivariate Procedures for the Behavioral Sciences*, New York: John Wiley & Sons, Inc., 1963) found, using only six attitudinal items which tap perception of internal communism, a *Gamma* of .87 between his classification of Rightists and Non-Rightists and the full Index scores (in quartiles), using 25 items.

classified as nonrightists, and organizational rightists (see Table 1); the relationship between Index scores and voting for Goldwater in the 1964 Presidential election (see Table 2); and the association between scores and conservative political beliefs (see Table 3).

TABLE 1

Index versus Original Sample Classification (percentaged down)

			NON-RIGHTIST	PROBABLY NON-RIGHTIST	PROBABLY RIGHTIST	ACTIVE ORGANIZA-TIONAL RIGHTIST
Radical	(low)	I	39	32	4	2
Rightism		II	44	36	10	7
Index		III	16	28	32	39
	(high)	IV	1	3	54	52
		(N)	(97)	(102)	(81)	(56)

TABLE 2

Index versus Candidate Voted for in 1964 Presidential Election (percentaged across)

			GOLDWATER	JOHNSON	OTHER	(N)
	(low)	I	19	76	5	(75)
Radical		II	36	58	7	(92)
Rightism		III	74	21	6	(92)
Index	(high)	IV	95	3	3	(77)

TABLE 3

Index versus Liberal-Conservative Attitudes (percentaged across) [a]

			LIBERAL		CONSERVATIVE		
			I	II	III	IV	(N)
	(low)	I	47	39	8	7	(75)
Radical		II	25	38	29	8	(92)
Rightism		III	15	21	35	29	(92)
Index	(high)	IV	1	9	31	58	(77)

[a] *Gamma* = .62

The first test, Table 1 is a case of validation against criterion groups. The other two tests represent examples of construct validity.[26] While not all Goldwater supporters were rightists, Goldwater did have the support of nearly all rightists. (Some rightists did not believe that any politician could effectively stop the Communist conspiracy. They believed the best strategy was to let Johnson win. Then, after a year or so of Great Society programs, the advances of communism would be so apparent that a real war against communism could be waged. These pessimistic rightists, who believe that activity would be somewhat futile, would fall into category III of the Index. This group does, in fact, manifest the greatest degree of feelings of personal powerlessness on an empirical measure.)

While I have argued that the beliefs of the radical right must be differentiated from those of legitimate conservatives, it is nevertheless the case that one facet of rightist ideology encompasses traditional conservative concerns. The items for the liberal-conservative scale are taken from the Survey Research Center's well known measure [27]; the scale was constructed using a type of item-analysis procedure, the resulting internal consistency, using a conservative version of the Kuder-Richardson equation for internal reliability,[28] was .83. Controlling for possible response-set effects did not significantly affect the relationship reported.[29]

Examination of Table 1 reveals that the two rightist subsamples (publicly active and organization members) are almost equally committed to rightist beliefs and participation in rightist activities. They are similarly matched on the two other correlates of rightism used to validate the Rightism Index —candidate preference and liberal-conservative political attitudes.[30] Later on I will delineate some important differences between the two types of Rightists, but for now they will be combined in the analysis. Persons who are *empirically* classified into the two upper quartiles of the Radical Rightism Index are called "Rightists" with a capital R; lower-case "rightists" refers to the generic aggregate of individuals associated with the political

---

[26] The classic discussion of "construct validity" is L. Cronbach and P. Meehl's "Construct Validity in Psychology Testing." This article, and several other important ones on types of validity, are reprinted in W. Mehrens and R. Ebel (eds.), *Principles of Educational and Psychological Measurement* (Skokie, Ill.: Rand McNally & Company, 1967).

[27] See A. Campbell and others, *The Voter Decides* (New York: Harper & Row, Publishers, 1954).

[28] G. F. Kuder and M. W. Richardson, "The Theory of Estimation of Test Reliability," *Psychometrika, 2* (1937), 151–160. (This article is also reprinted in Mehrens and Ebel.) For details of the scale construction technique, see footnote 20.

[29] See footnote 20.

[30] While there are in fact some differences between the two subsamples on the measure, the statistical probabilities that they represent random error are $P = .95$ for the liberal-conservatism scale (using the Kruskal-Wallis H-Test), and $P > .30$ for candidate preference (using the *Chi*-Square text). We thus accept the null hypothesis and reject the assertion that there are significant differences between the two groups *on these measures.*

movement called radical rightism. Upper-case "Non-Rightists" refers to individuals whose empirical scores put them in the lower two quartiles (I and II) of the Index.

ANALYSIS

While the right's beliefs about internal conspiracies are distorted renditions of the real world, they can be explained when we examine their holders' distinctive values, personality needs, and attitudes about their social circumstances. The goal of this study is to offer a theory of the etiology of rightist behavior, buttressed by empirical data whenever possible. Briefly, radical-rightist behavior and beliefs may be viewed conceptually as the end-products of an interaction between *personal discontentments* over values, status, and power and certain *personality factors*, particularly simplistic cognitive style and extrapunitiveness. Under these circumstances rightism allows its adherents:

1. to express their discontentments with rewarding personal and social consequences;
2. to enhance their sense of self-esteem;
3. to understand their social environment in terms psychologically congruent with their personal needs; and
4. to regain a sense of political effectiveness and control over their lives.

DISCONTENTMENTS

Values

The right's belief that the country is controlled by communists and their agents can be understood if we recognize the *affective* and *evaluative* beliefs which underlie this peculiar interpretation of social reality.[31] A dominant

---

[31] An analytical distinction is being made here between three *types* of beliefs: (1) *cognitive* beliefs, which consist of concepts and "knowledge" claims about the world; (2) *affective* beliefs, basically emotional responses to stimuli-objects; and (3) *evaluative* beliefs, which are essentially criteria or standards of preference (values). Cognitive, affective, and evaluative beliefs combine together and constitute *belief-systems*; particular types of organizations or cluster can be called ideologies, opinions, views, and orientations. M. Rokeach, *Beliefs, Attitudes, and Values* (San Francisco: Jossey-Bass, Inc., 1968).

See T. Parsons, *The Social System* (New York: The Free Press, 1951), chap. 8; M. J. Rosenberg, "Cognitive Structure and Attitudinal Affect," *J. Abnorm. Social Psychol.*, 53 (1956), 362–372; D. Katz, "Functional Approach to Study of Attitudes," N. Jenkins, "Affective Processes in Perception," *Psychol. Bull.*, 54 (1957), 100–127. For political applications of these distinctions see G. A. Almond and G. B. Powell, Jr., *Comparative Politics* (Boston: Little, Brown & Company, 1966); G. Almond and S. Verba, *The Civic Culture* (Princeton, N.J.: Princeton University Press, 1963); and A. Campbell and others, *The American Voter*, chap. 2.

characteristic of the right's programs and proposals is that they are heavily charged with *negative* affect; rightist groups and organizations are always advocating the repeal of this law or that, changing some practice or other, removing someone from office or position. A fundamental and intense hostility toward many facets of the current social and political order is one of the right's most distinctive characteristics, and one on which nearly all observers comment profusely.[32] The primary sources of these *affective* reactions are the rightists' *values*—emotionally charged standards, criteria, or rules, with deep psychological import, that in the case of the rightists press cognitive beliefs into their service. That is, when values are invested with considerable psychological significance, they greatly influence what stimuli are selected, how they are organized, and what meaning is imputed to them.[33]

The specific evaluative standards (values) which play such an important role in the rightists' reaction to today's social and political events stress religious morality, individualism, and the affirmation of hard work, saving, investing, and personal initiative, in sum, the Protestant Ethic.[34] People who believe strongly in these precepts see governmental activities in relief, health insurance, public housing, urban renewal, and other welfare measures leading, they believe, to a weakening of individual initiative and self-reliance. Politically, these ideas are, quite naturally, represented in demands that social security, Medicare, the progressive income tax, and government intervention in the economy be terminated.

Those who uphold traditional values are also deeply distressed by what they see as a decline in moral and religious principles in modern America. Crime, juvenile delinquency, obscene literature, corruption in politics and business, all are blamed on moral decay. This blight will not end, such persons believe, until proven religious, moral, and family practices of the past are again followed.[35]

---

[32] See references cited in footnotes 2 and 3.

[33] Two of the best discussions of values as influencers of behavior are: T. Parsons and E. A. Shils (eds.), *Toward a General Theory of Action* (Cambridge: Harvard University Press, 1951) and R. M. Williams, *American Society: A Sociological Interpretation*, 2d ed., revised (New York: Alfred A. Knopf, 1963), chap. 11.

[34] Max Weber, *The Protestant Ethic and the Spirit of Capitalism*, translated by Talcott Parsons (New York: Charles Scribner's Sons, 1958); also, Benton Johnson, "Ascetic Protestantism and Political Preference," *Public Opinion Quart., 26* (1962), 35–46.

[35] One need only recall Barry Goldwater's campaign speeches during the 1964 presidential election for political examples of this particular view of American life. Again and again Goldwater dwelled on the theme: "the moral fiber of the American people is beset by rot and decay." This explains, according to Goldwater and his followers, "wave after wave of crime in our streets and in our homes . . . riots and disorder in our cities . . ." and so forth. This speech, made at Prescott, Arizona, on Sept. 3, 1964, is quoted and analyzed in Richard Hofstadter, *The Paranoid Style in American Politics and Other Essays* (New York: Alfred A. Knopf, 1965), chap. 4, "Goldwater and the Pseudo-Conservative Politics."

While these values may be suited to rural and small-town life, to small businessmen and farmers, migration has brought into urban places and occupations an increasing number of persons raised with these values.[36] Finding their values repudiated in these more cosmopolitan environments, some of these people are attracted to rightism because it opposes and ideologically identifies as "Communistic" those aspects of a complex, modern society which are strange and disliked. Rightism provides a standard ("anti-Communism") behind which those who are intensely discontented with prevailing values and moral standards can rally.[37] Although "Communism" is the symbolic enemy, one primary function of rightism is its operation as a protest movement trying to counter the fact that America has moved away from Ascetic Protestant values.[38]

FINDINGS.   The Rightists we studied are strongly committed to traditional values and greatly disturbed over the values prevailing today. Rightists overwhelmingly subscribe to such statements as: "What this country needs most is a return to the simple virtues of individual initiative and self-reliance," "Thrift and industriousness are the most important traits a man should develop," and "What youth needs most is strict discipline, rugged determination, and the will to fight for family and country" (see Table 4).

------

[36] As Harold Laski put it in his classic observations about America (*The American Democracy*) (New York: The Viking Press, Inc., 1948): ". . . to work hard, to lead an orderly life, to have a name for integrity and fair dealing, not to spend one's substance in reckless display . . ." is part of the basic traditions of America. On the values of the independent entrepreneur and the farmer, see respectively, John Bunzel, *The American Small Businessman* (New York: Alfred A. Knopf, 1962), and Henry Smith, *Virgin Land: The American West as Symbol and Myth* (Cambridge: Harvard University Press, 1950) and E. Z. Vogt, *Modern Homesteaders* (Cambridge: Harvard University Press, 1955).

[37] This interpretation has been most developed in Seymour Lipset's "Backlash and Republican Prospects" (mimeographed paper, 1964) and Murray Havens, "The Radical Right in the Southwest: Community Response to Shifting Socio-Economic Patterns," paper delivered at the 1964 meetings of The American Political Science Association. See also Lipset's *Revolution and Counterrevolution: Change and Resistance in Social Structures* (New York: Basic Books, Inc., 1968), chapter 9.

[38] An insightful book on this type of phenomenon is J. R. Gusfield's *Symbolic Crusade: Status Politics and the American Temperance Movement* (Urbana: University of Illinois Press, 1963). The conflict between traditional values and more modern ones has been described in different ways. Some writers see it as a contest between "urban" and "rural" virtues, others as the struggle of tradition vs modernity, of "cosmopolitans" against "localities." David Riesman sees these conflicts between groups as "characterological struggles," since they are based primarily on cultural and ideological differences rather than on economic factors. David Riesman, *The Lonely Crowd* (New Haven, Conn.: Yale University Press, 1950); James Coleman, *Community Conflict* (New York: The Free Press, 1957); A. J. Vidich and J. Bensman, *Small Town in Mass Society* (New York: Doubleday & Company, Inc., 1960); Amitai Etzioni and Eva Etzioni (eds.), *Social Change* (New York: Basic Books, Inc., 1964), particularly part III, "The Modern Society"; Robert Merton, "Patterns of Influence: Local and Cosmopolitan Influentials," in *Social Theory and Social Structure.*

TABLE 4

*Traditional Values Scale*ᵃ *versus Radical Rightism Index*ᵇ
(percentaged across)

| DEGREE OF RADICAL RIGHTISM | | TRADITIONAL VALUES | | | | |
		(high) I	II	III	(low) IV	(N)
(low)	I	12	11	33	44	(75)
	II	17	26	29	27	(92)
	III	30	28	28	13	(92)
(high)	IV	30	36	27	7	(77)

ᵃ The other items in this scale are: "Too many people today are spending their money for unnecessary things, instead of saving or investing it for the future," "A man can't be respected unless he's worked hard for some important goal," and "Obedience and respect for authority are the most important virtues children should learn." The internal consistency of this scale (the Kuder-Richardson Coefficient) is .87.
ᵇ Kruskal-Wallis H-Test $= 41.5$, $P < .001$. *Gamma* $= .38$

Religiously our Rightists are greatly influenced by fundamentalism: 42 percent (compared to 17 percent of the Non-Rightists) attend churches of fundamentalist denominations, and their religious beliefs include "The Bible is God's word, and all that it says is true," and "In the next life people will be punished by God." [39] Fundamentalism is evidently an important source of the rightists' moral beliefs and fervor. Their writings bristle with indictments against "liberal theology" and the "social gospel," and prominent organizations such as Billy James Hargis's *Christian Crusade*, Carl McIntire's *Twentieth Century Reformation Hour*, Fred Schwarz's *Christian Anti-Communism Crusade*, and Edgar Bundy's *Church League of America*, are headed by fundamentalist ministers (or in the case of Schwarz, a former "lay" preacher) who combine Biblical rhetoric and anti-Communism.[40]

---

[39] The Index of Religious Fundamentalist Beliefs was drawn from G. Lenski's *The Religious Factor* (New York: Doubleday & Company, Inc., 1961). The association between the Fundamentalism and Rightists indexes, *Gamma*, is .31 (P < .001). The coding for fundamentalist church denominations was taken from B. Johnson's "Ascetic Protestantism and Political Preference in the Deep South," *Amer. J. Sociol.*, 49 (1964), No. 4.

[40] In "The Genesis of Political Radicalism: The Case of the Radical Right," in *Learning about Politics: Studies in Political Socialization*, edited by Roberta Sigel (New York: Random House, Inc., 1969), I systematically answer the question, "What in religious fundamentalism makes its adherents so ripe for radical rightism?" I propose, and offer empirical evidence and theoretical support for, two general answers: one, that fundamentalist values produce an ideological proclivity in its adherents to readily accept rightist political views, and second, that

Throughout the interviews our Rightists showed themselves to be individuals very disturbed by the disestablishment of their own values and their replacement by newer ones. We asked, "Are there any differences between what you believe should be the American way of life, and the way things are done in the country nowadays?" and "In what way are things different?" Rightists more frequently said "yes," ($P < .001$) [41] and gave answers which indicated that their dissatisfactions are rooted in current values and morals ($P < .001$). Typically, from the Rightists:

> Morality and standards are going bad; the American way of life is deteriorating because of a suppression of morality; we need a moral and spiritual revival among our leaders; we need to follow the Ten Commandments more.

Still more expression of value discontentments were elicited by the question, "To what extent do you think other people today share your beliefs about the importance of individual initiative, taking care of oneself more, respect for authority, and the other things just mentioned?" (This was asked just after being quizzed about their personal commitment to Protestant Ethic beliefs.) Again it is a disproportionate number of Rightists ($P < .02$) who specifically mention that the evident declining state of morality in this country showed them that many persons do not share their values.

> I am worried about the drift of our country; the amount of crime and disrespect for authority shows things are going the other way; we must

---

the cultural milieu of fundamentalism produces and reinforces, through socialization processes, authoritarian syndrome personality traits, which find in rightism a conducive political outlet.

Ralph Lord Roy's *Apostles of Discord* (Boston: The Beacon Press, 1953), although not current, still remains the best single work on these types of fundamentalist groups. For an updated discussion of contemporary groups, see his essay "Conflict from the Left and Right" in *Religion and Social Conflict*, edited by R. Lee and M. E. Marty (New York: Oxford University Press, 1964). For detailed discussions of rightist-fundamentalist groups and their leaders see Forster and Epstein, *Danger on the Right*; Overstreet and Overstreet, *The Strange Tactics of Extremism*; and J. H. Redekop, *The American Far Right: A Case Study of Billy James Hargis and the Christian Crusade* (Grand Rapids, Mich.: Wm. B. Eerdmans Publishing Co., 1968). For general discussions see David Danzig, "The Radical Right and the Rise of the Fundamentalist Minority," *Commentary*, April 1962; "Special Supplement on the Far Right," *The Reformed Journal*, Jan. 1965; and Richard Hofstadter, *The Paranoid Style in American Politics and Other Essays*.

[41] To conserve space, the table is not reproduced, but a probability statement is given which indicates the statistical likelihood that the relationship represents simply random sampling variation. The statement ($P < .001$) means that the probability of this particular difference having occurred by chance, given normal sampling error, is, in this instance, less than one in a thousand. Given these odds, we would usually conclude that the difference is statistically meaningful and thus worth noting.

Throughout the text the practice of listing probability estimates will be followed; complete tables are found in *The Radical Rightists: An Empirical Study*, unpublished doctoral dissertation, Michigan State University, 1967.

instill more emphasis on respect, integrity, and individual responsibility; parents aren't teaching their children the right things anymore.

Two fixed-item scales which explicitly measure evaluations of the state of current morality in the country and the teaching of traditional values in the schools show a striking monotonic relationship with the Rightism Index, with *Gammas* of .66 and .59 respectively (see Table 5). Statements which

TABLE 5

Moral Breakdown and Traditional School Values Scales versus Rightism Index (High and Low Quartiles Only, percentaged across)

| | MORAL BREAKDOWN [a] | | TRAD. SCHOOL VALUES [b] | |
	high	low	high	low
Non-Rightists (I)	2	57	3	49
Rightists (IV)	53	3	39	4
	Gamma = .66		*Gamma* = .59	

[a] *Moral Breakdown Scale items:* (1) Modern education is resulting in the loss of American moral values; (2) There has *not* been a general breakdown of moral standards in our country (reversed scoring); (3) What this country needs most is a return to love of country and old-fashioned patriotism; (4) If we could return to the religious, moral, and family values of the past, we could solve most of today's problems. Kuder-Richardson Coefficient = .87.

[b] *Traditional School Values Scale items:* (1) The schools should increase their emphasis on teaching Americanism; (2) We should increase the teaching of respect for authority in the school; (3) Modern education is resulting in the loss of American moral values. Kuder-Richardson Coefficient = .86.

drew emphatic agreement include: "[We now have] a general breakdown of moral standards in our country," "If we could return to the religious, moral, and family values of the past, we could solve most of today's social problems," and "Modern education is resulting in the loss of American moral values."

That traditional morality and values elements dominate many Rightists' perceptions of political and social reality also showed up in questions which had little evident connection to them. No matter what the topic—things they worried about, what community concerns they had, what qualities they admired in people—many Rightists tended to see them in value-laden terms.[42] Our findings are thus clear: Rightists are greatly dissatisfied with

---

[42] In all, 12 open-ended questions in the interviews elicited enough value-type responses to establish separate codes. In counting the number of such responses per interview, many more ($P < .001$) Rightists gave multiple responses than did Non-Rightists. (The mean number of such value responses per interview was .62 for

the values of contemporary American society because they adhere to the "old truths" and believe everyone else should "return" to them.

Status

The hypothesis that rightists are individuals experiencing severe discontentments or frustrations over their "status" in the community and nation is probably the most prevalent theme in the analytical literature on rightism.[43] The argument, essentially, is that for a variety of reasons, some persons who are either dissatisfied or insecure about their place ("status") in society or who have objective status incongruities such as low education coupled with high income, feel that others do not esteem them sufficiently, express their frustration over this difficulty, and compensate for it, by political and social acts which give them emotional identity and support.

The term "status" has several usages, but we are principally interested in the psychological consequences of a man's social status.[44] In this sense, the position a person occupies within his society's social stratification system significantly determines the approval, admiration, deference, and other forms of positive and negative evaluations he receives from others, and these social cues in turn greatly affect his sense of self-regard.[45] Many psy-

---

the Non-Rightists, and 1.2 for Rightists, although these figures obscure the distribution of multiple responses; for example, 42 percent of the Non-Rightists gave *no* value responses in their interviews, in contrast to 15 percent of the Rightists.)

[43] See Schmuck and Chesler, "On Super-Patriotism," and the articles in Bell (ed.), *The Radical Right*.

[44] See H. H. Hyman, "The Psychology of Status," *Arch. Psychol.* (1942), No. 269. For major reviews of status and the stratification system see Bernard Barber, *Social Stratification: A Comparative Analysis of Structure and Process* (New York: Harcourt, Brace & World, Inc. 1957); Joseph A. Kahl, *The American Class Structure* (New York: Holt, Rinehart and Winston, Inc. 1957); Reinhard Bendix and Seymour Lipset (eds.), *Class, Status and Power* (New York: The Free Press, 1953); and Milton Gordon, *Social Class in American Sociology* (Durham, N.C.: Duke University Press, 1958). An excellent synthesis is provided by R. Williams's *American Society: A Sociological Interpretation*.

[45] As used here, "status" is the socially defined measure of a man's prestige. Sociologists usually make an analytical distinction between the "prestige" which is associated with a particular social role or position and the "esteem" accorded for performing in a specific capacity. (Kingsley Davis, *Human Society* (New York: The Macmillan Company, 1949), chap. 4). Yet in the real world such fine distinctions are seldom made and people usually combine "prestige" and "esteem" into a single judgment when ranking others. (W. L. Warner, and others, *Social Class in America* (Chicago: Science Research Associates, 1949); A.B. Hollingshead, *Elmtown's Youth* (New York: John Wiley & Sons, Inc., 1949).

That the way an individual feels about himself is considerably determined by how other people judge him is not a new idea. C. H. Cooley, *Human Nature and the Social Order* (New York: Charles Scribner's Sons, 1902) referred to this process as the "looking-glass self": "the self that is most important is a reflection, largely, from the minds of others. . . ." George Herbert Mead similarly emphasized the processes of social appraisal involved in the individual's development of his self-image:

chologists consider the striving for self-regard (self-esteem, self-worth) as a primary psychological need.[46] Thus we can offer the psychological axiom that persons who feel downgraded or ignored defend themselves. Our corollary is that individuals who perceive or experience a significant discrepancy between their *socially* defined and *self*-defined prestige ranking will resist this state by adopting social maneuvers which restore their sense of self-regard. Persons experiencing relative status deprivation can be described as "status anxious" or "status frustrated," and may be drawn to radical rightism because its activities and ideology operate to heighten their threatened self-esteem.[47]

". . . the self arises in conduct, when the individual becomes a social object in experience to himself." (*Mind, Self, and Society* (Chicago: University of Chicago Press, 1934.)

[46] W. McDougall, *The Energies of Men* (New York: Charles Scribner's Sons, 1933); A. H. Maslow, *Motivation and Personality* (New York: Harper & Row, Publishers, 1954); H. A. Murray and others, *Explorations in Personality* (New York: Oxford University Press, 1938). Gordon Allport, a constant codifier of psychological literature on personality, states: ". . . the individual's desire for personal status is apparently insatiable. Whether we say that he longs for *prestige, self-respect, autonomy,* or *self-regard*, a dynamic factor of this order is apparently the strongest of his drives." ("The Psychology of Participation," *Psychol. Rev., 52* (1945), 122.)

[47] In a later section I discuss certain personality factors which seem to be necessary conditions for susceptibility to rightism, since obviously not all persons who experience status-frustrations are attracted. Psychological defense-mechanisms like rationalization, denial, and suppression can also be used to block feelings of relative inferiority. Or, the individual may endeavor to actually improve his social position and resultant prestige-rank by gaining more education, working harder, acquiring social skills, etc. So in the final analysis we are here talking only about a certain subgroup of status-frustrated individuals, who, for the reasons spelled out in this paper, adopt rightism as a strategy for enhancing their low subjective status.

This does not mean that the distribution of status-anxious individuals in the population is random. Indeed, the argument is that certain social groups contribute *disproportionately* to extremist movements because their situation in society exposes them disproportionately to status threats. (This assumes that the other factors which determine the response of political activism are relatively equally distributed among all segments of the population.)

Unfortunately, many analysts cast the status frustration thesis too broadly, without making these distinctions clear, and thus we find that almost all social groups, because they are either going up or down, or standing relatively still, have been catalogued at one time or another as predisposed toward extremist movements. (See Nelson Polsby's "Toward an Explanation of McCarthyism," in Polsby (ed.), *Politics and Social Life* (Boston: Houghton Mifflin Company, 1963), especially pp. 810–815, for an excellent discussion of this problem in the analysis of Senator Joseph McCarthy's supporters in the early 1950s.) Unless the multiple responses to frustration are considered (see references in footnote 85), and a clear effort is made toward explicating both the sources of discontent and why certain mechanisms are employed in resolving them, the status frustration explanation becomes so general that it is virtually worthless.

For elaboration of the important concept "relative deprivation" see Robert K. Merton and Alice S. Rossi, "Contributions to the Theory of Reference Group Behavior," in *Continuities in Social Research: Studies in the Scope and Method of "The American Soldier,"* edited by R. K. Merton and P. F. Lazarsfeld (New York: The Free Press, 1950).

Three categories of people who undergo status frustrations are relevant for our study of rightism: the *decliners*, the *newly arrived*, and the *value keepers*.

THE DECLINERS. The *decliners* are people in our modern, changing society who are going down in the social scale—undeservedly, as they see it.

Many criteria affect people's ranks in a prestige hierarchy. Varying with culture, nation, and even community, people are classified as superior or inferior on the basis of their family, authority, power, ownership of property, income, possessions, consumption patterns, style of life, occupation, skills, achievements, education, values and attitudes, race, ethnic background, and other personal attributes.[48] A man's occupation is an important measure of his social standing;[49] it provides him with an income which affects his style of living; it reflects his education; it tells something about his influence, the type of people he associates with, and is a gauge of his achievements. If a man's occupation declines in social standing, he may personally experience a loss of respect and, ultimately, self-esteem.

Such is the plight of many treated unkindly by recent social changes which have upset traditional status and power relationships. Modern technology and modern organizations increasingly require new skills, new orientations, more education. Those trained under different and outmoded disciplines, and those with insufficient or outdated educations, feel their positions becoming more and more insecure. Managerial and white-collar employees with anachronistic educations and dated skills thus find their social and occupational status seriously threatened.[50]

Also menaced by the vast social transformation taking place in modern America is the independent professional and entrepreneurial class. The independent physician, farm owner, real estate man, home builder, gas-station owner, and small businessman increasingly discover that status and influence are derived from association with large organizations; that technical knowledge and ability to coordinate group efforts are more valued than sheer hard work or individual initiative; that trying to survive in the shadows of giant corporations, large labor unions, and big government agencies is no simple task. College-educated professionals and corporate executives are taking over the small businessman's leadership role

---

[48] See references in footnote 44.

[49] W. L. Warner and P. S. Lunt, *The Social Life of a Modern Community*, Yankee City Series, vol. I (New Haven, Conn.: Yale University Press, 1941); Maryon K. Welch, "The Ranking of Occupations on the Basis of Social Status," *Occupations, 27* (1949), 237–241; Alex Inkeles and Peter Rossi, "National Comparisons of Occupational Prestige," *Amer. J. Sociol., 61* (1956), 329–339, Richard Centers, *The Psychology of Social Classes* (Princeton, N.J.: Princeton University Press, 1949); Barber; Kahl, chap. 3.

[50] Kahl, chap. 10; Daniel Bell, "The Dispossessed—1962," in Bell (ed.), *The Radical Right*.

in the community. He is being shoved aside; the hard work and independence on which he built his self-esteem and his concept of the good and righteous life becomes increasingly worthless. Briefly, in a society emphasizing concentration, centralization, and bigness, the independent businessmen and professionals find themselves more and more socially displaced.[51]

A similar process affects workers, both white- and blue-collar, displaced by new methods and machines. They, like their skills, are regarded as obsolete and therefore of little worth. The elderly and retired are in even a worse situation. No longer working, in a society which values productivity, and being old when youth and vitality are emphasized, they find themselves relegated to the ranks of the socially useless.[52]

As the actual status and influence of these groups declines, their consciousness of loss and rejection is made even more acute by the rise of those formerly considered low-class or rejected. An Irish Catholic, grandson of an immigrant, is elected president; a Negro "agitator" receives many honors and frequently visits the White House. Jews are found everywhere in prominent places and high office. The frustrations of these displaced groups are thus compounded by their awareness that formerly low-status immigrant, ethnic, religious, and racial groups are increasingly occupying important positions in industry and government.

Confronted by such changes, with their social and political status threatened by new groups rising to power, *declining status groups* become fertile sources of potential support for a political movement like radical rightism which opposes these disturbing social changes while allowing its adherents to feel respected and influential again.

THE NEWLY ARRIVED. Status frustrations occur not only in persons on the way down, but among those on the way up. There is almost always a lag between the time those who have risen quickly in economic position or occupation and achieve material success and the time when those who already possess high social status accept them as equals.[53] Thus arises an-

---

[51] Arthur Vidich and Joseph Bensman's *Small Town in Mass Society* (New York: Doubleday & Company, Inc., 1960) contains a vivid description of the plight of the small businessman in modern American society, which would seem generalizable to the urban scene as well. See also George Stone and William Form, "Instabilities in Status," *Amer. Sociol. Review, 18* (1953), 149–163; and Martin Trow, "Small Businessmen, Political Tolerance, and Support for McCarthy," *Amer. J. Sociol., 64* (1958), 279–286.

[52] See Frank Pinner, Paul Jacobs, and Philip Selznick, *Old Age and Political Behavior* (Berkeley, Calif.: University of California Press, 1959) for a discussion of status anxieties and their political consequences among the old.

[53] Bernard Berelson and Gary Steiner, in their book *Human Behavior: An Inventory of Scientific Findings* (New York: Harcourt, Brace & World, Inc., 1964), point out the universality of this kind of status lag: "As new groups come to positions of power and wealth in the society . . . prestige in the system of stratification attaches to them, but only with some lag; power and wealth are attained well before the commensurate prestige," p. 465.

other type of situation in which an individual's sense of self-regard is jeopardized because others fail to grant him the deference he believes his due. The newly mobile—people from humble origins, recent migrants to the cities, successful new small-businessmen and minor level semiprofessionals, and those who have moved upward from the factory to the white-collar class—often discover that a significant discrepancy remains between their material advancement and power within a particular enterprise and their influence and social standing in the community at large.

Other anxieties beset the newly arrived. For those who are employees, their influence is relatively transitory, without secure roots in property or established tradition.[54] With their status precariously linked to their occupational achievements, social change becomes threatening when lowered barriers, continued social mobility, and economic redistributions jeopardize their own, hard-won positions.[55] The attempt of the civil rights movement to attain better opportunities for Negroes, the efforts of the "War on Poverty" to help the poor find jobs (and possibly acquire political power), and federal aid to schools making higher education available to increasing numbers, all menace the status of those who have just made it themselves.

Because radical rightism is often used as a weapon against those who currently occupy positions of leadership and social influence, it attracts to its ranks some individuals who are frustrated by discrepancies between their economic achievements and their social acceptance. Under the guise of being "anti-Communist," rightists express their hostility toward, and try to defame, the established elite by calling them "Communists." At the same time, rightists use their identification with Super-Americanism to reinforce their own claims for higher status. Rightism appeals as well to persons who feel threatened by social changes, since opposition to civil rights, the War on Poverty, and similar programs constitute major items on the right's agenda of political activities.

THE VALUE KEEPERS.   All too often, in our concern for easily measured categories, we forget that an individual's social status is the result of a combination of many factors. The kind of status that is generally most emphasized by sociologists is social class, but an individual's "class" position in the stratification system is really a way of summarizing his type and quality of possessions, interaction patterns, occupational achievements, values, manners, and style of behavior in general.[56] While admittedly there

---

[54] See C. Wright Mills, *White Collar* (New York: Oxford University Press, 1951).

[55] David Riesman and Nathan Glazer, "The Intellectuals and the Discontented Classes—1955," in Bell (ed.), *The Radical Right*.

[56] A person's occupation, education, and income—commonly used measures of achieved status—have been called "positional attributes" by Kingsley Davis. These variables are, of course, only a few of the many personal characteristics which

is a very strong relationship between class and economic activities, social classes represent, ultimately, distinctions in styles of life. Status groups essentially reflect shared ways of living, which mean common values, attitudes, mores, manners, customs, and behavioral patterns.[57]

We therefore must consider the values he holds among the determinants of a person's status, since they shape his behavior (by establishing goals and defining what acts are appropriate and inappropriate) and in turn significantly affect how other people think and feel about him. Any societal reevaluation of these values may correspondingly affect his claim to prestige and respectability. If his values become dishonored, his status suffers. This is another experience which many rightists undergo because they cling to traditional values no longer respected.

For many today, perhaps the majority, many of the traditional rural or small-town ways or virtues are no longer useful or honored by practice. Modern society requires education and expertise more than simple hard work and self-denial; an expanding economy more than thrift; organized community welfare programs rather than primary reliance on savings, personal charity, and relatives' generosity. Moreover, the preponderance of political and economic power has shifted from the country with its white settlers to the metropolitan areas with their combinations of minority popu-lations, who often maintain strikingly different life-styles. Those whose beliefs and behavior were shaped by older traditions—who, as they see it, settled and built this country—now find themselves, in effect, increasingly disinherited.

We now see that the right's attacks on these societal changes serve multiple functions: to protest new and different values and life styles; to reassert the virtues of older ones; and to regain lost personal status. Thus an important prize at stake in this cultural conflict is the social respect its

---

combine to form what Goldhammer and Shils have called the individual's overall or "total status judgment." Kingsley Davis, "A Conceptual Analysis of Stratification," *Amer. Sociol. Rev., 7* (1942), 309–321; Herbert Goldhammer and Edward Shils, "Types of Power and Status," *Amer. J. Sociol., 45* (1939), 171–182.

[57] This extended meaning of class was early noted by Max Weber: ". . . *status groups* are communities . . . In contrast to the purely economically deter-mined 'class situation,' we wish to designate as 'status situations' every typical com-ponent of the life fate of men that is determined by a specific, positive or negative, social estimation of *honor*. . . . In content, status honor is normally expressed by the fact that above all else a specific *style of life* can be expected from all those who wish to belong to the circle." From "Class, Status, Party," in *From Max Weber: Essays in Sociology*, translated by Hans Gerth and C. Wright Mills (New York: Oxford University Press, 1946), pp. 186–193, emphasis added. Systematic research by Centers and Warner (see fn. 49) has also shown that prestige is accorded on the basis of styles of life and beliefs. For a classic description of class differences based on values, customs, and behavior, see Erving Goffman, *The Presentation of Self in Everyday Life* (New York: Doubleday & Company, Inc., 1959), and his "Symbols of Class Status," *British J. Sociol., 2* (1951), 294–304.

victors will gain. Because people's status is closely linked to the values they pursue, a dispute over values also becomes a contest for prestige and social position, with victory meaning deference and higher status for the winners, and degradation and loss of status for the losers. The fight against the "Communist conspiracy" thus represents the rightists' efforts to be recognized as the proper inheritors of America, deserving respect from neighbors and nation alike for their fight against alien and destructive forces.

. In summary, the concept of "status frustration," as I have used it, refers to the *psychological* state of individuals who, though exposed to diverse social circumstances, are commonly anxious and frustrated because they experience (a subjective state) a significant discrepancy between their own and other peoples' evaluations of their relative prestige.[58] The concept of status-frustration thus links up with what sociologists call "status inconsistency," "status mismatching," "status discrepancy," or lack of "status crystallization." [59] The basic idea is that when people's status is judged on the basis of multiple criteria, some individuals' positions on various rankings will be significantly discrepant, presumably affecting how they are treated, and thus, in cases of discrepancy, creating psychological stress.[60] Inconsistencies may produce a condition of marginality with deviant attitudinal and behavioral consequences. In this study, radical rightism is hypothesized to be one of these consequences.[61]

---

[58] Since rightists strongly subscribe to principles of hard work and achievement, and link these to social status and personal worth, it seems likely that they are extremely sensitive to any discrepancies between the social status they feel they properly deserve and the deference they actually receive from others. This sensitivity illustrates the highly *subjective* nature of personal status. The association between social position and personal worth is not made by everyone, since people vary in their proneness to measure themselves in terms of their occupational achievements. Some persons simply do not place a high value on hard work and self-improvement. Others, who may accept such beliefs, are also aware that social inequalities produce unequal opportunities for advancement. Neither of these groups is likely to connect their sense of self-esteem directly to their social achievements, as it is hypothesized many rightists do, because of their commitment to the Protestant Ethic.

[59] Leonard Bloom offers a good definition of this concept in "Status, Status Types, and Status Interrelations," in Robert Merton and others (eds.), *Sociology Today*, (New York: Basic Books, Inc., 1959), pp. 429–441. See N. J. Demerath's *Social Class in American Protestantism* (Skokie, Ill.: Rand McNally & Company, 1965) for a detailed (and critical) discussion of this concept.

[60] Elton Jackson, "Status Consistency and Symptoms of Stress," *Amer. Sociol. Rev.*, 27 (1962), pp. 460–480.

[61] The classic piece on this thesis is Gerhard Lenski's "Status Crystallization: The Non-Vertical Dimension of Social Status," *Amer. Sociol. Rev.*, 19 (1954), 405–413; continuations are: William F. Kenkel, "The relationship between Status Consistency and Politico-Economic Attitudes," *Amer. Sociol. Rev.*, 21 (1956), 365–368; Irwin G. Goffman, "Status Consistency and Preference for Change in Power Distribution," *Amer. Sociol. Rev.*, 22 (1957), 275–281. For applications of this thesis to the right see Bell, (ed.), *The Radical Right* and Gary B. Rush, "Status Consistency and Right-Wing Extremism," *Amer. Sociol. Rev.*, 32 (1967), 86–92.

FINDINGS.   Remarkably little empirical evidence actually supports the status frustration theory considering it is so prevalent in the analytical literature on the right. Lipset reports a study done by Robert Sokol which found that the more the ". . . conscious concern with status inconsistency . . . the greater the tendency to be a McCarthy supporter." And in an analysis of a California poll, Lipset found a weak but suggestive relationship between incongruent education and occupational attainments and favorable attitudes toward The John Birch Society.[62] Gary Rush finds a similar tendency among Oregon right-wingers.[63] In more impressionistic studies, the descriptions given by Chesler and Schmuck, Broyles, and Havens of rightists around the country, fit well the characterization that status frustrated individuals are attracted to radical rightism.[64]

While these data are hardly conclusive, the Wolfinger and associates study of persons attending a San Francisco area "Anti-Communism" school run by Schwarz's Christian Anti-Communism Crusade presents findings that counter the status frustration thesis—at least in terms of demographic variables.[65] Only one quarter of the adult participants were willing, however, to answer Wolfinger's questions, but on almost all measures these respondents showed themselves to be considerably different from the typical rightist described in the large body of literature on right-wing politics. These deviant findings suggest two conclusions: that the entire literature is either grossly inaccurate or, that the Wolfinger sample itself is not representative of the kind of persons most analysts have in mind or have observed when describing radical rightists. This latter explanation seems more credible, particularly in light of the clear evidence that the sample is primarily composed of college-educated, upper-middle class, conservative Republicans (which the authors openly acknowledge).[66] A third inference may also be drawn from these data: that a distinction be-

---

[62] Robert Sokol, *Rank Inconsistency and McCarthyism: An Empirical Test*, unpublished paper, Dartmouth College, cited in Lipset, "Three Decades of the Radical Right," in Bell (ed.), *The Radical Right*, p. 334. The California data is presented on p. 363.

[63] Gary Rush, "Status Consistency and Right-Wing Extremism."

[64] M. Chesler and R. Schmuck, "Participant Observation in a Super-Patriot Discussion Group," *J. Social Issues, 19* (1963), 18–30; Broyles, *The John Birch Society*, p. 155 and throughout the text; and Havens, "Radical Right in Southwest . . .", p. 12 especially.

[65] Raymond E. Wolfinger and others, "America's Radical Right: Politics and Ideology," in this volume.

[66] In comparing Wolfinger and others' sample with Fred Grupp's national sample of John Birchers (see his article in this collection) and my own on education and occupation, striking differences are apparent. There is also a serious question about equating attendance at a Schwarz Crusade with being a rightist. And lastly, the major difference between our two samples on a variety of attitude measures, reinforces the above arguments. The evidence for this case is presented in *The Radical Rightists* (New York: Basic Books, Inc., in press).

tween *types* of rightists is both a necessary and useful strategy to properly understand right-wing political groupings.

In confronting our data, we knew it would be difficult to find out if a person is "frustrated," since few people are likely to admit (particularly to a stranger) that they are not liked or respected. Consequently, we adopted a multiple-indicator strategy, and sought to build a cumulative case to test hypotheses derived from the status frustration theory, based on a number of objective status indicators and indirect questions.[67]

OBJECTIVE ATTRIBUTES. Our Rightists are drawn disproportionately from occupations of decreasing social prestige (see Table 6). The data shows that only 10 percent of Rightists are in the highest occupations, such

TABLE 6

Occupational Comparison between Male Radical Rightists and Nonrightists (percentaged across)

| | OCCUPATIONAL GROUP [a] | | | | | | | | |
	I	II	III	IV	V	VI	VII	VIII	(N)
Non-Rightists [b]	24	13	19	4	18	11		12	(95)
Radical Rightists [c]	10	12	17	15	14	9	2	21	(112)

[a] Occupational Classification based on Hollingshead's Index of Social Position—Seven Socio-Economic Scale Positions (Unpublished Manuscript, Department of Sociology, Yale University, N.D.), with separate category for retirees.

    I. Higher executives of larger concerns, proprietors, and major professionals

    II. Business managers, proprietors of medium-sized businesses, and lesser professionals

    III. Administrative personnel, owners of certain small businesses, and minor professionals

    IV. Clerical and sales workers, technicians, and owners of certain small businesses

    V. Skilled manual employees

    VI. Machine operators and semiskilled employees

    VII. Unskilled employees

    VIII. Retired

[b] Non-Rightists = I and II on Radical Rightism Index

[c] Radical-Rightists = III and IV on Radical Rightism Index

[67] One never "proves" or "disproves" a theory. Empirical evidence is assembled which validates empirical inferences derived from the theory, but a theory is, among other things, a system of explanations for a variety of phenomena subsumed within its scope. The validity of the status frustration thesis, as applied to rightists, thus ultimately depends on how well a number of subhypotheses, empirically tested across several sections, fare. See Abraham Kaplan, *The Conduct of Inquiry* (San Francisco: Chandler Publishing Company, 1964), especially chap. 7, and Eugene Meehan, *Explanation in Social Science: A System Paradigm* (Homewood, Ill.: Dorsey Press, 1968), especially chap. 5.

as executives and professionals compared with 24 percent of Non-Rightists, and that Rightists are over-represented among the lower-middle class (such as clerical and salesworkers) 15 percent to 4 percent.[68] Further, nearly twice as many Rightists as others are retired—removed, for most practical purposes, from economic importance to society—and they tend to be older (median age 54 compared to 45). There is a tendency ($P < .15$) for more Rightists (or their husbands, in the case of female Rightists), to be self-employed businessmen and independent professionals.

Occupation, alone, is not enough to measure adequately an individual's social standing. In our increasingly technologically oriented society, education is not only an occupational necessity but also a mark of prestige, especially in the middle and upper classes. Following the practice of Hollingshead and Warner,[69] a more refined gauge of status-rank was computed using both educational attainment and occupational standing.

A disproportionate number ($P < .05$) of Rightists are found in the middle-status groups—they are the minor professionals, owners of small businesses, clerical and salesworkers, and technicians, with only moderate educational achievements at best. Twenty-seven percent of the Rightists (compared to 42 percent of the Non-Rightists) are in the two highest objective status ranks. But even within these upper and middle occupational strata the Rightists have less education than their Non-Rightist equivalents. In the *highest* levels (high executives, ranking businessmen, major professionals) almost twice as many Non-Rightists as Rightists have graduate degrees (64 percent to 33 percent), while three times as many Rightists (12 percent to 4 percent) never went beyond high school ($P < .05$). In the *middle* levels over twice as many Non-Rightists had college degrees (27 percent to 12 percent) while more than twice as many Rightists (54 percent to 24 percent) never went further than high school ($P < .02$).[70] Education is very important in upper and middle-class persons' evaluations of membership in their class, since it importantly shapes friendship and consumption patterns and general style of life.[71] Our Rightists, with less education than is typical of their occupational group, seem likely to experience anxiety about their occupational advancement and social acceptance.

What about status mobility? Stated most simply, the status frustration thesis argues that relative changes in social status produce anxieties which are, for rightists, resolved through right-wing activities. Intergenerational

---

[68] The same relative relationship holds when women are included, basing their status rank on their husband's occupation.

[69] See Warner, *Social Class in America* and August Hollingshead and Frederick Redlick, "Social Stratification and Psychiatric Disorders," *Amer. Sociol. Rev., 28* (1953), 161–169, which describes the justification for assigning weights.

[70] The relationships remain essentially unchanged when controls for sex are introduced.

[71] Centers, *Psychology of Social Classes*, pp. 92–98.

status mobility was assessed by comparing a male Rightist's (or a female Rightist's husband's) occupation and education with those of his (or her) father. We found that Rightists, as hypothesized, did undergo much more status mobility than Non-Rightists, most often downward.

In the *lowest* occupations (typically, unskilled blue-collar, manual, and service workers) the Rightists had fallen farther and more consistently than Non-Rightists. Thirty-eight percent of Rightist men compared to 6 percent Non-Rightist had declined sharply from their father's occupation. ($P < .05$). Rightist laborers were quite apt to have middle-class or farm-owning parents. In the *middle* groups (white-collar, technicians, minor professional, small-businessmen), Rightists tended to be more mobile, both up and down, than Non-Rightists ($P < .20$). Relatively few had stayed at the same occupational and educational level as their fathers (14 to 29 percent); [72] these clusters would correspond to our categories of the "newly arrived" and the "decliners." In the *highest* status classification, Rightists have experienced a greater jump in status-rank than Non-Rightists (69 percent compared to 46 percent moved three or more positions upward ($P < .05$ for all respondents). It is not surprising that such rapid occupational ascendency should be accompanied by considerable status anxiety; this fits well the "newly arrived" thesis.

Our distinction between "decliners"—persons who use rightism to ward off anxieties caused by a decline in status as newly emergent groups displace them in the status structure and introduce new values into the community—and the "newly arrived"—who use rightism to gain acceptance into higher status groups (at least in their own mind)—appears not only in the data on intergenerational mobility but again when we examine our respondents' length of residence in their communities.

Controlling for age (since young people move much more frequently than older ones), Rightists under 50 tend to fall into two groups. One seems to be primarily composed of people new to the community (less than five years)—21 percent to 14 percent ($P < .30$)—who have declined in status (44 percent experienced a loss of status-rank, compared to only 13 percent of the geographically mobile Non-Rightists—$P < .02$). The other is composed of old-time residents who have lived in the same community most of their adult lives. The latter group, likely to resent the invasion of newer, influential persons into their community's status structure, is even more pronounced when we examine persons over 50; 46 percent of the Rightists have lived in the same community for more than 30 years, compared to 25 percent of the Non-Rightists ($P < .02$). Among this older group, the disproportionate degree of downward status mobility among Rightists noted above is also evident ($P < .10$).

---

[72] When only males are examined, status decliners among Rightists become even more pronounced (32 percent versus 18 percent).

SUBJECTIVE STATUS REACTIONS.   In profile, the typical Rightist is older, more often has a low- or middle-prestige level occupation or is thrown on his own resources—retired, or the operator of an independent business, he has significantly more status mobility, especially downward, and less education than the comparable Non-Rightist. This picture is consistent with the status-frustration hypothesis. These persons, as we have already seen, identify with an older and dominant tradition; they could hardly help feeling frustrated. So much for inferences, however; the significant question is how do these people themselves actually view their current status position?

Some Rightists tend to overrate themselves socially. Although on objective measures twice as many Non-Rightists as Rightists fell into the highest social class, Rightists, two to one, claim to be "upper class" ($P <$ .10). Support for the contention that Rightists feel improperly esteemed is further displayed in their perceptions of how social acceptance and higher position work. When asked, "How hard do you think it is for people today to move upward from one social class to another?" and "Why do you say this?" the Rightists' answers revealed a personalized view of society as essentially closed, dominated by personalities, controlled by the wrong people:

> depends on who you know; having money; not too much opportunity anymore, doors are closed as to who gets in; got to know the right people.

The views of the Non-Rightists (60 percent to 27 percent—$P < .01$) were much more objective and impersonal:

> depends on an education; people must work hard and have abilities to get it; if you have the desire and goal, then you can accomplish what you want.

The disparity in perceptions would seem to result from the two groups' dissimilar experiences, and is quite consistent with the right's contention that both nations and communities are controlled by a cabalist elite which they of course bitterly resent.[73] We asked: "Do you think that the people who are influential in this community are, in general, friendly people willing to help you out, or are they cliquish and keep to themselves?" Rightists answered "cliquish and unfriendly" more often than Non-Rightists ($P <$ .20), with the response most pronounced among status decliners. When

---

[73] The belief that a cabalist group secretly controls things is historically endemic and rather widespread in the population. For historical examples see Hofstadter, *Paranoid Style* . . . , especially Chapter 1, and Gustavus Myers, *History of Bigotry in the United States*, edited by Henry M. Chistman (New York: Capricorn Books, 1960). Hans Toch, in his *Social Psychology of Social Movements*, has a valuable discussion of the psychological functions of this kind of belief. See also Robert Lane's *Political Ideology* (New York: The Free Press, 1962), chapter 7.

those answering "cliquish" were asked to give reasons, Rightists again more often indicated belief in a closed structure run by a small group:

> Old residents tend to look on new people as outsiders; certain families run things here; segregated groups want their own way; all have common political views.

The typical Rightist, then, more often sees himself as an outsider, discriminated against in a closed society run by an elite.

Do Rightists feel deprived of their contemporaries' respect and acceptance? "In your own case, for example, do you think that *everyone* gives you as much respect as *you feel you* deserve?" Although bluntly worded, twice as many Rightists (16 percent to 7—$P < .02$) replied "No" to our question. This is true both of Rightists on the way up and down; but the decliners said "No" twice as often as those on the rise—suggesting that it is the losers who are most responsive to rightism. A variant on the respect question asked, ". . . do you feel you are accepted and part of the community or still considered an outsider?" (asked of everyone not born in the community where they then resided). Again more Rightists than Non-Rightists replied, relatively, that they felt unaccepted (16 percent versus 10—$P < .25$).

Although these latter findings are statistically weak individually, the cumulative case favors the conclusion that Rightists are persons who are disproportionately discontented with their degree of social acceptance, position, and influence.

THE STATUS-ENHANCING FUNCTIONS OF RIGHTISM. The argument being developed is that people resist being depreciated by others, and that radical rightism is a device used by some such individuals to enhance their threatened sense of importance, status, and self-respect. Two tactics are employed: through its emphasis on patriotism and anti-Communism, rightists identify themselves with "true Americanism," an association inducing respect and honor. Second, those with more education and higher social position can find their reputation seriously blemished by the status-reducing accusation they are "Communists," either really or at least in the eyes of the rightist accusers who label them such.

Rightist organizations and literature constantly reinforce their members' feelings of self-importance by emphasizing the significance of the job they are doing:

> And finally we can fortify our spirits with a realization of the historic and humanitarian importance of the job we have undertaken; of the staggering responsibility that now rests on our shoulders. That responsibility is not just for the future freedom of our own country, our children, and ourselves. To an increasing number of the best informed and

most honorable citizens of other nations throughout the world, The John Birch Society now appears as the last hope of saving their country, *their* children, and *themselves* from Communist slavery.[74]

Another communiqué is worth quoting to illustrate how rightists mutually reinforce their precarious sense of personal worth:

> There is, I submit, no organization on the American scene today in which there is to be found more of the quality of God-serving, dedicated, informed, courageous, patriotic Americans than there is in The John Birch Society . . . they are, in every sense, Americans of the finest calibre. (*JBS Bulletin*, June 1967)

Our interviews showed clearly that Rightists assimilate a highly desirable self-image as a result of their rightist activities. We asked them to select two "great Americans" and then describe what is admirable about them. Later, we asked them to describe "the typical member of anticommunist groups, like The John Birch Society, for example"—that is, in effect, an idealized version of themselves, *qua rightists*. The qualities which Rightists chose more often than Non-Rightists to describe "great people" consistently turn out to be the same ones they disproportionately used to characterize themselves.

Their great people, they said, were "true" Americans, concerned with their country, and "very patriotic" (35 percent to 21 percent of the Non-Rightists—$P < .01$); 75 percent found the same things true of themselves (compared to 22 percent of the Non-Rightists [$P < .001$], who tended to use extravagant terms as well).[75] Courage, strength, and "guts" were likewise qualities which they shared with the great, as were deep Christian faith and high moral standards. Fifty percent saw the great to be honest,

---

[74] This quotation was reprinted from an article written by Ezra Taft Benson which appeared originally in the December 1964 issue of *American Opinion*, the Birch Society's magazine. In the highly personalized style in which Welch writes the society's monthly bulletins, he attempts to make his followers feel they are real team-mates in their common war against Communism. Welch's inclusion of this selection from Benson, former Cabinet member, is no accident; every issue includes praise for members of the Society. For example, in referring to a professional politician's report that "in a political campaign one Bircher is worth over a hundred volunteer workers," Welch added this comment: "This is an excellent reputation to maintain—industriousness, judgement, courage and dedication—and this is a good time to maintain it." (*JBS Bulletin*, Oct. 1965) And here is Welch's final sentence in the same issue of the *Bulletin*, where he wishes ". . . to thank all of our members once again for all of their devotion to our high ideals which makes of The John Birch Society the finest body of men and women in the world." Similar status reinforcing statements can be extracted from other rightist publications.

[75] Our Rightists heightened sense of Americanism is also reflected in their responses to a scale which measures nationalistic feelings. Representative items include "I'm for my country, right or wrong," "America may not be perfect, but the American way has brought us as close to a *perfect* society as human beings can get," and ". . . I, for my part, feel that I am first, last, and always an American." *Gamma* = .23 ($P < .02$).

truthful, and sincere—like themselves. Non-Rightists, however, viewed Rightists very differently—"dishonest," "hypocrites," "no integrity," "use character assassination."

This tactic of Rightists to acquire status and importance by associating themselves closely with the great and good (and to cast such persons in their own preferred image) is well illustrated by their emphasis on "self-education." They are, in fact, less well-educated than the Non-Rightists. But the world of radical rightism is filled with self-styled "experts," study groups, monographs, footnotes, and extensive bibliographies—almost all with no standing among scholars. The rightists study them avidly, more often mention intelligence and education among those things they particularly admire in the great, and give themselves strong ratings as "intellectuals," "brilliant," "well-informed," "people with sound judgment, good reasoning," and "lots of sense" ($P < .001$). The special brand of education which rightists pick up not only allows them to feel educated, but also provides weapons which they use against opponents with more formal education and higher status.

The Rightists' *modus operandi* is to crusade publicly against the evils of communism and communists. These public expressions serve several functions: to elevate their own standing by defaming those in higher positions; to try to influence the institutions which form values (schools, churches, media) to reemphasize traditional morality; and to draw attention to themselves as citizens worthy of respect and consideration, since they are only "trying to save America from an impending doom."

We tested the hypothesis that Rightists seek attention and thus derive personal satisfaction from their activities by asking all interviewees who had written letters to newspapers or had been publicly active (circulated petitions, involved in political campaigns, and so on) about the reactions of people to these activities, and how they themselves felt about it. Rightists were first of all much more convinced that people paid attention to them than were the active Non-Rightists ($P < .02$),[76] and tended more to feel encouraged by these reactions to continue their activities ($P < .15$). Finally, when asked directly, "Would you say that because of this activity of yours, people are more likely to listen to you and pay more attention to what you have to say about public affairs?" Rightists answered "definitely yes" significantly more frequently ($P < .001$) than did Non-Rightist activists.

The followers of Billy James Hargis, Carl McIntire, Kent and Phoebe Courtney, Dan Smoot, Robert Welch, and other rightist leaders, all accept

---

[76] Interestingly, Rightists who had experienced *upward* social mobility (in terms of intergenerational occupational status) were most sensitive; this suggests that *public* rightist activity is more likely to be used as an attention-seeking device to enhance status claims than to protest their loss.

the same message: because you are involved in a great cause, battling the forces of evil (communism), you are good people, deserving respect and influence. The empirical data shows that Rightists believe this.

Powerlessness and Alienation

The drastic reshuffling of social and occupational positions that has accompanied a society changing from individualistic entrepreneurial forms to a corporate state heavily dependent upon technological skills, has contributed greatly to a deep and lasting sense of displacement and dispossession among persons drawn to the right. Rightists, in a word, feel powerless and alienated in contemporary American society, as it is now constituted.

The cry that individual freedom is rapidly being lost, that people like themselves cannot influence anything of importance any more, is one of the rightists' basic tenets. Political power is perceived as residing almost exclusively in the hands of a few powerful individuals and pressure groups, who, they believe, conspire to deny them influence. They also feel generally unable to control their lives, that what happens to them is beyond their ability to affect or change.[77]

Is "the federal government . . . extending too much of its power into too many areas of everyday life?" Nearly 70 percent of the Rightists (compared to 25 percent of the Non-Rightists ($P < .001$) "agree very much" with this proposition. "Are there any groups in America that you think have too much power and influence?" "Yes," the Rightists said significantly more often ($P < .001$) than Non-Rightists, and listed labor (and its leaders), "communists," big government, and such groups as the ADA, ACLU, and Council on Foreign Relations. Who has "too little power in America?" They mentioned twice as many groups as Non-Rightists, most

---

[77] There is a vast literature, both theoretical and empirical, on the concepts of alienation, powerlessness, estrangement, and so on. In the study, I subsume them under the term "anomy syndrome," taking the position that the concepts represent dimensions of anomy. A factor analysis substantiates this position, at least for these data.

See Robert Merton, *Social Theory and Social Structure,* for a discussion of the sociological development and uses of this term. An article by Herbert McClosky and John Schaar, "Psychological Dimensions of Anomy," *Amer. Soc. Rev., 30* (1965), 14–40, is extremely valuable both in terms of theory and empirical data. Other important works in this area include Leo Srole, "Social Integration and Certain Corollaries: An Exploratory Study," *Amer. Soc. Rev., 21* (1956), 709–716; Melvin Seeman, "On the Meaning of Alienation," *Amer. Soc. Rev., 24* (1959), 783–790; Murray Levin, *The Alienated Voter* (New York: Holt, Rinehart and Winston, Inc., 1969); Elizabeth Douvan and Alan Walker, "The Sense of Efficacy in Public Affairs," *Psychol. Monographs, 70* (1956), Whole No. 429; Morris Rosenberg, "The Meaning of Politics in Mass Society," *Public Opinion Quart.,* 15 (1951), 5–15.

often the two surrogates for themselves: the individual "common man" and "conservative" organizations.

Further empirical evidence that Rightists feel personally powerless is found in their agreement with three items which make up a reliable psychometric scale: "More and more I feel helpless in the face of what is happening in the world today," "Life is primarily a matter of struggle for survival," and "It is only wishful thinking to believe that one can really influence what happens in society at large." [78] A significant proportion ($P < .01$) of Rightists also pointed out that their idealized "great Americans," with whom they identify, were "maligned" and "mistreated": "Got a raw deal; treated badly by others, his country; a victim of injustice."

We found our Rightists to be significantly more alienated politically than the Non-Rightists, to feel that their elected public officials do not actually represent them, that local officials avoid or ignore them, responding only to special issues. The political alienation scale—"People like me should have more of a say about how things are run in this country," "Public officials really care how people like me want things to be done (reversed in scoring)," "I wish public officials would listen more to people like me," and "If it were possible, I'd throw most public officials out on their ears" —correlated (*Gamma*) .38 with the Rightism Index ($P < .001$). Other questions, employing different formats, asking about national and local leaders, drew essentially the same basic alienated response pattern.

Rightism offers these people the means to overcome or compensate for their feelings of social and political powerlessness. Rightism serves several functions here: it provides its followers with a vehicle to protest their state of powerlessness; members of organizations can feel protected because they belong to an influential group directed by a strong leader; and, isolated and estranged, they find a sense of community and social closeness with others who share similar feelings. [79]

Rightist groups repeatedly emphasize the "great strength" and "influence" of their organization; these pronouncements serve to ward off

---

[78] The Kuder-Richardson internal consistency coefficient = .77; *Gamma* = .21 ($P < .05$) between the scale and Rightism Index.

[79] Generally, we found that the Rightists in our sample were less often involved in social and community organizations ($P < .05$), and were more distrustful of other people ($P < .05$). The items on the "Trust of Other People" scale were: "If you don't watch yourself, most people will take advantage of you," "No one is going to care too much what happens to you when you get right down to it," and "Human nature is fundamentally cooperative (reversed in scoring)." The Kuder-Richardson Coefficient = .80, and *Gamma* = .23 running the scale against the Rightism Index.

For insightful discussions of this concept, see Morris Rosenberg, "Misanthropy and Political Idelogy," *Amer. Sociol. Rev., 21* (1956), 69–75, and Robert Lane's *Political Ideology*, Section II.

members' feelings of being insignificant. Members are also given leaders to follow and with whom to identify. The "leader" always knows what is going on and what to do to overcome it. He usually also provides an image of self-sufficiency, fortitude, confidence, and great personal ability, an image his followers can share in and thus negate their own inadequacies.

Today's radical right operates through national organizations and local "study groups" or "chapters." These local face-to-face groups provide the specific mechanism whereby rightists derive support, a sense of community, feelings of influence and self-worth, and information and direction. Bonds of friendship can be established with other persons who share common feelings of isolation, lack of self-worth, and frustration. Through the group, members are immersed in rightist information and guided activities which function to enhance their sense of status. Activity, often fervent, is very important, for it gives members meaning and a sense of influence.

Support for the contention that Rightists compensate for their feelings of powerlessness by political activity is provided by their responses to an index of political efficacy, where they claim that "working in a group which takes stands on public issues is a way people like me can influence the government," "voting is a way for people like me to have a say about how government runs things," and "writing my Congressmen and other public officials is a way people like me can influence the government's policies." [80] The seeming contradiction between these responses and their other alienated ones is explained, I believe, by a subtle difference in the questions. On the one hand, the previous scales tapped general anomic feelings, but when we asked Rightists about specific activities which their organizations engage in (letter-writing, working together in a group, circulating petitions), the *expectation* that these activities will have an effect is tapped. To believe otherwise would be an admission of complete futility, something hardly likely to make them feel powerful and influential, which is why they joined the rightist movement.

PERSONALITY AND RIGHTISM

We have seen that Rightists are persons discontented over modern value trends, their social status, and the allocation of power in this country. Their adoption of rightism allows them to combat cultural values which do not conform to their feelings of status and self-esteem, and to feel politically potent again. These discontentments alone, however, do not satisfactorily explain why only some and not all dissatisfied and anxious individuals in like circumstances are attracted to rightism. The operation of certain personality dynamics and appeals must be considered to understand more completely why some persons become Rightists.

---

[80] Rightists feel as politically efficacious as Non-Rightists ($P < .95$).

Cognitive Structure

One of rightism's most important appeals is its ideology, which offers its adherents, traditionalists adrift in a seemingly chaotic world of profound social and cultural change, an easily grasped explanation for what was previously unintelligible. The theory that history and current affairs can be attributed to communist machinations primarily appeals to the confused because of its remarkable simplicity. In the midst of great complexity, the rightist deliberately chooses a principle which provides him with a massive over-simplification. Politics, world events, civil turmoil, everything which baffles and disturbs him, all can be reduced to one overriding cause— conspiracy.

Considerable psychological research shows that persons who so readily accept such oversimplified views do so because they have a general psychological need for uncomplicated, firm, stereotyped views of people and events; there is no place in their beliefs for ambiguity or ambivalence.[81] Such people reject, in a closed-minded fashion, individuals who disagree with—or merely fail to share—their beliefs, and they hold their opinions so rigidly that compromise is impossible. Lack of self-guidance makes them unusually dependent upon external authority-figures and "experts" for guidance and information. This simplistic and closed-minded mode of cognizing is amply manifested in rightist ideology, in its literature, and its organizations.

In right-wing literature the conspiracy principle reappears again and again to cut through complexity. Every issue, no matter how involved, is presented and resolved as though it involved only two sides: the moral versus the immoral, the pro-American versus the anti-American, the procommunist versus the anticommunist. Closed-minded persons hold their beliefs so inflexibly that any compromise is impossible. Among rightists, compromise is equivalent to betrayal—differing points of view and political

---

[81] Milton Rokeach's *The Open and Closed Mind* (New York: Basic Books, Inc., 1960) provides one of the best discussions of this form of cognitive style, as well as reporting original research in this area. Other major sources include: T. W. Adorno and others, *The Authoritarian Personality* (New York: Harper & Row, Publishers, 1950); Else Frenkel-Brunswik, "Intolerance of Ambiguity as an Emotional and Personality Variable," *J. Personality, 18* (1949), 108–143; J. S. Bruner, J. J. Goodnow, and G. A. Austin, *A Study of Thinking* (New York: John Wiley & Sons, Inc., 1956).

It is, of course, axiomatic in social psychology that the cognitions of individuals are selectively organized, and little education and limited experiences also affect cognitive selectivity (see Seymour Lipset's "Working Class Authoritarianism," in *Political Man*). But it is also the case that *personal factors*, which I am labeling "cognitive structure," are also significant. (See Gordon Allport, *The Nature of Prejudice* (New York: Doubleday & Company, Inc., 1964), chaps. 2 and 10; David Kretch, Richard Crutchfield, and Egerton Ballachey, *Individual in Society* (New York: McGraw-Hill, Inc., 1962), chap. 2.)

systems cannot coexist; as the "General Beliefs and Principles of The John Birch Society" states, for example: "We believe that the continued co-existence of Communism and Christian-style civilization on one planet is impossible. The struggle between them must end with one completely triumphant and the other completely destroyed." [82]

The closed-minded person's lack of multiple and differentiated cognitions forces him to be overly dependent on accepted leaders and authorities to provide him with information and understanding. Rightists give un-wavering credence to their literature, organizational leaders, and self-styled "anti-Communist experts." Most rightist organizations are leader-centered and authoritarian in structure; the initiative always flows directly from the top downward (usually through weekly or monthly bulletins) and elected leaders are unheard of.

Rightist ideology thus both meets and reflects psychological needs for simple and dogmatic beliefs. Our empirical data strongly confirm the hypothesis that the cognitive style of Rightists is closed-minded and sim-plistic. Their views on matters concerning communism and Russia are ex-tremely rigid, absolute, and uncompromising; they emphatically agreed with items such as: "Communism is a total evil," "As philosophies of gov-ernment, modern liberalism, socialism, and communism are all essentially the same," and "the United States and Communist Russia have nothing in common." [83] That the political dogmatism of Rightists is a manifestation of more general personality traits is confirmed by their responses to psycho-metric measures of cognitive style; Rightists, compared to Non-Rightists, are characteristically more intolerant of ambiguity, opposed to compromis-ing their beliefs, and generally closed-minded and opinionated (see Table 7).[84]

Extrapunitiveness

The strident negativism and combativeness displayed in rightism points to another important psychological function: it satisfies the need to express

---

[82] Entered into the Congressional Record of the 87th Congress, Second Session, June 12, 1962 by John H. Rousselot, former Congressman from California. Rousselot was Director of Public Relations for The John Birch Society for some time, and still is publisher of its magazine, *American Opinion*.

[83] The other two items on this scale were: "The current fight between the Russians and the Communist Chinese shows there are some great differences between them," and "The Soviet Union is 'mellowing' and the way is opening for peaceful cooperation between the Russians and the United States." Both items were reversed in scoring, and the Kuder-Richardson Coefficient = .82.

[84] It is unfortunate that each scale consists of so few items, but time limitations and the decision to assess three theoretically separate traits required this. The items do, however, display excellent unidimensionality, as shown by their very high Kuder-Richardson Coefficient: .79, .86, and .73 respectively.

While one can differentiate three separate dimensions, empirically the three dimensions should intercorrelate. This in fact occurs, with the three scales correlating at levels of .43 to .65 with one another (product moments).

TABLE 7

*Cognitive Style Measures vs Radical Rightism Index
(High and Low Quartiles Only, percentaged across)*

		DOGMATIC ANTI-COMMUNISM VIEWS		
Non-Rightists	(I)	5	57	*Gamma* = .69
Rightists	(IV)	68	3	(*P* < .001)
		INTOLERANCE OF AMBIGUITY [a]		
Non-Rightists	(I)	15	44	*Gamma* = .46
Rightists	(IV)	49	6	(*P* < .001)
		ANTI-COMPROMISE [b]		
Non-Rightists	(I)	4	47	*Gamma* = .60
Rightists	(IV)	47	19	(*P* < .001)
		CLOSED-MINDEDNESS [c]		
Non-Rightists	(I)	23	45	*Gamma* = .22
Rightists	(IV)	36	25	(*P* < .05)

[a] *Intolerance of Ambiguity Scale items*: (1) Of all the different philosophies which exist in this world, there is probably only one which is correct; (2) There is usually only one right way to do anything; (3) People can be divided into two distinct classes: the weak and the strong; (4) You can classify almost all people as either honest or crooked. Kuder-Richardson Coefficient of Internal Consistency = .79.

[b] *Anti-Compromise Scale items*: (1) The compromising of principles leads to nothing but destruction; (2) To compromise with our political opponents is dangerous because it usually leads to the betrayal of our side; (3) To compromise with our political opponents is to be guilty of appeasement. Kuder-Richardson Coefficient of Internal Consistency = .86.

[c] *Close-Mindedness Scale items*: (1) It is a terrible thing for a person to attack publicly the people who believe the same things he does; (2) In this complicated world of ours the only way we can know what is going on is to rely upon leaders or experts who can be trusted; (3) In the long run, the best way to live is to pick friends and associates whose tastes and beliefs are the same as one's own; (4) A group which tolerates too much difference of opinion among its own members cannot exist for long.

personal discontents in the form of hostility directed against scapegoat enemies. The acceptance of the conspiracy theory not only greatly simplifies its believers' system of reasoning and conception of social causation, but provides concrete targets against whom anger can be discharged. Rightist ideology and activities provide a mechanism by which frustrations generated by status anxieties and value conflicts can be relieved.

Aggression is a common consequence of frustration. When someone is thwarted in achieving some important goal, aggression may be directed towards either the self or others. This dynamic is well known to psychologists as the concept of "frustration-aggression displacement." [85] Frustration

[85] The classic statement of this formulation is John Dollard and others, *Frustration and Aggression* (New Haven, Conn.: Yale University Press, 1939). An

can also be externalized by displacing hostility against some convenient target. Such behavior, if general, reflects the personality trait "extra-punitiveness." When confronted by frustrating situations, individuals who employ this mechanism typically react: (1) by manifesting anger; (2) by making judgments which blame others or the outer world for their personal difficulties; and (3) by directing aggression outward, against their environment.[86]

The two main features of the extrapunitive personality style—the display of considerable *aggressive needs* directed against supposedly blameworthy objects, and selective *perceptions* which justify these hostile attacks—are profusely exhibited by rightists.

Aggressive feelings emerge as hostility aimed at persons labelled as "Communists." Hostility permeates not only the literature of the right but frequently is expressed during their organizational meetings and at social gatherings; the prevailing atmosphere usually is one of animosity and bitterness. Virulent anticommunism not only allows its advocates to express hostility, but to do so without feeling guilt. Rightists vent most of their anger against people who are influential or whose ways of life differ from their own, but they justify their behavior in the name of pro-Americanism. Aggressiveness is thus rationalized in legitimate political, intellectual, and moral terms.

The rightists' distorted perceptions of a communist conspiracy reflects a simplistic, closed-minded cognitive style. That they grossly exaggerate certain traits which communists possess and attribute them to all persons they label communists to justify their hostility is characteristic of extra-punitive individuals. Communism, it is apparent, is not the real "cause" of the right's concern, but instead serves as a convenient symbol against which its followers can direct hostility. Rightists sanction their need to hate by portraying communists as "power- seeking gangsters," "megalomaniacal criminals," "degenerates," "foul creatures," "sex perverts," and "mass murderers"; attaching so much evil to them makes them legitimate enemies, against whom the employment of nearly any tactic is fair.

How does this distorted imagery come about? The answer is a psychological process which I call the projection-attribution mechanism. This concept emphasizes that a "projector" attributes onto others those personal qualities which he finds personally repugnant. Because rightists have ideological disagreements with, or dislike someone for almost any reason, they associate all kinds of other negative traits with this person. This occurs because their *disbelief-systems* have little differentiation within them; one

---

excellent review and critique of this concept is found in Aubrey Yates' *Frustration and Conflict* (New York: John Wiley & Sons, Inc., 1962), particularly chap. 3.

[86] Adopted from Saul Rosenzweig, "The Experimental Measurement of Types of Reactions to Frustrations," in Henry Murray's *Exploration in Personality* (New York: Science Editions, 1962), p. 586.

negative element is thus automatically associated with all other negative elements. If someone is tagged with being a "Communist," every other trait viewed with equal disfavor also becomes linked to this individual.[87]

We tested for aggressiveness in the interviews by noting expressions of hostility against safe scapegoat adversaries, such as communists and individuals who violate cultural morés. When asked what should be done about American communists, Rightists more often called for punitive sanctions ("take them out and hang them; punish them; tighten laws") than Non-Rightists ($P < .01$). Their *generalized* hostility showed up more clearly in their attitudes toward nonpolitical deviants. Studies have shown that hostile responses on items such as "sex crimes, such as rape and attacks on children, deserve more than mere imprisonment: such criminals ought to be publicly whipped or worse," "There is hardly anything lower than a person who does not feel a great love, gratitude, and respect for his parents," and "Homosexuals are hardly better than criminals and ought to be severely punished" (Kuder-Richardson Coefficient $= .89$), measure displaced feelings of general anger and aggression.[88] *Gamma* $= .31$ ($P < .001$) between the hostility towards deviants scale and the Rightism Index.

Whether the image which Rightists hold of "communists" reflects selec-

---

[87] Experimental evidence shows a definite relationship between the personal qualities which individuals attribute to others and their own attitudes. Victor Vroom, "Projection, Negation, and the Self-Concept," *Human Relations, 12* (1959), 335–344. For a discussion of disbelief systems see Rokeach, *Open and Closed Mind.* Theodore Newcomb, Ralph Turner, and Philip Converse employ the concept of belief system throughout their recent text, *Social Psychology: The Study of Human Interaction* (New York: Holt, Rinehart and Winston, Inc., 1965).

My amalgam "projective-attribution" is similar to what some clinical psychologists call the "mote-beam mechanism"; see G. Ichheiser, "Projection and the Mote-Beam Mechanism," *J. Abnorm. Social Psychol., 42* (1947), 131–133. "Complementary projection" is another type of defense mechanism which parallels my dynamic; see Gordon Allport, *The Nature of Prejudice,* p. 367, and H. H. Murray, "The Effects of Fear upon Estimates of the Maliciousness of Other Personalities," *J. Social Psychol., 4* (1933), 310–329.

[88] A strong element of adherence to traditional values is involved in these items, since they involve acts which violate conventional norms. The correlation (r) between the scale and the Protestant Ethic scale is, in fact, quite high, being .60. Controlling for this effect does attenuate the original association between the Rightism Index and the hostility measure: r decreases from .286 to .113, which is still statistically significant.

But this is not to say that the measure is totally determined by values; after all, nearly two thirds (minus reliability error) of its variance is *not* accounted for by the Protestant Ethic scale. Actually, the hostility scale correlates as much with personality measures as with traditional principles; in a factor analysis, it loads nearly as highly on a personality dimension as it does on a value dimension.

A good bibliography of these studies is contained in Yates, *Frustration and Conflict.* Of particular pertinence to the measure employed here are Adorno, *Authoritarian Personality*; M. S. Siegel, "The Relationship of Hostility to Authoritarianism," *J. Abnorm. Social Psychol., 52* (1956), 369–372; and W. Weiss and B. J. Fine, "Opinion Change as a Function of Some Intrapersonal Attributes of the Communicatees," *J. Abnorm. Social Psychol.,* 51 (1955), 246–253.

tively organized cognitions and projective-attribution of personal hatreds was tested by asking them to describe "the typical American communist" and "the kinds of things they believe in." Their answers make it clear that our Rightists associate with, or attribute to, their enemies traits which are the absolute antithesis of things they value most. Inordinately concerned with religious and moral principles, Rightists disproportionately describe communists as atheistic and anti-Christian, as immoral people dedicated to the destruction of "decent moral standards," the family, and "God's word" $(P > .01)$. Often threatened occupationally by better educated persons (see section on "Status Discontentments"), Rightists more often $(P > .07)$ describe "communists" as "well-educated."

Perhaps the clearest example of Rightists associating their enemies with "communism" came from their responses to the question: "From what racial or religious groups are communists most likely to come?" Rightists not only specified many more groups than did the Non-Rightists (who denied more vigorously that race or religion was relevant $(P > .01)$, but they more frequently designated "atheists," and liberal religious groups like "Unitarians" and "modernistic churches" as sources of Communism. Thus we come full circle: we have seen that many Rightists are religious Fundamentalists and bitterly oppose modern religious ideals, and they freely label these as communist.

A NOTE ON RESPONSE-SET AND SAMPLE REPRESENTATIVENESS

The possibility of response-set type phenomena affecting the results of this study was guarded against by employing a variety of question formats and building in a measure of "sensitivity to content." The problem is to take account of the well demonstrated fact that people's responses to questions are often affected by the interviewing situation, the design and wording of the questions, and a variety of factors.[89] All relationships between Rightists and Non-Rightists based on scales were reexamined with content-sensitivity controlled, and only one difference (out of 15 reported here) was significantly attenuated, this being the "trust of other people" scale results in the "powerlessness and alienation" section. The basic pattern remained unchanged, but it decreases in magnitude. We thus conclude that response-set

---

[89] For major reviews on a vast literature on response-set and the like, see D. N. Jackson and S. Messick, "Content and Style in Personality Assessment," *Psychol. Bull.,* 55 (1958), 243–252; S. Messick, "Response Style and Content Measures from Personality Inventories," *Educ. Psychol. Measmt.,* 22 (1962), 41–56; and Lee Cronbach, *Essentials of Psychological Testing,* 2d ed., (New York: Harper & Row, Publishers, 1960), Part III.

For details of the construction of the Content Sensitivity measure employed in the study see Rohter, *The Radical Rightists,* chap. 2.

does *not* account for the differences noted in this paper between Rightists and Non-Rightists.

Given the nature of the Rightist sample, the feasibility of generalizing the findings is a legitimate concern. Earlier, we found that the sample of publicly active Rightists did not differ significantly from a sample of randomly selected members of a rightist organization on Rightism Index scores, conservative political attitudes, and choice of candidate in the 1964 presidential election. Comparing these two groups on many of the variables covered in this paper, we discovered that both the publicly active and organizational Rightists are similar in their degree of concern about community issues and matters involving traditional values.[90] They also take part equally in *nonpublic* political activities (attend rallies, meetings, write letters, and so on), and there are no significant differences in their responses to several indicators of anomy. But the sample of Rightists who are organizational members does differ significantly from that of the publicly active Rightists on three dimensions: they possess lower objective status, score higher on measures of subjective status frustration, and are more "authoritarian" on personality measures—hostility, closed-mindedness, intolerance of ambiguity, and anticompromise. These differences are consistent with other research which has found these same characteristics significantly associated with less political activity.[91]

CONCLUSIONS: A TENTATIVE CAUSAL MODEL AND TOPOLOGY

The etiology of radical rightism seems to follow this pattern: Persons with certain personality traits, finding themselves in stress-filled social circumstances, react by feeling powerless, dispossessed, estranged, and threatened. They participate in rightism because it allows them to combat these feelings—to oppose, often through action, cultural changes which disturb them, to restore their sense of importance and self-worth, and to understand what is causing their difficulties.

In a preliminary effort to operationalize and more systematically test this theory, the following quantitatively based causal model seems most fruitful (see Figure 1).[92] A varimax factor analysis was performed on 18 scale

---

[90] See Rohter, *The Radical Rightists*, chap. 8, for details.

[91] See Lester Milbrath, *Political Participation* (Skokie, Ill.: Rand McNally & Company, 1965), pp. 115–128 especially, and Lane's *Political Life*, chap. 9.

[92] The construction of "causal models" is a technique for validating *empirically* the causal relationship between variables, an extremely necessary step in theory building. For three recent applications of this technique to political data see T. L. Boyle, "Contested Elections and Voter Turnout in a Local Community," *Amer. Pol. Sci. Rev., 59* (1965), 111–117; C. F. Cnudde and D. J. McCrone, "The Linkage

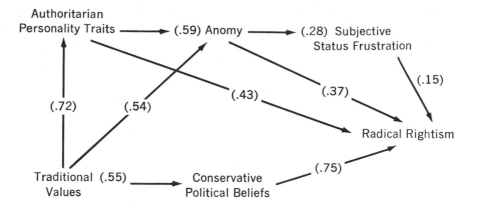

FIGURE 1
Causal Model of Significant Factors
Related to Genesis of Radical Rightism
(Correlation Coefficients)

measures, and four dummy variables were constructed, using factor scores
as weights. The four factors were labeled "Authoritarian Personality Traits,"
"Traditional Values," "Anomy," and "Conservative Political Beliefs." [93]
A fifth dummy variable, measuring "Subjective Status Frustration" was
also constructed. Regression and partial-correlation analysis show that
conservative political beliefs are almost totally determined by traditional
value orientations, that anomy is largely the product of authoritarian personality traits, and that each contributes something to rightism.

This model, to repeat, is highly tentative, and is offered here not as
conclusive but to illustrate the type of further analysis that is being pursued
in the effort to build a viable theory explaining rightism.

A second avenue of analysis being explored is a *typology* of radical
rightists. While the study has up to now tended to treat rightists as a mono-
lithic group, it seems apparent that some important differentiations between *types* of rightists are necessary. Two "types" currently being studied
are "Status Seekers" and "The Culturally Alienated." This first group seems
to fit best the model that status frustrations and the desire for social esteem
are primary motivational factors. Among these rightists matters of social
status, acceptance, and the attainment of influence are most salient." "Cul-

between Constituency Attitudes and Congressional Voting Behavior: A Causal
Model," *Amer. Pol. Sci. Rev.*, 60 (1966), 66–72; and A. S. Goldberg, "Discerning
A Causal Pattern among Data on Voting Behavior," *Amer. Pol. Sci. Rev.*, 60
(1966), 913–922. While there is a vast technical literature on this method, Hubert
M. Blalock's *Causal Inference in Nonexperimental Research* (Chapel Hill: Univer-
sity of North Carolina Press, 1964) is a readable introduction to the subject.

[93] See *The Radical Rightists*, chap. 8, for details of the factor analysis.

turally alienated" rightists conform closest to the conceptualizations about value alienation, social isolation, and anomy. Unlike Type I Rightists, who desire to be accepted into society and achieve positions of social importance, the alienated rightists do not want to be part of a society whose dominant values and practices are incongruous with their own basic values and behavior. These Rightists are extremely religious, usually belong to Fundamentalist churches, view the world in terms of ascetic Protestant values, and equate "Communism" with all they find wrong with today's world.

A typological approach offers at least two distinct advantages in studying radical rightism. It first calls attention to the multiple appeals of rightists by emphasizing that persons may become rightists for a variety of reasons. Rightism performs many functions, and participation can be for one or a combination of them. While some of these factors may cluster naturally, there is no simple explanation of "why people become rightists." Secondly, a typology is usefully applied to the study of rightist organizations. Obviously some groups appeal more to one type of potential rightist than others. "Culturally alienated" types would probably be attracted to religious-oriented organizations, such as Hargis's Christian Crusade, while "status seekers" might find the Birch Society or Liberty Amendment Committees more appealing. We could thus order rightist groups on a spectrum, with different membership compositions and ideological themes emphasized. Again, these are only hypotheses which need to be explored and tested empirically.

PART 3

THE CONVENTIONAL RIGHT: GOLDWATER CONSERVATIVES

Conservatism or Extremism: Goldwater Supporters in the 1964 Presidential Election

JAMES McEVOY III

The purpose of this study is to explore and describe the policy preferences, political activities, and social attitudes of persons in the electorate who gave early support to the candidacy of Senator Barry Goldwater in the 1964 national election. The character and degree of attitudinal and ideological constraint among their opinions, behaviors, and attitudes is viewed with an eye to the question: was Goldwater's candidacy supported by a social movement of an extremist, that is to say radical sort or, instead, was "Goldwaterism" a conservative political impulse? Furthermore, was there sufficient constraint among the beliefs of Goldwater's supporters to justifiably consider them ideologues in a political setting that has been shown to harbor few political animals of an ideological stripe. Finally, was "Goldwaterism" primarily an elite or a mass movement?

In his important book on the McCarthy period, Michael Rogin has pointed out the implications of these questions for the analysis of the supporters of the late Senator McCarthy.[1] Attacking the ex-radical pluralists'[2] view of McCarthyism, which was in part based on their assumption of the equivalency of Populism, Progressivism, and McCarthyism as mass (that is, antidemocratic, and anti-institutional) social movements, Rogin accuses the former radicals of an elite bias—a bias which caused them to identify McCarthy with mass politics and to avoid consideration of institutional and elite support for his activities. It is unfortunately true that the same biases have already begun to color the interpretations of the causes of the nomination and analysis of the social support for Senator Goldwater. Writing in the *Saturday Review*, for example, the late Arthur Schlesinger, Sr., identified the appearance of Goldwater as a remanifestation of an "extremism" which pervaded the A.P.A., Know Nothing, Ku Klux Klan and the McCarthy "movements."[3] Much of the liberal and not-so-liberal commentary on Goldwater not only reinforced this picture of the backers of Senator Goldwater as "nuts," "cranks," "neo-Nazis," and the like, but also, in a less pejorative vein portrayed the senator and his supporters as "irresponsible." Responsibility was a catchword among political commentators in 1964;[4] and while the seeming lack of consistency (responsibility?) which governed the Republican candidate's conflicting pronouncements on foreign affairs and domestic policy should not be lost in consideration of the outcome of the election of 1964, it does not follow that the supposed irresponsibility of an aspiring decision-maker should be used as the single tool in the analysis of the persons who supported him.

Theodore H. White, author of *The Making of the President: 1964*, carried this style of analysis into the Republican party itself. White identifies the conflict in the party over the nomination as one between the "Eastern Establishment" on the one hand and the "Primitives" on the other. This differentiation, while convenient shorthand and far less disparaging in intent than the Schlesinger comparison, nevertheless points to the same general

---

[1] Michael P. Rogin, *The Intellectuals and McCarthy: The Radical Specter* (Cambridge, Mass.: MIT Press, 1967).

[2] Rogin, especially his first chapter, "Radicalism and the Rational Society: The Pluralist View," pp. 9–31.

[3] Arthur M. Schlesinger, Sr., "Extremism in American Politics," *Saturday Review* (November 27, 1965), pp. 21–25. See also Lionel Lokos, *Hysteria 1964: The Fear Campaign against Barry Goldwater* (New Rochelle, New York: Arlington House, 1967), for an interesting collection of articles in which Goldwater was described as a "fascist," "Nazi," "racist," and so on. Lokos' volume is a post-campaign, pro-Goldwater tract attempting to "set the record straight." Nevertheless, it is an interesting record of one important aspect of the 1964 campaign.

[4] Angus Campbell, "Interpreting the Presidential Victory" in Milton Cummings, Jr., *The National Election of 1964* (Washington, D.C.: The Brookings Institution, 1966), pp. 260–264.

conclusions that Rogin and others [5] have shown to be the conceptual down-fall of the pluralists: the portrayal of American rightist politics as prac-ticed primarily by unsocialized political actors lacking either the prerequi-sites or the stability to be trusted with political power and as representing segments of the society which are, by definition, anti-democratic. As we shall see in the following pages, there is evidence to suggest that Goldwater sup-porters are not advocates of mass politics, are highly socialized political actors, come from normally conservative sectors of the society, and hold social attitudes and policy preferences which may seem to many as irre-sponsible and ill-thought out but which are held, nevertheless, by persons with extraordinarily high levels of formal education and political involve-ment—conditions which even the most ideologically blinded commentator would have to admit are associated, in the United States at least, with politi-cal responsibility. The evidence suggests that Goldwater's supporters did not lack continuity in their political norms with the remainder of the American electorate. As we shall also see, there were very few persons in the mass public who favored Senator Goldwater's nomination; even among Republi-cans he was a fourth or fifth choice.

The organization of this study is fairly straightforward. First, there is a consideration of the demographic characteristics of Goldwater's supporters; second, an analysis of their opinions on the important domestic and foreign issues in the 1964 campaign—civil rights, American foreign policy, and social welfare. The third and most extensive section deals with the political activity, partisan preference and involvement, political information, ideo-logical structure, and political efficacy of the Goldwater supporters.

The responses of Goldwater supporters to various items from the Survey Research Center's 1964 Election Studies are the data from which this analysis is drawn. This group of respondents is broken down into early (pre-convention) supporters of the senator and late (post-convention pre-election) backers of his candidacy. Comparisons are made among the pro-Goldwater group as a whole and its two subgroups and other groups of the electorate in 1964, including Johnson supporters and undecided voters. For the most part, the analysis considers the segments of the mass public who were, relatively speaking, politically involved and sophisticated to at least the extent that they had a vote intention and/or a candidate preference at the time the SRC conducted its pre-election survey, September through October, 1964.

As I have suggested, Goldwater's early supporters were drawn from relatively high socioeconomic strata. Among the early Goldwater supporters,

---

[5] Raymond E. Wolfinger and others, "America's Radical Right: Politics and Ideology" in David E. Apter (ed.), *Ideology and Discontent* (New York: The Free Press, 1964), pp. 262–293 and Nelson W. Polsby, "Toward an Explanation of McCarthyism," *Political Studies* (October 1960), 250–271.

the percentage of college graduates, persons with incomes of $10,000 or more per year, and those employed in professional and technical occupations, or who were self-employed businessmen or managers, was remarkably high. Slightly more than one quarter of the early supporters had a college education, half of them held professional or technical occupations or were self-employed businessmen, and more than a third had incomes above $10,000. See Table 1.

TABLE 1

Demographic Characteristic of Candidate Preference Groups[a]

	EARLY SUPPORTERS		LATE SUPPORTERS		JOHNSON SUPPORTERS		UNDECIDED OTHER		TOTAL	
CHARACTERISTICS	N	%	N	%	N	%	N	%	N	%
Region										
East and Middle										
Atlantic	8	7.7	45	20.6	222	26.6	70	18.1	345	22.3
Midwest	32	30.4	76	34.7	267	31.9	109	28.2	484	31.3
South and Border	46	43.8	64	29.2	210	25.1	154	39.8	474	30.6
Mountain and										
Pacific	19	18.1	34	15.6	137	16.4	54	14.0	244	15.8
	105	100.0	219	100.0	836	100.0	387	100.0	1547	100.0
Population										
Central cities of										
12 largest SMSA's	10	9.5	15	6.8	121	14.5	43	11.1	189	12.2
50,000 and over	18	17.1	41	18.7	162	19.4	85	22.0	306	19.8
10,000–49,999	15	14.3	38	17.4	155	18.5	78	20.2	286	18.5
2500–9999	33	31.4	56	25.6	151	18.1	74	19.1	314	20.3
Rural	29	27.6	69	31.5	247	29.5	107	27.6	452	29.2
	105	100.0	219	100.0	836	100.0	387	100.0	1547	100.0
Sex										
Male	60	57.1	98	44.7	374	44.7	159	41.1	691	44.7
Female	45	42.9	121	55.3	462	55.3	228	58.9	856	55.3
	105	100.0	219	100.0	836	100.0	387	100.0	1547	100.0
Age										
21–30	16	15.2	21	9.6	113	13.5	72	18.6	222	14.4
31–39	18	17.1	37	16.9	175	20.9	63	16.3	293	18.9
40–49	24	22.9	52	23.7	184	22.0	70	18.1	330	21.3
50–59	21	22.9	40	18.3	179	21.4	73	18.9	313	20.2
60 or older	26	24.8	69	31.5	184	10.1	109	28.2	388	25.1
	105	100.0	219	100.0	835	100.0	387	100.0	1546	100.0
Race										
White	105	100.0	218	100.0	721	86.5	332	87.8	1376	89.6
Negro	0	0	0	0	113	13.5	46	12.2	159	10.3
	105	100.0	218	100.0	834	100.0	378	100.0	1535	100.0
Marital Status										
Married	88	83.8	156	71.2	641	76.7	290	74.9	1175	76.0
Single	6	5.7	14	6.4	52	6.2	28	7.2	100	6.5
Divorced/										
separated	5	4.8	10	4.5	52	6.2	27	7.0	94	6.1
Widowed	6	5.7	39	17.8	91	10.9	42	10.9	178	11.5
	105	100.0	219	100.0	836	100.0	387	100.0	1547	100.0

TABLE 1 (cont'd)

Demographic Characteristic of Candidate Preference Groups [a]

	EARLY SUPPORTERS		LATE SUPPORTERS		JOHNSON SUPPORTERS		UNDECIDED OTHER		TOTAL	
CHARACTERISTICS	N	%	N	%	N	%	N	%	N	%
Level of Formal Education										
Grade school or some high school	24	22.9	67	30.6	378	45.4	218	56.9	687	44.6
High school graduate	16	15.2	53	24.2	189	22.7	72	18.8	330	21.4
Some college	38	36.2	69	31.5	190	22.8	53	13.8	350	22.7
College graduate	27	25.7	30	13.7	76	9.1	40	10.4	173	11.2
	105	100.0	219	100.0	833	100.0	383	100.0	1540	100.0
Income: [b]										
0–3999	12	11.5	49	23.2	217	27.0	142	38.6	424	28.5
4000–6000	16	15.4	45	21.3	168	20.9	78	21.2	307	20.6
6000–7499	11	10.6	22	10.4	136	16.9	45	12.2	214	14.4
7500–9999	22	21.2	38	18.0	130	16.1	46	12.5	236	15.9
10,000–14,999	22	21.2	38	18.0	107	13.3	37	10.1	204	13.7
15,000 or more	17	16.3	19	9.0	47	5.8	12	3.3	103	6.9
	104	100.0	211	100.0	805	100.0	368	100.0	1488	100.0
Occupation [c]										
White-Collar:										
Professional and Semiprofessional	12	11.7	26	11.9	77	9.4	33	8.7	148	9.7
Self-employed business, artisans, manufacturers	29	28.4	45	20.6	123	15.0	48	12.7	245	16.1
Clerical and sales, buyers, agents, brokers	21	20.6	24	11.0	84	10.2	29	7.7	158	10.4
Total White-Collar	62	60.8	95	43.6	284	34.6	110	29.1	551	36.3
Blue-Collar:										
Skilled and semiskilled	15	14.7	41	18.8	260	31.7	119	31.5	435	28.6
Unskilled, service, farm laborers	2	2.0	11	5.0	79	9.6	38	10.1	130	8.6
Protective service	1	1.0	4	1.8	17	2.1	6	1.6	28	1.8
Total blue-collar	18	17.6	56	25.7	356	43.4	163	43.1	593	39.0
Farm operators	2	2.0	18	8.3	38	4.6	17	4.5	75	4.9
Retired	17	16.7	35	16.1	101	12.3	55	14.6	208	13.7
Housewife	3	2.9	13	6.0	32	3.9	25	6.6	73	4.8
Unemployed	0	.0	1	.04	10	1.2	8	2.1	19	1.3
	102	100.0	218	100.0	821	100.0	378	100.0	1519	100.0

[a] This and other demographic tables are percentaged down rather than across.
[b] Combined family—expected
[c] Head of Household

As an inspection of this table shows, not only were Goldwater's early supporters disproportionately higher in educational, occupational, and income levels with respect to the population as a whole, but they were also an elite group among probable Republican voters. Since Republicans have generally higher levels of education and higher occupational status than either Democrats or the undecided voters, the findings of high-status bias among pro-Goldwater Republicans is interesting. The division in the Republican voting bloc was the reverse of that suggested by White: the relatively elite segment of the Republican party's mass base disproportionately supported the "primitive's" candidate. Of course, the data in Table 1 do not account for the probable shift of approximately 10 percent of normally loyal Republicans to the Johnson ticket. In any case, the rather high absolute level of social status possessed by the early pro-Goldwater group is still apparent; and while the effect of that shift may have been to remove persons of fairly high status from the group of later supporters of Senator Goldwater, it was not likely to be of sufficient size to obviate this finding.[6]

There were a few other important differences between early and late supporters of the senator. Regionally, Goldwater's early support was drawn heavily from the South and border states (43.8 percent) and West (18.1 percent) with very little support from the Middle Atlantic and Eastern states, (7.6 percent). The later supporters, in contrast, were more evenly distributed among the various regions of the country with 20.6 percent from the East and Middle Atlantic states, 34.7 percent from the Midwest, 29.2 percent from the South and border states and 15.6 percent from the West. These compare with the sample's distribution of 22.3 percent from the New England and Middle Atlantic states, 31.2 percent from the Midwest, 30.7 percent from the South and border states, and 15.8 percent from the Mountain and Pacific states.

There was a heavy over-representation of males in the group of early supporters: 57.1 percent of these respondents were males; only 44.7 percent of the later supporters and 44.7 percent of the sample as a whole was male. This distribution, probably an artifact of the high levels of political activity among Goldwater's early supporters, will be discussed in some detail in the final section of this essay. Table 1 gives the distribution of all the various groups in the analysis on these and a number of additional demographic characteristics; the concluding section of this essay will discuss the contents of this table in greater detail.

The age breakdowns, also reported in Table 1, show that the early pro-Goldwater group was *less likely* to have older (60 years or more) persons in it than the later pro-Goldwater group and more likely to have

---

[6] The question of defection rates is discussed in Campbell, "Presidential Victory," and is treated later in this discussion.

relatively young members in the 21–30 age brackets. Between Johnson backers and all Goldwater supporters, however, there was an extreme difference in the percentage of older persons supporting either candidate. Goldwater, with 21 percent of the electorate supporting him, had 31 percent of the persons 60 years or older behind him. Put differently, only 10 percent of Johnson's supporters were 60 or older, almost 30 percent of Goldwater's backers came from this age cohort. There was not a single Negro in the sample who supported Goldwater either before or after his nomination.

CIVIL RIGHTS, PREJUDICE, AND THE SUPPORTERS OF SENATOR GOLDWATER

If a single overt issue of domestic policy in 1964 could be said to have been the crux of the conflict among Republican political elites, it was the Civil Rights Act of 1964. The conflict over this act and its implications for further extension of federal power into the area of civil rights for Negroes was followed by a series of riots in American cities in which the antagonists were police and Negroes. These issues, coupled with George Wallace's success in the Wisconsin and the Indiana primary elections, lent an impressive facade to the supposed power of "White Backlash." By the time of the Republican convention, there had been a clear split among liberal and conservative Republicans over the civil rights issue, drawn primarily along the dimension of federal intervention on behalf of the civil rights movement. While the following paragraphs do not form a comprehensive analysis of the racial and civil rights issues in 1964, they do at least suggest that there was, among Goldwater's early supporters, a distinct opposition to both federal intervention in the civil rights area *and* a fairly high level of approval of segregation and other anti-Negro attitudes and policy preferences.

Table 2, Parts A and B, presents the responses of the various groups to several questions dealing, first, with federal intervention in the civil rights area (Part A) and then with a series of questions which attempted to tap the electorate's feelings about the civil rights movement, segregation, and property rights.[7]

Table 2, Part A points to a fundamental division between Johnson and Goldwater supporters on the issue of federal intervention to establish equality of job opportunity and integrated schools. In each case, the response most hostile to such intervention was given by the early pro-

---

[7] The intercorrelations between these two types of questions were low, but they were rather strongly associated within their category. The correlation between the two items in Part A of the table was $+.308$; the mean correlation between these questions and the school integration items $+.133$.

TABLE 2

Part A: Government Action on Civil Rights [a]

| | EQUAL JOB OPPORTUNITY | | | | | | INTEGRATION OF SCHOOLS | | | | | |
| | For Intervention | | Against Intervention | | Total | | For Intervention | | Against Intervention | | Total | |
	N	%	N	%	N	%	N	%	N	%	N	%
Early supporters	17	16.8	70	69.3	87	86.1	24	23.1	69	66.3	93	89.4
Later supporters	43	20.5	131	62.4	174	82.9	69	32.4	588	43.8	657	76.2
Johnson supporters	387	48.0	278	34.4	665	82.4	402	49.8	266	32.9	668	82.7
Undecided/other	160	50.3	134	42.1	294	92.4	149	47.2	140	44.3	289	91.5
Totals	607	45.6	613	46.1	1220	91.7	644	47.8	588	43.8	1232	91.6

TABLE 2

Part B: Responses to Civil Rights Movement, Segregation and Property Rights [a]

| | SEGREGATION | | | | | | CIVIL RIGHTS MOVEMENT | | | | | | PROPERTY RIGHTS: OPEN OCCUPANCY | | | | | |
| | Favor | | Oppose | | Total | | Mostly Violent | | Mostly Peaceful | | Total | | Favor | | Oppose | | Total | |
	N	%	N	%	N	%	N	%	N	%	N	%	N	%	N	%	N	%
Early supporters	29	28.4	27	26.5	56	54.9	67	70.5	22	23.2	89	93.7	48	45.7	38	36.2	86	81.9
Later supporters	58	27.5	51	24.2	109	51.7	149	75.6	43	21.8	192	97.4	114	52.3	63	28.9	177	81.2
Johnson supporters	154	18.8	306	43.8	460	62.6	442	59.6	265	35.7	707	99.3	519	62.4	190	22.8	709	85.2
Undecided/other	104	27.9	101	27.1	205	55.0	220	57.9	89	23.4	309	81.3	202	52.8	109	28.5	311	81.3
Totals	345	22.9	485	32.2	830	55.1	878	64.7	419	30.9	1297	95.6	883	57.4	400	26.0	1283	83.4

[a] Percentages are computed only for those responding to the question. Responses reported exclude "no interest" and include "other" categories of response to each question as part of the percentage base. Total columns refer to percentage of respondents replying to the question in the manner indicated in the table. Tables read from left to right.

Goldwater group—in the case of school integration they were 13 percentage points above the later group in opposition to federal intervention and 33 points above Johnson's early backers. The difference between the early and later group of ʿupporters on the issue of federal intervention to insure equality of job opportunity was small, but again a gulf separated all Goldwater supporters from those backing Johnson and, it is interesting to note, from the electorate as a whole on both issues raised by the questions in Part A of Table 2.

The second part of this table reports the responses of the same groups to a series of questions on civil rights issues which were not at the same time related to the issue of federal power over traditional local matters. Here the difference between Goldwater supporters and the pro-Johnson group are in the same direction as they were in the first part of the table but are by no means so extreme. Nor (with one or two exceptions) do the early or late backers of the senator deviate so strikingly from the entire electorate as they did on the civil rights-federal power issues. Nevertheless, it seems clear that not only was there a strong reflection of the Republican elites' controversy over the issue of the role of the federal government in civil rights among Goldwater's supporters but also a distinct tendency on their part to favor racial segregation, oppose open occupancy, and perceive the civil rights movement as more often violent than peaceful. Part of this probably may be explained by the heavy representation of Southern (37 percent) and Border state (11.4 percent) respondents in the early pro-Goldwater group (see Table 1); but the differences between the early and late groups of supporters are fairly small and the later group had a slight underrepresentation of Southerners based on the distribution of the sample as a whole. (See Table 1.) Obviously, then, the critics of Goldwater who identified his campaign and its supporters as generally opposed to equal opportunity for Negroes were in part correct; but Goldwater, on the other hand, properly identified the overriding issue surrounding civil rights as one of federal power and intervention in local and state affairs, not simply racism or segregation.

Clearly, the responses to the questions reported in Table 2 do not necessarily imply that the pro-Goldwater groups were necessarily bigoted, prejudiced, or hate-mongering, no more than do the seemingly more liberal responses of the Johnson supporters to the same questions mean that these respondents were integrationist, fair-minded contributors to the Southern Christian Leadership Conference. Part of the difference between Johnson and Goldwater supporters is simply a matter of adherence to their perceived party or candidate position on the issues raised by the questions. But it is rather surprising that groups with such extraordinarily high levels of formal education as the pro-Goldwater supporters possessed would favor segregation to the degree they did and so often oppose the right of a Negro to buy a house wherever he might choose to do so. Was prejudice a distinct characteristic of this group? There is some data that bears somewhat more directly on this point; let us examine it briefly.

Employing an evaluative measuring technique known as a "feeling thermometer," the Survey Research Center asked the respondents in the 1964 election studies to indicate the degree (on a scale of 100) of approval or disapproval of a number of ethnic groups and voluntary associations known to large segments of the mass public. While this scale gives great flexibility to the measurement of the intensity and direction of an opinion, it has been found to be a relatively unreliable indicator of attitudinal constraint except among persons with high levels of education; that is a high rating of, say, "liberals" may be coupled with an equally high rating of "conservatives." Among respondents with higher formal education, however, this tendency is attenuated, thus making the scale of some limited value for an analysis of the groups with which we are primarily concerned.

Two groups other than Negroes who have been traditional targets of prejudiced persons are Jews and Catholics. The feeling thermometer scores of the partisan segments on these two groups and on Negroes are reported in Table 3. And as a preliminary glance at this table shows, there appears to be a general pattern of antagonism towards Jews, Catholics, and Negroes on the part of the early pro-Goldwater group. They were twice as negative in their response to Jews as the sample as a whole, slightly more hostile in their responses to Catholics, and about one and one-half times as negative in their views of Negroes as was the entire sample. Of course, it is evidently the case that a small subset of this early pro-Goldwater group was responsible for this distribution of responses because of the fact that the early pro-Goldwater group also provided a very high percentage of persons with positive attitudes towards these groups. Nevertheless it is clear that there was a consistent and disproportionately high level of antagonism to these three minority groups by this subset of the early group which was not present in the responses of the group of later supporters. Thus it appears, although the issue is by no means a closed one,[8] that prejudice—defined as expressed "coldness" to minority groups—was higher (with one exception) among a larger proportion of the early supporters of Senator Goldwater than among any other of the groups isolated here for analysis, and substantially higher than for the electorate as a whole. Again in the case of the group of early supporters, this finding seems especially significant considering the exceptionally high educational and socioeconomic status of that group, conditions which normally are associated with low levels of racial and religious prejudice.

---

[8] Due largely to the issue of overrepresentation of southern respondents in the early group—a control of South/North on this variable would, in a sample of this size, reduce the N in the cells to the point where analysis would be fruitless, with a random distribution producing only ten cases per cell.

TABLE 3

Evaluation of Jews, Catholics, and Negroes [a]

| | JEWS | | | | | | | |
| | Negative ≤ 49° | | Neutral 50–59° | | Positive > 59° | | Total | |
	N	%	N	%	N	%	N	%
Early supporters	19	18.4	27	26.2	58	56.6	104	100
Later supporters	18	8.5	82	38.5	113	53.1	213	100
Johnson supporters	67	8.2	307	37.4	447	54.4	821	100
Undecided/other	34	9.2	191	51.6	145	39.2	370	100
Sample	138	9.2	607	40.3	763	50.6	1508	100

| | CATHOLICS | | | | | | | |
| | Negative ≤ 49° | | Neutral 50–59° | | Positive > 59° | | Total | |
	N	%	N	%	N	%	N	%
Early supporters	13	12.5	25	24.0	66	63.5	104	100
Later supporters	26	12.1	67	31.2	122	56.7	215	100
Johnson supporters	63	7.6	236	28.7	523	63.6	822	100
Undecided/other	40	10.8	152	41.2	177	48.0	369	100
Sample	142	9.4	480	31.8	888	58.8	1510	100

| | NEGROES | | | | | | | |
| | Negative ≤ 49° | | Neutral 50–59° | | Positive > 59° | | Total | |
	N	%	N	%	N	%	N	%
Early supporters	24	23.1	21	20.2	59	56.7	104	100
Later supporters	36	16.7	52	24.2	127	59.1	215	100
Johnson supporters	97	11.9	211	25.8	510	62.3	818	100
Undecided/other	67	25.3	109	41.1	89	33.6	265	100
Sample	224	16.0	393	28.0	785	56.0	1402	100

[a] Table is read from left to right.

FOREIGN POLICY: MILITARISM, ANTICOMMUNISM AND POLITICAL INVOLVEMENT

The issue of the questionable "responsibility" of Senator Goldwater was, as I suggested in the introduction, a very salient one for the American electorate in 1964. Campbell summarizes the different areas of the Senator's image at which the electorate directed its criticisms:

It has been pointed out that Mr. Goldwater was much more commonly spoken of unfavorably than favorably. While he was more often referred to as a man of integrity than Mr. Johnson, and less commonly as a "politician," in most other respects he suffered from the comparison. He was especially weak in the public assessment of his past record and experience. His speeches drew much more criticism than Johnson's. His policy positions, as they were seen by the public, drew an exceptional number of comments, most of them unfavorable. While Mr. Goldwater obviously had many ardent admirers, the total public reaction to his personal qualities, his campaign appearances, and the policies with which he was identified was on balance clearly negative.[9]

And no single policy area drew as much criticism as did the electorate's belief that Goldwater was a militarist. Of a total of 738 unfavorable references to Senator Goldwater's policy positions, 213 were directed at his "militarism," 177 at his stand on social security and only 81 at his opposition to civil rights. The remainder were distributed among the issues of his conservatism, opposition to Medicare, and a general disagreement with his policies.[10] Very clearly, then, militarism and, by extension, foreign policy concerns were strikingly influential in the electorate's relatively negative evaluation of Senator Goldwater. This perception is even more remarkable when one looks at the data on the same issue from the 1960 election study. There only 12 mentions of either candidate as being too militaristic occurred, four attributed to Nixon and eight to Kennedy.[11]

There is a rather broad range of policy preferences and beliefs to which the larger issue of Goldwater's supposed militarism might be presumed to be related. Among these are, of course, overt concern about war in general and specifically the then relatively low-key conflict in Vietnam. But in addition such issues as foreign aid, the perceived position of the United States in world affairs, strength of anti-Communist feelings and the respondents' views on negotiation and trade with Communist nations all appear to tap concerns which if not identical to a direct concern with militarism at least are related to each other along the dimension of the respondents' preference for either a relatively conciliatory, flexible foreign policy or a rigid, aggressive-isolationist posture on the part of his government.[12] There were a number of questions in the 1964 election study which explored these dimensions of opinion and attitude. Let us see to what extent the preferences and beliefs of Goldwater's supporters on these issues differed or concurred with those of the other members of the electorate in 1964.

Table 4 regarding American involvement and policy in Vietnam presents an interesting, seemingly asymmetrical, distribution of opinion on this question of foreign policy which has, of course, become the central issue of American politics in the years since these data were collected. While

---

[9] Campbell, "Presidential Victory," p. 263.

[10] Campbell, pp. 261–62.

[11] Campbell, p. 261.

[12] These dimensions of policy preference seem to be the major ones to which the electorate as a whole responds. See Angus Campbell and others, *Elections and the Political Order* (New York: John Wiley & Sons, Inc., 1966), pp. 355–356.

TABLE 4

Policy Preferences on the War in Vietnam

| | INVOLVEMENT | | | | | | | |
| | Approve | | Other | | Disapprove | | Total | |
	N	%	N	%	N	%	N	%
Early supporters	45	59.2	1	1.3	30	39.5	76	100
Late supporters	74	51.7	4	2.8	65	45.5	143	100
Johnson supporters	329	66.1	5	1.0	164	32.9	498	100
Other	103	51.2	4	2.0	94	46.8	201	100
Totals	551	60.0	14	1.5	353	38.5	918	100

| | SOLUTION FAVORED | | | | | | | |
| | Pull Out | | Retain Troops Try to End Fighting | | Take Stronger Stand—Including Invasion | | Total | |
	N	%	N	%	N	%	N	%
Early supporters	9	11.3	8	10.0	63	78.9	80	100
Late supporters	18	12.2	30	20.3	100	67.6	148	100
Johnson supporters	64	12.5	230	44.8	219	42.7	513	100
Other	34	18.3	84	45.2	68	36.6	186	100
Totals	125	13.5	352	37.9	450	48.5	927	100

undecided voters were most likely to disapprove of Americans' involvement in Vietnam, they were closely followed by both groups of Goldwater's supporters who were 14 and 7 percentage points respectively above the pro-Johnson group's level of disapproval on this question. On the other hand, the Goldwater groups differed markedly from the remainder of the electorate in the option they favored as a solution to America's presence in Vietnam: the early supporters of the senator favored "escalation," including the invasion of North Vietnam, by a factor of almost 2:1 over Johnson's partisans and the undecided voters. The later supporters of the senator were only slightly less aggressive in their choice of solutions.

It is somewhat ironical, given the immense growth of the conflict in Vietnam under Johnson's administration, that the majority (57.3 percent) of Johnson's supporters in 1964 favored either a maintenance of the conflict at its 1964 level or pulling out of Vietnam entirely; and furthermore that the undecided voters also favored these alternatives even more strongly. Vietnam was the issue in 1964 around which the electorate's fear of militarism was organized, and although the electorate as a whole was almost evenly divided (48.5 percent for escalation, 51.4 percent against it) on this issue, the broad thrust of the Johnson vote was anti-escalation.

Evidently the militaristic segments of the electorate—with respect to the issue of Vietnam, anyway—were disproportionate in the ranks of Goldwater's early backers. But although there is no clear split between the early and the late group on this question, there was a difference of 11.3 percentage points between these two groups, indicating that the voters who stayed with Goldwater, even though preferring another candidate, were likely to differ in a somewhat less militaristic direction from his earlier supporters on the issue of prosecuting the war in Vietnam. However, this difference is small when compared with Johnson's supporters and the sample as a whole. Since this group of later supporters was made up largely of what might reasonably be termed the "party faithful" (42 percent identified themselves as "strong Republicans" and an additional 38 percent said they were either not very strong or independent Republicans), the apparent militarism of Goldwater's campaign, while no doubt offending the defectors from the Republican ticket and Independents, and causing some concern among his later supporters, was not objectionable to the majority of Republicans in 1964. Evidently it would be a mistake to identify Goldwater's campaign as specifically responsible for the mobilization of militaristic sentiment among the electorate. It appears that, among Republicans, a large majority favored an aggressive policy in Vietnam and would do so regardless of who was heading the Republican ticket. Of course, this may simply be an artifact of Republicans' loyalty to their perception of the policy position of their party's candidate. As we shall see in the following paragraphs, despite the relative similarity in the two pro-Goldwater groups along these two specific policy dimensions, they were widely divergent on another issue which might seem to be intimately related to the prosecution of a war against North Vietnam. This issue was anticommunism.

ANTICOMMUNISM

The American electorate is generally in favor of negotiations with Communist nations (84.3 percent favor this, only 11.4 percent oppose it) [13] but on several other issues appears to be somewhat less than willing to support policies which involve the United States more closely than at present with Communist nation-states. For example, almost 57 percent of the electorate stated that "farmers and businessmen should be forbidden to do business with Communist countries." And a large majority (74.9 percent) of those having an opinion on the issue opposed the admission of Red China to the United Nations. (However, only 11.5 percent felt that if Communist China were admitted, the United States should withdraw its membership in the U.N.) The support of the electorate for American intervention to remove Communist governments seems fairly strong: 39 percent favored doing ". . . something to get the Communist government

---

[13] All percentages are based on the number of persons responding.

out of Cuba," but almost a majority (48 percent) felt that it was "up to the Cuban people to handle their own affairs."

Aggressive, interventionist anticommunism as a strong theme of Goldwater's campaign and, as we would expect, his early supporters were most likely to echo this theme in their responses to questions concerning American foreign policy. In order to measure the general level of anticommunist feeling among the electorate an "Anti-Communism Index" (ACI) was constructed by intercorrelating three items dealing with American policy toward Communist nations, and then, after establishing that a sufficiently high relationship between them existed for the purposes of an index (mean inter-item correlation $= +.422$), the individual items were trichotomized into a 3-point scale: 1 = low, 2 = medium, 3 = high, a 0 was recorded for missing data. To determine scores the sums of these values were added for the three items and the range of possible scores $(0 - 9)$ was again trichotomized with total scores of 1, 2, or 3 becoming a 1 in the final scale, 4, 5, or 6 becoming 2's, and 7, 8, or 9 becoming 3's. The scores of the groups were then summed and expressed as percentages.[14]

Table 5 presents the distribution of scores for the various groups on

TABLE 5

Scores of Groups on Anti-Communism Index (ACI)

	LOW		MEDIUM		HIGH		TOTAL	
	N	%	N	%	N	%	N	%
Early supporters	10	10.6	33	35.1	51	54.3	94	100
Late supporters	40	21.4	87	46.5	60	32.1	187	100
Johnson supporters	267	38.5	330	47.6	96	13.9	693	100
Other supporters	117	41.6	125	44.5	39	13.9	281	100
Totals	434	34.6	575	45.8	246	19.6	1255	100

the ACI. Looking at the high end of the distribution reveals extremely large differences between every group with a candidate preference. The early Goldwater backers were more than 20 percentage points above the later group on this index, and Johnson supporters were slightly more than 20 percentage points below the later Goldwater group.

Anticommunism was not by any means an issue uniting all of the eventual supporters of Goldwater in 1964, but it was one of the stronger discriminators between the blocs of Johnson and Goldwater supporters. But while

---

[14] This same procedure was used to develop all additional indices reported here. The questions making up this index were those concerning trade with Communist nations, military policy in Vietnam, and admission of Red China to the U.N.

the conception (evidenced by some critics) of the Republican party and its supporters in 1964 as monolithically anticommunist is simply not borne out here, this is not to say that anticommunism as a political style was unimportant in Republican politics at the mass level. Goldwater supporters, while at the time accounting for only about 21 percent of the electorate, contributed 45 percent of all the individuals scoring at the high end of the ACI. And inasmuch as the groups isolated here for analysis occupy a relatively elite political status, the extreme differences found here between Johnson and Goldwater supporters, like the similarly strong division between these groups on civil rights issues, suggests, as we would expect, that these issues are ideologically distinct ones for these groups in a very general sense of that term. Intense anticommunism—a Goldwater campaign theme—was very well received by the majority of his early supporters.

Table 6 presents data about three additional areas of foreign policy on which some interesting differences are found between the groups. Like the ACI scores for the early Goldwater, late Goldwater, and Johnson groups the patterns of response on the first two issues in the table (success in foreign relations and world position) are rather widely divergent from each other. Clearly, Goldwater's early supporters were extraordinarily agitated about these issues, and those who supported him soon after his nomination also appear very disturbed. That dissatisfaction was so high among Goldwater supporters may, of course, simply reflect their allegiance to the Republican party's position on foreign affairs, or it may reflect a genuine concern for the state of U.S.-foreign relations. If this is the case, these respondents might be expected to take something other than a traditional isolationist position on the question of foreign aid and, as can be readily seen, they do.

As column 3 of Table 6 indicates, both the early and late group of Goldwater backers supported foreign aid about half the time. Johnson's partisans backed it in two-thirds of the cases. But the spread between the

TABLE 6

Perception of America's World Position and View of Foreign Aid

	U. S. Not Doing As Well As It Should In Foreign Affairs		U. S. Position In The World Has Become "Less Strong"		Favor Giving Aid to Foreign Countries Who Need Help	
	N	%	N	%	N	%
Early	86	86.0	61	61.0	47	46.15
Late	117	59.4	81	41.8	102	49.0
Johnson	170	23.9	102	14.4	490	65.1
Other	105	40.5	78	25.2	180	54.1
Totals	478	37.75	322	24.5	819	58.7

early Goldwater group and the Johnson group is only nineteen percentage points—a spread that is relatively small when compared with the ACI scores or the responses to the "success" and "world position" questions. Thus, while a more traditional isolationism may be reflected in the tendency for Goldwater supporters to object more often to foreign aid than their Democratic counterparts (and also in their opposition to America's initial involvement in Vietnam), a relative consensus on the issue is at least implied by these data and its direction is clearly "internationalistic."

SOCIAL WELFARE

In the previous two sections of this study, I have pointed to two broad sets of variables which clearly differentiate Johnson supporters from Goldwater supporters. As we might have expected, among these groups there were some extraordinarily intense divisions of opinion over the issues of federal intervention in the civil rights struggle and in their expressed levels of hostility to communism. The final issue area to be examined—social welfare—is one that is, not surprisingly, equally polarized (see Table 7). And like the civil rights and foreign policy-militarism issue areas, there was some discontinuity between the early and late pro-Goldwater groups in the level of their support for these social welfare policies. For example, the later group of Goldwater supporters was 18 percentage points higher in approval of Medicare, 10 points higher in aid to employment, and 9 points higher in approval of aid to education than the early pro-Goldwater group. But again these differences are relatively small when compared with those found when comparing the responses of both sets of Goldwater's supporters to those of either Johnson's backers or the undecided voters. Typically, spreads of 30 and 40 percentage points are the result of such comparisons.

From the three areas of American national and foreign policy that have been examined here, it is evident that some unusually large differences of opinion existed between the relatively politicized segments of the electorate in 1964. Also, and certainly of greater interest, is the fact that the early and later pro-Goldwater groups were often significantly divided on these questions, the later group manifesting a distinctly liberal bent in its preferences. This consistent discrepancy between the direction and intensity of the attitudes and opinions of these two groups is, of course, a finding which only confirms our commonsense judgments.

The evidence suggests that Goldwater's candidacy resulted in a substantial shift of voters from the Republican to the Democratic party;[15] and the data reported here show that the "party faithful" who stayed with Goldwater by no means responded to the themes of his campaign in a con-

---

[15] Campbell, "Presidential Victory," pp. 279–281.

TABLE 7

Social Welfare

	Favor Medicare		Oppose Medicare		Favor Aid to Employment		Oppose Aid to Employment		Favor Aid to Schools		Oppose Aid to Schools	
	N	%	N	%	N	%	N	%	N	%	N	%
Early supporters	13	13.4	72	74.2	8	8.2	78	80.4	12	12.2	81	82.7
Late supporters	62	31.3	123	62.1	35	17.6	146	73.4	41	20.8	147	74.6
Johnson supporters	501	72.5	140	20.3	311	44.1	289	40.9	311	45.5	332	48.6
Undecided voters and others	189	62.4	94	31.0	127	40.4	152	48.4	122	42.2	150	51.9
Totals	765	59.3	429	33.3	481	36.6	665	50.5	486	38.4	710	56.0

sistently supportive way. It appears very likely that Goldwater not only got all the support he could expect from ideologically conservative Republicans, but also managed to attract a sizable segment of the electorate whose views, as a group, were rather less conservative than this pure and early group of his supporters. These groups made up respectively 7 percent and 14 percent of the electorate.

These divisions of opinion and candidate preferences among the American electorate inevitably led to a conclusion so obvious historically and in 1964, that it may not be worth stating except for the fact that the Republican party's decisions in 1963–1964 appear to have neglected its implications: There is not a sufficiently large corps of conservatives in the United States to place a conservative in the White House.

Perhaps, then, in the decisions that were made prior to the Republican convention of 1968, the Republican conservative elites expressed a clear understanding that the nomination of a candidate whose views appeared to be as divergent as did those of Goldwater from even those of their loyal party members, cannot succeed in a national election. While there was a segment of the electorate who mobilized themselves around Goldwater's candidacy, the major thrust of their activities and his campaign was to polarize the elite of the Republican party and to make more than obvious the fact that the levels of support for the policy positions favored by Goldwater and his followers were insignificant in comparison with the remainder of the American electorate who felt, on the whole, very differently about the issues that faced the American people in the election of 1964.

THE CAMPAIGN OF 1964

If the level of political involvement in the 1964 Republican campaign seemed to many observers to be entirely out of proportion to the actual percentage of the electorate that supported the Republican candidate, it was because Goldwater's early supporters were by far the most active and involved segment of the electorate during 1964. They manifested a high sense of political efficacy and involvement, and even for persons of their rather high educational achievements, they possessed high levels of political information and high rates of exposure to the political process, the media, and the campaign.

For example, 70 percent of the early pro-Goldwater group fell at the high end of the SRC's index of political involvement, while the pro-Johnson group and the later pro-Goldwater group each had only about 40 percent of their members at this point or higher on the scale. As Converse, Clausen, and Miller point out in their article, "Electoral Myth and Reality: The 1964 Election," the early pro-Goldwater segment of the electorate was not only involved in the sense of being concerned about the outcome of the election and being very interested in the campaign—it was sufficiently active to produce, in absolute numbers, more pro-Goldwater letters sent to elites and the media than any other segment of the electorate who supported any other candidate.[16] And there is every reason to believe that this preconvention activity was carried over with redoubled effort into the campaign itself.

Converse and his colleagues suggest that a portion of the rational basis (that is, the premise that Goldwater could win) of the Goldwater campaign may have rested upon this high level of activity on the part of Goldwater's early supporters and in particular on the high media visibility that their preferences presumably commanded by reason of their high rate of political letter writing.

But visibility in the national media was not the only probable reason for the misjudgment of support for Goldwater by Republican conservative elites. As the following discussion reveals, Goldwater, while very much a minority candidate, was able to field a greater number of involved and active supporters than was Johnson. Surely at least part of the decision as to Goldwater's probability of success was also influenced by the presence of this field of dedicated supporters. Certainly it must have seemed to many Republican elites that a Goldwater boom was not simply in the making but was already a fact of American political life in the summer and fall of 1964. And while the previous sections of this study demonstrate—as, of course, did the election itself—that there was a fatal discrepancy between the general ideological orientation of the early supporters of Goldwater and much of the remainder of the electorate, the scope of this discrepancy, if it was visible to the conservative Republican elites, was no doubt balanced by what they also knew to be true: many extraordinarily dedicated people supported Goldwater. Perhaps that was all he needed to win.

A simple measure of political activism was constructed in the same fashion as the ACI with seven items dealing with opinion leadership, attendance at political meetings, working for a party or candidate, and the like. The mean inter-item correlation for these seven variables was $+.924$. Table 8 presents the distribution on this index among the various groups using a control for high and low levels of political involvement.

As is evident from an inspection of this table, the early supporters of Senator Goldwater were much more likely than the other groups to have accompanied their involvement (that is, interest in and concern about outcome) in the campaign by actual political activity. Even where the involvement with the campaign was low, this group was extraordinarily active in politics. In the case of the high-involvement group, of course, the

---

[16] Philip E. Converse, Aage R. Clausen, and Warren E. Miller, "Electoral Myth and Reality: The 1964 Election," *Amer. Pol. Sci. Rev., 59*, No. 2 (June 1965), 321–366.

TABLE 8

Levels of Political Activity—Political Activity Index (PAI)
Controlled for High and Low Levels of Political Involvement [a]

| | HIGH POLITICAL INVOLVEMENT | | | | | | | |
| | Low Activity | | Medium Activity | | High Activity | | Total | |
	N	%	N	%	N	%	N	%
Early supporters	0	0	35	50.7	34	49.3	69	100
Later supporters	0	0	50	62.5	30	37.5	80	100
Johnson supporters	2	0.7	231	79.4	58	19.9	291	100
Other	0	0	48	77.4	14	22.6	62	100
Total	2	0.4	364	72.5	136	27.1	502	100

| | LOW POLITICAL INVOLVEMENT | | | | | | | |
| | Low Activity | | Medium Activity | | High Activity | | Total | |
	N	%	N	%	N	%	N	%
Early supporters	1	3.6	17	60.7	10	35.7	28	100
Later supporters	11	8.9	99	80.5	13	10.6	123	100
Johnson supporters	41	8.2	434	87.1	23	4.6	498	100
Other	61	20.5	229	77.1	7	2.4	297	100
Total	114	12.1	779	82.3	53	5.6	946	100

[a] Respondents dichotomized on the basis of high and low scores on the SRC index of political involvement.

differences between the late and early supporters may simply be an artifact of their own preferences prior to the convention, with Goldwater partisans simply backing their man more strongly during the campaign, as would be expected in any factional situation. Yet while this effect may be present to some degree, the later supporters of the senator were still, regardless of the degree of their involvement in the campaign, much higher on the PAI than any other group except the initial backers of the Republican nominee.

While these findings are very much in line with what we know about Republicans and persons of high socioeconomic status as participants in the political arena—namely, that they are usually much more active than Democrats—it is interesting to note the much higher consistency that existed between high involvement and high activism among the early Goldwater group than among all others. As we have seen, 71 percent of this group scored at the high end of the involvement index and half of this subset fell at the high activity end of the PAI. Only 39 percent of the later Goldwater group manifested the same degree of involvement and only a little more than a third of them scored at the high end of the PAI. Johnson supporters, with 40 percent of their members at the high-involvement end of the SRC index showed only about one fifth with high levels of political activism.[17] Goldwater was able to muster supporters whose level of consistent dedication to his cause was without parallel among the electorate in 1964.

Unfortunately, from the point of view of his election, these dedicated persons made up only about 4 percent of the electorate even though they accounted for almost 40 percent of the high-activity—high-involvement subset of the public and more than 50 percent of the active-involved group with a candidate preference. Thus, the Goldwater strategists were correct in proposing the theory of the existence of a hard core of conservatives willing to give almost everything for the election of a conservative Republican candidate. Many persons did support Goldwater with a degree of faithfulness and dedication that certainly appears to be extraordinarily high.

But, of course, they were mistaken in believing that there was a sufficiently large number of such persons to make enough of a difference. That Goldwater did as well as he did on the third of November may very well be attributed to the fact that he had, during the campaign of 1964, more politically active and involved supporters than the winner of the election, Lyndon B. Johnson.

PARTISAN CHOICE

Earlier in this study some mention was made of the partisan makeup of the early Goldwater supporters and of the rates of infusion and defection from partisan ranks in the 1964 election. Table 9 provides some data about the party identification of Goldwater's supporters and of the probable net shifts between the parties in 1964. What is immediately evident from these data is that, although heavily Republican in their party identification, Goldwater's early backers were more likely to identify themselves as independent Republicans or as Democrats than were his post-convention supporters. Evidently the early pro-Goldwater group was composed of persons with an unusually high degree of independence from political party structure. These findings also seem to reinforce the contention of the conservative Republican elites that either (a) persons alienated from (that is, independent of) the Republican party would support Goldwater more strongly than anyone else by reason of the party having at last supplied them with an acceptable candidate—which seems to have, in fact, been the case; or (b) that a coalition of conservatives would form, irrespective of their party identification, and back Senator Goldwater for the presidency. These both evidently occurred, but, of course, the number of such persons was insufficient to effect a victory.

---

[17] When these groups are controlled for level of political involvement the differences between them become even more extreme.

TABLE 9

Party Identification

	Strong Democrat		Not Very Strong Democrat		Independent Democrat		Independent		Independent Republican		Not Very Strong Republican		Strong Republican		Total	
	N	%	N	%	N	%	N	%	N	%	N	%	N	%	N	%
Early supporters	6	5.8	13	12.5	2	1.9	7	6.7	23	22.1	15	14.4	38	36.5	104	100
Later supporters	9	4.1	21	9.7	4	1.8	10	4.6	17	7.8	65	30.0	91	41.9	217	100
Johnson supporters	350	42.0	245	29.4	93	11.2	38	4.6	17	2.0	72	8.6	19	2.3	834	100
Undecided voters and others	51	14.2	103	28.8	43	12.0	58	16.2	30	8.4	51	14.2	22	6.1	358	100
Total	416	27.5	382	25.2	142	9.4	113	7.5	87	5.8	203	13.4	170	11.2	1513	100

How much the Republicans lost and how much the Democrats gained from the short-term influence of Goldwater's candidacy is an extremely complicated question,[18] and the answer suggested here is by no means definitive—first and foremost because this is not an analysis of voting as such. But some idea of the effects of his candidacy on the more politically involved segment of the electorate may be gained from brief consideration of the data in Table 9. Of all Johnson supporters, 12.9 percent identified themselves as Republicans of some type, the majority saying that they were "not very strong" Republicans. This amounts to about 11 percent of the subset of the sample with a partisan choice shifting to the Democratic ticket. Among the supporters of Goldwater (early and late), 17.1 percent volunteered a Democratic identification, or about 4 percent of the same partisan-choice subset. Proportionally speaking, therefore, Goldwater got slightly more Democratic support than he lost from Republicans; but in absolute terms, of course, his net loss to the Democrats was almost three times that of the gains he made by attracting conservative or dissident Democrats to his candidacy. And as Campbell has shown, the overall percentage of votes gained by the Democratic party in 1964 was several percentage points greater than could be accounted for by either sampling error or the normal net variation in the vote of something less than 6 percent.[19] Goldwater's nomination resulted in some sharp turnover among persons with high and moderately high levels of party identification; and, if this pattern of identification is retained in these strata of the electorate, it suggests that a first step in the realignment of American parties may be occurring. Based on the other data we have considered, the direction of this realignment is toward a greater polarization along the well-worn, but in this case useful, dimensions of liberalism and conservatism.[20]

THE POLITICAL SOCIALIZATION OF GOLDWATER'S SUPPORTERS: DEMOCRATIC INSTITUTIONS AND THE QUESTION OF "EXTREMISM"

In addition to the questions of the strength and nature of the partisan identification of the various groups that we have examined, there is another issue, raised loudly during the 1964 campaign, concerning the extent to which Goldwater's supporters were or were not socialized political actors. That is, to what degree did they overtly support and practice American-style democratic politics? Or were they, as charged by Richard Rovere, simply a group of infiltrators? [21] Part of this question resulted from the

---

[18] Campbell, "Presidential Victory," pp. 279–281.
[19] Campbell, "Presidential Victory," pp. 279–281.
[20] Campbell, "Presidential Victory," pp. 279–281.
[21] Richard Rovere, "American Letter," *Encounter, 23* (October 1964) p. 49 in "Two Faces of Republican Leadership: Goldwater and Rockefeller Elites in California," by Edmond Costantini and Kenneth Craik (Berkeley, Calif.: University of California, Institute of Governmental Affairs, 1967), mimeographed.

high number of new (and pro-Goldwater) delegates to the Republican Convention.[22]

Costantini and Craik, in a paper dealing with the political and psychological characteristics of the two competing California delegations (Goldwater and Rockefeller) to the convention, found, however, that the Goldwater delegation, from California at least, was new neither to politics nor to the Republican party. In fact, the Goldwater delegates' commitment to their party, in terms of holding county and state office, length of participation in party affairs, proportion of income contributed to the party, and attendance at national party conventions, was in every case greater and often twice as great as was that of the Rockefeller delegates. In part, of course, these findings are unique because of the nature of California's somewhat unusually polarized party system. But they neverthelesss point out that at the elite level the Goldwater backers do not necessarily seem to have been "seditious insurgents" or antiparty grass roots anarchists. As we have seen at the mass level, the early backers of Goldwater expressed a relatively independent party identification and had a lower rate of party consistency in their voting history (45.2 percent stated they voted for "different parties" versus 34.0 percent of later supporters and 34.4 percent of Johnson's supporters). But at the same time the high PAI scores of these early pro-Goldwater respondents argue for a rather high level of political socialization on their part.

A somewhat tangential approach to answering the questions raised about the political socialization of Goldwater backers can be taken by looking at several different sets of variables. One of these concerns the degree of legitimacy that the various groups of respondents assign to American political institutions such as elections, the Congress, and political parties. Presumably, persons who see little effectiveness in these institutions (that is, think of them as being unrepresentative and unresponsive to the "will of the people"), also are likely to harbor doubts about their value. Of course, it is the nature of an opposition party to question the decisions of such institutions when they are controlled by the opposing party. But nonetheless, the rejection of these institutions, if common among Goldwater's early supporters, might be taken as some very tenuous confirmation of the argument put forth by Rovere and others that Goldwater's backers lacked a commitment to the democratic political order. Secondly, if Goldwater's supporters approve of "extremist" political organizations, such as the Ku Klux Klan and The John Birch Society (although these organizations are in no real sense comparable except in the mind of the American press), as they were so widely said to do, we might infer that the support of organizations like these is inconsistent with support for democratic norms. If some evidence could be found that Goldwater's partisans were backward-looking political dreamers, rejecting the present in favor of the idyllic past, it could

---

[22] Costantini and Craik, "Two Faces."

be argued that this view of political life was essentially "unrealistic" and dysfunctional. Finally, if his early supporters are dogmatic and inflexible in their approach to life, might they not also be dogmatic and inflexible in their political actions, thus violating democratic norm of compromise and respect for the opposition's point of view? The remainder of this essay will attempt to examine and perhaps answer these questions.

Let us look first at the electorate's perceptions of the legitimacy of the government and of American political institutions. A five-item series of questions in the post-election survey dealing with "different ideas people have about the government in Washington" was combined in an index of the type used earlier in the essay. Labeled the Legitimacy of Government Index (LGI), the distribution of responses to this index is reported in Table 10. The modal score on the LGI is the midpoint—very few respondents were willing to describe the government in perfectly rosy terms. Dissatisfaction, however, was much more common among Goldwater's early backers than the other groups. While this finding in itself is of somewhat dubious meaning, having the character of a more or less standard opposition response, it is paralleled by a similar pattern of responses to several

TABLE 10

Distribution of Scores on
Legitimacy of Government Index (LGI) [a]

	HIGH LEGITIMACY		MEDIUM LEGITIMACY		LOW LEGITIMACY	
	N	*%*	*N*	*%*	*N*	*%*
Early supporters	1	1.0	38	39.2	58	59.8
Late supporters	9	4.4	95	46.8	99	48.8
Johnson supporters	26	3.3	557	70.7	205	26.0
Other supporters	20	5.6	219	61.9	115	32.5
Total	56	3.9	909	63.0	477	33.1

[a] The items were as follows:
1. Do you think that quite a few of the people running the government are a little crooked, not very many are, or do you think hardly any of them are crooked at all?
2. Do you think that people in government waste a lot of the money we pay in taxes, waste some of it, or don't waste very much of it?
3. How much of the time do you think you can trust the government in Washington to do what is right—just about always, most of the time or only some of the time?
4. Do you feel that almost all of the people running the government are smart people who usually know what they are doing, or do you think quite a few of them don't seem to know what they are doing?
5. Would you say the government is pretty much run by a few big interests looking out for themselves or that it is run for the benefit of all the people?

The mean inter-item correlation for these five questions is +.763

TABLE 11

Legitimacy of Political Institutions

	GOVERNMENT DOES NOT PAY MUCH ATTENTION TO WHAT THE PEOPLE THINK WHEN IT DECIDES WHAT TO DO.		POLITICAL PARTIES DO NOT HELP MUCH TO MAKE THE GOVERNMENT RESPONSIVE TO THE PEOPLE.		ELECTIONS DO NOT HELP MUCH TO MAKE THE GOVERNMENT RESPONSIVE.		CONGRESSMEN DO NOT PAY MUCH ATTENTION TO THEIR CONSTITUENTS WHEN MAKING DECISIONS.	
	N	%	N	%	N	%	N	%
Early supporters	42	43.7	18	19.1	10	10.3	20	20.8
Late supporters	60	30.6	33	17.4	20	10.2	35	17.8
Johnson supporters	146	19.7	79	10.7	28	3.7	102	13.6
Undecided voters and others	90	29.0	50	16.6	32	10.2	60	19.6
Total	338	25.2	180	13.6	90	6.6	217	16.1

questions concerning American political institutions. These responses were not reduced to an index but are presented individually in Table 11. In every case, the early supporters of Senator Goldwater gave a slightly greater proportion of responses questioning the effectiveness of the three agencies of representation (Congress, parties, and elections) and were 13 percentage points above the later supporters of the Senator in their overall belief in the unrepresentativeness of the government.

I do not believe that any but the most tentative conclusions may be drawn from these two patterns of responses; but it does seem reasonable to conclude that the early pro-Goldwater group does manifest a very slight tendency in the direction proposed by Rovere and others. They were, in fact, more often willing to give pessimistic and disaffected responses to questions concerning American political institutions and government than most of the mass public. Whether or not this pattern simply reflects their role as an opposition force or if it simply reflects a "realistic" attitude toward the facts of American political life is hard to say. In any case, the evidence does not support any particular interpretation very strongly, and there is most certainly no strong support here for an interpretation of Goldwater's followers as being generally alienated or hostile to the forms and institutions of American political life.

Another related issue, raised loudly during the 1964 Republican convention and the ensuing campaign, revolved around "extremism" or, more specifically, about the supposed "extremist" support for Goldwater and his supposed reciprocal encouragement of "extremist" groups. The most prominent of these was The John Birch Society, an organization with which Goldwater had cooperated while he was a senator although he later became critical of its founder, Robert Welch.[23] The measure of support for this organization employed in this survey was the "feeling thermometer" discussed above and the responses of the various groups to the Birch Society are reported in Table 12 along with data about the Christian Anti-Communism Crusade and the Ku Klux Klan, two other organizations often described as extremist.

As Table 12 clearly demonstrates, the two groups of Goldwater's sup-

TABLE 12 [a]

Support for Three "Extremist" Organizations:
The John Birch Society, the Christian Anti-Communism Crusade,
and the Ku Klux Klan

	J.B.S.		C.A.C.C.		K.K.K.	
	N	%	N	%	N	%
Early supporters	43	47.3	16	41.0	4	4.2
Late supporters	35	19.9	19	31.1	12	6.0
Johnson supporters	36	5.8	56	28.7	24	3.2
Undecided voters and others	13	5.4	13	18.8	11	3.5
Total	127	11.3	104	28.6	41	3.0

[a] Table should be read from left to right. It reports only the indicated percentage of the candidate preference group responding as stated in the table. Scores $\geq 60°$ on feeling thermometer.

porters were much more likely to give favorable evaluations of these groups than Johnson's backers or the undecided voters; and the early pro-Goldwater group was particularly strong in its support of The John Birch Society and the Christian Anti-Communism Crusade. In view of this high level of support for these two groups by Goldwater's early backers it may seem appropriate to answer our original question in the affirmative; that is to accept the notion that Goldwater's early supporters were "extremists." If we equate support for these groups with radical or "extremist" political values (a highly dubious assumption considering the fact that they tend to work

[23] Specifically, by signing, with Welch and a number of members of the Council of the Society, an advertisement urging Eisenhower to cancel a then impending visit to the U.S. by the former Russian Premier Nikita Khrushchev. This advertisement was reprinted in *The Blue Book* of The John Birch Society.

within the system), there is no question that the early Goldwater supporters were disproportionately pro-"extremist." But as we have seen, this high level of approval of the Birch Society and the C.A.C.C. was not accompanied by any wholesale rejection of political institutions. This is not to say, however, that the three sets of findings presented here do not give some support to the Rovere thesis, they do. But with the exception of the data on the "extremist" groups, this support is not terribly strong.

The last measures which bear on this point are two attempts to assess the degree of personal dogmatism and of yearning for the past among the respondents—two sets of concepts which have frequently been associated with the psychological components of conservatism. The first of these, personal dogmatism, was tapped by three items reported in Table 13 concerning the respondents' ability to change his mind, his success in winning

TABLE 13

Personal Dogmatism (Self Reported)

	ALWAYS GETS "OWN WAY" IN ARGUMENTS		HAS STRONG OPINIONS		HARD TO CHANGE MIND	
	N	%	N	%	N	%
Early supporters	22	23.9	72	74.2	81	84.4
Late supporters	43	21.9	94	46.5	145	72.5
Johnson supporters	197	25.5	347	44.5	546	69.5
Undecided voters and others	66	19.6	123	43.9	232	67.8
Total	328	23.4	636	44.9	1004	70.5

arguments, and the strength of his opinions. As can be seen, some interesting differences do emerge between the early pro-Goldwater group and the remainder of the electorate on the two items having to do with strength of opinion and flexibility in changing one's mind. Goldwater's early backers are about 30 percentage points above all of the other groups of respondents in their self reported characteristic of "having strong opinions" and about 15 points higher than the others in their reported resistance to changing their minds. A certain mental rigidity definitely appears, at first, to characterize this group vis-a-vis all other groups isolated here for analysis but, in fact, this finding is largely an artifact of the high level of education and political sophistication that is present among the early supporters of the Senator.

Somewhat surprising, however, is the data reported in Table 14, for contrary to much popular wisdom there was no universal identification of

TABLE 14

Nostalgia for the Past

	STATE LIFE WAS BETTER 50 YEARS AGO		LIFE MORE SATISFYING 50 YEARS AGO		HARDER TO LEAD A GOOD MORAL LIFE NOW	
	N	%	N	%	N	%
Early supporters	25	26.3	44	47.3	62	69.7
Late supporters	47	23.7	84	43.5	142	74.7
Johnson supporters	120	15.7	233	30.9	517	69.1
Undecided voters and others	77	23.3	119	36.4	234	73.4
Total	269	19.4	480	35.1	955	71.0

the past as personally or morally idyllic on the part of Goldwater's early or later supporters. Rather, only a slight tendency exists for the pro-Goldwater groups to value the past over the present—a finding that is somewhat confusing when one considers their profound dissatisfactions with the course of much current American foreign and domestic policy.

CONCLUSION

The theoretically relevant conclusions that may be drawn from the data presented in this essay appear to fit quite well with the findings of Nelson W. Polsby in his re-analysis of survey data on support for McCarthy represented elsewhere in this volume and Raymond Wolfinger and his collaborators in their study of The Christian Anti-Communism Crusade.[24] Their work diverged from a tradition in political sociology which attributed the origins of "right-wing extremists" to social-structural discrepancy. This idea had a good deal of influence on Lipset, Bell, and Hofstadter, and has also strongly influenced two major pieces of empirical research on the "Radical Right" which were published as recently as 1966 and 1967,[25] one of which is also represented elsewhere in this volume.

While it is a highly questionable enterprise to equate Goldwater's early supporters with "right-wing extremists" and to proceed with an analysis of prior theory by determining the degree of fit between the statements of

---

[24] Raymond E. Wolfinger and others, "America's Radical Right: Politics and Ideology," in David E. Apter (ed.), *Ideology and Discontent* (New York: The Free Press, 1964), pp. 262–293, and Polsby, "McCarthyism."

[25] See especially, Gary B. Rush, "Status Consistency and Right-Wing Extremism," *Amer. Sociol. Rev., 32*, No. 1 (February 1967), 86–92.

the theories and the behavior of these individuals, a brief review [26] of five separate areas of theoretical speculation about the origins of "right-wing extremist" groups may nevertheless serve as an appropriate conclusion to this essay.

A number of writers have proposed that right-wing "extremists" are "alienated." That is, they have suffered economic dislocation or some serious breakdown in primary group associations, lack secondary group memberships, and are detached from politics and political institutions.

We may say quite firmly that these are statements which do not generally apply to the early supporters of Senator Goldwater. In fact, the opposite seems the case. The early Goldwater group is highest in the proportion of its members who are married and second (to the later pro-Goldwater respondents) in the lowest proportion of divorced or separated members. They are also the most frequent church-goers in the population. Almost 62 percent of the early pro-Goldwater group had some college education or more and nearly 40 percent had incomes of $10,000 or more per year. As we also know, their economic condition, as measured by a number of variables such as home ownership and their reports concerning the comparative cost of the neighborhoods into which they have moved, seems largely secure and comfortable. We have seen their very high level of participation in politics and their extraordinarily high sense of political efficacy and involvement. These are conditions which argue rather strongly against describing the early supporters of Senator Goldwater as alienated—at least in the meaning usually assigned to this term.

Although not covered in detail in the body of the essay, the issue of status discrepancy (that is, the presence of an imbalance in one or more components of socioeconomic status, such as very low income with very high education) will be examined at this point. As we just noted, high income and educational attainment mark Goldwater's early supporters. The same is true of their occupational roles. They are highest in the proportion of white-collar workers (by almost 20 percentage points) and correspondingly lowest in the percentage of blue-collar workers. They are especially high (28 percent) in the category of self-employed businessmen, artisans, and managers, a finding which parallels that of Martin Trow in his important study of small businessmen's support for McCarthy in Bennington, Vermont.[27]

As we shall see in the following pages, however, Goldwater's supporters,

---

[26] For further detail on these points consult James McEvoy III, "The American Right in the National Election of 1964," (unpublished doctoral dissertation, University of Michigan, 1968).

[27] Martin Trow, "Right-Wing Radicalism and Political Intolerance: A Study of Support for McCarthy in a New England Town," (unpublished doctoral dissertation, Columbia University, 1957).

while disproportionately sharing the economic roles Trow found to be associated with support for McCarthy, had quite a different orientation toward the major economic institutions of American society. In their social class identifications, the early pro-Goldwater group was overwhelmingly middle class (70.6 percent), 18 percentage points above their nearest rival, the later group of Goldwater supporters. It does not appear then, that there is very much status discrepancy at the group level among Goldwater's early supporters. Furthermore, upward intergenerational mobility appears to be no greater among the early pro-Goldwater respondents than among the later group or the Johnson supporters. Each group reports a gain of about 8 percent in middle-class status over the reported status of their parents.

Additionally, in a series of cross tabulations *within* the various groups between the variables of occupations, income, and education, no important differences were found between the early pro-Goldwater group and the other groups in the proportion of their members who were status discrepant. Table 15 gives the results of these tabulations. As this table indicates, the proportions of each of the candidate preference groups that falls into any of the discrepant conditions is rather small, having a maximum value of about 13 percentage points. And there is no consistent pattern of upward or downward discrepancy found here either. Put differently, the three discrepant conditions which imply upward social movement (a grade-school education paired with an income of $10,000 or more; a grade-school education and an upper white-collar occupation, and a blue-collar occupation with an income of $10,000 or more) are distributed about equally among all three of the candidate-preference groups as are the three remaining discrepant conditions implying downward social mobility.

Finally, Table 16 reports the proportion of respondents in the various groups that are mismatched in terms of their reported social class membership and their educational level. In the case of persons with a low (grade-school) level of education who report a middle class identification we might attribute such a report to *status anxiety*, a psychological variant of the status discrepancy theory which is manifested as anxiety about one's status irrespective of its actual consistency and has usually been measured by questions concerning one's acceptance in his local community. Table 16, while obviously not fully tapping this dimension of behavior, might be considered to reflect either actual upward or downward mobility which is correctly perceived by the respondent, or it could be taken as indicating a perverse self-aggrandizing or self-effacing tendency on the part of the respondents and as such be indicative of some sort of status anxiety. As can be seen from the table, the early pro-Goldwater group is slightly below the mean percentage of mismatched respondents. Thus, if this is a measure of status anxiety, it does not support the notion of status anxiety as causally related

TABLE 15

Status Discrepancy—Comparison of Groups on Selected Status Variables: Occupation, Income, Educational Attainment [a]

CONDITION OF DISCREPANCY

	Grade School Education and Income ≥ $10,000.00		Grade School Education and Upper White-Collar Occup.		Some College or More and Income ≤ $6,000.00		Some College or More and Blue-Collar Occupation		Blue-Collar Occupation and Income ≥ $10,000.00		Upper White-Collar Occup. and Income ≤ $6,000.00	
	N	%	N	%	N	%	N	%	N	%	N	%
Early supporters	3	2.9	7	7.1	11	10.6	8	8.1	3	3.1	7	7.1
Later supporters	7	3.3	7	3.4	28	13.3	16	7.8	15	7.5	13	6.6
Johnson supporters	44	5.5	44	5.6	86	10.7	74	9.4	42	5.5	40	5.2
Undecided voters and others	12	3.3	23	9.7	27	7.3	21	8.9	13	5.7	20	8.7
Mean %		3.8		6.5		10.5		8.6		5.5		6.9

[a] Table is to be read from left to right. Numbers and percents refer to proportion of candidate preference group matching the given condition of discrepancy.

TABLE 16 [a]

Status Anxiety: Comparison of Self-Reported Social Status with Level of Formal Education

| | MIDDLE CLASS ID GRADE SCHOOL | | WORKING CLASS ID SOME COLLEGE OR MORE | |
	N	%	N	%
Early supporters	9	9.9	6	6.6
Late supporters	23	11.3	22	10.8
Johnson supporters	70	8.7	106	13.1
Undecided voters and others	36	9.9	23	6.3
Mean %		10.0		9.2

[a] Table is to be read from left to right. Numbers and percentages refer to proportion of candidate preference group matching the given condition of discrepancy.

to political "extremism" if we accept support for Goldwater as in any sense being the equivalent of being an "extremist."

The thesis which equated support for McCarthy with populism, so well refuted by Michael Rogin in his recent volume on McCarthy, cannot really be tested as applicable to the Goldwater movement by the data we have here. But it is interesting to note that Goldwater got almost no early support in the New England states and very little in the Middle Atlantic area. He received disproportionate support from the southern and the border states and slightly disproportionate early backing in the West. Although there was no overrepresentation of rural respondents among the early Goldwater group, there was considerable (11 percentage points above the mean) overrepresentation of persons living in very small towns of 2500–9999 persons. Thus a slightly small-town southern caste to the group does exist but this, of course, is a far cry from being coextensive even with southern populism. Finally, the early Goldwater group was less likely than any of the others to have grown up on a farm and more likely to have come from larger cities of 250,000 or more.

Religious fundamentalism, a trait often associated with right-wing political extremism, was not found disproportionately among the early Goldwater group. In fact, they were lowest in the proportion of members in pietistic Protestant and neofundamentalist denominations and highest in the traditionally upper-status Reformation protestant churches—Presbyterian, Episcopal, Lutheran, and the like. They did, however, go to church more often than any other group.

Earlier, Martin Trow's work on support for McCarthy in Bennington was mentioned because of the similarity between the early Goldwater supporters and Trow's McCarthy supporters in the overrepresentation of small-businessmen and self-employed persons in these two groups. Almost 30 percent of the early pro-Goldwater group was self-employed. About a quarter of the later supporters of the Senator were also self-employed, but only 17 percent of Johnson's backers showed this occupational attribute. Trow's analysis of the political divisions in Bennington led him to construct a four-fold typology of political outlook based on the attitudes of his respondents toward two of the major economic institutions of American society: big business and labor. Trow's four groups were "19th-Century Liberals" or persons holding unfavorable attitudes to *both* business and labor. It was in this group that his McCarthy supporters were overwhelmingly located. Secondly came "Right-Wing Conservatives" or persons holding negative attitudes toward labor and favorable opinions toward business. This group was followed by "Moderate Conservatives" or respondents with favorable attitudes towards both business and labor. Lastly were the "Labor Liberals," the obverse of the Right-Wing Conservatives, who liked labor unions but opposed big business.[28]

Table 17 reports the distribution of the candidate preference groups among these four categories of political orientation. The categories were prepared by selecting out persons responding to the feeling thermometer measures in the manner dictated by Trow's formulation. For example, "19th-Century Liberals" were designated by reason of the fact that they rated both business and labor 49° or lower on the feeling thermometer. As this table shows, however, 19th-century liberals, the group Trow found to be so dominantly pro-McCarthy, were not very strong among the supporters of Senator Goldwater. Only five percentage points separate the early pro-Goldwater group from the Johnson group on this measure. However, Trow's category "Right-Wing Conservative" has a good deal more discriminating power between all Goldwater's backers and those supporting Johnson. In this case, about 27 percentage points separate these groups from each other. Unfortunately, though, there was no substantial difference between the early and late pro-Goldwater groups on this measure, so it may only indicate a difference that we would normally expect to find between Republicans and Democrats.

Finally, of course, first Polsby and later Wolfinger have noted the importance of party identification in the composition of many of America's recent rightist and conservative movements. It may seem that a perfectly circular argument on this point would be the only one possible in this essay because of the dependence of the construction of the analytic groups on candidate preference and therefore, by extension, partisan identification. However, there is some rather convincing evidence that Republicanism (of

---

[28] Trow, "Right-Wing Radicalism."

TABLE 17

Distribution of Candidate Preference Groups among Trow's Four Structural Categories of Political Orientation

	19TH-CENTURY LIBERALS		MODERATE CONSERVATIVES		RIGHT-WING CONSERVATIVES		LABOR LIBERALS		TOTAL	
	N	%	N	%	N	%	N	%	N	%
Early supporters	9	13.2	27	39.7	30	44.1	2	2.9	68	100.0
Late supporters	12	9.3	54	41.9	56	43.4	7	5.4	129	100.0
Johnson supporters	37	8.2	267	58.9	76	16.8	73	16.1	453	100.0
Undecided voters and others	21	13.9	79	52.3	34	22.5	17	11.3	151	100.0
Total	79	9.9	427	53.3	196	24.5	99	12.4	801	100.0

an Independent variety) is an important and almost unique aspect of the early Goldwater group's make-up if the dimension of attitudinal consistency is added as a criterion for Right-Wing reference group membership.

In order to test this, all the respondents in the sample were isolated who rated The John Birch Society at 60° or higher on the SRC "Feeling Thermometer." This resulted in the isolation of 127 "pro-Birch" respondents. Of these, 43 or 33.4 percent were also early supporters of Senator Goldwater. The remaining 84 had other candidate preferences or lacked a presidential preference. These two groups were then compared on some other measures which appear to denote the level of attitudinal or perhaps ideological consistency among the two groups—their feelings toward liberals and labor unions. The results of this comparison were interesting: 74 percent and 61 percent of the early pro-Birch/pro-Goldwater group had negative attitudes ($\leqq 49°$ on feeling thermometer measures) toward liberals and unions respectively. The proportion of negative responses among the other "pro-Birch" group was 28 percent negative toward liberals and 32 percent negative toward unions. Evidently there was much higher consistency among the pro-Goldwater segment of the pro-Birch respondents. It thus appears that the more consistent "rightists" did, indeed, support Goldwater more often than anyone else and as we have seen, these respondents are largely Republican (even though independent Republican) in their partisan identification.

And it is most certainly the case that the dominant partisan identification among both the early and late pro-Goldwater groups was Republican. In the case of the early group, of course, there are a greater proportion of Democrats and Independent Republicans than were present in the later group of his partisans, but nevertheless, to the great majority of persons in the American electorate who possess consistently conservative approaches to political matters, the Republican Party is their political home. No great wave of right-wing Democrats fell into Goldwater's camp even though the defection rate from the Democratic party in the South, a trend visible for many years, was larger in 1964 than usual.

The questions raised at the beginning of this study have, I hope, largely been answered. We have seen that "Goldwaterism" was hardly a mass movement in the sense of the sweeping abandonment of political norms and processes, and that in many respects its members are traditionally conservative both in their social and economic roles and in their political beliefs. Some evidence has been examined which suggests that at least the early pro-Goldwater group shows a reasonably clear-cut set of conservative political values—perhaps a conservative ideology. The liberal charges of "extremism" and "racism" directed at Goldwater's followers have been shown to have some foundations in fact; but, at the same time, these tendencies among his supporters have been found to a somewhat lesser degree than many commentators seemed to believe in 1964.

What emerges from these data is a portrait of a small but active segment of Republican conservatives, people with strong opinions, money, middle-class status and education. They are, or were, committed more heavily than was any other group in 1964 to the election of their candidate. They did all they could, but as an ideological, elite minority their views had virtually no general appeal. That they captured the party at the national level attests to their dedication. If they still remain in control it will be due to their perseverance in the face of the fact that they represent minority opinion both within and without their party.

The Goldwater movement was, in its essentials, conservative. The data presented here strongly suggest that "radicalism," "extremism," "mass politics" and the other pejoratives of popular political sociology are rather inaccurate labels for Goldwater's supporters. Instead, in their social and demographic locations, their policy preferences and their attitudes about contemporary American society, Goldwater's supporters occupied traditionally conservative territory.

As a suggestion for future theory-builders of political extremism, I call attention to the vast discrepancies between the policy preferences and social attitudes that have emerged between the portion of the electorate who supported Goldwater's candidacy from the beginning and those who took some other course in 1964, whether Republican, Democratic, or those who avoided the election altogether.

The early pro-Goldwater group's values—if we may translate their strong beliefs and their commitment to political action as a value-oriented characteristic of their behavior—are grossly divergent from those of the larger society. In many respects they are "extremists" in the statistical sense of deviating strikingly from the society's "mean" on any number of policy variables. But it is evident from the data presented here that we are dealing not with a group of pure fanatics but with a well socialized set of political actors. These people not only mouth the Americanisms of citizen participation and political interest, they practice them as well. Their support of Senator Goldwater was a manifestation of that practice. These individuals are also reasonably well-educated and presumably sensitive to the drift of American society and American politics and have been so for a long time.

That this drift is distinctly to their displeasure seems evident: the welfare state, the rise of the bureaucratically oriented family, the increasing proportion of the economy controlled by large-scale organizations, and the beginnings of collapse of traditional status-deference patterns, such as those between Negroes and whites, are, if not directly opposed by these persons, the cause of much concern among them. It is certain that the direction of the society has resulted in political trends which are simply unacceptable to them. In a sense, the society has moved past these people. They are victims of what I term *transitional unrepresentation*, a process which will, eventually, reduce their views to those of an historical anachronism.

In an earlier study I attempted to assess the size, growth rate, and contemporary importance of American rightist groups. In that study I concluded that despite somewhat fragmentary evidence there seemed to be an increasing mobilization of interest in rightist causes, possibly within a segment of the population that has traditionally held extremely conservative and rightist opinions, but which is now in the process of increasing its ideological solidarity and raising its levels of political interest, activity and involvement. Perhaps the nomination of Barry Goldwater may, very cautiously, be taken as further support for this view.[29]

Certainly, the behavior of the Republican party in its choice of candidates in 1964 was directed by ideological rather than politically rational considerations. Thus, while the Right as a political force may not have grown in size, it appears to have been successful in redirecting the course of one of America's major parties in a way that may have had long-term effects on voter alignment. If Goldwater's nomination is viewed as the triumph of the American Right within the framework of the legitimate political system, it was a triumph which has made even clearer the power that is available to an active, even though immensely unrepresentative, minority within the American political system. That this minority achieved success in its own terms cannot be doubted. Its goal was the articulation of a political ideal. The 27 million votes that were registered for Goldwater were seen by his supporters, however misguidedly, as an affirmation of the validity of that ideal at the mass level. The American Right therefore has achieved a victory which, unfortunately, may have been won at the expense of meaningful two-party politics.

---

[29] McEvoy, chap. I.

The New Conservatives: A View from the East[*]

ROBERT A. SCHOENBERGER

INTRODUCTION

The empirical study of political ideology in mass publics must ultimately be related to political behavior; otherwise, the ideological description of such publics exists in an action vacuum. Yet the most detailed and sophisticated descriptions and analyses of American conservatives and their characteristics are those which have most notably failed to connect their findings (about opinions, attitudes, and ideologies) with consistent or predictable political activity of any kind.[1]

* A shorter version of this selection appeared under the title, "Conservatism, Personality and Political Extremism," in *The American Political Science Review, 62* (1968).

1 T. W. Adorno, E. Frenkel-Brunswik, D. J. Levinson, and R. Sanford, *The Authoritarian Personality* (New York: Harper & Row, Publishers, 1950); H. McClosky, "Conservatism and Personality," *Amer. Pol. Sci. Rev., 52* (1958), 27–45,

This absence of systematic linkage between belief and behavior is primarily a consequence of the general absence of ideological structure in the political orientation of the broad American electorate.[2] But it is also a consequence of the researchers' reliance on a priori ideological measures of doubtful validity.[3]

Hence, when the student of politics is informed that reputed conservatives are, or tend to be, authoritarian, anti-Semitic, and ethnocentric,[4] or imbued with ". . . feelings of worthlessness, submissiveness, inferiority, timidity . . ., . . . hostile and suspicious, . . . rigid and compulsive, . . . inflexible and unyielding . . .,"[5] he must question the adequacy of the political designation, conservative, both on descriptive and predictive grounds.

Because of these methodological and empirical problems, I suggest that the findings of prior research and hypotheses related to them be tested in a different manner. For example, if one examines the membership and/or known supporters of organizations which exist to aggregate and channel conservative political demands, the analysis of political ideology and its correlates can be conducted in a definitively political context, with the labels being supplied (or implied) by the actors themselves.[6]

Such an approach, using a criterion of *active* self-definition, avoids the ambiguities both in abstract, a priori definitions of ideological propensity and in the passive self-definition occasionally employed by pollsters ("Do you consider yourself a conservative, a liberal, or a middle-of-the-roader?").

By shifting the focus to the level of conscious, deliberate, and specific

---

especially 44–45. See also M. Rokeach, *The Open and the Closed Mind* (New York: Basic Books, Inc., 1960); and B. Anderson and others, "On Conservative Attitudes," *Acta Sociologica, 8* (1965), 189–204.

[2] A. Campbell, P. Converse, W. Miller and D. Stokes, *The American Voter* (New York: John Wiley & Sons, Inc., 1960), p. 249; P. Converse, "The Nature of Belief Systems in Mass Publics," in D. Apter (ed.), *Ideology and Discontent* (New York: The Free Press, 1965), pp. 206–261.

[3] See, for example, the critiques by R. Christie, H. H. Hyman and P. Sheatsley in R. Christie and M. Jahoda (eds.), *Studies in the Scope and Method of 'The Authoritarian Personality'* (New York: The Free Press, 1954); M. Rokeach, pp. 3–30; R. Brown, *Social Psychology* (New York: The Free Press, 1965), pp. 526–546. Campbell and others, pp. 209–214, 512–515; W. Kendall, "Comment on McClosky's 'Conservatism and Personality,'" *Amer. Pol. Sci. Rev., 52* (1959), 1111–1112; M. J. Rosenberg, "Images in Relation to the Policy Process: American Public Opinion on Cold-War Issues," in H. Kelman (ed.), *International Behavior* (New York: Holt, Rinehart and Winston, Inc., 1965), chap. 8.

[4] Adorno and others, pp. 179, 265.

[5] McClosky, pp. 37–38.

[6] S. H. Barnes, "Ideology and the Organization of Conflict: On the Relationship Between Political Thought and Behavior," *J. Politics, 28* (1966), 513–530, especially 521–524. For relevant, not necessarily deliberate, examples of this approach, see M. Chesler and R. Schmuck, "Participant Observation in a Super-Patriot Discussion Group," *J. Social Issues, 19* (1963), 18–30; R. Wolfinger and others, "America's Radical Right: Politics and Ideology," in this volume; F. Grupp, Jr., "Political Activists: The John Birch Society and the ADA," a paper delivered at the Annual Meeting of the American Political Science Association, New York, 1966.

supportive behavior, comparisons are facilitated both among ideologically-based groups and between aggregates who "know" what they are, ideologically, and those who, operationally, must be told.[7]

SETTING

One major effort to mobilize conservatives for political action has been made in New York state. There in 1961 a group of intellectuals, journalists, business and professional men founded the Conservative party of New York, with the stated aim of (1) offering a conservative alternative to the relatively liberal programs and candidates of the two major parties and the seemingly influential Liberal party, and (2) eventually pressuring the state Republican (and conceivably, the Democratic) party to move to a suitably conservative posture.[8]

The Conservative party, a segment of whose membership will be discussed herein, has experienced slow but steady growth since 1962. Its gubernatorial poll increased from 141,877 (2.4 percent) in 1962 to 510,023 (8.4 percent) in 1966. Three Conservative congressional candidates (in 1966) and the party's candidate for Mayor of New York City (in 1965) have received more than 10 percent of the total vote in their constituencies. The party's mean vote percentage in 16 New York State Congressional Districts was 6.4 percent in 1966.

The core of the Conservative party's supporters can be readily located from public registration lists. This analysis is based upon the interview responses of a random sample of male Conservative party members in Monroe County, New York, which comprises the city of Rochester and its suburbs.[9] Interviews—lasting about 90 minutes—were completed with

---

[7] The mere act of joining an ideologically-oriented group or party does not guarantee either ideological support or even interest. A discussion and justification of certain analytical exclusions can be found in R. A. Schoenberger, *Conservatives and Conservatism* (unpublished Ph.D. dissertation, University of Rochester, 1966; University Microfilm No. 67–8976), pp. 40–41.

[8] The key points of the Conservative Party platform, derived from ". . . the American tradition of individual liberty, limited constitutional government, and defense of the Republic against its enemies," include belief in balanced budgets, opposition to or curbing of ". . . centralization of governmental power, monopoly union power, deficit spending and oppressive taxation . . . ," the wish for the confinement of ". . . the Supreme Court . . . to its proper judicial functions," support for the "Neighborhood School" principle, opposition to state legislative reapportionment, public housing, and foreign aid (except for "our friends"). See "Introducing: The Conservative Party of New York State" (New York, 1965), unpaged pamphlet. Available from Conservative Party State Headquarters, 141 E. 44 St., New York, N.Y. 10017.

[9] The 1966 Conservative congressional candidate in the district dominated by the eastern, and most populous, half of Monroe County polled 6.4 percent of the vote. Females were excluded primarily because of the need to economize resources. Informal inquiries discovered, as one would suspect, that numerous Conservative females registered as they did only at their husband's request.

45 Conservatives,[10] in a universe of 325, and with a control sample of 48 Republicans, the latter intended to provide a contrast between Conservatives (all but one of whom had been a Republican) and their unchanged, generally less ideological, former fellow partisans.

FINDINGS

PERSONALITY

Conservatives do not appear to differ substantially from Republicans on either of the two psychological measures employed. On specific assertions of social trust and distrust (Morris Rosenberg's "misanthropy" scale),[11] the results are, at best, ambiguous. Comparing total male sample responses to each of the items (Table 1), it is apparent that the dominant direction of

TABLE 1

Misanthropy

PERCENT WHO AGREE THAT	CONSERVA- TIVES ($N = 45$)	REPUB- LICANS ($N = 48$)
1 "Most people can be trusted."	91	92
2 "People are more inclined to look out for themselves than to help others."	(89) [a]	(75)
3 "Human nature is fundamentally cooperative."	78	92
4 "No one is going to care much what happens to you, when you get right down to it."	(40)	(35)
5 "If you don't watch yourself, people will take advantage of you."	(58)	(71)

[a] Proportions in parentheses are those giving the misanthropic response.

Conservative response is the same as that of the Republican sample. Moreover, the intersample differences are not consistent in direction, Conservatives appearing to be more trusting than the Republicans on item five and notably less so on items two and three.

Since there is a long-recognized tendency for poorly educated people to respond uncritically to such assertions, and because of the disproportionate number of Conservatives with relatively high educational achievement,[12] I

---

[10] The upper-case "C" is used only when referring to registered Conservative party members or to the party itself.

[11] M. Rosenberg, "Misanthropy and Political Ideology," *Amer. Sociol. Rev., 21* (1956), 690–695; and "Misanthropy and Attitudes Toward International Affairs," *J. Conflict Resolution, 1* (1957), 34–45.

[12] Eighty-nine percent had attended college, 62 percent received the Bachelor's degree, and 31 percent had started or completed graduate or professional school requirements.

TABLE 2

Misanthropy, by Respondents with at Least Some College

PERCENT WHO AGREE THAT	CONSERVA-TIVES (N = 40)	REPUB-LICANS (N = 20)
1 "Most people can be trusted."	93	95
2 "People are more inclined to look out for themselves than to help others."	85	80
3 "Human nature is fundamentally cooperative."	78	90
4 "No one is going to care much what happens to you when you get right down to it."	37	50
5 "If you don't watch yourself, people will take advantage of you."	58	60

TABLE 3

Authoritarianism-Equalitarianism

PERCENT WHO AGREE THAT	CONSERVA-TIVES (N = 45)	REPUB-LICANS (N = 48)
1 "Human nature being what it is, there will always be war and conflict."	73	77
2 "Most people who don't get ahead, just don't have enough will power."	51	52
3 "A few strong leaders could make this country better than all the laws and talk."	22	38
4 "An insult to your honor should not be forgotten."	22	33

have isolated this segment of the samples (Table 2). Here the distances between the resulting subsamples diminish, with notable but nonsignificant differences occurring only on two of the five items (3 and 4). Again, the differences are not consistent in direction.[13]

This absence of significant differences between samples recurs in an "authoritarian-equalitarian" scale, borrowed from a larger battery employed by the Survey Research Center in 1952 (Table 3).[14] Here, however, Conservatives tend to be less authoritarian on each of the four items, with the

---

[13] The average item-percentage difference between Conservatives and Republicans in Table 2 is —0.8 (sign indicates normative evaluation). The range is +13 to —12 across items.

[14] x^2, $p < .05$, df = 1. All subsequent references to significance refer to this statistical measure and convention.

largest difference appearing on the sole assertion with overt political content ("a few strong leaders . . . better than all the laws and talk").

Comparing the college-educated subsamples (Table 4), the gaps between samples increase; Conservatives continue to respond in a less authoritarian pattern. The normative differences between Conservatives and Republicans consistently favor the former.[15]

TABLE 4

Authoritarianism-Equalitarianism,
by Respondents with at Least Some College

PERCENT WHO AGREE THAT	CONSERVA-TIVES (N = 40)	REPUB-LICANS (N = 20)
1 "Human nature being what it is, there will always be war and conflict."	72	80
2 "Most people who don't get ahead, just don't have enough will power."	50	60
3 "A few strong leaders could make this country better than all the laws and talk."	20	40
4 "An insult to your honor should not be forgotten."	20	25

CIVIL LIBERTIES

The major politically relevant characteristic imputed to the maladjusted American conservative is his willingness to suppress, or to tolerate the suppression of, the civil liberties of his fellow citizens.[16] The discovery or expectation of such behavior underlies and justifies most analyses of radical-right organizations and joins the authoritarian personality to right-extremist, antilibertarian perspectives.[17]

To explore the possibility that Conservatives may not be attached to the

---

[15] The average item-percentage difference between Conservatives and Republicans in Table 4 is +10.75. The range is +5 to +20. Where sample responses are scored and indexed, with education controlled, the number of Conservatives in the high (normatively negative) range does not differ importantly or significantly from the Republicans. The percent "highly misanthropic" are: Conservatives—12; Republicans—15. The percent "highly authoritarian" are: Conservatives—17; Republicans—15. The scoring procedure is that used by G. Almond and S. Verba, *The Civic Culture* (Princeton, N.J.: Princeton University Press, 1963), pp. 262–263.

[16] The concept of authoritarianism is politically empty unless those persons it purports to describe are antilibertarian. See Peter Viereck's phrase ". . . authoritarian reactionaries . . . , hypocritically pretending to be devoted to civil liberties," in D. Bell (ed.), *The Radical Right* (New York: Doubleday & Company, 1964), p. 196.

[17] See, for example, S. A. Stouffer, *Communism, Conformity and Civil Liberties* (New York: Doubleday & Company, Inc., 1955), pp. 94–97; D. Bell, pp. 88, 358; R. Wolfinger and others, pp. 270–273.

standards of American civil liberties, I employed a ten-item measure covering key features of the Bill of Rights, a measure primarily derived from
one applied to a 1957 sample of Berkeley college students.[18]

Comparison of the responses (Table 5) indicates that Conservatives
offer predominant and broad support to libertarian assertions and comparable opposition to antilibertarian ones. Where this finding does not
obtain—on assertions supporting "double jeopardy" (item 8) and opposing
academic freedom of belief (item 9)—it is notable that the reservations of
Conservatives are largely shared by Berkeley respondents.

On nine of the ten items, Conservative responses are more libertarian
than those of the Republican sample, usually by significant margins.[19] Even
when only the highly educated respondents are considered, large intersample differences remain, with Conservatives demonstrating greater support for civil liberties than Republicans.[20]

Beyond the item analysis, a summary table of libertarianism (Table 6)
indicates that a large majority of Conservatives favor most of the libertarian
assertions, with an overwhelming difference between Conservatives and
Republicans. Moreover, 92 percent of the Conservatives and only 58 percent of the Republicans offered more prolibertarian than antilibertarian
responses.[21]

Although the measure is admittedly crude, weighing each item equally,
one is able to clearly differentiate Conservatives from Republicans along
lines of commitment to or at least acceptance of libertarian assertions. Of
most obvious importance is the consistently libertarian attitude complex of
both Conservatives and, to a slightly lesser degree, the small group of
Goldwater Republicans.

These findings do not permit the inference that Conservatives will be in
the forefront of any movement to expand or even protect the generality of
civil liberties. Robert Lane has suggested that this fight is usually led by a
triumvirate composed of the legal, clerical, and teaching professions,[22] none

---

[18] H. C. Selvin and W. O. Hagstrom, "Determinants of Support for Civil
Liberties," *British J. of Sociol.,* 11 (1960), 51–73.

[19] The average item-percentage difference between Conservatives and Republicans is +17.1; between Conservatives and Goldwater-voting Republicans, +8.4.
If any inference is to be drawn, it is that Goldwater Republicans are less antilibertarian than Johnson-voting Republicans.

[20] The average distance between college-educated Conservatives and Republicans diminishes to +11.6.

[21] The mean Conservative score (defined as the number of pro-libera-
tarian responses) is 7.8 of a possible 10; for Republicans it is 6.0. College-educated
Republicans have a mean of 6.75 and Goldwater-voting Republicans (8 of whom
have not attended college) a mean of 7.1. College-attending Conservatives achieve
a score of 7.9.

[22] R. E. Lane, "The Fear of Equality," *Amer. Pol. Sci. Rev.,* 53 (1959),
35–51. See also, S. A. Stouffer; J. W. Prothro and C. M. Grigg, "Fundamental Principles of Democracy: Bases of Agreement and Disagreement," *J. Politics, 22* (1961),
276–294.

of which is represented among the Conservatives. The latter are nearly all corporation employees working in executive, engineering, accounting, statistical, or technical capacities.

EXTREMISM

The relationship between conservatism and rightist extremism (or radicalism) has never been clear. It has not been possible to estimate the ratios of conservatives willing and desiring to effectuate policy changes through traditional democratic procedures, including third parties, to those who prefer or abide techniques of personal and group harassment, slanderous or libelous allegations and put forward or support wild—and probably unattainable—policy objectives (for example, "impeach Earl Warren," "get the U.S. out of the U.N. . . .," "abolish the 16th Amendment").

In current context, the extremist style is principally manifested by a perception (presumably common to Birchers, Christian Crusaders—both Hargis and Schwarz versions—Minutemen, and so on) that the group's enemies are engaged in a generally successful conspiracy against its continued well-being or even survival, having infiltrated and gained significant control over major decision-making and communications centers of American society.[23] Specifically, it is charged that the United Nations, the executive and judicial branches of the federal government, and major political parties, the schools, the press, unions, and financiers are all subject to control or major influence by the conspirators (that is, Communists) or their "pseudo-liberal," "Fabian socialist," fellow-traveling associates.[24]

Regardless of whether such beliefs are pervasive among members and supporters of "radical-right" organizations they do not, with rare exceptions, appear to dominate the *Weltanschauung* of Conservatives. Whatever their various perceptions of the influence of domestic communism, the subject seldom appears anywhere on their lists of problems confronting the political system. Only two Conservatives mentioned domestic communism in any form. (One, also a member of The John Birch Society, complained that the government was riddled with ". . . Reds and security risks"; the other —who claimed that The John Birch Society was ". . . a collection of neu-

---

[23] R. Hofstadter, *The Paranoid Style in American Politics and Other Essays* (New York: Alfred A. Knopf, 1965), chap. 1. See also J. Higham, *Strangers in the Land* (New York: Atheneum Publishers, 1955), pp. 81, 85, 180; E. Shils, *The Torment of Secrecy* (New York: The Free Press, 1952), chap. 1.

[24] J. Stormer, *None Dare Call It Treason* (Florissant, Mo.: 1964); P. Schlafly, *A Choice Not an Echo* (Alton, Ill.: Pere Marquette Press, 1964); C. Manly, *The Twenty Year Revolution* (Toronto: S. J. Reginald Saunders & Co., Ltd., 1954). See especially, A. G. Heinsohn (ed.), *Anthology of Conservative Writings in the United States: 1932–1960* (Chicago: Henry Regnery Company, 1962) and *any* publication of The John Birch Society or its Western Islands Press.

TABLE 5

Attitudes toward Civil Liberties by all Respondents and by Respondents with at Least Some College Education

PERCENT WHO AGREE THAT	ALL CONSERVATIVES (N = 45)	ALL REPUBLICANS (N = 48)	BERKELEY STUDENTS [a] (N = 894)	COLLEGE REPUBLICANS (N = 20)	COLLEGE CONSERVATIVES (N = 40)
1 "There should be a law to prevent people from making speeches against our form of government."	2 [d]	27	[c]	20	2
2 "Books which oppose churches and religion should be removed from local public libraries."	4 [d]	27	[b]	15	5
3 "A high-school teacher whose loyalty has been questioned before a committee of Congress should be fired, even if he swears under oath that he isn't a Communist."	7	8	[c]	10	5
4 "State governments should have power to pass laws making public speeches against racial and religious groups illegal."	7 [d]	31	10	25	2

5 "When the police are looking for evidence against a suspected criminal, they should not have to have a warrant to search a house."	13 [d]	33	11	30	13
6 "Large-scale roundups of 'undesirables' are proper as long as they are restricted to people with known criminal records."	22 [d]	58	19	45	20
7 "The government is acting properly when it refuses a passport to a Socialist."	27	44	10	40	22
8 "If a man accused of a major crime is acquitted, and apparently incriminating evidence is later discovered, he should be retried."	53 [d]	79	53	70	50
9 "Legislative committes should not investigate the political beliefs of university faculty members."	(44) [a]	(35)	(61)	(40)	(55)
10 "It is not reasonable to suspect the loyaly of a lawyer who represents accused Communists before a Congressional Committee."	(67)	(77)	(79)	(90)	(65)

[a] The proportion giving the libertarian response is parenthesized. Data from H. C. Selvin and W. Hagstrom, "Determinants of Support for Civil Liberties." British J. Sociol., 11 (1960), 52–53. I have reversed one and slightly altered four of their items. Responses are not controlled by sex.

[b] Question not used by Selvin and Hagstrom.

[c] Phrasing employed by Selvin and Hagstrom or Stouffer unsuitable for comparison.

[d] Differences beween Conservatives and Republicans are X^2 significant, $p < .05$, df $= 1$.

TABLE 6

Relative Support for Civil Liberties (in Percent) [a]

	CONSERVATIVES ($N = 45$)	REPUBLICANS ($N = 48$)
Stronger	69	21
Weaker	31	79
Totals	100	100

[a] The cut is made at the place where the frequency distributions for the two groups of respondents intersect, that is, at eight prolibertarian responses.

rotics and buffoons"—complained about ". . . the increase of leftist sub-version in education . . . and in civil rights groups.")

Conservatives do not rationalize their act of joining the new party as an anticommunist step. Rather, they view it as either a protest against the liberal policies and leadership of the state Republican Party or a positive identification with the conservative movement or philosophy or both.

When asked if they could think of any organization hurting the conservative cause (only 7 of 45 thought *any* was helping), 71 percent named The John Birch Society, with 60 percent including the members as well as the leadership in their indictments. Their comments were dotted with such epithets as "kooks," "radicals," "bigots," "a WASP front," and some barely printable phrases. Among the far-right groups, only The John Birch Society and the American Council of Christian Churches (led by C. C. McIntyre) received any praise, each from one respondent. Sixteen percent could think of no organization either to praise or to damn.

It would appear, based on their responses to the questions discussed above, that the large majority of Conservatives consciously avoid adopting both the presumed perspective and the group identification of right-wing extremists. A final check on the accuracy of this finding is contained in an analysis of their responses to the items on a "domestic communist threat" scale (Table 7). Conservative responses to each assertion, covering American society in general, college faculties, and each of the major political parties were, in the aggregate, similar to the Republicans but consistently, though not significantly, more threat-perceiving. Only once, with regard to communist influence in colleges and universities, did even a bare majority of Conservatives reject one of the assertions.

Although the data does not support any inference that most Conservatives are totally devoid of a belief in serious communist influence in major domestic institutions, only a minority (26 percent) accepted at least three

TABLE 7

Perceptions of Communist Danger or Influence in American Society

PERCENT WHO AGREE THAT	CONSERVATIVES [a] (N = 45)	REPUBLICANS (N = 48)	COLLEGE REPUBLICANS (N = 20)
1 "Communist professors do *not* have very much influence in American colleges and universities."	42	48	45
2 "The danger to the United States from communists living here is *not* as great as the danger from Russia or China."	56	73	75
3 "Communists do *not* have very much influence in the Democratic party."	67	81	75
4 "Communists do *not* have very much influence in the Republican party."	84	85	90

[a] Within arithmetic limitations, the five non-college-educated Conservatives, responded exactly as did their colleagues to each of the items.

of these extremist assertions.[25] If the extremist criteria are tightened somewhat, to include either a desire to see the U.S. withdraw from the U.N. or to impeach Earl Warren, the percentage in this category drops to 17 (eight respondents). (Only one, the Bircher, responded negatively to all six items.) No Republicans were found in the latter group of extremists.

THE POLITICS OF CONSERVATIVES

As most Conservatives are quick to acknowledge, it is their political views which separate them importantly from other segments of the population.

In their responses to a series of general open-ended and specific closed-ended questions, both the most salient political interests of Conservatives and those dimensions on which they stand farthest apart from the sampled Republicans coincide.

Analysis of the verbal responses indicates clearly that the major political interest of Conservatives is in the role, direction, and/or activities of the federal government in domestic economic affairs, with a concomitant fear for the present and future freedom of the individual in a "government dominated" society. A substantial majority of Conservatives (60 percent)

---

[25] Fifty-eight percent accepted no more than one; 31 percent accepted none of them. Comparable figures for college-educated Republicans were 65 percent and 30 percent; for all Republicans, 72 percent and 29 percent.

commented at some length about their dislike of (1) government intervention into the affairs of business and businessmen, (2) the "socialistic" direction in which the nation's economy is moving, or (3) the size and power
of the government in general.[26]

An additional 25 percent focused upon the individual rather than the
government acting upon him. They expressed the belief that people were
becoming dependent upon "government handouts," distracted by "bread
and circuses," and they bewailed the prospective "disappearance" of the
individual and "subjugation of his rights."

This general antipathy to the activities, or "consequences" of the activities, of the federal government is illustrated in Table 8. When asked spe-

TABLE 8

Attitudes toward Federal Social and Economic Roles [a]

PERCENT OPPOSED TO ANY FEDERAL ROLE IN	CONSERVA-TIVES ($N = 45$)	REPUB-LICANS ($N = 48$)
Financing education (building and operating costs)	91	54
Financing public housing	78	25
War on poverty	80	31
Medical care for the aged	60	6
Combating depressions	24	
Combating depressions through public expenditures	58	19
Setting minimum wage rates	62	33

[a] All intersample differences in Table 8 are significant, $p < .01$.

cifically, Conservatives rejected every listed federal welfare program enacted
since 1932, usually by overwhelming majorities. Only when it came to combating depressions did they indicate a slackening of hostility to a federal
economic or welfare role. Yet even on this issue, no longer a subject of
major party controversy in principle, the majority endorsed either a summary statement of the Hooverian approach ("balance the budget, increase
tariffs, and lower interest rates") or absolute non-interference with the
business cycle (the federal government "should not interfere at all except,
possibly, to stop regulating business").

While most Conservatives (78 percent) disagreed with the assertion that

---

[26] The segregation of responses into these, and allied, categories is for
the purpose of expository convenience. There is evidence that respondents falling
into only one category would quickly endorse the remarks of their colleagues in the
others. For example, 80 percent of the Conservatives (36 of 45) agreed that "it
seems clear that the United States is on the way to becoming a Socialist country,"
although only ten mentioned the word "socialism" during the interviews. Seventy-
four percent (34 of 48) of the Republicans disagreed with the assertion.

"this country would be better off if the federal income tax were abolished" (as did 94 percent of the Republicans), nearly half (47 percent) would prefer a flat-rate to a graduated structure. Only 15 percent of the Republicans accepted this view.

Conservative opposition to governmental economic and welfare activity is not restricted to the federal branches. Given the choice of a variety of governmental programs which included state *or* national and state participation, substantial numbers of Conservatives opted for neither (Table 9).

TABLE 9

Attitudes toward Governmental Social and Economic Roles [a]

PERCENT OPPOSED TO ANY GOVERNMENTAL ROLE IN	CONSERV-ATIVES ($N = 45$)	REPUB-LICANS ($N = 48$)
Financing public housing	29	4
War on poverty	38	13
Medical care for the aged	58	6
Combating depressions	24	
Regulating public utilities	49	17

[a] All intersample differences in Table 9 are significant, $p < .01$.

Whereas no Republican respondent could accept a policy of total government inaction during a depression, 25 percent of the Conservatives had no such inhibition. An equal number were at most localists on all three specific social welfare items, relating to public housing, the antipoverty program, and medical care for the aged. Only one respondent, a follower of Ayn Rand, would deny the government any role in any endeavor (except defense of life and property).

Allied to the Conservatives' general pro-business, anti-governmental attitudes is a widespread antipathy toward labor unions. Eighty percent believed that they ". . . do more harm than good," compared with 40 percent of the Republicans.[27] No other political dimension, including civil rights and foreign policy, ranked so high on their lists of interests or elicited such near-uniformity of response as did the areas of economic regulation and welfare.

CONSERVATISM AND STATUS STABILITY

As an alternative, or at least supplementary, explanation of rightist attitudes and behavior, it is commonly argued that rightists are likely

---

[27] Forty-five percent of the Conservative respondents volunteered anti-union comments.

to be characterized by what Hofstadter calls "status insecurity." This frustrating situation, which may occur as a result of social mobility or status incongruence, is assumed to make the victim unsure of and anxious about his status in society, and hence, for socially protective reasons, to project his anxieties onto political objects through, for example, super-patriotism and vocal anticommunism.

Although the applicability of this hypothesis to extreme rightists is debatable,[28] it clearly does not apply to the generality of this sample. Conservatives possess as much or more objective status stability as either the Crusaders in Wolfinger's sample (which, as Rohter argues, may overrepresent the status-stable) or white business and professional men in the 1956 SRC election study (Table 10). (I did not test for personal, subjective

TABLE 10

Occupational Mobility among Conservatives, Crusaders, and White Northerners with Business or Professional Occupations (in Percent)

FATHER'S OCCUPATION [c]	CONSERV-ATIVES (N = 38)	CRUSADERS [a] (N = 179)	WHITE NORTHERNERS [b] (N = 290)
Business or professional	45	41	37
Clerical or sales	16	8	6
Blue-collar	26	12	38
Farmer	11	16	16
No answer	3	23	3
Totals	101	100	100

[a] Source: Wolfinger and others, "America's Radical Right," p. 278.
[b] Source: SRC 1956 Election Study (see Wolfinger).
[c] My question was: Do you remember what your father did for a living while you were growing up? If so, what? (In case of multiple responses, the highest in status rank was coded.)

status anxiety.) Moreover, the upwardly mobile cannot be differentiated from the status-stable respondents on any crucial measure, political or psychological.

An associated proposition points out the attractiveness of the radical right for downwardly mobile individuals because it supposedly provides an explanation for their failures and a scapegoat (and an outlet) for their hostilities. The Conservative party sample does not contain a single downwardly mobile person.

Still another proposition relating status to rightist activity asserts that

---

[28] See the selections in this volume by Wolfinger, Rohter, and Elms.

individuals with "status discrepancies" (for example, college-educated mailmen and street cleaners or semiliterate college presidents), are likely to resolve the resentments created by these incongruities by joining in the anti-elitist and anti-intellectual attacks of the extreme right.[29] Again, no support for this hypothesis can be found. Conservatives are less likely to exhibit status incongruities than either Crusaders (who exhibit few) or white northerners (Table 11). Seven of the eight noncollege graduate professionals were technicians, bringing that little incongruence which may be inferred from this data down to a minimum. Status discrepancies appear to account for fewer Conservative party memberships than would be expected by chance.

DISCUSSION

Monroe County Conservatives differ substantially, on the measures employed, in their psychological make-up, their attitudes toward civil liberties, and their susceptibility to the doctrines of and admiration for the behavior of the "radical right," from other conservatives and rightists examined by social scientists. The large majority of them cannot be classified as authoritarian or misanthropic, anti–civil-libertarian or currently vulnerable to the obsessive anticommunism of right-wing fringe groups.

But there are common political and social denominators by which Conservatives can be distinguished from other political aggregates. The Conservatives examined here are mostly well-educated, well-paid family men, with upper-status occupations and suburban residences.[30] They are bound together politically by a consistent and highly salient opposition to the modern welfare and regulatory role of the federal government, combined with a solid hostility to the perceived power and influence of labor unions. While other political dimensions attract their interest and concern, they rarely rank as high, occur as frequently, or elicit such near-uniformity of attitude.[31]

In short, Monroe County Conservatives can be characterized by their average relatively high socioeconomic position and by their possession of a distinct and coherent ideology which, while limited in breadth, is appropriate (within the American political tradition) to their socioeconomic position.

These findings seriously contradict the conclusions of McClosky and the

---

[29] S. M. Lipset, "Three Decades of the Radical Right," in D. Bell (ed.), pp. 402–403.

[30] The median family income for Conservatives in 1964 was nearly $12,000; 85 percent earned more than $8,000. Ninety-six percent were employed in white-collar jobs, 84 percent in business, managerial, professional, or technical capacities.

[31] The Party platform, summarized in footnote 8, is an accurate, if too short and general, summary of the views of the majority of the sample.

TABLE 11

Occupation by Education among Conservatives, Crusaders, and White Northerners (in Percent)

OCCUPATION[b]	COLLEGE GRADUATES			SOME COLLEGE			ATTENDED HIGH SCHOOL[a]		
	Conservatives	Cru-[c] saders	North-[d] erners	Conservatives	Cru-[c] saders	North-[d] erners	Conservatives	Cru-[c] saders	North-[d] erners
Professional	75	54	59	50	25	34	40	7	6
Business	21	31	19	25	30	17		37	12
Clerical and sales	4	11	14	17	22	23	40	26	20
Blue-collar		3	9	8	22	25	20	30	62
	100	99	101	100	99	99	100	100	100
Number of Respondents	28	140	108	12	63	149	5	43	545

[a] All the Conservatives had attended high school, therefore no lower categories are used.
[b] All Conservatives are subsumed by these categories. Farmers, students, etc., are excluded from the other samples.
[c] Source: Wolfinger, p. 280.
[d] Source: SRC 1960 Study (see Wolfinger).

Berkeley group. Most Conservatives do not fit the mold of psychic mal-adjustment, anomie, alienation, and outgroup hostility found jointly or separately by these scholars. There are two possibilities which may account for the strong psychological-political correlations heretofore discovered and their general absence from my sample. One is that the kind of conservatism represented by the New York Conservatives is crucially different, in terms of key issues and social and demographic sources, from the variants(s) manifested by the radical right. Recent research into the background and attitudes of radical-right activists suggests that this is likely.

A large segment of Ira Rohter's sample of Oregon rightists is dispro-portionately older, rural-born, less well-educated, lower in income and occupational status, and likely to belong to fundamentalist religious de-nominations than is my sample.[32] His respondents are found to be com-paratively maladjusted on 11 of 12 psychological measures.[33] (They *were* politically efficacious.) Mark Chesler and Richard Schmuck have found similar, though fewer, associations in their midwestern samples, but suggest that a political "value strain"—the unhappy perception of the difference between what *is* (or will be) and what *should be*—underlie adoption or acceptance of radical-right perspectives.[34] It must be noted that heavy concentrations of older, less well-trained and economically successful, fundamentalist, and rural-born individuals have been found by all students of the subject except Wolfinger, who believes that San Francisco-area Christian Anti-Communism Crusaders, at least, ". . . are not social and psychological cripples." [35]

Despite some elements of overlap, it may be in order to hypothesize that two major strains of right-wing attitudes and behavior are distinguishable on the basis of (1) political grounds—one concerned primarily with ques-tions of economic and social policy, the other with a powerful and conspira-torial domestic communist threat; (2) social differences—one a segment of the young, educated, technologically competent, and economically success-ful middle to upper-middle class, the other older, less competent, and less "successful" on these dimensions; and (3) psychological differences—one reasonably well adjusted to their environment and able to cope with, though dissenting from, the major political tendencies of their time, the other hostile toward many of the social forces of the era and less able to main-tain their social-psychological balance when confronting them.

---

[32] I. S. Rohter, *Radical Rightists: An Empirical Study* (unpublished Ph.D. dissertation, Michigan State University, 1967), pp. 124–144.

[33] Rohter, pp. 154–265.

[34] M. Chesler and R. Schmuck, "Social Psychological Characteristics of Super-Patriots," above.

[35] R. Wolfinger and others, "The Radical Right . . . ." Another recent study, of Dallas rightists, concludes that the availability of rightist organizations may better account for rightist behavior than psychological predispositions. See A. C. Elms, "Psychological Factors in Right-Wing Extremism," above.

It is urgent to separate analytically the type of conservatism displayed by the New York State Conservative Party and the radical variant(s) which provide support for The John Birch Society. The persistent political warfare between William Buckley's *National Review* (the major journalistic supporter of New York Conservatives) and The John Birch Society, among other things, indicate that those differences are strongly reflected in the political arena. The distinction seems to me to be that between reasonable political intelligence and its absence, with their associated causes and correlations.

The second explanation of the discrepancy between my findings and those of McClosky and the Berkeley group is that "conservatives" attitudinally defined and derived from a population cross-section and those surveyed on the basis of overt, politically relevant behavior are actually two distinct empirical universes sharing the same label. The former group of inactive, inefficacious, alienated and largely not well-educated individuals may be *psychologically* conservative, but no evidence has been offered to demonstrate a consistent relationship to any broad variant of *political* conservatism. (That many radical rightists are recruited from McClosky's universe of "extreme conservatives" appears probable, however.)

McClosky himself found that the correlations ". . . between classical conservatism . . . and . . . party affiliation, attitude on economic issues and liberal-conservative self-designation . . . tend to be fairly low. . . ." [36]

It is clear, from the evidence presented here, that some of the people who identify, register, and vote as Conservatives do not possess the personality attributes assigned to "conservatives" selected on other bases. For this group, at least, politics is primarily a legitimate means to express political and economic dissatisfactions and desires. Also, it is a means which dominates, if not supersedes, its utility as a political outlet for clinical and social psychological maladjustments.

---

[36] H. McClosky, "Conservatism and Personality," pp. 44–45.

Notes on Contributors

MARK CHESLER (Ph.D., University of Michigan) is a Project Director at the Center for Research on the Utilization of Scientific Knowledge and Assistant Professor of Sociology, University of Michigan. His publications include several articles and monographs on racial change and conflict, educational roles and attitudes, and political extremism.

ALAN C. ELMS (Ph.D., Yale University) is Assistant Professor of Psychology, University of California, Davis. He taught previously at Southern Methodist University and has contributed articles to several scholarly journals.

FRED W. GRUPP, JR. (Ph.D., University of Pennsylvania) is Assistant Professor of Government at Louisiana State University. He has also taught at the University of Wisconsin, Racine, and has published an article on the reading habits of political activists.

SHEILAH R. KOEPPEN (Ph.D., Stanford University) is Assistant Professor of Political Science at the University of Minnesota. She has taught previously at San Francisco State College and the University of San Francisco.

JAMES MCEVOY III (Ph.D., University of Michigan) is Assistant Professor of Sociology, University of California, Davis, and Visiting Assistant Professor of Political Science, University of California, Berkeley. He was recently a special consultant and Project Director for the National Commission on the Causes and Prevention of Violence. His publications include articles on political conservatism and right-wing extremism.

SCOTT G. MCNALL (Ph.D., University of Oregon) is Assistant Professor of Sociology at the University of Minnesota. His publications include articles on the sociology of religion.

IRA ROHTER (Ph.D., Michigan State University) is Assistant Professor of Political Science at the University of Hawaii. He has also taught at the University of California, Berkeley and the University of Wisconsin, Milwaukee. He is the author of scholarly articles on both the radical right and the "new left."

ROBERT A. SCHOENBERGER (Ph.D., University of Rochester) is Assistant Professor of Political Science at the University of Michigan. His publications include articles on political conservatism, the electoral effects of campaign decisions, and political mobilization.

RAYMOND C. WOLFINGER (Ph.D., Yale University) is Associate Professor of Political Science at Stanford University. He has published articles on ethnic politics, community power, and political regions.

Index